GANGSTERS AND OTHER STATESMEN

Gangsters and Other Statesmen

Mafias, Separatists, and Torn States in a Globalized World

Danilo Mandić

PRINCETON UNIVERSITY PRESS

PRINCETON AND OXFORD

Copyright © 2021 by Princeton University Press

Requests for permission to reproduce material from this work
should be sent to permissions@press.princeton.edu

Published by Princeton University Press
41 William Street, Princeton, New Jersey 08540
6 Oxford Street, Woodstock, Oxfordshire OX20 1TR

press.princeton.edu

Library of Congress Control Number 2020943969
Cloth ISBN 978-0-691-18787-7
Paperback ISBN 978-0-691-18788-4
E-book ISBN 978-0-691-20005-7

British Library Cataloging-in-Publication Data is available

Editorial: Meagan Levinson and Jacqueline Delaney
Production Editorial: Jill Harris
Cover Design: Pamela L. Schnitter
Production: Brigid Ackerman
Publicity: Kate Hensley and Kathryn Stevens
Copyeditor: Cindy Milstein

Cover image: Feodosian regiment of Zaporozhian Cossack troops polices the
lakes around Feodosia, Crimea, 2010. Photograph by Anastasia Taylor-Lind

This book has been composed in Adobe Text and Gotham

Printed on acid-free paper. ∞

Printed in the United States of America

10 9 8 7 6 5 4 3 2 1

This book is dedicated to survivors in torn states around the world.

CONTENTS

TABLES

ABBREVIATIONS

AKSH Albanian National Army
DNR Donetsk People's Republic
EULEX EU Rule of Law Mission in Kosovo
FBI Federal Bureau of Investigation
HEU highly enriched uranium
IAEA International Atomic Energy Agency
ICG International Crisis Group
ICTY International Criminal Tribunal for the Former Yugoslavia
INGO international nongovernmental organization
IS Islamic State
IQB Izz ad-Din al-Qassam Brigades
JCC Joint Control Commission
JPKF Joint Peacekeeping Force
JSO Special Operations Unit
KFOR NATO Kosovo Force
KGB State Security Committee
KGK Kongra-Gel
KLA Kosovo Liberation Army
LNR Lugansk People's Republic
MFDC Movement of Democratic Forces of Casamance
MNJ Movement of Nigeriens for Justice
MNLA National Movement for the Liberation of Azawad
NATO North Atlantic Treaty Organization
NGO nongovernmental organization
NLA National Liberation Army
OSCE Organization for Security and Cooperation in Europe

PKK Kurdish Workers' Party
UNHCR United Nations High Commissioner for Refugees
UNMIK United Nations Interim Administration Mission in Kosovo
UNODC United Nations Office on Drugs and Crime
WDR *World Drug Report*

Separatism, Meet Mafia

1

Introduction

The day he believes that separatism pays, on that day he will certainly become a separatist.
—ROLAND GIRARD, *FRANCO-AMERICANS OF NEW ENGLAND*

That people fighting for their independence will take aid from wherever they can find it is clear. To win our independence we should even take aid, as they say, from the devil himself.
—AGOSTINHO NETO, *THE SKULL BENEATH THE SKIN*

Separatism in the late twentieth and early twenty-first centuries poses a paradox. On the one hand, the world is ostensibly coming together through globalization. On the other, the territorial integrity of nations appears fragile in most regions. How are these two trends related? This book argues that countries torn by separatist movements since the Cold War cannot be adequately understood without an appreciation of organized crime. Far from passive by-products or trivial catalysts, mafias can play a decisive, autonomous role in shaping state-separatist relations, promoting or hindering secession, and fueling war. Transnational processes—of mafia expansion, chronic smuggling, and patrimonial governance—critically shape national processes of ethnic mobilization, border reconfiguration, and state collapse. Through a comparative historical analysis of the role of organized crime in West Africa, Eastern Europe, and the Middle East, I examine understudied dynamics of territorial consolidation in torn states. By nourishing, infiltrating, and even co-opting governments and separatist movements, mafias have the power to mold the basic political units of our world.

Separatist movements are a hallmark of globalization. Since 1990, new nation-states have emerged at an average rate of one per year. By a conservative estimate, over three hundred separatist movements likewise aspire to state-hood.[1] Some—such as Scots in the United Kingdom, the Flemish in Belgium, or Québécois in Canada—are moderate and unsuccessful. Others—like Crimea, Kurdistan, or South Sudan—revived questions about how separatism develops and what can be done to accommodate it peacefully. Seemingly never-ending territorial consolidation in torn states appears to dispel the hope and promise of globalization. These disintegrative domestic processes, it would appear, are impeding integrative global ones.

This book suggests not. I propose that transnational organized crime significantly shapes the politics of borders in torn states. While economic, historical, geopolitical, religious, and demographic factors explaining separatism have been widely explored, a distinguishing feature of torn states has been neglected: their deep criminalization. Unlike in consolidated nations, the existence and operation of globalized mafias *matter* in separatist cases. Counterintuitively, furthermore, organized crime has the capacity to both promote and obstruct separatist movement success by: determining the stability and capacity of weak host states engaged in curbing separatism, with a fateful impact on the trajectories of secession; supplying separatist movements with criminal resources and allies, without which they are doomed to demobilization; generating or prolonging separatist confrontation and war; and promoting stalemate and ethnic reconciliation. Given these realities, globalized mafias and separatist politics are deeply symbiotic. In developing a framework for understanding these processes, I will rethink what is typically a tale of two sides—the host state and separatist movement—as instead a story about a triad: states, separatists, and mafias. Then I will develop a typology of organized crime in three regions rife with torn states, grounded in two dimensions: how *state dependent* and *partisan* mafias are.

This approach entails demystifying organized crime, as we disown—perhaps reluctantly—many cherished folk sociological beliefs about lawbreaking, impropriety, and deviance. Mafia mythology carries a twofold danger: romanticization and demonization. On the one hand, organized crime is glorified as Robin Hoodism.[2] Since precapitalist societies, social banditry has been a potent form of primitive resistance: a religion of the oppressed. From Jesse James to Al Capone, the gangster served as a symbol of revolutionary change that is otherwise impossible: "a surrogate for the failure of the mass to lift itself out of its own poverty, helplessness and meekness."[3] For pragmatic and symbolic reasons, gangsters cultivate an aura of purity, righteousness, and invincibility. Public opinion—or is it public madness?—often ranks criminals higher than elected officials.

On the other hand, no slur is complete without invocations of mafia villainy. Knee-jerk labeling of "gangster" regimes, firms, and movements settles policy disputes before they begin. Politicians paint criminals black. Law enforcement (the leading data collectors on the subject) exaggerate mafias' sinister influence, and omit continuities between state and criminal sectors. Regarding torn states, scholars dispute caricatures of separatist statelets as "criminalized badlands," cautioning that "this image was overplayed" in many quarters.[4] Indeed, gangsters play a special role in modern demonology for good reason. The histories of countless nation-states are replete with mafias as forces to be reckoned with—serious contenders for not only economic monopoly but for political legitimacy itself. The Japanese Yakuza, Russian organized crime, and four Italian syndicates were pivotal in nationalist development.[5] Today, global organized crime raises between $800 billion and $1.6 trillion yearly, or 2 percent of the world economy.[6] Yet existing approaches treat mafias as apolitical nuisances, neglect to conceptualize organized crime as an autonomous actor, and fail to differentiate between mafias associated with *host state* territory and institutions, and those associated with *separatist* territory and institutions. Overcoming these limitations, we open new horizons for understanding torn states.

A related task is to recognize the singular opportunity structure in which separatist movements find themselves. Contemporary nationalism has transformed radically, both as ideology and practice.[7] What used to be a unificationist force seeking to transcend petty tribal and ethnic cleavages—the Italian Risorgimento or the Pan-Slavic movement—evolved into a disintegrative force proliferating tiny, unsustainable ministates. "For [separatist] elites," if not necessarily their constituents, "small is indeed beautiful; it provides them with the prerogatives, the prerequisites, and the trappings of power."[8] In Albert O. Hirschman's (1970) classic formulation, most movements seek "voice" and "loyalty." Separatist movements are interested strictly in "exit." But the recursive trap of separatist logic has yet to be surmounted.[9] Secession within a region within an autonomy within a province is all too common, and reminiscent of the parodied Harvardian stranded on a desert island: he launches three political parties and ten newspapers, all violently disagreeing.

In such separatist contexts, mafias have unique choices. Whereas in normal circumstances gangsters "are very often satisfied with the existing rules of the political and economic game in which they move," those rules are unstable and opaque in torn states.[10] Mafias can undermine both conflict resolution (which may reimpose clear laws and border control) and conflict escalation (which may further destabilize the existing, lucrative lack of jurisdiction, law, and order). Alternatively, they can co-opt or support the separatist movement, hedging bets on a newly emerging polity where the criminal fiefdom can reign supreme under a novel, sovereign political umbrella. Finally, they can co-opt or support the host state in crushing separatists, hoping for a return to the initial environment with which they are familiar and comfortable. Such an opportunity structure affords mafias exceptional power.

Through comparative-historical analysis this book inquires into how transnational organized crime impacts separatism by examining border disputes in sixteen countries (n = 16) in three regions.[11] First, by comparing two cases in depth, I explore the conditions under which organized crime enhances separatist movement success (part 2). Second, by analyzing fourteen cases across three regions, I explain the variety of roles mafias play in torn states (part 3). The investigation is, the reader will notice, fairly exploratory and conducive to provisional explanatory conclusions—not extravagant, definitive causal claims. Nevertheless, through careful comparison of cases, process tracing of separatist trajectories, and synthesis of the best available sources on the role of organized crime in these societies (see "Sources" in the appendix), I unveil understudied and counterintuitive patterns of mafia influence on separatist dynamics. These recurring patterns across cases should, at minimum, give us pause regarding torn states globally. I do not propose a "theory" of separatism, and still less a refutation of extant approaches that disregard organized crime entirely. Rather, the reader is invited to a shift in emphasis in their comprehension of border disputes in torn states and offered a set of tools for explaining separatist outcomes. No oddity, the convergence of torn states and mafias is—I argue—perfectly normal.

The first half of the analysis compares two paired cases of separatism (n = 2) in Serbia/Kosovo and Georgia / South Ossetia, and the second investigates fourteen cases (n = 14) across three regions (West Africa, the Middle East, and Eastern Europe). Accordingly, the first half offers greater depth with lesser generalizability, and the second supplies greater breadth with a more generalizable typology of mafias.[12]

In part 2, the paired sampling of Serbia/Kosovo and Georgia / South Ossetia is due to their fortuitous similarities but contrasting outcomes. Namely, despite remarkable resemblances in separatist trajectory, Kosovo's movement is more successful. Exploiting their resemblances, I first process trace the separatist trajectories of Kosovo and South Ossetia from 1989 to 2012 with an eye to the divergent roles played by organized crime vis-à-vis the state, on the one hand, and separatist movement, on the other. Then I examine why organized criminal opportunity in two particular rackets (drug and arms smuggling) resulted in separatist benefit in Kosovo, but not in South Ossetia. Finally, I compare two episodes of nefarious organized crime (in organs and uranium) to see why, despite four contextual reasons to the contrary, South Ossetia was harmed more than Kosovo by the scandal's exposure. No paired comparison is perfect—and it remains, of course, impossible to exhaustively synchronize or control all variables in the manner of quantitative matching techniques. But these two cases are, for a qualitative comparison of different outcomes, the best-possible selection (see "Logic of the Pairing" in the appendix).

In part 3, the fourteen cases are a comprehensive sample of the remaining separatism-torn countries in the three regions. Identifying sufficiently similar patterns across regions, I typologize the variety of roles that mafias play—along the two dimensions of state dependence and ethnocentrism—in border disputes. The case-oriented, purposive sampling of the regions (nonprobabilistic and nonrandom) was motivated by four considerations: a majority of nation-states in these three regions have simultaneous (1989–2019) separatist divisions, enabling contextualized comparisons; all but a few of the separatism-afflicted nation-states have conspicuous and documented organized crime, guaranteeing relevance; there is considerable intraregional diversity and cross-regional convergence of mafia-separatism patterns, allowing discoveries that undermine extant nation- and region-centric interpretations; and the abundance, accessibility, and quality of the primary and secondary sources on organized crime in these regions is rare, presenting an opportunity in an otherwise-malnourished research field. Furthermore, omitting the relative rarity and idiosyncrasy of separatisms in Western developed democracies (as elaborated on in chapter 2), it is reasonable to conjecture that the sampled regions are not especially atypical for the universal set of separatist movements globally in the post–Cold War period.

The technique of process tracing in comparative-historical research is a powerful, if somewhat speculative, engine for generating plausible causal associations (see "Process Tracing" in the appendix). By "analyzing a case into a sequence (or several concatenating sequences) of events and showing how those events are plausibly linked given the interests and situations faced by groups," process tracing gives us reasons to believe that two sets of phenomena are causally related.[13] The method does not pretend to be definitive or resolve the problem of spuriousness. Rather, linkages in a causal chain—especially ones that connect sets of phenomena previously thought to be unrelated—increase the confidence with which we can draw more macrolevel causal inferences.[14] In part 2, using a Simmelian model of triadic relations between host states, separatist movements, and mafias, I will process trace the cases of Kosovo and South Ossetia to demonstrate that divergent mafia roles in the two cases caused different outcomes, mafias function as "filters" determining whether regional smuggling opportunities are transformed into separatist gains at critical junctures, and three aspects of mafia capacity "immunized" one separatist movement, but not the other, from public exposure of a nefarious criminal episode. In part 3, I argue that the extent to which mafias are state dependent and ethnocentric explains the disparate effects they have on separatist movements. The purpose of the mafia typology (see table 1) is to generalize insights hitherto restricted to a handful of countries, underline cross-regional similarities, and reinterpret separatist outcomes in terms of a neglected agent.

The argument is *not* that mafias necessarily or always impact separatist trajectories. Rather, it is that they have—conditionally—the potential for an immense impact on separatist escalation and demobilization, violence and conciliation, victory and defeat. The purpose is not to postulate grandiose causal claims holding for separatism sans context, nor to recommend explanatory reductionism of any sort. Given the normal limitations of the research design and sampling strategy, I am content to restrict my conclusions to mere causal conjectures: tentative, plausible proposals of how mafias affect separatism based on recurring patterns in three theoretically interesting regions.

What about Catalonia, Brexit, or Hong Kong? Why aren't Flemish separatists racketeering in Switzerland? Are the Yakuza planning a declaration of independence? Where, exactly, is the mafia in Quebec? And why did El Chapo refrain from proclaiming a People's Republic of Sinaloa? This book is not about border disputes in general, crime in general, or the advanced societies. Temporally and spatially, we restrict this exploration to the post–Cold War period (1989–2019) in three regions: West Africa, the Middle East, and Eastern Europe (see "Regional Scope" in the appendix for geographic individuation).

A more general expression of methodological humility is also in order. As a qualitative sociologist, I readily concede that quantitative studies of separatism are preferable social scientific approaches.[15] I have no qualms about relegating qualitative research on the topic—including the present study—to the task of apprenticeship to statistical analyses with greater confidence in their validity, reliability, and generalizability. Sadly, a single solitary attempt has been made to operationalize mafias for quantitative purposes: Jan van Dijk's (2007) audacious but crude Composite Organized Crime Index. Fully *zero* scholars have utilized it to explain separatism. In my judgment, this is a failure of qualitative sociology, which has not succeeded in presenting empirically driven, conceptually compelling accounts of mafias as agents.[16] Thus, if statistically minded students of separatism adopt insights from this book to imaginatively and rigorously introduce organized crime variables into their regressions, the effort will have been amply vindicated.

Finally, this analysis restricts itself to a confined range of phenomena by adopting fairly narrow conceptualizations (chapter 3) and technical definitions (to which we now turn). Namely, they exclude most insurgencies, criminal entities, and ethnonational divisions, leaving mere subsets of each (separatist movements, mafias, and torn states, respectively). Definitions are matters of convenience, not fact; their value is only in the context of the explanatory argument at hand (see "Coding" in the appendix). This book has little to say to analysts of separatism and criminologists who proceed with more inclusive definitions (e.g., that "organized crime" should include kleptocratic regimes, multinational corporations, or mere gangs), and does not purport to persuade scholars with incompatible definitions (e.g., that "separatism" is strictly nonethnonational, legal, or premodern). Such alternatives, I wholly concede, have their own value elsewhere.

Charting the Terrain

A plethora of labels has emerged to characterize separatist movements: "de facto states," "statelets," "unofficial states," "breakaway provinces," "unrecognized states," "frozen conflicts," "contested states," "disputed territories," "self-proclaimed states," "informal countries," and—the author's favorite—"nonstate states." Ominous prefixes and adjectives (quasi-, pseudo-, proto-, near-, semi-, mini-, contested-) are nervously attached to "government," "nation," "society," "state," and "country" in every conceivable permutation.[17] Most are synonymous. The terminological morass has produced much confusion, but also insights into how misleading political maps in the twenty-first century are. What is missing is an understanding of separatism as a *social movement*.

Not to be outdone, organized crime has inspired a dictionary's worth of definitions (one meticulous compiler gathered more than two hundred).[18] Of eleven popular elements in definitions, the top two are a continuing hierarchy and rational criminal profit—both of which are misleading in separatist contexts.[19] Furthermore, most definitions of organized crime assume a sharp distinction between state and mafia, relegating the latter to an informal, abnormal, and apolitical phenomenon. Yet separatist conflict creates a unique space for mafia agency that does not exist in weak but untorn—or even collapsing—states. What is missing is a recognition of mafias as *independent political agents*. In what follows, I individuate and delineate a set of terms related to separatist movements and organized crime. Some of these definitions will appear idiosyncratic and counterintuitive, but are—I maintain—necessary for the heterodox argument and context to which they apply.

"Separatism" is a stigmatized term. For host states, it is a euphemism for traitors, terrorists, and criminals. For separatist movements themselves, it is a slur; they are liberators, democrats, and patriots. For conservatives, the term conjures a stable and benign political order threatened by unreasonable, disruptive renegades. For revolutionaries, there is no such entity to "separate" from, only emancipatory justice fighting against oppression. Before proceeding, we must abandon sympathetic and pejorative connotations alike. Separatist movements are *nationalist movements*. That is, they rely on identity claims based on ethnonational markers and claims of territorial sovereignty that contradict formally existing borders. Separatists are nationalists in Ernest Gellner's (1983, 1) strict sense: they hold that "the political and national unit should be congruent." Unlike unificationist nationalists, separatists feel trapped in an "internal incongruence" of the host country, from which they wish to withdraw.[20] *Separatist movements*, then, are social movements claiming increased independence from the centralized government for a territorially concentrated population or the surrender of some of the centralized government's sovereignty to a foreign state. I restrict the scope to movements that have exercised territorial control for at least a year.[21] The level of violence is undefined: a secessionist movement that has waged multiple wars is just as separatist as a peaceful one. Separatists exist within *host states*, formally recognized members of the United Nations with at least one major separatist challenger. When referring to the country's territory excluding separatist turf, we will call it the host state *proper* (e.g., Israel proper is Israel without Gaza and the West Bank).

Note that separatists fight for independence, not necessarily statehood. Rogers Brubaker (1998, 238) recognized that nationalism in general "should not be conceived as essentially or even primarily state-seeking"—and the same applies to this subset. Rather, they are interested in greater separation from their polity's center, which only occasionally means secession. Demands often evolve dramatically: from increased regional autonomy within the extant constitutional framework to full sovereignty with new, internationally recognized borders. These demands are variously formulated as "independence," "self-determination," "autonomy," "decentralization," "partition," "secession," or simply "liberation." Sometimes separatists opt for *irredentism*: greater integration into neighboring nation-states.[22] We will call these countries *patron states*. The unificationist nationalisms of patrons are "resources which help shape the character and achievements of the separatist" movement enjoying patronage.[23] Separatist movements often lack the capacity to exist as independent entities and therefore cling to irredentist options even if they would prefer outright independence. Other movements eschew irredentism because they have the capacity to function without merger, even if patrons want integration. But in both cases, separatists are never mere marionettes of their neighboring states.[24]

Why emphasize that separatist movements are *social movements*? Why not operationalize them as civil wars, revolutions, or insurgencies? There are two reasons. First, drawing attention to separatist movements qua movements highlights their autonomous agency vis-à-vis patron and host states. All too often, we define separatism in such a way as to relegate it to a mere side effect of external forces.[25] Partition, decolonization, and secession, for example, are frequently conflated.[26] But the differences matter: the first is done "from outside and above," the second "from within and above," and the third—for our purposes—"from within and below."[27] Framing the phenomenon as a social movement reminds us that we are dealing with an indigenous force inside the locality. Second, it is important that separatists—like any competent political actors—display tremendous tactical and ideological flexibility. There is a great temptation to define nationalist movements according to their provisional demands vis-à-vis the state.[28] These demands are highly unstable, however. Separatist elites are rarely unanimous, factionalism is ubiquitous, and ad hockery in narrative framing is common. Hard-line supporters of violent secession often sit alongside moderate autonomists seeking modest concessions ("goats" and "sheep," as Bruce Baker [2001] calls them). Some of them reserve greater contempt for each other than for their national out-group enemy. Nevertheless, such divisions can be an asset: movements pressure the host state with modest demands by pointing to uncompromising extremists in their ranks. Hard-line separatists, in turn, are rarely die-hard ideologues or nationalist purists. They say what they think is politically expedient to particular audiences. In sum, separatists oscillate effortlessly between hard-line maximalist and accommodationist demands—as social movements tend to do.[29]

Before defining mafias, let us fix their essential activity and source of power: a *racket* is a monopoly on a good (primarily narcotics) or service (primarily protection) considered illegal or otherwise illegitimate, backed by violence.[30] This violence need not be exercised frequently or at all. But at minimum, credible threat is necessary to safeguard contraband, storage sites, smuggling routes, and people who purchased protection. Phil Williams and John Picarelli (2001, 116) call it "the capacity to hurt"—as economical a definition as there is. Rackets include the criminal infiltration of at least one state or quasi-state institution such as a ministry, public enterprise, or army. In addition to bribing or strong-arming officials, mafias hire lawyers, journalists, drivers, guards, accountants, clerks, medics, and scientists—all legally. Though they specialize, criminals often diversify and transition across rackets. For instance, they initially seize an opportunity of sudden market demand for Kalashnikovs, but then adapt their infrastructure to smuggle refugees as well. Most rackets—such as those in marijuana in Senegal (chapter 6) or food in Palestine (chapter 7)—are widely considered popular and legitimate. But certain smuggling enterprises—in human organs or highly enriched uranium (HEU) (chapter 5)—carry a special burden of ignominy and prohibition, posing unique challenges to separatists and governments involved. I will call such high-stigma rackets *nefarious organized crime*.

Rackets are violent and illegal, but not entirely secretive. The criminal underworld (n.b., "under") is mistakenly thought to be absolutely clandestine and anonymous, shying away from public light. In fact, visible displays of violence are critical for deterrence, credibility, and administrative efficiency.[31] The strategic placement of mutilated corpses, for instance, is a deliberate instrument of public relations. Just as Mexican cartels place headless bodies in a pile in Yucatán to communicate in a turf war, most of the rackets in this book are advertised publicly. That is not to say that there are no *codes of conduct*: rules governing discipline, communication, and duties. But traditional secrecy codes such as the Sicilian omertà (incidentally, it meant "manliness," not "silence") survive only in cinema and shrinking ethnic enclaves. The globalization of media has eroded them. Eager to capitalize on mafia mystique, a cavalcade of gangsters has exposed the inner workings of these criminal milieus in television interviews, tell-all tabloids, and court testimonies. In torn states, silence is arguably even rarer, with gangsters embracing celebrity to solicit political patronage and sustain violent authority. Rackets require discretion, but also credibility.

The mafias in this book are *transnational*: they run rackets—smuggling enterprises, protection rings, or both—across recognized international borders. They also operate domestic ones. Yet the seductive lure of illicit cross-border profiteering is chronic. *Contraband*—narcotics, heavy weaponry, or prostitutes—is illegal even if it is not smuggled. Other goods—cigarettes, light weaponry, or migrants—are smuggled, but may otherwise be legal. Some—like the stimulant qat—are legal within a torn state (Yemen), but are contraband in neighboring countries (Saudi Arabia). As we will see in chapter 4, whether rackets are concentrated in *separatist* or *host state* territory makes quite a difference. Transnational smuggling takes two forms: administrative, traversing legitimate checkpoints or crossings governed by states or proto-state representatives; and physical, bypassing governments altogether via illegal routes.[32] Some mafias are purely administrative smugglers, such as the Sinai Clans of Palestine through Hamas-controlled Gaza-Egypt tunnels. Others are physical smugglers, like the Agadez mafias of Niger across the Sahel and Sahara. But most combine and alternate between the two methods. Smuggling insinuates surreptitious concealment from governments, yet this is misleading.[33] Most mafias are partially integrated into government or separatist movement institutions, and their smuggling rackets enjoy considerable official support. We must therefore recognize a peculiarity of torn states: where separatist movements progress, opportunities multiply for *both* administrative and physical smuggling. Therein lies one of the greatest incentives for separatist officials to patronize rackets. Rackets are ominous enough in advanced, rule-of-law societies. In torn states, however, mafias can conduct what Jesse Driscoll (2015, 52) termed "aggrandized extortion": the capacity to threaten state elites with substantial instability and chaos through economic sabotage, public disorder, seizures of power, and political violence. Simply put, racketeering in torn states is a matter of the highest politics.

A *mafia* is a relatively centralized criminal network of at least twenty actors engaged in a sustained racket for at least a year. For convenience, "mafia" will be used synonymously with the long-winded "organized criminal group." Despite its etymology, the term has acquired a helpfully nonethnic colloquial meaning. It also signals that organized crime is an agent, not merely an abstract activity.[34] Within mafias, tensions between old and young, traditionalists and adventurists, and the political and the agnostic generate competing as well as sometimes incoherent strategies. Mafias consist of at least two *gangs*: smaller, compact subunits engaging in consistent, profitable criminal activity in a locality. Rivaling formal authorities, a gang can exercise significant control over a neighborhood, village, or even entire city. Surpassing recreational theft and violence, its activities are patronized by a clique of mafia heads. Gangs— whether Nigerian area boys, Turkish *babastures*, or Russian *brigadas*—often dissolve, merge, splinter, or integrate into government or separatist organizations (notably, militias).[35] *Gangsters* will refer to individuals—higher-ups or rank and file—who supervise or administer coercion or extraction to sustain rackets. They are not exclusively from the "criminal milieu," as is often assumed; many gangsters "act directly within law-enforcement institutions or within the private security sector."[36] Vadim Volkov's (2002) pioneering study called them "violent entrepreneurs."

An important implication of these definitions is that mafias do not necessarily undermine government. On the contrary, political figures themselves often create and sustain organized crime to boost administrative capacity. The "hypothesis that the strengthening of illegal networks automatically undermines state power" has been rejected even for stable democratic societies, let alone for separatist regions.[37] Embarrassingly, mafias can be corrosive *or* conducive to state making.

Mafias are notoriously hybrid in organizational structure. There is no single model of organized crime across the world. As a rough approximation, I identify an economic branch, which handles the profiteering, and a governance branch, which monitors agents, mediates disputes, and creates and enforces rules. The administrative functions are frequently divorced from extractive and trading activities, with highly centralized committees for the former, but loose, diffuse associations for the latter.[38]

How do mafias fit into the broader, *dis*organized crime scene? For our purposes, they are between corruption, on the one hand, and banditry, on the other. At one end of the spectrum, systemic corruption is the target of World Bank and Transparency International reports: graft, nepotism, bribery, embezzlement, and influence peddling in government and civil society bureaucracies. Mafias certainly make use of corruption, "the oxygen for organized crime."[39] Rackets necessarily involve at least a few—and sometimes hundreds of—politicians, police officers, judges, customs officers, border guards, and so on. (For transnational smuggling, they may span a dozen bureaucracies.) But systemic corruption—no matter how endemic—is largely consensual and voluntary. Mafias, in contrast, sustain their activities with a conspicuous degree of compulsion and coercion. At the other end of the spectrum, banditry—piracy, marauding, or vandalism—is spontaneous and unsystematic crime lacking penetration of at least one state or quasi-state institution. Bandits are nomadic, lonesome, and independent criminals. Mafias, in contrast, are stationary, sizable, and highly organized with codes of conduct, a division of labor, and patrimonial networks. Bandits may be clustered in free-roaming gangs, but it is only when they acquire higher criminal patronage that they become a mafia constituent. As we will see, one of the hallmarks of a successful mafia, separatist movement, or government is the capacity to organize extant banditry.

Finally, if a mafia operates a transnational smuggling racket in the post–Cold War era, it is labeled a *globalized mafia* or *transnational organized crime*.[40] Today's organized crime boasts an unprecedented diversity of ethnonational composition and territorial reach.[41] As we will see, this endows mafias with the speed, flexibility, and leverage to be major actors on the stage of separatist politics.

The Road Ahead

Chapter 2 will review the literature and conclude part 1. I then proceed to a mesoanalysis of Serbia/Kosovo and Georgia / South Ossetia in part 2 (chapters 3–5), move to a macroanalysis of West Africa, the Middle East, and Eastern Europe in part 3 (chapters 6–8), and arrive at the conclusion (chapter 9). In part 2, I argue that the differences in separatist outcomes between Kosovo and South Ossetia were due to organized crime. In part 3, I suggest that four types of globalized mafias—varying in state dependence and ethnocentric partisanship—mold torn states in three regions. The book is organized as an ascending "zoom out" from an in-depth, high-resolution look at two outstanding cases of separatism, to a broader, more generalizable analysis of fourteen countries.

Chapter 2 reviews scholarly approaches to the issue. Though both are rich, the compartmentalized literatures on separatism and organized crime have not suitably addressed each other. To cross-fertilize insights on the two phenomena, I propose two analytic tools: a Simmelian triadic model of relations between the state, separatist movement, and organized crime, defining three formative roles that mafias play; and a typology of organized crime across three regions, according to how state dependent and partisan they are.

Chapter 3 process traces host state, separatist movement, and mafia relations in Serbia and Georgia, 1989–2012. Though organized crime in both countries began as a *rejoicing third*, the mafia's role in Kosovo evolved into a *divider and conqueror*, while in South Ossetia it evolved into a *mediator*. These differing trajectories account for the greater success of Kosovo's separatist movement.

Chapter 4 compares the organized criminal filtering of regional smuggling opportunities (in drugs and arms) into separatist movement benefit. Mafia *capacity* and *predisposition* in these rackets at critical junctures—1999 in Kosovo and 2008 in South Ossetia—enhanced and stagnated separatism, respectively.

Chapter 5 examines organ smuggling in Kosovo (1999–2000) and HEU smuggling in South Ossetia (2006), comparing three dimensions of mafia capacity: *infrastructure*, regarding control of borders and sites; *autonomy*, concerning the ability to leverage separatist ideology and instrumentalize movement institutions; and *community*, apropos levels of fear, discipline, and clan-based solidarity. Nefarious crime harmed Kosovo's separatists less because mafia capacity was greater, thereby containing the damage.

Chapter 6 begins regional overviews in West Africa during 1989–2019. Three of the host states (Mali, Senegal, and Nigeria) were significantly torn by ethnocentric, separatist-controlled rackets in drugs and migrants (Azawad), marijuana (Casamance), and extortion (Boko Haram). Nigeria employed ethnocentric Niger Delta mafias to fight its northern separatists. In Niger's Agadez and Cameroon's Ambazonia, however, organized crime promoted cohesion.

Chapter 7 surveys four torn states in the Middle East. The Turkish government mobilized gangsters (gunrunners, mercenaries, and assassins) as instruments of antiseparatist crackdown. Mafias sustained Kurdish separatists in Turkey (through narcotics, arms, extortion, and money laundering), the Islamic State (IS) in Iraq and Syria (oil, extortion, theft, and gangs), and Gazan Palestinians in Israel (tunnel smuggling). In contrast, Yemen and the Houthis were both sabotaged in their efforts by a state dependent—but utterly disloyal—mafia operating qat and arms rackets.

Chapter 8 analyzes Eastern Europe, where ethnocentric organized crime dominated the separatist movements of Greater Albania (Macedonia), Transnistria (Moldova), and Nagorno-Karabakh (Azerbaijan). The Azeri host state deployed gangsters to combat separatists in wartime and sustain its oil regime in peacetime. In the cases of the Autonomous Province of Western Bosnia (Bosnia-Herzegovina) and Donbas (Ukraine), mafias' indiscriminate smuggling from within government structures obstructed separatists and host states alike.

Chapter 9 concludes with five propositions that may inform future research and, more quixotically, policy.

2

Normal Bedfellows

The people cannot decide until somebody decides who are the people.
—IVOR JENNINGS, *THE APPROACH TO SELF-GOVERNMENT*

The organized crime boss of today is the insta-patriot and freedom fighter of tomorrow.
—ANDREW BOWEN, "COERCIVE DIPLOMACY AND THE DONBAS"

This chapter develops three concepts: separatism, organized crime, and the relation between the two. I begin by drawing on social scientific insights to dispel some common misconceptions about, in turn, separatist movements and mafias. By bridging two compartmentalized subfields, we discover just how natural the connections between them are. Finally, I delineate two tools—a Simmelian triadic model of state-separatist-mafia relations, and typology of mafias across three regions—for explaining the phenomenon.

Separatism

Scholars have tackled the timing of secessions, patron state support for separatism, structural determinants of torn states, the effect of military intervention on separatist movements, border reconfigurations as "rightsizing," separatism as ethnic politics, Asia-Europe similarities in separatist-government interaction, and international recognition of secessionist identities and borders—all without attention to organized crime.[1] But there are compelling reasons to inject mafias into the core of our conceptualization of separatism.

UNDERDEVELOPMENT

Though Western separatist movements receive tremendous attention, global dynamics can hardly be understood from this subset of exceptional cases.

Investigations of torn states in underdeveloped regions tend to be regimented by area studies. For example, an outstanding literature on "de facto" and "unrecognized" states is limited to post-Communist Eurasia.[2] Other works, on warlord politics and "subnationalism," are restricted to sub-Saharan Africa.[3] Even as they overlap, both hesitate to generalize insights to separatism globally. Meanwhile, studies generalizing from the advanced democracies are bold and sweeping. Abstract conceptualizations of separatism disregard non-Western torn states entirely.[4] John Doyle (2010) puts greater emphasis on the United States, Canada, and Western Europe than on the rest of the world combined. Ian S. Lustick's (1993) explanation of border reconfiguration as state expansion/contraction dynamics essentially uses the British (Ireland) and French (Algeria) cases to theorize about Palestine, and then the world.[5] The likes of the Québécois, Catalans, and Flemish often serve as empirical templates for "theorizing" separatism globally.

But separatism is not the proverbial first world problem. It is overwhelmingly located in poor, underdeveloped societies with weak, undemocratic, and criminalized states. The most comprehensive data set of 464 self-determination movements found that affluent and democratic countries have hosted a modest minority of separatist cases from 1945 to 2012.[6] After the Cold War (1990–2012), their share fell further.[7] Moreover, separatists in wealthy and stable countries are tamed because states with rich democratic traditions are more effective at preventing separatism. The mere existence of a meaningful federalism, confederalism, or regionalism preempts movement mobilization. David Siroky and John Cuffe (2015, 41–43), coding 115 ethnic groups from Asia, Europe, and North America, found that those without autonomy status launched separatist movements much more frequently (45 percent) than those with some semblance of autonomy (19 percent). Those constituencies that *had* had autonomy before it was taken away from them were particularly likely to mobilize: 89 percent of ethnic groups that lost autonomy status turned to separatism, but only 21 percent of groups that have autonomy currently and 2 percent that never had it. Full of institutionalized safety valves, Western rule-of-law democracies have deep structural hinderances to separatist escalation.[8]

When compelled to compromise, furthermore, wealthy democratic host states are more likely to make concessions. They are also less likely to restrict the rights of rebellious constituencies. Separatists in rich countries have a 50 percent chance of extracting concessions; in medium-income countries, their chances are below a third; in poor societies, negligible.[9] The reason, Michael Hechter (2000) argued, is that indirect rule inhibits separatism. But high-capacity indirect rule is a luxury of prosperous, stable countries. Accordingly, the agendas of Western separatist movements are much more modest. Most of them have tempered their demands to benign reformist ones, notably native-language use. Some of their grievances are incomprehensible elsewhere; northern Italians, Flemings, and Catalans, for instance, boast a superior economic position compared to the host state proper. While the rest of the separatist world resents underprivilege, these three are tired of footing the bill for their unproductive compatriots.

When separatist conflict *does* escalate in rich countries, it is remarkably pacifistic. There have been zero post-1990 wars to adjudicate separatist quarrels in the advanced democracies. Elsewhere, separatism is a more pugnacious affair; 61 percent of movements globally are violent.[10] These "violent movements tend to be in poorer and less democratic societies."[11] Among separatist elites globally, Palestine's Yasser Arafat is normal, while Tibet's Dalai Lama is an outlier. Among separatist elites in developed societies, Catalonia's Carles Puigdemont is typical, while the Irish Republican Army's Thomas "Slab" Murphy is exceptional. One need only look at the pathos-laden spectacle of a recent Basque press conference to appreciate the chasm between separatism in the West versus the rest. The ETA—the militant wing of Basque secessionism—issued a public apology for the deaths caused in forty years of terrorism.[12] I have searched in vain for a single, comparable instance of a separatist spokesperson *apologizing* (for violence or otherwise) outside the Western democracies.

One final divergence: organized crime plays no role whatsoever in the vast majority of Western separatist movements.[13] Elsewhere, as we will see, mafias are integral to separatism.

BORDERS

Separatism is about borders—and not merely symbolic ones, at that.

Rational choice theorists have attributed considerable cost-benefit certainty to the choices of separatists and host states.[14] The decision to engage in violence, especially, has been modeled on expected government benefits, reasons for trust in civil war contexts, and economic gains and losses.[15] Even the most seemingly irrational and chaotic wars, Stathis Kalyvas (2006) argued, have a logical structure to them, as the deliberate strategies and interests of elites and local actors intertwine. Separatism through civil war emerges, quite simply, when it "is profitable for potential insurgents, in that they can both survive and enjoy some probability of winning the state," while "secession is seen to be the outcome of a series of collective decisions made by regional leaders and populations."[16] Furthermore, ethnic secession is more likely as the dilemma of "credible commitment" intensifies: the more distrustful minorities are of majorities' willingness to secure protection and rights, the more rational separatism becomes.[17]

But these approaches rarely acknowledge the border-specific interests involved. First, borders determine peacetime smuggling dynamics. Separatist movements are compelled to rely on extrainstitutional funding channels. The goods they hope to deliver to their constituency instead of the host state—food, medicine, fuel, and so on—often require smuggling. The contraband that fills separatist coffers (notably narcotics) requires black marketeering. One possibility is moving across unadministered frontier zones (typically, mountains and desert). Another is to smuggle across existing host state checkpoints: via bribery, document forgery, or creative concealment. But a third option—much preferable—is to have *separatist*-controlled border infrastructure: passports, ramps, booths, watchtowers, guards, roadside sentries, license plates, and tariff stamps. The profits to be made are enormous, and the special interests involved (notably mafias) may be directly at odds with nationalist goals, complicating the instrumental rationality calculus. Second, access to war matériel is critical during violent conflict. Successfully importing arms can mean the difference between victory and annihilation. Little wonder that separatist elites are obsessed with checkpoints, buffer zones, frontline trenches, and the no-man's-lands between them. Quite apart from the symbolic value, the separatist administration of checkpoints enables espionage and the surveillance of supply lines. The cost-benefit analysis of civil war therefore frequently has more to do with securing merchandise around strategic border positions than with nationalism per se.[18]

These realities are not easy to admit publicly. Nominally, separatists are maximalist in their calls for self-determination. As good nationalists, they insist on the doctrine that national and state boundaries must coincide.[19] In practice, however, they settle for less than statehood, administered by a combination of host state agents, international peacekeepers, and partial (even emblematic) separatist representation. Host states are extremely sensitive about their borders, often engaging in futile symbolic gestures to keep up appearances of territorial control. "For weak states in particular," Justin Hastings (2010, 39) points out, "borders are one of the most visible manifestations of their (sometimes otherwise nonexistent) sovereignty." On the ground, then, disputed frontiers operate through implicit agreement between separatist and host state institutions to share overlapping, ambiguous, and criminalized jurisdictions at checkpoints. Utterly inconsistent with official nationalist pieties on either side, such unofficial arrangements make certain constituencies very powerful—and very wealthy.[20]

Rogers Brubaker (1996) has conceptualized the separatist imbroglio as a product of three forces: nationalizing states, national minorities, and external homelands.[21] In practical terms, this is frequently manifested as porous checkpoints administered by weakly centralized governments, minority non-officials levying "taxes" on behalf of separatists or warlords, and minority, diaspora communities on either side of the "border" that informally regulate trade and movement. Africa, notably, hosts voluminous "gray zones": quasi-state territories that contradict formal borders but are themselves fragile, precarious polities.[22] Far from resisting such arrangements, separatism thrives on them.

Accordingly, one should not exaggerate the importance of separatist rhetoric in defining rational separatist actions. "Discoursive dynamics" and "frames" about ethnic boundaries do not themselves create new nation-states.[23] When disputed borders are lucrative, separatists are perfectly capable of suspending nation building altogether. Indeed, as we will explore, one thing that gangster bosses, separatist leaders, and government figureheads have in common is a superb instinct for self-preservation at the public's expense. Hard-line positions on national perimeters change accordingly.

HETEROGENEITY

Secession is one matter, but ethnic homogenization is quite another.

Separatists promise stability and justice through "natural" ethnonational boundaries. Yet border reconfigurations aimed at ethnic or tribal homogeneity are often counterproductive. Instead of harmonizing new neighboring nations, "ethnic unmixing" perpetuates instability, civil war, and more of itself.[24] Brubaker (1998, 233–34) attributed this to the "architectonic illusion": the mistaken belief that "the right territorial and institutional framework can satisfy nationalist demands, quench nationalist passions and thereby resolve national conflicts." In this sense, separatists are the ultimate architectonic illusionists.

First, "the people" being separated remains a mystified concept with elusive boundaries.[25] Who, exactly, enjoys the right of secession? Groups (like nationalities) or polities (like republics)? If the former, do they have to be large enough, old enough, different enough? Should borders be political, geographic, or ethnic? If the first, should they be provincial, regional, or federal? In which historical period—Soviet, British colonial, ancient African—are "authentic" and "natural" frontiers to be found? What survey, election, or tribal council map can we possibly accept as a legitimate benchmark? Above all, who decides any of this?

Second, taken to its logical conclusion, separatist logic inspires infinite regress. Every entrepreneurial patriarch with a grievance, surveyor, and flag could warrant a new nation-state. "Why should I be a minority in your country," a Balkan proverb asks, "when you can be a minority in mine?" More than a third of new post–Cold War entities bred their own separatist movements within the new polities. Some, like Bosnia-Herzegovina, Georgia, and Ukraine, host *two* major separatist challengers; territorially noncontiguous, these secessionists within secessionists tear the young countries on two sides. "Once the logic of secession is admitted," Immaneul Wallerstein (1961, 88) noted, "there is no end except in anarchy."

Third, separatism often appears a remedy worse than the disease. Postcolonial and post-Communist state making creates leftover communities— "orphans of secession," as John McGarry (1998) called them—stranded in new polities in which they do not feel they belong. Within newly seceded entities, separatist success creates a perverse incentive to displace and dispossess minorities.[26] In principle, nationalism offers two elegant solutions: "rightsizing the state"—through annexation, partition, or secession—and "rightsizing the people"—through assimilation, expulsion, or genocide.[27] In practice, neither looks appealing:

> The assumption has usually been that secession produces homogenous states. In point of fact, neither secessionist states nor rump [i.e., host] states are homogenous. They can be made more homogenous only by the clumsiest and most unfair methods of population exchange or by policies of expulsion, always carried out with a massive dose of killing.[28]

At a minimum, such separatist homogenization projects create perpetual refugee crises.[29] At most, this "dark side" of self-determination is genocidal.[30]

Nowhere is this Gordian knot tighter than in former imperial borderlands such as Eastern Europe, the Middle East, and West Africa. In Yugoslavia, the incongruence of republics with nationalities—stemming from the Anti-Fascist Council for the National Liberation of Yugoslavia, a 1943 makeshift wartime administration—fed manipulations of identity categories by regional elites, international actors, and tendentious scholars.[31] Titoism congealed the Macedonian nation, while Bosniak became a brand-new, salient ethnic category among Muslims. Similarly, the USSR's fifteen republics created a tenuous ethnofederalism in tension with emergent post–Cold War conceptions of nationhood and belonging.[32] Moldova-Transnistria, for example, has been repeatedly reconfigured by the Russian Empire, Romania, and the Soviets, while Joseph Stalin personally (as commissar of nationalities) switched Nagorno-Karabakh from Armenia to Azerbaijan.

Imperial carvings likewise cast a long shadow on Arab and African nationalisms.[33] It was Ottoman, Persian, and European compromises that scattered Kurds across four states, while Ottoman and British endowments molded north and south Yemenis, respectively. In Senegal, the Portuguese (Casamançais) and French (northerners) left their trace. In Nigeria, the British empowered the Hausa, Ibo, and Yoruba at the expense of the Ogoni. In Cameroon, the carving up of Germany's colony between France and Britain continues to pit the anglophone southerners against the francophone majority. When separatist cleavages mirror centuries-old colonial divisions, nationalist fantasies are difficult to reconcile with the heterogeneity of today's torn states.

We arrive at an important observation. If a transnational network—a mafia, for instance—traverses disputed borders in such regions, it is certain to be embedded in the dilemmas of ethnic politics.

LEGITIMACY DEFICIT

Separatism is a Sisyphean endeavor. It is difficult enough that separatists are deemed inherently illegitimate by their host state, disruptive by neighboring states, and criminal by the international community. But adding insult to injury, even the very people they purportedly seek to emancipate are often hesitant to sacrifice and fickle in their nationalist enthusiasm.

Born of the Treaty of Versailles, Woodrow Wilson's Fourteen Points, and Leninist nationalities policies, the doctrine of self-determination has survived the Cold War.[34] In principle, "nationalism can be employed equally in the service of unification or secession."[35] In practice, however, there is no doubt which prevailed in the twenty-first century. Of two unificationist cases (Germany and Yemen, both in 1990), one was a spectacular success. But the premature integration of North and South Yemen boomeranged into separatist bloodshed in a single generation. The harmonious secessions of Slovakia from Czechoslovakia (1993) and South Sudan from Sudan (2011) are exceptions; the likes of Namibia (1990), Eritrea (1993), and East Timor (2002)—whose border demarcations plagued them with war, displacement, and bankruptcy—are the rule.[36]

In defense, modern nation-states have rushed to criminalize separatism. Constitutions treat it not only as offense but as *the* supreme crime. From China's Uyghurs to South Africa's Zulus, entire ethnic groups have endured persecution under the banner of antiseparatist legalisms. The UN Charter sanctifies territorial integrity. Through technicalities, International Court of Justice opinions carefully avoid condoning secession qua secession.[37] Host states refuse to recognize each other's separatist entities, crafting multilateral treaties—such as the Shanghai Convention against separatism—to nip secession in the bud. Compared to other insurgencies, "separatist movements tend to get less foreign support because most governments are reluctant to encourage secession even from their enemies."[38] Even radical proponents of the right of secession struggle to relativize its illegality under international law.[39] The stigma of unconstitutionality and treason lingers even after independence is achieved.

The legitimacy deficit does not end there. Frequently, the disjuncture between separatist elites and the population they represent is colossal. In a classic early statement on separatism, Anthony Smith (1979, 21)—never one to downplay ethnonational solidarity—insisted that the phenomenon cannot be reduced to "an outlet for the expression of ethnic identity and social regeneration." Rather, opportunistic power centers pursuing self-interest. "One of the chief sources of separatism's continuing appeal," Smith argued, is that it "affords a new set of avenues to power and privilege for members of strata hitherto excluded from a share in both." The separatist demos, meanwhile, often knows not what it wants. Consider referenda. When the separatist motion is proposed in democratic conditions with free and fair elections, "the people" tend to be deeply divided. It is only when the question is put in staged, *un*democratic, and *un*free conditions of censorship and repression that separatism wins—and with above 90 percent consensus at that. One need only compare the referenda in Quebec (1995), in Scotland (2014), on Brexit (2016), and in Catalonia (2017) with those of the Iraqi Kurds (2005, 2017), Montenegrins (2006), and Crimeans (2014) to appreciate the difference. When the separatist dilemma is put without coercion, abstentions and "no" votes carry the day.

Secessionism's unpopularity should not be surprising: human beings are risk averse and biased toward the status quo.[40] Citizens are much more afraid of what they might lose than hopeful of what they might gain. This dominates ordinary political decision making, let alone abnormal, high-uncertainty dilemmas such as separatist rebellions.[41] Secession is a gambit; it may increase isolation, provoke host state retaliation, create an unsustainable Bantustan in the international system, or destroy the economy. The benefits of a new nation appear abstract, but the stakes in safety, livelihood, and property are concrete and salient.[42] Ex-Yugoslavia was a striking example. Supposedly a paradigm of nationalisms outrivaling each other in mass popular support, separatism was in fact overwhelmingly opposed prior to the outbreak of war.[43] In summer and fall 1990, the population was asked, "Do you agree that every (Yugoslav) nation should have a national state of its own?" Sixteen percent agreed completely, 7 percent agreed partly, 61 percent did not agree at all, and 10 percent disagreed partly.[44] In regional scholarship, nationalist mythology has dispatched such facts into George Orwell's memory hole.

Separatist movements—especially successful ones—are adept at retrospectively constructing narratives of popular support. One of nationalism's most cherished "invented traditions" is commemorating precisely the mythology of consensus at the time of nationalist founding.[45] From Zionism to Hindu nationalism, ethnic "origin myths" not only whitewash massacres and expulsions of out-groups. They also erase in-group heterogeneity from history. In real time, however, separatists face chronic legitimacy challenges both before and during fabled periods of ethnonational awakening. The "Sleeping Beauty" view of separatism, as Hechter (2000, 6, 15) mockingly labeled it, distorts the fact that a deeply ambivalent, skeptical "Beauty" is hardly thrilled to waken.

We arrive at a paradox. On the one hand, given their structural circumstances, separatists are especially predisposed to nonlegal and extrainstitutional (i.e., organized criminal) means. Denied normal legal channels to achieve their aims, they naturally turn elsewhere. On the other hand, precisely because of their reliance on criminal means, separatists assume an impossible burden of illegitimacy: a double stigmatization—one for their treasonous ends, and another for their criminal means. Host states relish in portraying separatist elites as criminals, repelling sympathy and support both domestically and internationally. When separatist movements do in fact ally with mafias—a perfectly normal association, we will find—the legitimacy deficit amplifies.

LONG-DISTANCE SEPARATISM

Separatism appears to be a purely domestic dispute. It is not.

External threats are the sine qua non of ethnonational identification and mobilization.[46] Just as nineteenth-century nationalists defined themselves in opposition to colonial empire, twenty-first-century separatists exist in relation to their host state opponent. It is by resisting the titular ethnicity that separatists define their own. The movement's trajectory is always an imperfect compromise between the host state's nation-building efforts, negotiations with the minority ethnicity seeking to separate, and international stakeholders.[47]

The notion that foreign intervention molds separatist success is practically a truism.[48] Military intrusions were decisive for separatists from Southeast Asia to the Balkans.[49] Explaining Soviet secessions, one analyst remarked, "One can do worse than answer with the crude observation that 'Political elites in Russia just wanted it that way.'"[50] Nominally "domestic" factors (such as separatist tactics, ethnic identification processes, and resource mobilization) always interact with "foreign" ones (economic sanctions, ethnic migrations, neighboring state collapse, and—crucially—transnational smuggling).

To be sure, foreign support matters. Great powers routinely abuse international law regarding secession as they see fit.[51] Russia detests Chechen separatism, but generates Crimean. China pressures Taiwan, but sends state-building peacekeepers to independent South Sudan. The United States deplores Ossetian independence, but celebrates Kosovo's. Secessionists cunningly navigate these diplomatic discrepancies to their advantage. Geopolitical reductionism, according to which separatists are mere pawns in grander, strategic chess games, is tempting but inadequate.[52] Host states themselves paint their estranged foes as puppets on the strings of foreigners to discredit their indigenous base. But Nina Caspersen (2008) argues persuasively that the tendency to relegate separatists to mere instruments of their patron state sponsors is mistaken.[53]

Separatism is also inherently international because diasporas are bedrocks of movement success.[54] Diasporas provide funding, recruit militants, and lobby patron states and other international sponsors. Refugees are especially consequential, as forced migration instigates ethnic identification and mobilization.[55] Suffering the "anguish of displacement, the nostalgia of exile, the repatriation of funds or the brutalities of asylum seeking," these displaced communities are often more nationalistic than their brethren in the motherland.[56] Zlatko Skrbiš (1999) calls this "long-distance nationalism": the exaggerated attachment to national territory on the part of dislocated people. Striking examples are Tuaregs in Mali and Niger, Albanians in Serbia and Macedonia, and Kurds in Turkey, Iraq, and Syria. Cycles of population dispersion and resettlement are among the most powerful contributors to separatist momentum.

Furthermore, separatist movements observe each other through diaspora organizations and communication networks. As with other social movements, the tactics, frames, identities, and demands of separatist trailblazers are diffused regionally.[57] Albanian secessionism in Serbia ignited separatism in Macedonia. Uses of Palestinian and Kurdish symbols—flags, anthems, and uniforms—were emulated by smaller separatist movements across the Middle East. In Africa, the fiascos of Biafra and Katanga loom as a dark cloud over secessionist dreams, while the successes of Eritrea and South Sudan entice would-be governors to gamble.[58] A "tidal" effect of separatist movements inspiring each other was critical to post-Soviet nationalist mobilizations.[59] The rapid series of secessions across Eurasia prompted scholars to say "separatism is contagious" like "the common cold."[60] Ethnic diasporas—to continue the unsympathetic metaphor—are indispensable transmitters of the disease.

One final observation. Diasporas also tend to reside where transnational organized crime happens to be embedded. An ethnocentric mafia can be a critical ingredient for the mobilization of people and extraction of resources from coethnics across disputed borders.

Transnational Organized Crime

Organized crime scholarship typically neglects separatist cases altogether or confounds them with nonseparatist ones.[61] Yet today's globalized mafias have deep structural reasons to flourish, especially in torn states.

NETWORK

A pervasive myth about organized crime is its hierarchy.

Ironically, it was not even true of the archetypal Sicilian mafia.[62] Experts iterate that "there does not exist—and there never has existed—any secret, hierarchical and centralized criminal organization called the *mafia*."[63] "Mafioso," moreover, was "not a rank or position within a secret organization. Rather, it represented a type of position within a patron-client relationship of Sicilian society itself."[64] With globalization, hierarchy in transnational mafias became unattainable.[65] Even if top-down command chains were maintained nationally, cross-border ties are loose and polycentric internationally. Thus today's Sicilian mafia is one cluster in a decentralized network of Albanian, Nigerian, and Turkish mafias stretching from Benin City to Berlin.

Organized crime remains what it has always been: a patrimonial, horizontal social structure (of the sort Max Weber observed in noncapitalistic societies). Mafias are *not* bureaucratized, impersonal hierarchies (of the type Weber saw in armies, states, and firms). Instead of pyramids, we may visualize spider webs. Hierarchy, however, is not the same as centralization. Mafia webs do indeed have a focal middle—vague, shifting, and cacophonic as it may be. Without this center, a criminal network is an assortment of vaguely interconnected gangs— mere *dis*organized crime. Additionally, "the governmental structure of mafia families is not the same as the economic structure of the organisations that actually undertake criminal activity."[66] The political decision-making center is therefore coupled with a highly diffuse profit-making enterprise.

The *political structure*—a governing group of under ten leaders—creates rules, adjudicates disputes, regulates membership, and punishes transgressors. Much of the leaders' power is supervisory, not managerial. They themselves cannot administer smuggling, conduct extortion, or even issue commands to individual gangsters. Rather, they define and enforce the limits of rackets— often after criminal schemes have been created without their approval. This political body may include figures associated with governments, separatist institutions, legal private enterprises, civil society groups, or other enablers. A gangster boss may control one racket (e.g., narcotics), but not another (e.g., protection); one might handle brokers in the locality, and another abroad. Rarely does a single personality—like the Turkish mafia's Dündar Kılıç— dominate. Instead, some sort of collective decision making and power sharing emerges, frequently ad hoc, inconsistent, and defensive. While elite conflicts may produce internal rotations and external substitutions, this agenda-setting body is relatively cohesive and centralized.

But the *economic structure*—which physically administers rackets on the proverbial ground—is far more decentralized and compartmentalized within an allotted turf. This is the profit-making machine of organized crime: enforcers, informants, distributors, collectors, fixers, smugglers, and wheeler-dealers. Members often simultaneously serve in armies, militias, or other armed formations. Clustered into gangs, many of them have no idea what broader organization they are a part of except via middlepersons who liaison with the political center. For instance, Kurdish narco-distributors in the Netherlands and United Kingdom—under the same mafia umbrella—were fully unaware of each other. For a price, gangs largely administer their own rackets without interference. Through neighborhood solidarity, surveillance, and recruitment, gangsters create lasting subcultures as well as lucrative markets. Their connections to formal institutions are restricted to low- and midlevel bribed officials.

These two structures constitute a dynamic but nebulous network. Mafias have no manifestos, membership lists, or organizational charts. We thus abandon the fetching image of criminal command pyramids on chalkboards in scenes from *The Godfather* (1972) and *The Sopranos* (1999–2007). Instead, *Once Upon a Time in America* (1984) and *Gomorrah* (2008) give better portrayals of the typical organizational structure: decentralized economic networks overlapping with a centralized political governing body.

Two implications are worth bearing in mind: this kind of network is akin to guerrilla groups, revolutionary cells, and social movement organizations; and given their structure, mafias will tend to overlap with political and economic institutions in environments where hierarchical, bureaucratized governments are limited or contested.

ROOTS AND TERRITORY

Globalization has allegedly made mafias deterritorialized, denationalized, and hypermobile. In actuality, they remain rooted.

Organized crime is notoriously embedded in extant community relations: patriarchal, occupational, residential, and above all, ethnic.[67] Tribal, clan, and kinship networks—the Albanian *fis*, the Tuareg *tawshet*, or the Palestinian *hamulas*—are the indispensable fabric into which criminal rackets are sown. The logic of rootedness is simple: "trust in the criminal world is highly fragile, particularly when one moves beyond the ties of family, kinship, ethnicity and other forms of bonding." Consequently, Williams (2002, 79) argues, globalized organized crime remains—unlike multinational corporate conglomerates—deeply fractured and connected by loose alliances instead of organizational integration. "The flow of organized crime products and services is transnational; however, control of the flow is local."[68]

Mafia mobility is also exaggerated. The growth of cybercrime, offshore finances, and modern smuggling technologies has exacerbated the illusion.[69] But mafia transplantations are rare, difficult, and highly undesirable for gangsters. Federico Varese (2011) demonstrated that, transnational as it may be, organized crime is extremely hesitant to uproot itself. Between Mancur Olson's (2000) "stationary" and "roving" bandits, globalized gangsters are decidedly the former.[70] On the rare occasions when mafias *are* mobile, they hardly acculturate in the destination society. Transplanted gangsters code switch and negotiate their own ethnicities as well as cultural reputations, precisely the way everybody else does.[71] Thus the uprooted "Turkish" and "Russian" mafias strategically instrumentalize ethnic stereotypes of Turkishness and Russianness to enforce obedience, instill fear, deter competitors, and avoid capture.

If anything, globalization has accentuated mafias' territoriality. As the modern nation-state refined its monitoring and surveillance capacities, organized crime has retreated from what Peter Andreas (2013) calls the "front door" (stations, harbors, and airports), to the "backdoor" (forests, deserts, and mountains) of transnational smuggling. Technical innovation tightened as many border crossings as it created: "The technologies, methods of transportation, and processes that are most liberated of territory are also the ones that move through global chokepoints, that have received the most aid from states, and thus, are the ones most subject to curtailment by state power, sometimes even nominal states power [i.e., separatists]."[72] Pressured to bypass such dangers, mafias and other "clandestine transnational groups," Justin Hastings (2010, 39) found, have increasingly become "dissociated from the state, and hence more dependent on difficult natural terrain." A globalized gangster must be competent at navigating obscure topography in periphery areas.

Where exactly are these territories in which today's global mafias are rooted? As it happens, they are precisely in regions rife with separatism. First, torn states tend to be in the middle of transnational organized crime routes. They are bridge societies for global smuggling paths: links between demand/destination and supply/source regions.[73] Of the sixteen host states examined in this book, eight are bridges for one traffic (in narcotics, arms, or people), six countries are bridges for two, and two cases are bridges for all three contraband. The world's most lucrative migrant trafficking route—from sub-Saharan Africa to Europe—traverses Mali's breakaway Azawad. Global heroin flows, from Afghanistan and Pakistan to the United States and Western Europe, cross Kurdish and Albanian separatist lands. Nagorno-Karabakh, South Ossetia, and Kosovo may be landlocked, but are otherwise advantaged: these territories are situated in the middle of massive post-Soviet arms traffics. In global criminal supply chains, the mafia "middleman minority" lives in and around separatist lands.

Second, separatists are disproportionately concentrated in tough topographies—what James C. Scott (1998) called "illegible" spaces—where host state penetration is historically difficult. It is no coincidence that *Nagorno* in Nagorno-Karabakh means "mountainous." Kurdish and Albanian guerrillas hide in highlands, while desert terrain conceals Boko Haram, Agadez, and Azawad separatists. Among the cases in this book, Senegal's Casamance has arguably the most fortuitous separatist geography: amble forest, bushes, and mangroves to hide from the host state in all directions, not to mention an oddly slim territory (480 by 80 kilometers) tailor-made for narco-trafficking.[74]

If separatism is common in rough terrains, and rough terrains provide mafia opportunities, it is only natural that mafias are rooted in disputed territories.

PATRIMONIAL GOVERNANCE

Mafias are undoubtedly animated by greed, profit, and market share. But they are just as vigorously dedicated to governance.[75]

Organized crime operates on patrimonialism: informal networks of patron-client relations enforced by personalistic rulers.[76] When governments are unable to meet security demands, mafias supply private protection to clients: citizens, families, tribes, businesses, churches, political parties, and—to be sure—social movements and insurgencies. A mafia "is performing governmental functions—law enforcement and criminal justice—in that sphere where the legal judicial system refuses to exercise power."[77] Given how hybrid mafias are, organized criminal governance has been overtheorized.[78] For our purposes, suffice it to acknowledge that the administration underpinning this kind of rule can reach startling levels—including state-like capacities for extraction, surveillance, and service provision. Even Kalyvas (2015, 17), a leading skeptic regarding mafias' impact, invites greater attention to how "criminal groups can out-administer the states they operate in and can evolve into institutions that resemble actual governments. Insofar as their rule is perceived as more real, and often even more legitimate, compared to the actual government's, this strengthens their capacity to grow and develop." This does not mean that profiteering is less important than patrimonial rule. A tired criminological debate has attempted to reduce mafias' function to purely economic (profit) or purely political (governance) motivations. The two desiderata are inseparable.[79]

Governance is, of course, not statehood. But in torn states, by definition, the aforementioned "sphere" of government capacity and legitimacy is narrow. As separatism escalates, mafias can inherit ever-larger spatial scope and power over sizable populations. Desperate to curb full-on secession, host states frequently sacrifice proper territorial sovereignty for tenuous, informal arrangements with regional tyrants. An "oft-observed truth of the Saharan political economy" of Niger and Mali, for instance, is that "for governments, controlling men is far more important than controlling territory."[80] This presents opportunities for mafias to feign statehood and gangsters to become statesmen.

But there is a liability. Patrimonial systems, as Weber recognized, are inherently unstable. In patron-client ties, personalities matter and individual gangsters often prove irreplaceable. Charismatic leaders tend to delegate and deputize against meritocracy. Ambitious regional bosses routinely form alliances without permission, diversify their businesses beyond their turf, and attempt to replace higher-ups. Reluctant to abdicate, mafia heads frequently meet their demise in a violent blaze of glory. Disintegration is therefore common, after which criminals reconfigure whatever network ties were operant into new ones. Accordingly, contrary to popular portrayals, organized crime is a short-term, fleeting enterprise. Durable mafias that persevere more than five years are exceptional, with the rule being "small groups of operators [who] take advantage of fortuitous opportunities, pulling off a few 'deals' before vanishing."[81]

Finally, mafia governance is a cultural force to be reckoned with. Patrimonial systems enjoy certain advantages over tiresome, rationalized organizations like governments. They celebrate private interest, offer space for charismatic personality, and suggest visible, sensational pathways to success. In torn states, criminal icons serve as bulwarks against anomie and moral disintegration. Russian mafias, for example, "regard themselves as bastions of order and morality in the community."[82] From the United States to Nigeria, ethnographic studies of gangs document remarkable convergence: gangsters tend to be young, male, socioeconomically disadvantaged, and inspired by dynamic cultural templates of masculinity, empowerment, and justice.[83] In many societies, mafias are defenders of ethnic tradition and dominant employers offering paths to social mobility. Due to parental absence or displacement, gangster children typically lack adult supervision. Thus "the gang becomes a surrogate family," a potent source of psychological and cultural fulfillment.[84]

Profit aside, then, mafia governance is a vigorous moral order.

STRUCTURAL AMBIVALENCE

Most definitions of mafias begin in relation to the state, conceptualizing organized crime as a by-product. This not only underestimates mafias' overall societal role. It neglects their twofold capacity for state building *and* state deformation—a crucial dualism that serves them especially well in torn states.

Mafias, like separatist movements, are technically nonstate actors. But all too often, "nonstate actors" serve as conceptual placeholders in societies we do not fully understand: "This term is unfortunate, as it does not accurately convey the nature of these groups. Organized crime may begin as a nonstate actor, hidden in the contours of the informal economy, but it can emerge into a state actor very quickly. Deposed racketeers can also transition into post-state actors or deterritorialized militias."[85] The "state" to which nonstate actors are contrasted is typically understood as a strong, consolidated government. The custom is then to distinguish three criminal interactions—predatory, parasitic, and symbiotic—with this government.[86] In this perspective, mafias are modest, apolitical agents who react to—but cannot determine—the fate of states.

This outlook is modeled on countries that are convenient to study, lush in data, and recognizable to traditional criminology. In torn states, the biological metaphor quickly fails. The "social organism," as Durkheimians would put it, is literally splitting in separatist contexts. Mafias have choices as to which of two and sometimes three "organisms" to be predatory, symbiotic, or parasitic toward. Even without separatist war, torn states offer multiple sets of mutually exclusive institutions—political offices, security forces, financial bodies, and border administrations—to engage. Mafias in torn states have the luxury of being picky.

An alternative approach is to conceptualize mafias as agents involved in state building and state destruction—not as peripheral aids or spoilers, but as independent players determining government capacity and steering nationalist politics. When conditions allow, "criminal syndicates function like mini-states."[87] Charles Tilly (1985, 169) immortalized this theme in calling modern states our "largest examples of organized crime." Even outside separatist zones, mafias are independently capable of co-opting and even creating state structures. The trajectory from mafia to state organ has been case studied in Pakistan, Indonesia, Japan, and New York City.[88]

In torn states, the path from organized crime to government is even shorter. Separatist movements, after all, are states in the making. When mobilizing successfully, they create lawless zones of governmental retreat. Host states often respond with administrative overstretch. Conveniently enough, both too little *and* too much of the state generates mafias. "Excessive bureaucratic power" incubates organized crime just as easily as sudden power vacuums or "abdications" by the government.[89] Since both options are signatures of torn states, the incentive to multiply governments grows. "Contrary to a widespread perception," Francesco Strazzari (2003, 158) explains, the "emergence of small, almost stifled states, devoid of institutional autonomy and of margins of maneuver in the international arena, seems to be the condition in which mafia structures and practices thrive. In this way, mafias can often go as far as to take hostage the development of state structures." On the one hand, then, organized crime can certainly be a force of "state deformation."[90] On the other, mafias can just as easily be nation builders, creating administrative apparatuses for extraction and coercion in their turf.[91] This remarkable dualism—the ability to thrive off both state strength and weakness—is the singular power of mafias in separatist contexts.

WAR

Not all separatists wage war. But when they do, it is easier with a mafia in one's corner.

The genealogy of states through war making has endowed a fundamental similarity between what states and gangsters do. "Banditry, piracy, gangland rivalry, policing and war making all belong on the same continuum."[92] In torn states—where civil controls over militaries are weak, the flow of armed personnel and equipment is unregulated, and unaccountable foreign troops circulate—criminal opportunities arise.

Mafias may originate as mere servants of warring parties. But their power can grow spectacularly, frequently matching a "side" in civil war. The "ability of criminal war economies to subsist in post-war environments," Jessica West (2002, 8) argues, "suggests that in many cases the control of territory is dependent on criminal organizations more so than on a guerrilla or terrorist presence." Organized crime, Andreas (2004a, 49) adds, "can contribute to the outbreak and persistence of war, but also to its conclusion." When a separatist entity is borne of war, "criminal actors can contribute to the looting of the country, but also to its survival." Once up and running, mafia gains can be irreversible.[93] Afghanistan is a paradigmatic case, where the clash between the Taliban and Northern Alliance was fatefully determined by narco-mafias: "Both parties relied heavily on income from the opium economy to finance the war, however neither one of them controlled the drug trade."[94] Waves of violence in Afghanistan have come and gone ever since, but this autonomous organized crime continues to dominate politics and the economy.[95]

Lastly, separatist zones have another mafia magnet: foreign troops. The mere presence of an international administration—civilian or military—is a natural opportunity for transnational organized crime, notably in narcotics and sex trafficking. The discomforting public secret of international peacekeeping—armed, lonely young men on dull missions—is that it unfailingly produces blossoming prostitution in the locality.[96]

Modeling the Relationship

What remains is to take up Kalyvas's (2015) challenge to cross-fertilize crime and insurgency research. On this path, I follow in the footsteps of a set of inventive interdisciplinary studies that bridge the analytic gap between torn states and organized crime.[97] Subsequent chapters develop two ways to understand the relationship between separatism and mafias: a Simmelian triadic model of state-separatist-mafia relations, and a typology of mafias according to how *state dependent* and *partisan* they are. The triadic model is a high-resolution analytic tool, useful for the in-depth analysis of separatist trajectories in a limited number of cases (Serbia and Georgia). The mafia typology is a lower-resolution tool, useful for macroanalytic overviews across entire regions (West Africa, the Middle East, and Eastern Europe). Below I sketch each in turn (for details, see the appendix).

SIMMELIAN TRIADS

In part 2, I conceptualize mafia roles in Serbia (Kosovo) and Georgia (South Ossetia) from 1989 to 2012. By "zooming in" to these paired cases, we begin to understand what it means for organized crime to be an independent agent, not mere epiphenomenon (chapter 3), which can filter regional smuggling opportunities into separatist success (chapter 4) and manage the stigma of nefarious criminal activity (chapter 5). The mafia's role, I argue, was a major reason that separatism was more successful in Kosovo than in South Ossetia.

Intuitively, we imagine a two-sided contest between the separatist movement and government. Yet students of mafia-infested torn states rightly conclude that this dyadic vision is limited. "But once one abandons the analytic simplification of the two-player approach—the state vs. the insurgent terrorists, the red team vs. the blue team, our guys vs. their guys—where does one go next?"[98] One goes to Simmelian triads. Georg Simmel's great insight was that seemingly tangential social actors can fundamentally shape the relationship between another pair of actors who appear—due to our analytic bias—to be solely relevant. His examples ranged from impish bachelors vis-à-vis a troubled married couple to power-hungry kingdoms vis-à-vis Anglo-Saxon and Norman nations. In triadic forms, what matters is not so much the relative strength of the two most salient parties. Rather, the overall relational form can empower a less apparent third party to play a decisive role.[99] When spouses fight, a mischievous bachelor can destroy the marriage. When two nations bleed each other dry, an ambitious regional power can devour both. In such circumstances, neglecting the third yields poor explanations of what happened.

Applying this approach, instead of thinking about separatism in terms of two actors, we must consider three: the host state, separatist movement, *and* mafias. Their triadic relations taken holistically help us better understand torn states. To be sure, tremendous asymmetries exist between the first two and organized crime. But it is precisely because separatists and governments confront each other that mafias gain in relevance. Just as small parliamentary parties, otherwise weak and insignificant, sometimes acquire decisive voting leverage when larger political parties collide, so can mafias acquire enormous power when host state and separatist movement collide. Concretely, three mafia roles in triadic forms prove useful for our purposes: the rejoicing third, divider and ruler, and mediator.

First, a rejoicing third (*tertius gaudens*) has an advantage "resulting from the fact that the remaining two hold each other in check and he can make a gain that one of the two would otherwise deny him," as when a financial broker plays parties against each other, or "because action by one of the two parties brings [advantage] about for its own purposes—the *tertius* does not need to take the initiative," as when foreign investments in a region increase as neighboring regions' rioters disrupt each other's economies. In Serbia and Georgia, as we will see, mafias initially grew as rejoicing thirds. Second, a divider and ruler (*divisor et imperator*) proactively creates conflict between the two in order to secure a dominant position or other gains, as when an empire creates borders to sever the ethnic or religious unity of potentially rebellious populations. In Kosovo, the mafia assumed a spectacular role of divider and ruler, propelling the separatist movement into secession. Finally, a mediator assuages the factors that produce tension between the remaining two—he "functions as an arbiter who balances . . . their contradictory claims against one another and eliminates what is incompatible," as when a child brings parents together, or mediators boost negotiations between labor and management.[100] In South Ossetia, organized crime played an incredible role as mediator, deflating secession and boosting Georgian-Ossetian cooperation through smuggling.

TYPOLOGY OF MAFIAS

What kinds of mafias are there in separatist zones more generally? In part 3, we zoom out to survey four types of mafias in torn states in three regions: fourteen countries with separatist movements (four in West Africa, five in the Middle East, and five in Eastern Europe) from 1989 to 2019. In each of these cases, I argue, territorial consolidation was vitally molded by organized criminal agency.

I will arrive at two simple findings: some mafias are more embedded in governments (*state dependent*) than others, and some mafias are more ethnocentric (*partisan*) than others. Regarding state dependence, I differentiate between organized crime that is largely controlled—often created—by host state institutions, and organized crime that largely operates autonomously. Regarding partisanship, I differentiate between mafias that are highly ethnocentric, and those that are less so.

State dependent mafias are indispensably patronized by host state institutions (government, military, police, and state enterprises), sustaining their rackets from within the state apparatus. Independent mafias, though they engage corrupt government officials (through bribery, blackmail, and cooptation), largely operate autonomously and sustain rackets despite—not through—host state institutions. The basic litmus test is: If the host state were to collapse at dawn, would this mafia persevere and sustain its basic racket?

Partisan mafias are ethnocentric in their composition and territorial localization, which gives them a strong preference for one side or another in separatist disputes. Even if transnational, their rackets are clearly tilted in favor of either the separatist movement or host state. Impartial mafias, in contrast, lack allegiances: they just as easily finance, protect, arm, or agitate for separatism as against it. Here the litmus test is: When separatist tensions escalate, does this mafia take sides in the dispute?

These are idealizations. No mafia is entirely independent of governments, nor are state-run mafias entirely loyal to their patrons and creators. Even the

TABLE 1. Typology of Mafias

	Partisan	Impartial
State dependent	*Mafias in uniform* in Nigeria, Turkey, Serbia, Georgia, and Azerbaijan	*Minderbinder mafias* in Bosnia-Herzegovina / **Autonomous Province of Western Bosnia**, Yemen / **Houthi North**, and Ukraine/**Donbas**
Independent	*Rebel mafias* in **Azawad**, **Casamance**, **Boko Haram**, **Kurdistan**, **Gaza**, **Islamic State**, **Greater Albania**, **Kosovo**, **Crimea**, **Transnistria**, and **Nagorno-Karabakh**	*Cosmopolitan mafias* in Niger/**Agadez**, Cameroon/**Ambazonia**, and Georgia / **South Ossetia**

Notes: Separatist movements are in bold. Mafias in uniform is inspired by Élise Massicard's (2010) analysis of Turkish "gangsters in uniform" against Kurds. Minderbinder mafias refers to Joseph Heller's immortal character in *Catch-22*, Milo Minderbinder, the prototypical war profiteer; embedded in the military, Mindbinder undermines war efforts on all sides.

most fanatically ethnocentric gangsters sometimes sabotage their ethnonational "side" in a separatist conflict, while impartial gangsters sometimes adopt pro- and antiseparatist actions. But polarization on both dimensions is a critical, if neglected, reality of today's torn states. The resulting two by two produces a four-category typology of mafias explaining their varying roles. Table 1 summarizes the types, plotting all upcoming cases of separatism.

Mafias in uniform. In this type, gangsters are subcontractors. The host state—typically the security apparatus—either creates a mafia or instrumentalizes existing organized crime to fight separatism. Recruiting in prisons and neighborhoods as well as from its own corrupt ranks, the host state coordinates hired guns, procures dirty money, and smuggles precious contraband. Supplementing legal antiseparatist measures, mafias in uniform are a clandestine tool for infiltrating, subverting, and killing separatists. These loyal gangsters are typically enlisted from the titular ethnic constituency, but may include "turncoats" from the targeted separatist community. In this scenario, gangsters become statesmen at the behest and invitation of the government. Regime self-defense and sometimes survival depends on them. In this sense, mafias in uniform are a force for conservation.

Minderbinder mafias. Here, gangsters are loose cannons. Initially, the host state empowered—and may have even created—them as servants of the state. Their independent criminal capacity grows, however, as they "convert their political resources (principally their links with official actors and their skill in the use of violence) into criminal activities" outside the state's initial purpose.[101] Due to government incompetence or weakness, the gangsters' ability to smuggle, extort, and profiteer with impunity takes on a life of its own. Their rackets—notably selling government arms to "the enemy"—subvert and undermine their host state patrons. By catalyzing conflict, perpetuating divisions, and incentivizing confrontation with separatists, Minderbinder mafias are a centrifugal force.

Rebel mafias. These gangsters are allies of the separatist movement. Unlike mafias in uniform, rebel mafias become statesmen *un*invited—through coups, rebellions, and wars. They were not created or monitored by government organs, nor do they require state patronage to profiteer. Rebel mafias are firmly rooted in minority ethnic communities, where rackets service their separatist brethren at the expense of the host state. Control over smuggling routes—cocaine into Azawad, oil into Iraq, and arms into Kosovo—empowers gangsters as brokers, suppliers, and partners to separatists. In desperate moments of nationalist liberation, a rebel mafia can be the decisive ingredient for secessionist success.

Cosmopolitan mafias. In this category, gangsters are peacemakers. True wonders of globalization, these organized criminals connect divided ethnic communities that share a demand for security, employment, and contraband. Multiethnic in composition, cosmopolitan mafias specialize in smuggling transnationally across polarized populations. They are skeptical of ethnonational confrontation and conflict, which—given their rackets—is bad for business. They prefer stalemate (sometimes called "frozen conflict"), where borders remain disputed, jurisdictions unclear, and cross-ethnic trading illicit. They have little desire to become formal political figureheads. Unlike Minderbinder mafias (disintegrative and centrifugal), cosmopolitan mafias are an integrative, centripetal force.

To be clear, predatory opportunism characterizes all four types. Whatever their politics, mafias form cynical "marriages of convenience" to protect their rackets.[102] But they do not do so arbitrarily. Gangsters pursue opportunism *within* the structural confines of their levels of dependency (Are they state creations or clients?) and ethnocentrism (Do they have a dog in the separatist fight?). Impartial mafias reject both nationalist projects (separatist and host state) because it suits their interests. Partisan mafias, similarly, take nationalist positions because there is a congruence of one nationalism (or another) with their profiteering. Across the board, it is a Weberian elective affinity between profit and ideology.

PART II

Kosovo and South Ossetia

3

The Third Man

Normally, countries have mafias. But in Yugoslavia, mafias have created their own countries.

—ZORAN DJINDJIĆ, SERBIAN PRIME MINISTER ASSASSINATED BY THE ZEMUN CLAN, *PEŠČANIK*

Peacekeepers? (*Laughs.*) You know who the real peacekeepers were? *We* [Ergneti smugglers] were the peacekeepers. *We* made the peace. Yes my friend. While we worked, nobody wanted to fight, nobody was crazy. Everybody had something. Every side needed us. The politicians were with us. Everybody was happy. If someone was getting killed, it was for business. No politics. The people *understood* this. Georgian, Russian, no difference. Nobel Prize should be for us. Instead, they hit us. . . . So, they got war. Now, enjoy!

—ATSAMAZ, FORMER OSSETIAN SMUGGLER AND VETERAN, AUTHOR INTERVIEW

Consider a romantic couple on the brink of divorce. Unsophisticated accounts of their separation tend to focus on the husband and wife alone—their personalities, grievances, and expectations. Their relationship—dependent, distrustful, abusive, and so on—is readily understandable in terms of the two of them. We have an analytic bias toward *dyads*.

But suppose there is a third man. Perhaps a mischievous bachelor happens to be the wife's lover. Suppose he is more than a disinterested, passive bystander to the marriage. Suppose he connives to ruin it. He may incite the husband's abusive jealously, inspiring the wife to leave. In such circumstances, it might make sense to explain the divorce in terms of more than two actors. Suppose, alternatively, that the couple has a son who is the principal reason keeping the marriage intact. Imagine, further, that the child is proactively bringing his parents together. He fosters their intimacy, organizes family activities, and distracts them from their acrimony with his own needs and concerns. In such a family, the son mitigates the pressures toward separation; he is obviously a vital part of the story. In less trivial (but no less intriguing) circumstances, mafias play such roles in torn states. All too often, we analyze state-separatist relations dyadically, without considering a critical force between them. Torn states should be understood as stories of *triads*.

A Tale of Two Torn States

Kosovo and South Ossetia (1989–2012) are the most similar pair of separatist stories in the ex-Yugoslav and ex-Soviet spaces. Their unique mix of wars (foreign and civil), separatist mobilizations (some successful, others less so), and mafia roles (sometimes tearing states, sometimes consolidating them) offers precious lessons on the agency of organized crime. In Serbia and Georgia, war was mafia as much as state business. Borders were made and unmade by smugglers. The black market was not an anomaly; the formal economy was. What separatists achieved depended tremendously on whether organized crime was multiethnic or not, violent or not, strong or not. Different mafia roles gave different results.

But what are these roles? Returning to Simmel's idea of triads, three kinds will be useful for our purposes:

1. A *rejoicing third* benefits from conflict but does not cause it; as the government and secessionists assault each other, gangsters thrive.
2. A *divider and ruler* proactively creates conflict to secure a dominant position or other gains; mafias provoke or create separatist clashes for their own ends.
3. A *mediator* assuages the factors that produce tension between the other two; organized crime undermines state-separatist conflict.

Both Serbia and Georgia concluded post–Cold War skirmishes in 1995. In the first phase (1989–95), organized crime played the role of a rejoicing third in both societies. In the second phase (1995–2012), however, a fateful divergence occurred. In Serbia, the mafia assumed the role of a divider and ruler—incapacitating the host state and ascending to dominance in Kosovo. In contrast, organized crime played the curious role of a mediator between Georgia and South Ossetia—undermining secession and promoting multiethnic cooperation.

The Rejoicing Third, 1989–95

The separatist trajectories of Kosovo and South Ossetia began the same way. The years 1989 to 1995 saw Communist fragmentation, civil war, and economic breakdown. Serbia and Georgia emerged as sovereign from larger socialist projects (Yugoslavia and the Soviet Union), and confronted separatists on multiple fronts. Hundreds of thousands of casualties and millions of refugees were among those trampled on. Not everyone suffered, however. When it came to organized crime in these countries, it not only grew but blossomed. Mafias swelled and congealed around both government and separatist institutions, becoming genuine social forces in the Balkans and Caucasus. This period marked the rise of mafias, the rejoicing third. In battles over secession—military, political, and cultural—mafias emerged to meet three pressing needs.

CANNON FODDER

First, both governments and secessionists needed fighters. The birth of a new criminal class was less an outcome of neglect or accident, but rather the deliberate mobilization of coercion in struggles over sovereignty. The Yugoslav wars first erupted in Slovenia (1991), then in Croatia (1991–95) and Bosnia-Herzegovina (1992–95). Georgia fought South Ossetia (1990–91), Abkhazia (1992–94) and most vigorously, itself in a civil war (1991–93) followed by a near-lawless interval (1993–95). Battle after battle, commanders on all sides would find themselves lacking in soldiers *to* command. Democratic conscription was underwhelming. Civilians were tired and reluctant. Discipline was low, and mass mobilization difficult. The inherited coercive apparatus was dysfunctional, if it existed at all. In conditions of military breakdown, criminal paramilitarism was the only salvation.

Serbia and Georgia thus converged on the same solution: create, nurture, and instrumentalize criminal cliques that—if not exactly symbols of virtue—will be loyal and effective. In Serbia, the resulting mafias were the Zemun Clan and Ražnatović group. In Georgia, it was the Mkhedrioni and National Guard.[1] They parasitically grew with the chaos, integrating themselves into the state and military apparatus. Opportunistic and brutal, they nevertheless delivered cannon fodder in the tens of thousands.

Among five rival Serbian gangs, the Zemun Clan rose to become the state's apprentice.[2] Its leader, Milorad Ulemek, joined the French Foreign Legion to evade arrest after a series of robberies in Europe. Deserting, he returned to Belgrade to head the region's most powerful mafia. In 1991, Slobodan Milošević created the Special Operations Unit (JSO) under his direct command, bypassing legal formalities. The Clan gradually merged with the JSO to become two wings (unofficial and sanctioned) of the same criminal enterprise. Publicly advertised as national heroes despite their psychopathic profiles, the gangsters were recruited to do the regime's bidding.[3]

Also renowned was Željko Ražnatović, a bandit-socialite and later presidential candidate. Topping Interpol's most wanted list in the 1970s and 1980s, he boasted warrants for violent crimes in six European countries. During heists, Ražnatović unmasked to smile for security cameras, gifting flowers to tellers. Putting on a dozen thick sweaters, he once escaped Swiss prison by rolling over two-meter-high barbed wire fences; mutilated, he reappeared in Belgrade two days later. On another occasion, he robbed a Stockholm bank with a Sicilian accomplice who was captured. During his trial, Ražnatović stormed the courtroom, battered the guards, threatened the Swedish judge, and absconded with his partner by jumping out the second-floor window.[4]

Folk legends ensued, and the security apparatus cultivated them.[5] Marrying a silicone-adorned folk singer in a televised nationalist spectacle, he became a symbol of patriotic glory. Youngsters idolized Ražnatović—and were willing to prove it on the front. His paramilitary Serbian Volunteer Guard, formed in 1990, featured football hooligans. The militia fought conspicuously in Croatia and Bosnia (and later in Kosovo) in an effort by Milošević to deny the existence of these wars. How can you fight a war, the party line held, if you do not recognize the "nation" you are fighting? Criminals naturally gravitated to such "covert" antiseparatist operations.[6]

Gangsters became a pillar of the Serbian war effort. Even as they earned worldwide publicity for war crimes and looting habits, they held no ranks or titles. Ražnatović registered as a pastry shop owner. His death squad enjoyed greater regime patronage than the Yugoslav National Army itself. Career military officers would suffer abusive visits in their own offices—with no repercussions. "Is it normal," one of them asked Milošević, "for a Serbian military commander to get slapped around in the face by a pastry chef?" In 1992, Ražnatović was immunized by a parliamentary seat. A fellow delegate remarked in a televised discussion, "This man has put stockings on his head more often than on his legs."[7]

Despairing of such spectacles in Belgrade, Kosovars were hardly inspired to reintegrate. Instead, separatists nurtured their own criminal infrastructure. The terrain was fertile. The community consisted of ten clans (*fis*), in which kinship loyalty reigned supreme—above ethnic Albanian solidarity. Many nurtured a tradition of blood feuds.[8] Clan elders issued disciplinary death sentences for minor transgressions like romance out of wedlock. This coercive infrastructure would suit criminal purposes well. In July 1990, Kosovo began creating its own hospitals, chambers of commerce, educational boards, and expanded municipalities. Among these "parallel institutions" were coercive organs: defense committees, coordinated military staffs, armed units in every municipality, a surveillance/intelligence network of informants, and a civilian police force.

Though dormant in this phase, these would become the infrastructure of future criminal endeavors.[9]

Two underground groups thrived. First, there was the (poorly) Armed Forces of the Republic of Kosovo founded by exiled nationalists. Second, there was the Kosovo Liberation Army (KLA), a front for drugs and arms traffickers. Against folklore, both were inchoate in this period, and preferred profit to politics.[10] They nevertheless created—like their Serbian counterparts—a pool of able and willing young mercenaries and fighters. Among their ranks was the promising Hashim "the Snake" Thaçi, a heroin trafficker and future prime minister of Kosovo.

Georgian society was likewise conducive to gangster burgeoning. For both host state and Ossetian authorities, organized crime was a matter of survival. The mafia centered on two groups: the Mkhedrioni and National Guard. Like their Serbian counterparts, both would integrate into successive governments.

The Mkhedrioni had a singular advantage: it was the only credible *armed* opposition. Created in 1989 by criminal chief Dzhaba Ioseliani, the group held regional extortion and smuggling rings. It "relied entirely on illegal sources of income," especially gasoline supplies.[11] Viciously seizing the protection market, it superseded the Thieves-in-Law (*vory-v-zakone*) of the Soviet era. By 1995, Ioseliani committed some thirty serious offenses, including sadistic murders. His seventeen-year prison stint for robbing a Leningrad bank in 1948 congealed his nationalist credentials. The discrete charm of his banditry attracted a loyal following among convicts, drug abusers, and the Russian underworld.

The National Guard was headed by the conspiratorial Tengiz Kitovani. A graduate of the Tbilisi Fine Arts Academy, the former painter was a plump, imposing figure who rode limousines and symbolized Georgian war crimes in Abkhazia. He dealt with opponents with murder, beatings, and raving accusations of homosexuality. Equally adept at espionage intrigues, high-level diplomatic negotiations, and frontline brutality against civilians, Kitovani would become a precious asset. His militia members—often recruited from prison—faithfully served the nationalist cause in both separatist conflicts as well as the civil war. For a brief Kafkaesque period, he served as defense minister.

The offensive against secessionists turned hoodlums into heroes.[12] Georgia's first president, Zviad Gamsakhurdia, turned to Ioseliani for help in subduing the Ossetians. Tbilisi's soldiers in the First South Ossetian War were largely uncoordinated bands—roughly six separate formations of fifty to two hundred people each. At least one of them "was made up of common criminals."[13] All of them engaged in conspicuous pillaging alongside the fighting. In 1991, Georgian troops began clashing with armed Ossetian villagers. Gamsakhurdia commanded the Mkhedrioni to recruit rowdy protesters through its paramilitary channels for two "people's rallies" toward Tskhinvali. Like the

JSO for Milošević, Ioseliani's mafia was pillar of the host state's military—and civilian—offensive.

The birth of Ossetian organized crime followed as a reaction—and mimicry. Mirroring the anti-Ossetian gangs, an impromptu National Guard was hastily formed within a year. In early 1990, the troops numbered only three to four hundred; within six months, there were fifteen hundred with another thirty-five hundred standby volunteers. As in Georgia's formations, convicts and violent offenders were overrepresented. They quickly mastered defensive paramilitarism. Volunteers included Ossetians from North Ossetia as well as Georgia proper. Like in Serbia, war was the mother of criminal invention.

Overall, however, treason in the Ossetian north was the least of Georgia's ordeals. The entire country was "divided into fiefdoms presided over by war-lords and their private armies." Nobody, least of all the state, could control the "gangs and paramilitary thugs [that] roamed the streets and terrorised towns and villages."[14] In a remarkable testimony to the chaos of 1993, the Tbilisi police chief begged Russian troops to help curb crime in the streets. Ioseliani and Kitovani, meanwhile, flourished in such conditions. Their war profiteering and pillaging during Abkhazia's blundering military effort (1992–93) signaled miserable failure for both the state and separatists, but solidified the mafia's grasp on the economy and culture.

CASH AND CONTRABAND

Second, host state and separatist movement alike needed smugglers. Virtually overnight, Serbia and Georgia transitioned from closed, centralized econo-mies with rigid one-party control into the market wilderness. Economically atrophied, regionally isolated, lacking private sector traditions, and without geopolitical allies, governments and separatists shared the same urgencies: cash flows for sustaining loyalists, access to trade routes, and black funds for arms, fuel, and combat equipment. Covert operations required covert resources.

Defeated in three wars, Yugoslavia was placed under crippling UN sanc-tions. Hyperinflation was rampant; in the peak month, January 1994, the rate reached a staggering 313 million percent.[15] Launching vast smuggling operations, the regime endured off the gray economy. Ex-convicts were put into business as war profiteers. Initial trafficking handled oil, cigarettes, and weapons, and later, more gainfully, narcotics. Profits went to Russian, Chi-nese, Cypriot, Lebanese, and Swiss accounts under Milošević's family's and associates' names. Estimates of regime plundering are imprecise, but they range in the hundreds of millions of dollars.[16] The chain of command was from Milošević to the chief of security command via a mediator from the JSO to its head, Ulemek. The mafia thus liasioned between Serbia's first and second in command. Naturally, sanctions busting was tax exempt; "tribute income from cross-border trade stayed within this command structure, under the control of the president, without ever being recorded or transferred to the Federal Government."[17] The smugglers effectively enabled Milošević's private ownership of an entire national import-export economy—for a modest fee.

Kosovar separatists, meanwhile, suffered double economic strangulation. Preoccupied and dismissive, Belgrade halved its aid to Kosovo between 1990 and 1995. Amplifying the deprivation, Albanians (supposed darlings of the West) "suffered more [than the Serbs] under the same sanctions" that the international community imposed on Yugoslavia.[18] The more isolated Kosovo became, the more dynamic its black economy. Inheriting the Balkan's poorest, most underdeveloped province, separatists desperately needed resources. Two channels were available: fraud and smuggling. Embezzlements from government funds served as budgets for parallel institutions. Defrauding host state aid through family ties and bribery became (unofficial) separatist policy. Fake pensioners would withdraw Yugoslav funds for dead friends and cousins. In one instance, a 112-year-old's pension was diligently claimed every month by the deceased's family through an accomplice clerk.[19] Similar networks extracted resources from Kosovo's meager natural resource industries, particularly the Trepča Mines. For every two deutsche marks entering Kosovo, one would vanish.[20]

But Serbia's punitive aid to the separatist authorities was so paltry that embezzlement alone could only hope to extract something out of nothing. Kosovo outlived the embargo by smuggling from neighboring Albania. The southward turn in the early 1990s was trumpeted as a glorious nationalist awakening: Albania recognized the Republic of Kosovo, called for boycotting Yugoslav elections, and demanded UN intervention. In reality, contraband was what nurtured the friendship. Though most trafficked commodities were not illicit, narco-dealers and gunrunners (both exceptionally violent) began flexing their muscles.[21] Herein, the seeds of a bitter struggle within the separatist movement were sown.

In Georgia, smugglers were correspondingly entrepreneurial. As early as the 1980s, "Georgia had an off-the-books 'shadow economy' that was estimated to be one of the largest anywhere in the U[SSR]."[22] But before independence, border control was tight, trade relations were limited and state dictated, and monetary flows were under police surveillance. Foreign trade was supervised by intelligence services, which were in turn run by a party clique. Suddenly this all collapsed. In its place was black market pandemonium. Assuming a state mantle, mafias would pick up the remnants and replace the centralized economic planner.

Lacking campaign financing, Georgia's second president, Eduard Shevardnadze, summoned Ioseliani to help seize power. By 1992, the Mkhedrioni and now-overlapping National Guard "controlled the newly constituted Military Council, the black economy, and most of the regions."[23] Their cigarette and arms smuggling operations were done under the Ministry of Internal Affairs, which absorbed the militia into its chain of command. In a concession, one Mkhedrioni commander ("a twice convicted criminal") became the minister.[24] Mkhedrioni "deputies took stakes in many of the private businesses that got started in Georgia in 1993–[9]4."[25] Patronizing the black marketeers, Shevardnadze financed budding government institutions.[26]

Filling government coffers, the National Guard's fundraising was unsentimental. Like the Mkhedrioni, gangsters sustained "targeted taxation of various shadow businesses . . . through a soft extortion racket."[27] Staffed by volunteers with their own weapons, they even traded in the abundance of illicit arms. (On the record, Kitovani imported bananas from Ecuador.) While the National Guard concentrated on oil and the Mkhedrioni on guns, they united to protect both markets from legalization. The mafia's "black budgets" were second to none during the civil war; they were de facto national treasuries.

Also craving money and guns, separatists formed new alliances. Ravaged by war, an economic blockade from Tbilisi, and Russian troops entering the province, South Ossetian leaders were left with few alternatives. Lyudvig Chibirov, chair of the separatist parliament (1993–96), "maintained a good position to exploit illegal trade and smuggling" through family ties to the Tedeyev Clan, "one of South Ossetia's most powerful families."[28] Chibirov's son, fittingly, was deputy head of the republic's State Security Committee (KGB), augmenting Moscow's collaboration. Russian arms from garrisons in North Ossetia flowed to the rebels. Formally free of charge, they were sold and resold by villagers and border officials. Self-defense militias began securing smuggler supply lines. With 80 percent unemployment and rampant poverty, bribery could open any border—disputed or otherwise. The Chibirovs and Tedeyevs had little difficulty transitioning from war profiteering to smuggling in peacetime. They had weapons, corruptible peacekeepers, and exclusive control of the Roki Tunnel—the sole northern crossing into Russia.

Finally, smuggling routes were established as a by-product of northward forced migration. By March 1992, some hundred thousand refugees had registered in North Ossetia's capital, Vladikavkaz (the true figure is surely greater).[29] Many had family in Russia. Some had KGB and mafia contacts. Russian distributors of gas, oil, and electricity—all of which intermittently shut down to punish separatists—met new business partners. Smuggling soared between the 1992 cease-fire and 1994 creation of the Joint Control Commission (consisting of Russia, Georgia, and North and South Ossetia), which installed a trilateral Joint Peacekeeping Force (JPKF). Multiethnic and not quite incorruptible, the JPKF was a harbinger of the all-important Ergneti market. The stage was set.

THUGS FOR HIRE

Third—and vitally—host states needed instruments of population control. Quelling rebels in remote front lines was important enough, but without protection and loyal coercion at home, contenders for statehood would risk instability in their capitals.

Again, gangster clientelism was only natural. In Belgrade, the Zemun Clan and JSO served as quasi-private security agencies for the government's shadow firms. Trained killers were redirected from the Yugoslav wars to regulating "internal enemies" in the nation's metropolis. The auspicious partnership blossomed into a decades-long collaboration between state security and organized criminal enterprises.[30] Under fire from a united opposition, Milošević ordered kidnappings, assassinations, and intimidations by the Clan. Journalists, political opponents, and businesspeople funding democratic reformists were threatened and killed. Even family friends of the Milošević clique (notably Ivan Stambolić) were murdered. Several opposition leaders fled the country from regime death warrants.

The Ražnatović mafia, for its part, rented thugs for hire through sports clubs.[31] Loyal convicts were appointed to head football associations, where hooligans were trained as regime voters and agitators.[32] Local kids were indoctrinated with nationalist fervor and recruited as extortionists. Gangs patrolled Belgrade neighborhoods around stadiums, vandalizing apartments displaying anti-Milošević emblems in their windows. Homeowners understood the message. On gentler occasions, undercover narco-dealers were sent as agents provocateurs to disrupt opposition rallies. At major protests in 1991 and 1996–97, Clan members and Ražnatović loyalists were videotaped inciting riots. They had been ordered to create an alibi for a police crackdown. The mafia also provided bodyguards for the ruling political parties of Milošević and his wife. With thousands of violent foot soldiers behind them, the mafia became regime guardians—champions of domestic order. They offered blackmail, beatings, and murders. In exchange, drug smuggling, car theft, and war profiteering—their real preoccupation—were tolerated.[33]

In Georgia, this pattern was grotesquely familiar. Gangsters transitioned from killing faraway enemies of the nation to killing conationals and associates "at home" in the civil war. Remnants of the Soviet apparatus, politicians, and businesspeople developed routines of hiring entire armed gangs for protection. Criminal bodyguards became part of the political culture. By centralizing control over gangs, the Mkhedrioni and National Guard monopolized the domestic protection racket. It is difficult to overstate how essential thugs for hire were in the early 1990s. Overreaching against separatists, the government collapsed, leaving the country in the hands of "paramilitary clans-cum-mafias fighting for power, gun-toting brigands collecting their own 'taxes' on the roads, and merchants wishing only for more orderly and predictable racketeers."[34] The gangs' firm grasp over large swaths of territory and their capacity to exert violence rivaled anything the government could muster. Disarmament was out of the question. Whoever wanted to rule needed criminal protection.

Nationalist posturing aside, the militias were motivated by profiteering.[35] Indeed, the chronology of the civil war suggests that pillaging and banditry were their sole coherent strategies in the early years; politics trailed as an afterthought.[36] Widespread infighting between renegade sectors of the state apparatus (military, police, and the National Guard) overtook the pro- and anti-Gamsakhurdia camps. Fierce battles were conducted over precious buildings, roads, and bridges of strategic importance for smuggling routes. Any contender for state power who preferred a head on their shoulders was invariably drawn to contracting the gangsters.

Having initially benefited from both militias, Gamsakhurdia sought to diffuse the criminal units.[37] His opponent Shevardnadze managed an alternative: in exchange for amnesty, the mafia would serve the emerging state apparatus under new leadership. Through a coalition with Gamsakhurdia's former ally Tengiz Sigua, Kitovani and Ioseliani became part of the democratic opposition. They ordered five hundred National Guard troops into the streets of Tbilisi, occupying government buildings in a coup on behalf of their new patrons. Thousands of Mkhedrioni took control of much of the capital. In the coming years, they would combine street fighting with theft, murder, and racketeering aimed at consolidating turf—all with exalted patriotic rhetoric.

Though anti-Gamsakhurdia oppositionists entered the uneasy mafia alliance grudgingly, it succeeded. One battering at a time, the National Guard and Mkhedrioni duet became guarantors of public safety. They were instrumental in securing foreign support—something the civic, nonviolent opposition lacked. In 1991–92, Russia reinforced any gangsters it could to ensure Gamsakhurdia's replacement with Shevardnadze. It donated military equipment, including tanks and heavy artillery, to Ioseliani and Kitovani.[38] Moscow even dispatched a modest number of soldiers to join opposition troops in the street fighting. As it became apparent he "could not fight for more than a week," Gamsakhurdia fled the country.[39]

Helping consolidate the state, the gangsters ascended from obscurity to national prominence. By murdering their chief criminal rivals, the Thieves-in-Law, Mkhedrioni, and National Guard fortified their positions.[40] They created political parties, ran for office, and entered state bureaus. The Georgian state propped them up as respectable candidates in the 1992 elections (presumably for a fee). For his campaign, Ioseliani sported a tuxedo with a white bow tie; in place of his familiar AK-47, he carried a cane. In parliament for the next three years, "Kitovani and Ioseliani did not weaken their links with the criminal world, as was hoped."[41] On the contrary, the Mkhedrioni members expanded their campaign of extortion throughout the country, particularly in Tbilisi and its suburbs. Georgia's dilapidated prison system replaced the education system as the *true* engine of social mobility and skills training. Even "violent young men of good Tbilisi families" were attracted to the mafia mystique.[42]

In sum, organized crime was a rejoicing third in both cases—but no more than that. Tied to authorities by profit, reputation, and security, it did not yet deviate or assume an independent role in shaping secession. Rising from petty convicts to wealthy nationalist heroes, the new criminal class remained an obedient instrument of its patrons. Governments and separatists supervised and legitimated gangsters in exchange for their services. They provided people, resources, and protection. Soon, mafias would outgrow their creators.

Divider and Conqueror in Serbia/Kosovo, 1995–2012

Organized crime began to spread its wings. In the host state, it nearly seized power in a coup. In breakaway Kosovo, it co-opted the separatist movement and created a parastate of its own. How could mafias become governments?

LOSING CONTROL

What Milošević had created during the Yugoslav wars was "effectively the largest criminal organization in the Balkans"—no small feat, given the regional competition.[43] Like Frankenstein, however, the regime lost control of its creation because peace brought globalization. The lifting of international sanctions following the 1995 Dayton Accords suddenly opened one of the most isolated countries in the world to international markets—legal or otherwise. War profiteers returned home from the front, but their pursuits could now extend outside the truncated Yugoslavia. Appetites grew. The criminal class purchased entire industries and connected them to international black markets. Pyramid scheme banks laundered war smugglers' money. In Belgrade, restaurants and other businesses blossomed.

Gangsters could now finance activities without state supervision.[44] Ražnatović's football club had been a paramilitary training camp. After 1995, it was a center for embezzlement and money laundering. Illegal trades of players coincided with Ražnatović's pledges to personally maim anyone who scored against his team. Stadium hooligans were mobilized to selectively produce disruption—on demand—for various clients. No longer loyal regime tools on standby for patriotic missions, thugs for hire were now available to the highest bidder. They settled everything from personal romantic disputes to industrial strikes. Effectively, they sold riots.[45] Mafia schisms ensued in 1996–97, disrupting the hierarchy leading to Milošević.[46] Rogue elements of the state apparatus deviated. Police chiefs, ministers, and military officers were killed in the dozens by gangsters they previously controlled. The Zemun Clan eliminated at least three rival narco-traffickers in 1999. Even Ražnatović met his demise in 2000 in a luxury hotel lobby. Losing control of the underworld, his patron Milošević would soon lose it all.

By 2000, the democratic opposition was near belated victory. It united a broad popular coalition as stolen elections mobilized a massive protest on October 5. Panicked, the regime explored its repressive options.[47] The Zemun Clan and JSO were prepared to violently crush the uprising at the orders of the beleaguered state security apparatus. Had they obeyed (as when Milošević turned tanks on nonviolent protesters in 1991), the fabled Bulldozer Revolution would have been a bloodbath. Thankfully, organized crime supported democracy. Faced with the prospect of loyalty to a sinking ship, the Clan sought secret negotiations with opposition leaders. Criminal leverage in the state apparatus made the Zemun Clan a compulsory negotiating partner for the incoming pro-Western reformers. Zoran Djindjić, Serbia's first democratic prime minister, personally negotiated with Ulemek. Barely three years later, he would pay for the devil's bargain with his life.[48]

Mafia defection thus enabled Milošević's removal—but not without considerable theatrical saber-rattling in the streets. JSO fighters descended on a television station during a riot. Armed to the teeth in militarized Humvee and shooting into the air, they prepared to open fire on demonstrators. Hesitating at the last moment, the "troops suddenly salute[d] the demonstrators and le[ft]," proceeding to a nearby boulevard to fraternize with activists. Posing for photographers, hugging female protesters, and kissing an Orthodox priest's hands, rank-and-file uniformed JSO members solemnly pledged to protect "the people" they nearly fired on moments earlier. Behind the scenes, Ulemek liasoned with army, police, state security, Milošević's inner circle, and the opposition to ensure his mafia's perseverance as events unfolded.[49]

Forsaking a bygone regime, and with minimal concessions to the new authorities, the chief murderers, smugglers, and racketeers of the war years emerged unscathed.[50] Outstanding criminals of the outgoing regime simply transitioned into cosmetically "reformed" institutions, while ministers experienced subordination to the security agencies they nominally headed. Extraditions to the Hague Tribunal (where embarrassing evidence was accumulating) met fierce resistance. In superb irony, the JSO itself arrested Milošević on behalf of the government; it was commissioned for lack of alternatives. In late 2001, the JSO blocked Belgrade's main highway with armored vehicles, in fully armed war gear. Ostensibly, it demanded an end to the extradition of Serbian commanders, whose patriotic heroism resonated with nationalist public opinion. Its actual request—made secretly—was the release of Zemun Clan foot soldiers from prison, where they found themselves for less praiseworthy deeds.[51] This act—an armed insurrection by the country's strongest mafia—was met with state impotence. "Do we have *any unit*," the deputy interior minister was asked, "which can break this up?" Bashfully shrugging, he conceded Serbia did not.[52]

Humiliating negotiations ensued to defuse the crisis. Djindjić—alone and unprotected—was escorted into mafia villas on the outskirts of Belgrade by armed narco-traffickers, summoned like a lowly errand boy. One could easily have confused which side was the state and which the mafia.[53] Celebrations followed. Firing weapons and rampaging through Belgrade in high-speed cars, gangsters threw lavish parties at a disco before burning it to the ground (the hapless owner, needless to say, failed to get satisfaction in court years later). Public displays of nationalist euphoria were matched by drug-infused depravity. Spanish police discovered a murder of one of their own members. Fearing that he would testify against them, senior Clan members tortured him, minced his body through a meat grinder, and *ate* him.[54] Jokes about the cannibalism were recorded on audio, but hardly seemed to repel young admirers.

Undeterred, Djindjić fought back. The government passed witness protection legislation, creating a specialized organized crime court. The JSO harbored no illusions about whom these might be for. With over fifty assassinations, dozens of kidnappings, and funds from Colombian narco-cartels, the JSO now marshaled enough audacity for a full-frontal assault on the state: a coup d'état. Three attempts were made on the prime minister's life, each revealing the government's feeble response.[55] On one occasion, the perpetrator—known to authorities as a mobster—was released in two days by local police under pressure. In March 2003, the Clan finally succeeded in killing Djindjić. In a political scramble, the mafia nearly reversed the entire democratic reform begun in 2000. It was a daring, unprecedented act, but ultimately a failure. A belated and partial crackdown thwarted full criminal co-optation in a month-long state of emergency. Most JSO members were captured or killed. After fourteen months in hiding (sometimes disguised as a bearded monk), Ulemek surrendered to sympathetic authorities under mysterious circumstances. Clan accomplices remained in the state apparatus, but out of government.[56]

All the while, separatist divergence continued. While Serbia proper was preoccupied—and shackled—by unruly gangsters, organized crime transformed into a veritable mafia state on the breakaway territory itself. What Serbian organized crime only attempted with the host state, the Kosovar mafia triumphantly achieved with the separatist movement.

MAFIA ASCENDANCE

In 1996, the KLA was an obscure and eccentric fringe of the (then-diverse) separatist movement.[57] National liberation head Ibrahim Rugova—"Kosovo's

Mandela"—publicly scorned the drug-peddling fugitives. Like their Serbian counterparts, Kosovar gangsters cloaked themselves in patriotism. The mainstream of the separatist cause maintained a prudent and firm distance from the KLA. But the bizarre cabal—comprised of gamblers, mercenaries, heroin peddlers, sex entrepreneurs, exiled convicts, and idolaters of the late Stalinist Envir Hoxha—would soon lead the secessionist struggle to victory. This was achieved in two steps: massive armament and drug funding, followed by the extermination of rivals.

The KLA had a fateful advantage: its transnational reach. Shunned by the puritanical separatist authorities, the mafia nevertheless controlled smuggling into Kosovo. When the opportunity for an arms bonanza appeared, it was prepared to seize it. In 1997, neighboring Albania descended into anarchy. Under Thaçi's coordination, 750,000 weapons were stolen and transported to KLA sites. Dozens of gangsters returned from exile for the occasion. Prominently, Ramush Haradinaj (who fled conviction in 1990) became a commander. A modest lawbreaker specializing "in cigarette and oil smuggling, as well as extortion rackets," he suddenly headed a gang in possession of the armed arsenal of an entire country.[58] Nearly overnight, the KLA transformed from a negligible set of ruffians to a full-fledged army. No Albanian unit in Kosovo had ever been so well equipped. With improvised uniforms to match the stockpile, the gang strode out of the shadows. At its first public appearance in 1997 near the village of Srbica, the invigorated KLA paraded, brandishing its armory and exciting the local population. It initiated attacks on postmen, lumberjacks, clerks, government officials, and civilians, eliciting a brutal crackdown by Serbian forces. The separatist struggle had a new, imposing—if boisterous—representative.

Guerrilla cycles of violence, naturally, strengthened the militants and discredited the pacifistic mainstream. In October 1997, twelve thousand Albanians attended a funeral of a KLA fighter killed by Serbian forces; double as many attended a subsequent one the following month. Recruitment skyrocketed. Twenty thousand armed members were stationed in training camps in Albania in 1998–99.[59] Low-level mafia foot soldiers became proud national liberators. While separatist authorities issued statements from ornate offices, it was conspicuous who ran Kosovo's streets. Spectacular, gruesome displays of mafia ritual engulfed the society, usurping attention and credibility from Rugova's institutions. Corpses were placed as markers of turf. Through *fis* patronage networks, the mafia initiated forced mobilization campaigns in 1998. Villagers were compelled to dig trenches. Health insurance cards and driver's licenses were confiscated to compel young men to take up arms. In a half-dozen villages, citizens naively returned drugs and weapons forcibly given to them by KLA recruits, begging the host state for protection. The request was in vain.[60]

Contrary to both Serbian and Albanian narratives, however, these measures were not primarily aimed at ethnic struggle. For the mafia, the separatist cause was an afterthought: "The KLA fought just as hard, and devoted arguably more of its resources and political capital, to maintain its advantage over its ethnic Albanian rival factions as it did to carry out co-ordinated military actions against the Serbs."[61] It was *intra*ethnic cleansing. The KLA concentrated on separatist rivals by enforcing obedience within the community. Between 1996 and 1998, more than half the KLA victims were Albanians accused of "collaboration."[62] In the peak violence year 1998, 45 percent of the civilians killed (77 out of 173) were coethnics opposed to KLA leadership. These included mafia "demonstration cases," when weak targets were made examples of: a household was besieged overnight, injuring two pregnant women; a suspected informant was assaulted, and his wife raped in front of him; and a Rugova supporter and her twelve-year-old daughter were murdered, and placed on the side of a busy road for publicly criticizing KLA tactics.[63] Loyalty to any other brand of separatism became an ill-advised proposition.

By the end of 1997, the fringe KLA had become the political, military, and cultural center of the separatist movement. By midsummer 1998, it controlled 40 percent of Kosovo territory, and the rest indirectly through its patronage networks. The educated, scarf-adorned Rugova and his pacifist negotiators could hardly compete. Smuggling across the southwest—where all movement was supervised by KLA patrols, customs, and checkpoints—skyrocketed between late 1997 and March 1999. Against Belgrade, Tirana, *and* Priština, the mafia put the Yugoslav-Albania border under new management.

STATEHOOD

The long-awaited war of national liberation ensued—with international support. The West had courteously ignored Kosovo's nonviolent authorities throughout the 1990s. With a fully armed transnational mafia waging guerrilla warfare, however, they were compelled to acknowledge a serious new player—and partner. The odd US Department of State report did express anxiety about KLA heroin ties, but the long-standing commitment to restrain Milošević prevailed. Continuing its strategic orientation from Bosnia and Croatia, the United States actively backed secession in early 1998, when the Central Intelligence Agency joined in training and equipping KLA fighters. After twenty thousand tons of bombs were dropped on it, Serbia withdrew its forces.[64] It was an unprecedented triumph for Kosovar sovereignty.

In the ensuing decade, Kosovo became "the world's first Mafia state," a singular phenomenon in post-1945 European history.[65] Despite the formal disbanding of the KLA, its commanders used newly minted government positions to expand a narco-trafficking empire. Interpol fugitives on top of a world-class drug-smuggling hierarchy—Thaçi, Haradinaj, and Agim Çeku—became prime ministers. Italian, Chechen, and Pashtun drug cartels eagerly collaborated with the parastate. Though Kosovo's share in the arms trade waned, the drug traffic skyrocketed. Separatist drug smugglers came to account for 70 percent of the total drug imports into Europe from the east. Narcotics could now fly. Priština International Airport became a hub of massive contraband transfers—the subject of seventeen romantic UN reports between 2004 and 2007.[66]

Rackets globalized, with flows to four continents. Offshore accounts from Kosovo broke European records. Diverse contraband began trailing the drug traffic. An elaborate organ-harvesting ring run by Thaçi extracted kidneys from (involuntary) donors and flew them to Turkish black markets. Hundreds of millions were embezzled from government funds or laundered through nepotistic privatization schemes. In Europe's poorest province, with unemployment between 40 and 75 percent, gangsters turned dignitaries built extravagant villas. One minister, Rexhep Osmani, publicly bragged of making €500,000 by swapping a ruined piece of real estate for underpriced state property. Another operated brothels servicing foreign troops. Hubris grew accordingly. Men known for their demented brutality were honored with Priština street names and socrealist bronze statues. Charged with war crimes at the Hague Tribunal, Haradinaj ended his legal troubles curtly: those planning to testify, along with their wives and their children, were systematically murdered or intimidated.[67] Lamenting the puzzling disappearance of its witnesses, the prosecution abandoned the case. Haradinaj returned home, exonerated, to a hero's welcome with fireworks, red carpets, and a marching band.

The North Atlantic Treaty Organization (NATO) Kosovo Force (KFOR) and its European successor, the EU Rule of Law Mission in Kosovo (EULEX), were hardly a match for the new mafia state. Some international officials were themselves not immune to corruption.[68] Most were simply impotent. In the 2000s, indigenous law enforcement institutions were either nonexistent or rudimentary. Foreigners avoided anticrime tasks, particularly prior to 2009. The top UN official stated publicly that addressing corruption and organized crime is not part of the international mandate.[69] Meanwhile, mafia law was still in effect. Police work froze for pervasive fear of retribution from KLA remnants above the law, with former commanders in the highest offices still running *fis*-based gangs.[70] Drug- and other crime-related murders numbered in the hundreds between 2004 and 2012.[71] Already perceived as alien intruders, many international peacekeepers understandably hesitated to meddle in such native traditions.

By 2012, Kosovo's criminal empire had truly globalized. Transcending the separatist territory, the mafia reached well beyond its region. Police reports across Europe documented the rise of Kosovo Albanian crime rings in Switzerland, Italy, the United Kingdom, Macedonia, and elsewhere.[72] The Balkan route for heroin—from Pakistan, through Turkey, and across Kosovo to Western Europe—represented the most coordinated transnational effort in Eastern

Europe and the Middle East. To this day, the racket is more coordinated and stable than the governments seeking to curb it.

Mediator in Georgia / South Ossetia, 1995–2012

In Georgia and South Ossetia, organized crime played a different role. Compromising, nonviolent, and multiethnic, the mafia that dominated separatist dynamics was a formidable force for peace and reconciliation. Its removal, in turn, sparked a separatist war. How could gangsters be peacekeepers?

INTERRUPTION

Since the Rose Revolution, the scholarly verdict on the Shevardnadze administration (1995–2003) has been unkind: he ran a criminal enterprise masquerading as a government. But his administration perceived—with justification—the grim choice between fraternizing with gangsters and lawlessness. Driscoll (2015, 121) disabuses us of the notion "that 'the state' suddenly became strong enough to take on militias and restore order. Rather, . . . 'the state' was itself formed from a subset of militias and warlords who had their armed checkpoints, bazaars, shadow-economy enclaves, and local tax collection legalized by the decrees of a government they installed." Just as Djindjić's post-Milošević government made mafias stakeholders in the new democratic order, so was Shevardnadze forced into power-sharing arrangements with the underworld. He took tremendous, if ambivalent, steps against organized crime, often in onerous conditions.

As early as 1995, Shevardnadze ordered the Mkhedrioni disarmed. He blamed Ioseliani for one of several failed attempts on his life. Like Ulemek in Serbia, the militia leader apparently ordered renegade subordinates in the security service to assassinate the president that he helped bring to power. Ioseliani was arrested and imprisoned, and the organization publicly stigmatized as criminal. Over two hundred Mkhedrioni members were jailed.[73] Kitovani was arrested in 1996 for planning yet another failed putsch. Anything reminiscent of the violent skirmishes, overt racketeering, and public coercion of the civil war days was dealt with swiftly. Shota Kviraia, the new minister for interior, was "effective, but excessively cruel."[74] He provoked infighting among criminal clans. Several top Mkhedrioni leaders were murdered. A wave of arrests was even made within the security service. Unlike in Serbia, patriotism was being publicly divorced from gangsterism.

To be sure, the regime compromised too. Shevardnadze co-opted criminal networks to solidify his position and strengthen state capacity as chronic intra-government divisions enabled criminal networks to increase their influence. In the late 1990s and early 2000s, "Ministries of Internal Affairs, Security and

Defense became competing fiefdoms," staffed with semiliterate thugs straight from the underworld.[75] Ministers used street gangs and prisoners to strengthen their autonomy from the rest of the government. These "fiefdoms" repeatedly forced concessions from the president and his inner circle.

Shevardnadze also created embezzlement schemes in private enterprise and government bureaucracies. Over a decade, he surrounded himself with allies that drained the economy through nepotism, kickbacks, and outright theft. His inner circle extracted vast wealth from Georgia's railroad, energy, aviation, telecommunication, and banking sectors.[76] Ministers of interior, defense, and security all participated in smuggling operations in contested territories under Shevardnadze, who ensured their loyalty by "allowing state or public theft." Most income was unregulated by legislation or presidential decree, ensuring that "they cooperated with their Russian counterparts and criminal networks to control drug flows and trafficking across Georgia's borders." Georgia became a prominent money-laundering destination for post-Soviet entrepreneurs. A single bank from the Shevardnadze era was found to have laundered $1 billion for transnational organized crime.[77]

Georgia's pivot toward globalization, however, unseated its initiator. Having consolidated the state as a coherent entity, Shevardnadze opened the society to Western markets. Georgia became the greatest per capita US aid recipient of all ex-Soviet territories. Every subsequent Georgian elite would remain dependent on Western aid. The government entered the International Monetary Fund, World Bank, Organization for Security and Cooperation in Europe (OSCE), and Partnership for Peace. Shevardnadze pledged to bring Georgia into NATO, which the United States was receptive to. The nation's reintegration into the world began stirring the Rose Revolution. These integrative processes brought new obligations and expectations by foreign evaluators. Georgian gangsters were now under international scrutiny. Local civil society monitors sprouted with Western aid, advocating transparency and accountability. Some four thousand nongovernmental organizations (NGOs) were registered. By the time of the Rose Revolution in November 2003, international and local campaigns to expose corruption brought public pressure to a boiling point. Though the immediate occasion for the uprising was electoral fraud (like in Serbia), the single most conspicuous demand was an end to organized crime (*un*like in Serbia). It was christened "Georgia's anti-corruption revolution."[78] Promising fierce, systemic reform, President Mikheil Saakashvili came to power peacefully—without negotiations with criminals.

All the while, mafias adapted: smuggling became quiet and inclusive. Public gun toting à la the Zemun Clan or KLA was kept to a minimum. Instead of armed insurrection or extermination of rivals, the mafia opted for a more profitable—and multiethnic—approach.

PEACE THROUGH SMUGGLING

While the Kosovar mafia came to fill the coercive vacuum left by the frail state, the Ossetian one filled the economic void. Instead of monopolizing violence, it monopolized the means of trade and major markets. The consequences for separatism would be fateful.

The Ergneti market was born in 1996, and would last until 2004.[79] At the heart of the disputed Georgian-Ossetian border—where blood had been shed for both nations—a veritable smuggling gold mine was erected. Around the vacated village of Ergneti, an accessible administrative area drew thousands of ordinary people daily from both sides of the border. They met, bartered, and exchanged services. Technically illegal, it became the epicenter of Georgia's gray economy (i.e., *the* economy). Hundreds of trucks and cars with questionable license plates inundated the area. Gangster suppliers struck informal turf agreements: vehicle sharing, protection rules, avoiding surpluses, designating schedules, and coordinating border crossings. The duty-free northern border was deluged with foodstuffs, oil, electronics, cigarettes, alcohol, stolen cars, and to a lesser extent, drugs and weapons. Just as the nearby Liakhvi River stretched from separatist into host state territory, Ergneti would link the two bickering societies. Indeed, it would reintegrate them. "In South Ossetia, the illegal trade benefits all sides," analysts noted. "It is partly for these reasons Tskhinvali and Tbilisi have generally been so cordial [before 2008], notwithstanding the lack of a final settlement."[80] Indeed, the absence of formal resolution was a blessing, not an obstacle.[81] Frozen conflict, with its jurisdictional confusion, was lucrative insofar as it remained unresolved and uncertain. Porous borders were profitable *because* they were disputed.

Separatist leaders were well aware that their survival depended on Ergneti.[82] They proceeded to crow secessionist demands in public, but were hardly sincere. Fostering Ergneti's inclusiveness meant good relations with Russia (i.e., an irredentist stance) and Georgia (i.e., a truce). South Ossetia's president even publicly supported Shevardnadze's candidacy for the Georgian presidency in early 2000. Ossetians were not prepared to jeopardize Ergneti and thus their livelihoods for secessionist daydreams—not at 70 percent youth unemployment.[83] As smuggling swelled, separatist demobilization was evident.[84]

Ergneti was a paradigm of multiethnic, equal opportunity organized crime.[85] Russian peacekeepers, Ossetian separatists, and Georgian officials alike tolerated Ergneti with agreements, implicit rules, and discretion. Ordinary people in both ethnic communities voted with their feet by conducting business there. Georgian car thieves sent vehicles northward through South Ossetia, while Ossetian forgers fabricated US currency to send to the West. Host state and separatist adjustments to Ergneti were almost indistinguishable.

True to the etymology of "nepotism," Shevardnadze's own nephew ran petroleum smuggling through South Ossetia on the host state side of the border.[86] In the early 2000s, a deputy governor of a Georgian region—along with three members of the national parliament—inherited these swindles. On the Ossetian side, former separatist leader Chibirov's son Alexei coordinated the traffic. In between them, the Tedeyev mafia ran day-to-day operations. Violence never exceeded exceptional, minor scuffles—all over criminal turf or profit, and none ethnic.[87] Smugglers hired drivers, vendors, and bodyguards in the thousands. Through Ergneti, organized crime was a leading employer in both societies.

Multiethnic reconciliation became so threatening that separatist ideologues were compelled to remind their constituency of the unfashionable anti-Georgian cause. Comical measures ensued. Pamphlets were printed railing against purchasing "Georgian goods." In reality, these were Russian goods sold by Ossetians, the taxation of which paid for the very printing presses churning the pamphlets out. The silly documents were distributed to truck drivers by their criminal suppliers at "administrative borders"—sometimes in lieu of wrapping paper, and sometimes as jokes and souvenirs. In the 2000s, separatist police demonstratively arrested several recipients of Georgian government aid—an exercise in futility.[88] Ossetian authorities routinely misrepresented Ergneti transactions as Georgian conspiracies, downplaying their multiethnic character. But the bluster failed to stop the routine mingling of ordinary folk in the open-air market, which grew from hundreds of cautious daily attendees in 1996 to thousands in 2003. Now a part of the average consumer's everyday life, Ergneti also catalyzed migration. The majority of Ossetians in South Ossetia acquired Russian nationality between the two wars, including through a 2002 Russian citizenship law. Ethnic Georgians got indirect access to Russian goods and business contacts. Remittances moved in both directions. The specter of ethnic reconciliation haunted the Caucasus.

Shevardnadze's criminal inner circle would stand to lose enormous money with a political settlement. Formalized, proper customs controls would be the worst possible outcome. Ossetian leaders felt the same way. Buttressed by the Tedeyev Clan, the separatist authorities were pressured to temper their nationalist tone. Their rule depended on regular salaries and social service provisions for the separatist bureaucracy. Yet South Ossetia's official GDP was supposedly $15 million, collected mainly through Russian border customs—a fraction of its actual spending.[89] Anti-Georgian extremism became heresy for criminal policy makers.

Ergneti emerged because mafias turned to nonviolent instead of violent profiteering. The criminalized militias of the 1990s abandoned resource extraction at gunpoint; they reoriented themselves to lucrative, politically neutral trading. The armed gangs that formed to resist Georgian aggression refrained from extortion, reapplying their skills to new market demands. Nobody asked—or cared—about their convict backgrounds. They became bodyguards, drivers, travel agents, customs liaisons, escorts, traders, and managers.[90] Separatist agitation simply did not pay. Furthermore, organized crime internationalized trade in the torn state. The multiethnic mafia enterprise brought Ossetian, Russian, Georgian, Turkish, Albanian, Armenian, Chechen, and Chinese enterprises together in profit—including individuals who killed each other's villagers, comrades, and families. One pair of veterans recalled nearly shooting each other in the First Ossetian War. Years later, they partnered through Ergneti to peddle stolen jewelry to Ukrainian housewives through a Turkish middleperson in Kiev. Not to be outdone in cosmopolitanism, the driver exporting their goods was Greek with fake diplomatic license plates.

In full bloom by 2004, Ergneti seemingly did the impossible. It reversed South Ossetia's northward economic turn, which had begun with the 1990s' blockade punishing the secessionist parliament. Having been forcefully tilted toward Russia, the Ossetian (North and South) economy was now reoriented toward Georgia. Indeed, organized crime accomplished what the host state only pledged to do in rhetoric: it reintegrated the separatist economy into the Georgian economy. Since separatist escalation or host state repression would have disturbed the criminal harmony, both were avoided. Despite international pressures on Tbilisi and Russian pressure on the separatists, Georgian–South Ossetian relations were conciliatory. Both sides, in effect, suspended hostilities in favor of the mafia economy.

ERGNETI'S AFTERMATH

Appealing to popular resentment, Saakashvili implemented the most sustained and aggressive anticrime reforms in Georgian history.[91] Indeed, this was "the first anti-corruption revolution in the Soviet Union."[92] By strengthening border controls, removing power from regional politicians, and firing corrupt police officers and state officials, the new administration reformed Georgia proper. Yet when he attempted to reintegrate Ossetians under the banner of curbing corruption, Saakashvili destroyed the only remaining adhesive between the host state and separatist territory. The tragic assault on Ergneti resulted in the 2008 Second Ossetian War.[93]

The host state first fired warning shots. Saakashvili's forceful removal of the president of nearby Adjara as a "test case for subsequent autonomy options for South Ossetia" left Tskhinvali unamused.[94] A public relations campaign from Tbilisi demonized South Ossetia as a criminal entity, insulting ethnic sensitivities and ignoring real grievances. By December 2003, the host state's Ministry of Interior conducted its first seizures of contraband. It began physically destroying major roads used for Ergneti, affecting tens of thousands of livelihoods. Ossetians were not the only ones publicly complaining about the assault on Ergneti. Paid advertisements in Georgian newspapers protested from both sides. One report conveyed a sense of betrayal and anger at Tbilisi's treatment of Georgian conationals in South Ossetia during the shutdown. Outraged citizens claimed—accurately—that Georgians around Tskhinvali were as harmed as the Ossetians.[95] The first onset of violence came after an effort to install customs booths in July 2004. This endangered not only Ossetians and their Russian accomplices but also Ministry of Interior officials who "profited from Ossetia's ambiguous political status and porous borders."[96] While the closing of Ergneti was sold as just another aspect of the anticorruption campaign, the host state's objective was clearly retaking South Ossetia by force.

When Ergneti was militarily assaulted, official Russia rejoiced.[97] The Ossetian leadership, now attracting popular support, began resisting the crackdown and inviting Russian patronage. Moscow and its preferred separatist leader, Eduard Kokoity, were the greatest victors of the clampdown. The secessionist regime in South Ossetia was extremely unpopular—a fact that Tbilisi misguidedly attempted to rely on. The proposal to merge South Ossetia with its northern neighbor was a minority view among the South Ossetians prior to Georgia's anticorruption offensive. Informal South Ossetian estimates put Kokoity's popularity at less than 20 percent, while Georgian estimates put it at 2 percent before May 2004. The tide turned quickly. Within two months of Tbilisi's onslaught on Ergneti, his popularity soared to 96 percent. A previously reluctant population, 95 percent of South Ossetians now rejected Georgian sovereignty and a staggering 78 percent reported being prepared to "personally fight if need be."[98] Ethnic polarization rose to a ten-year high.

Having opened Pandora's box, Saakashvili attempted damage control. The host state launched a farcical public relations campaign aimed at persuading Ossetians not to be Ossetians. In a fit of generosity (2004–7), Georgia suddenly invested into Tbilisi-controlled areas of South Ossetia. Concerts with German disco groups advertised the benefits of Georgian sovereignty over the region, among other stunts.[99] Ethnic enmity only worsened; separatist resolve grew. Desperate smugglers and their investors sent armed bands to revitalize crucial trafficking roads that had been destroyed. Violent skirmishes multiplied, as dormant Ossetian militias reorganized and rearmed. Defense of their illicit livelihoods combined with anti-Georgian nationalism. Gangsters who had collaborated with their Georgian counterparts for decades were again preparing to kill them. When war finally erupted in 2008, it took 850 lives and displaced 130,000.[100] Unlike the First Ossetian War, the reprise included brutal jingoistic violence and documented war crimes. The fragile but effective multiethnic cooperation that Ergneti fostered was radically reversed. In contrast to the First Ossetian War, the violence was conspicuously characterized *not* by criminal opportunism but by ethnic rancor instead.[101]

TABLE 2. Effects of Divergent Mafia Roles

When organized crime was *rejoicing third* (both cases)		When organized crime was *divider and ruler* (Kosovo)	When organized crime was *mediator* (South Ossetia)
Host state consolidated after war, chaos, and economic disaster . . .	→	is assaulted and provoked into war	It becomes collaborator or partner in crime
Host state aid to separatist territory wanes . . .	→	and "mafia state" emerges	Ergneti emerges
Host state crackdown on organized crime . . .	→	is not attempted	It reignites separatism
Gangsters with quasi-state credentials . . .	→	become nationalist heroes, freedom fighters, martyrs, and political figures	Gangsters become business-people, entrepreneurs, gatekeepers, and unwitting agents of interethnic cooperation
Unruly militias out of work . . .	→	became tools of war profiteering and nationalist politics	Militia members become smugglers, bodyguards, travel agents, and gatekeepers
Interethnic relations . . .	→	are polarized	Relations are improved
Intraethnic relations in separatist community . . .	→	are polarized	Relations are improved
Immunity for criminal leaders . . .	→	is ensured by intimidation, terror, and nationalist stigmatization (of "traitors")	Immunity is ensured by widespread collaboration (everyone "in on it")
Host state and separatist leaders seeking to mobilize for the national cause . . .	→	are co-opted, giving gangsters nationalist legitimacy	They are made unpopular and unpersuasive
Violent, militant wing of separatist movement . . .	→	is empowered	It is discredited
Victims of criminal turf wars . . .	→	are many and justified as collateral damage of liberation struggle, and contribute to ethnic mobilization	They are few and do not contribute to ethnic mobilization
Eager patron state . . .	→	becomes supplier of arms, intelligence contacts, militant training camps, and antihost state resources	It becomes supplier of food, oil, cigarettes, cars, and so on.

The Ergneti market had sustained an entire quasi-state apparatus on a territory lacking revenues, international support, and even people. It turned out, ironically, that "corrupt ties can mitigate ethnic violence," while "anticorruption movements such as the Rose Revolution in Georgia destabilized, rather than stabilized, the country's ethnic political situation."[102] By destroying the most important mediator between Georgia and South Ossetia, Saakashvili rekindled nationalism on both sides and revitalized a depressed separatist cause. No warring party achieved its objective. Nearly a decade later, experts on both sides lament the days when organized crime united them.[103]

When the mafia acted as divider and ruler, separatism progressed (Kosovo). When the mafia acted as mediator, separatism was hindered (South Ossetia). Some of the counterintuitive processes involved are summarized in table 2. What happened to these understudied societies is an illuminating lesson about what determines the fate of border disputes. The "third man" not only matters: their role can mean the difference between integration and separatist drift, consolidation and state collapse, peace and war.

4

Mafia Filter

Until that moment, the Kosovo Liberation Army (KLA) worked illegally, clandestinely. In 1999, they felt the moment was right. And even though they didn't liberate anything—namely, Kosovo was liberated by NATO—they declared themselves liberators.
—KOSOVAR JOURNALIST VETON SURROI, *PEŠČANIK*

South Ossetia is not a territory, not a country, not a regime. It is a joint venture of siloviki [ex-KGB] generals and Ossetian bandits for making money.
—RUSSIAN JOURNALIST YULIA LATYNINA, *RADIO FREE EUROPE*

For separatists, it is preferable to have transnational smuggling in their region than not. This is trivial, almost axiomatic. Movements are denied formal channels for various resources they sorely need—money, arms, fighters, and propaganda channels. What they cannot procure within host state borders, they must smuggle across them. When separatists have the fortuitous circumstance of regional smuggling routes, it is only natural they exploit it. But the advantage does not come automatically. When *exactly* do mafias help separatists? What are the conditions under which organized crime advances separatist success as opposed to hindering it? Why do some separatist movements fail to capitalize on regional smuggling opportunities, even if they have them?

Fortunate, Ready, and Willing

This chapter examines how transnational smuggling converted—or not—into separatist success at two critical junctures for Kosovo (Serbia) and South Ossetia (Georgia). Specifically, it looks at the 1999 Kosovo War, which gave Kosovo de facto autonomy under NATO occupation, and the 2008 South Ossetia War, which gave South Ossetia de facto autonomy under Russian occupation.[1] Both crises coincided with momentous trafficking opportunities in drugs and arms. Following data on transnational smuggling from 1989–2012 for the two cases, we can see the extent to which each criminal branch promoted separatism. In Kosovo, the mafia filtered both opportunities toward separatist success. In South Ossetia, it did neither.

Smuggling routes that traverse torn states incentivize various actors to profit from the transit of contraband across their territory. As transnational criminal opportunities—which they did not create—ebb and flow around them, local mafias' prospects benefit accordingly. But to speak of "geographic advantage" or a "criminal hub" begs the questions of precisely *what* smuggling, and *when*. Some traffics (e.g., in fuel) are readily applicable to the practical needs of separatist insurgency. Others (e.g., in qat) are not. More important, some global alterations in illicit flows precede critical junctures of separatist success (e.g., a war), but others do not.

Human trafficking, for instance, can be as profitable as narcotics when regional demand is high and steady (as we will see in Niger's Agadez). In South Ossetia, however, regional opportunities to smuggle people were consistently lacking. In Kosovo, human trafficking flows (mid-1980s–92) were too early and too difficult to convert into separatist gains. Poor timing was as crucial as the nature of the contraband. Exploiting migrants and prostitutes was a laborious task compared to narco-profiteering in the late 1990s—let alone diverting such resources to separatists.[2] Drugs, on the other hand, were effortlessly sold for KLA arms.

I focus on narcotics and weapons as two contraband with the most direct, salient separatist benefit. The division into two smuggling branches is of course an idealization. Both Serbia and Georgia—and their separatist territories even more so—had muddled "war economies" long after their wars, blurring differences between formal and informal trade, black and gray economies, contraband and goods.[3] Transnational mafias crossbred their dealings; drugs and guns were often trafficked by the same gangsters under similar circumstances at the same time. Nevertheless, disaggregating the two branches sheds light on an important mystery: How do regional and global trends in the flows of these commodities (exogenous and uncontrollable) interact with the domestic criminal reaction to those trends (endogenous and autonomous)?

Mafia "filtering" is the sine qua non of separatist benefit from smuggling. The filter model involves two aspects of mafia agency:

1. Organized criminal *capacity* to react to regional smuggling fluctuations. Is the local mafia up to the task?
2. Organized criminal *predisposition* to aid separatism. Is the mafia ethnocentric or multiethnic?

TABLE 3. Mafia Filtering of Regional Drug and Arms Traffics

	Drug traffic		Arms traffic	
	Kosovo	South Ossetia	Kosovo	South Ossetia
Regional opportunity	Yes	Yes	Yes	Yes
Mafia *capacity*	Yes	No	Yes	Yes
Mafia *predisposition*	Yes	Yes	Yes	No
Effect on separatist success	Positive	Negligible	Positive	Negligible

For regional criminal flows to aid the separatist movement at a critical juncture, three conditions must align: chance, ability, and will.

THE DRUG TRADE

With richer tradition and greater ethnocentrism, the Kosovo narco-traffic is in a league of its own. Compared to their Caucasian counterparts, Kosovar mafias are older, larger, more dynamic, and more adaptive to regional and global drug flows. The South Ossetian drug traffic is comparatively newer, smaller, relatively static, and unreactive to new commodities or fluctuating yearly volumes. More important, Kosovo is a major center for drug trafficking (largely independent of Serbia), where separatist control over illegal narcotics is a central aspect of its trajectory. South Ossetia, in contrast, accounts for a marginal share of overall Georgian traffic, and the drug trade was not a primary branch of organized criminal control in the separatist region. As a result, although mafias in both countries were *predisposed* to assist separatism, only Kosovar mafias had the *capacity* to do so. Separatist success in Kosovo was thus dramatic; in South Ossetia, it was negligible.

Supplementing Serbia's and Georgia's general geographic advantages, the end of the Cold War brought superb forecasts to drug entrepreneurs in the two countries. In the early 1990s, Serbia and Georgia were low-level transit sites, unworthy of mention in globalized narco-markets. The 1997–98 *World Drug Report* (*WDR*) found that both Serbia and Georgia were outside major world routes.[4] They were equally inconsequential at the regional level: while both states registered trafficking upsurges in the mid-1990s, neither was competitive with neighboring countries by volume—per capita, by territorial size, or in aggregate. The turn of the century, however, brought a dramatic reversal of fortunes. In the late 1990s and early 2000s, Turkey's disruptive campaign against hard drugs coincided with a wave of decriminalization and legalization measures by wealthy European government, notably the Netherlands.[5] The resulting reinvigoration of narco-trafficking in Balkan and Caucasus societies was then augmented by the 2001 invasion of Afghanistan, a world historic episode for narcotics globally.[6] In the 2000s, both Serbia and Georgia became vital transit hubs.

Serbia/Kosovo assumed their natural advantage as a bridge in the so-called Balkan route: a global drug path from Afghanistan to Pakistan, via Turkey, through the porous Balkan frontiers of Greece, Macedonia, Albania, and Serbia/Kosovo—onward to Western Europe. During Yugoslav-Albanian Cold War frictions and Communist Yugoslavia's rigid border control, the traffic through Serbia had been curbed. In the 1990s, the United Nations noted for the first time that the Balkan route developed "various offshoots as a result of the conflict in the former Yugoslavia."[7] Gradually, Serbia—by then a shrinking Yugoslavia—become the center of southeastern European narcotics smuggling, both by land and rail. In due course, it monopolized the westward stream of narcotics. By 1997, more heroin was seized in Serbia/Kosovo (with the region's most corrupt and inefficient law enforcement) than in all other Balkan countries combined.

Concurrently, in the late 1990s, the Georgia-Turkey route replaced previous passages from the east into western markets. With corrupt border officials, unregulated trading enterprises, and the region's largest unemployed majority, Georgia became a natural midpoint on the criminal furrow.[8] Before the government had consolidated after civil war, Azeri, Armenian, and Russian smugglers had already established partnerships—including with deckhands on the Kura River going through Tbilisi and Gori. Additionally, an alternative route emerged that bypassed Turkey altogether; instead of Afghan/Pakistani drugs flowing south of Georgia through Iran and Turkey directly into Greece, they tilted north—from Iran into Azerbaijan or Armenia, and then Georgia. This path, bypassing Turkey entirely, now took advantage of Georgia's Black Sea access to southeast Europe.

This rerouting through the Balkans and Caucasus enabled both separatist territories to diversify their range of drugs, assume greater market share in regional traffic, and most significant, adopt a bridge role hitherto held by neighboring states. Like Panama for the South American cocaine routes or Thailand for the Southeast Asian "Golden Triangle" of heroin, Serbia and Georgia became strategic conduits in global drug paths. Within the Caucasus, then, Georgia became a mirror image of Serbia's bridge position in the Balkans. The shift in regional flow was as favorable as the Balkan route transition was to Serbia. The two countries could have been equally vital branches of the same global drug chain—each in its region. The same potential volume moving westward could now cross both countries. Indeed, accounting for the "leakage effect" of longer transport chains, Georgia might even have had *greater* volume than Serbia, given its proximity to Afghanistan. Alas,

Georgian drug cartels squandered this opportunity. Neighboring states seized it.[9]

This divergence is particularly remarkable because Georgian narco-traffickers had another advantage: more domestic addicts. Both south Europe and the Caucasus have opiate prevalence rates below the world average.[10] But while Serbians have midrange drug prevalance by the standards of Balkan countries, Georgians are a notable drug-using population in their region with 200,000 to 240,000 addicts, 80,000 of whom are regular injection drug users. Serbia—nearly double Georgia's population—has 100,000 addicts, 27,700 of whom are regular injection drug users. Moreover, 1.2 percent of fifteen-year-old Georgians engage in drug abuse compared to 0.3 percent of Serbians. Into the mid-2000s, Georgia continued to be second only to Tajikistan in all Central Asia and Transcaucasia in abuse prevalence among its population.[11] In contrast, "although opiate abuse is a problem in Serbia & Montenegro . . . and is higher than in several other European countries, there are no indications that opiate abuse is higher than in neighboring countries."[12] In 2011, a standardized study of young people found that among sixteen-year-old Serbians, 0.8 percent had tried heroin, 0.9 percent had tried cocaine, and 6.7 percent had tried cannabis; among sixteen-year-old Georgians, 2 percent had tried heroin, 1.1 percent had tried cocaine, and 16.9 percent had tried cannabis.[13] Both in absolute and relative terms, Georgia had greater domestic demand than most countries of the Caucasus and Balkans.[14]

The volume and variety of drugs available within Georgia, not to mention its territory and population, are smaller. Yet Georgia captures many more citizens abusing and possessing drugs recreationally without the intention to sell. In 2005 and 2006, Serbia arrested 336 and 268 people, respectively, for drug-related crime/possession/abuse, and Georgia arrested as many as 1,427 and 1,926, respectively. But when it comes to the prosecution of dealers (not users), the pattern is reversed.[15] For abusers, then, better to be in Belgrade than in Tbilisi. For drug peddlers, though, Georgia was decidedly safer—and with a larger customer base.

Yet Serbian narco-entrepreneurs were distinctly more active than their Georgian colleagues. Nowhere is the divergence in mafia capacity more striking than in drug volumes.[16] Serbia and Kosovo—whether considered aggregated or separately—consistently held larger shares of their regional narco-traffic than Georgia ever did. Between 1992 and 1995, a separatist gangster, Musa Rifatu (known as the "brains of the Kosovo connection"), single-handedly smuggled 465 kilograms of heroin worth fifteen million Swiss francs.[17] This one operation is greater than *all* Georgian and Ossetian heroin seizures in the aggregate, over the same period.

By 2010 estimates, "the bulk" of the 55–60 tons of heroin moving yearly to Germany and the Netherlands went through Serbia, Bulgaria, Hungary, and Austria. Assuming, conservatively, that only half of this total transited to Serbia, the amount is still greater than the entire estimated heroin traffic through Georgia for a full decade (1995–2005). Georgia's record year (by far) in heroin traffic was 2009, when by liberal estimate, 15–20 tons of heroin went into Ukraine. But most Georgian years recorded less than a third of this volume. After prolonged stagnancy in the 1990s, the Georgian drug trade grew modestly to a $1 billion market annually by 2002.[18]

The Georgian mafias' trademark commodity is opium, a significant share of which flows through South Ossetian channels. In addition to a sizable domestic base of opium users, Georgia is a major transit country feeding neighboring countries' demands. One would expect Georgia's comparative advantage vis-à-vis Serbia *at least* in the opium realm, if anywhere. Indeed, the Serbia/Kosovo traffic is almost entirely devoid of opium, with zero or near-zero amounts seized over nearly three decades—except for one year. In a single year, 2007, Serbia seized 57 kilograms of opium, which exceeds the entire 1990s for Georgia *combined*. Even though this commodity was without precedent in Serbia's domestic traffic, was unpopular in the neighboring states, and had no significant demand inside the country, the Serbian-Kosovar mafias were again more accomplished.

If the Georgian narco-traffic was a two-chord ditty, its Balkan counterpart was an elaborate atonal symphony. Practically every few years, the dynamic Serbian drug trade had major variations in scope, drug kinds, and within-country routes. The most notable adaptation was the takeover of the traditional Balkan route, which was roughly divided between its eastern (bypassing Serbia) and western (through Serbia) halves. "In the early 1990s, prior to the disintegration of the former Yugoslavia, the West Balkan route accounted for 60% of all opiate seizures made along the European Balkan route."[19] Within this trail, Serbia's share was marginal compared to its neighbors, with only 8 percent of the heroin and morphine seizures in 1996. It was a modest link in a chain, which in turn competed with another chain. A decade later, when heroin first began flowing through Bulgaria and Macedonia, close to 60 percent of the seizures on the West Balkan route were made in Serbia alone. The country's narco-bosses also deftly adapted to an emerging cocaine market; by 2000, Serbian and Kosovo Albanian networks "started to expand their product range from heroin and hashish to include cocaine as well."[20] By 2004, the cocaine traffic was in a "notable increase."[21] Eventually Serbia progressed to being the sole, uncontested corridor of the Balkan route.

Increasingly organized, narco-entrepreneurs monopolized all manner of eccentric drug bonanzas. Uniquely among its neighbors, for instance, Serbia became a leading regional destination country for ecstasy.[22] Within two years, it became a "country of origin" for ecstasy in the European market and ceased to be a major importer.[23] Subsequently, a similar cycle—importing, improvising production, and exporting—drove multiple drug markets. From 2002 to 2004, the state suddenly became a country of origin for several kinds of amphetamines.[24] In 2009, it was a transit hub for Captagon, a specialized synthetic stimulant from the Near and Middle East—ephemeral but popular. Drug rackets repeatedly innovated and diversified. In the mid-1990s, the consumption of depressants ranged between zero and twenty tons; by the late 2000s, the range was sixty to eighty tons. Serbia/Kosovo, once at the bottom of the list for depressant drug smuggling, was now fourth in the entire world—trailing only Belgium, Uruguay, and Portugal—in the reported per capita consumption of illicit benzodiazepines.[25] In 2012, certain narcotics categories suddenly plummeted as depressants reached a zenith.

The Serbian narco-mafia, critically, was not altogether Serbian. Initially thought to be a Belgrade-centric business, narcotics increasingly traversed Kosovo Albanian drug routes at the expense of Serbia proper. "In [the early 2000s]," a report found, "criminal groups of Albanian origins (based in Kosovo, FYR of Macedonia and Albania) have gained in importance"—a harbinger of things to come.[26]

Such fluctuations of drug type and changes in origin-transit dynamics are conspicuously absent in the Georgian traffic. Two major regional "waves" of cocaine in the late 1990s and mid-2000s left no apparent mark on local mafia activity. Despite global fluctuations, including increasing demand in the neighborhood (notably, Azerbaijan and Russian Dagestan), the opium trade in Georgia remained remarkably stable. Ecstasy—which enjoyed brief hospitality in Serbia—remained an exotic item throughout Georgia's history as an independent nation.

NARCOTICS IN SEPARATIST TERRITORY

Separatist success is a matter of seizing opportunity, criminal or otherwise, when it appears. When the time came—in 1999 for Kosovo, and in 2008 for South Ossetia—to divert drug trade profits into the separatist crusade, Ossetian organized crime was nowhere near the capacity of Kosovar organized crime. There were four reasons.

First, Georgian organized crime was significantly less experienced. Kosovo mafias were not only prepared to seize the mid-1990s' drug upsurge that came their way but had decades of experience in narco-entrepreneurship too. The Albanian secret service established a heroin-smuggling base in Kosovo's capital, Priština, as early as the 1950s, shipping to Western European heroin distributors.[27] The newly founded Albanian network initially worked in zones uncovered by Italian organized crime. Gradually, cooperation and partnership ensued. By 1997, the Kosovo Albanian mafia alone accumulated threefold the funds of the entire GDP of the sovereign Republic of Albania.[28]

In Georgia, by contrast, the drug trade was only born in the 1990s, with little organizational precedent from administrative remnants of the USSR in North and South Ossetia. Once established, the narco-traffic was minor and fleeting. Local gangsters certainly *wanted* to narco-fund separatist institutions. For a short period, "that criminal enterprise become, together with Russian support, a major factor sustaining the separatist republic [of South Ossetia]."[29] But mafia capacity was modest. Minor quantities of marijuana and hashish were produced locally, while heroin and opium were the only transiting narcotics. The drug trade peaked in April 2002 at $1 billion (miniscule compared to Kosovo's). From 1999 to 2002, the Pankisi Gorge bordering Russia served as the primary focal point. In 2002, the state regained control over the gorge, effectively disabling separatist narco-profits.[30]

While narcotics were Kosovar mafias' primary business, drug smuggling was a tangential activity for Ossetian gangs. South Ossetia's organized crime includes four branches: the smuggling of nonlethal goods from Russia, kidnappings of Georgians, arms, and drugs. The last is decidedly the least. The stolen car market, to name a single instance, is so much more developed that "drug dealers . . . either sell the drugs or trade them for stolen cars from Georgia," apparently with equal ease, if not preference, for the latter commodity.[31] In a typical raid, 800 people were detained and 20 arrested as members of illegal armed groups in 2004. Characteristically, only 10 kilograms of drugs were confiscated compared to 70 firearms, 55,000 cartridges, and $140,000 worth of other contraband.[32]

Second, while Kosovo drug runners adapted to seasonal variation and unfavorable terrain, their South Ossetian counterparts were incapacitated by them. Both separatist territories are highly mountainous. Movement can be inconspicuous but treacherous. Thus the Kosovo heroin trade spiked in summer, when a sizable number of tourists, including Turkish citizens who live and work in Western Europe, travel through Serbia.[33] In winters, nonetheless, smugglers continued to be active on major railways and roads, supplementing them with obscure paths through some of the (near-sixty) mountain peaks 2,000 meters above sea level. Trafficking routes crossed the peaks of Tromeđa (at the tripoint bordering Albania and Montenegro), Pogled (bordering Montenegro and Serbia), and Sherupa (bordering Albania and Macedonia). These smuggling corridors were effective precisely because the hostile topography proved challenging for law enforcement.[34]

In contrast, Ossetian drug cartels never overcame cold temperatures and snow. Georgia's northern mountainous terrain limited ordinary traffic even in warm weather. Heavy trucks or risky cargo on slippery winter roads were not supplemented or superseded by effective alternatives. Indeed, *all* smuggling between Russia and South Ossetia ceased in wintertime.[35] Hundreds of hiking guides—many of them veterans of the First Ossetian War—escort tourists on climbs as high as Mount Khalatsa (3,900 meters above sea level) and Mount Kazbek (5,047 meters above sea level). Though they readily boast of smuggling escapades along obscure paths (flogging everything from heavy automobile parts and paintings to guns and babies), narcotics were not on offer. In the fifteen years preceding 2008, no successful drug routes through the Likhi Mountain range have been documented.[36] Considering the long-standing traffic in stolen cars through South Ossetia, the passivity of drug traffickers is striking.

Third, the separatist share of the total national narcotics market diverged vitally between the two cases. The Kosovo drug trade is incomparably greater, more adaptive, and more independent compared to South Ossetia's. Indeed, Kosovo's narco-business exceeds the entirety of Georgia's (including disputed territories), despite size. Georgian drug seizures near South Ossetia or involving Ossetians were negligible in the 1990s. Serbia, meanwhile, seized 30 kilograms of heroin from 49 Kosovars in 1995, 21.6 kilograms of heroin from 51 Kosovars in 1996, 20.6 kilograms of heroin from 71 Kosovars in 1997, and 16 kilograms of heroin with 3.8 kilograms of cocaine from Kosovars in 1998.[37] The trend only escalated in the 2000s. Between 2007 and 2012, the number of major yearly Kosovo heroin seizures ranged from 41 to 77, the quantity ranged from 36 to 94 kilograms, and the number of people arrested for heroin trafficking ranged from 71 to 102.[38]

While the Ossetian drug trade barely differentiated from Georgia's, the narco-mafias of Serbia and separatist Kosovo continued to diverge. The 2007 accession of Bulgaria and Romania to the EU Schengen Area enabled the Bulgaria-Hungary-Romania route to compete with the western Balkan route through Serbia. The Serbian drug trade declined accordingly. Yet "the territory of Kosovo became increasingly used for the storage of large quantities of heroin that is to be smuggled to west European countries via Albania (Durres harbor), Montenegro and Bosnia and Herzegovina."[39] In effect, Kosovo appropriated the share of the drug trade that Serbia had lost.[40]

When Kosovars took over a substantial part of the heroin wholesale market from Turkish and Kurdish groups, the narco-mafia in Kosovo was "well organized, with perhaps five regional strongmen controlling corners of the territory and distributing to diaspora clan members in specific destination countries."[41] In 2008, 300 kilograms of heroin went just from Kosovo to Switzerland weekly. Throughout this ascendency of the province, the profits went to separatists.[42] There is no evidence of any such development for South Ossetia. To this day, drugs move across separatist land in Serbia; in Georgia, they bypass it.

The fourth, most fateful difference was in ethnic closure. Namely, Kosovo's drug cartels were a more ethnocentric, kinship-based operation than their Ossetian counterparts. Initially the Serbian drug trade was a multiethnic, almost cosmopolitan affair.[43] Belgrade's Zemun Clan, largely financed by narco-trafficking, cooperated with the Albanian Šabani Clan (though both now deny it, for the nationalist embarrassment). But Kosovar cartels became increasingly independent, superseding Serbian drug traffic in scale. In 1998, Interpol data show 143 Yugoslav citizens detained for drug smuggling, and of those, 135 were Kosovo Albanians.[44] Albanian groups found new partners such as West African smugglers importing cocaine from the Netherlands to northern Italy—an operation noted for its complete autonomy from Serbia.[45]

Kosovo Albanians—and secondarily, Albanians from Albania—incontestably controlled the most profitable sector of the Serbian drug trade, abandoning gangs based in the host state. After all, what use were they? The four major zones of national traffic were Kosovo, Bujanovac/Preševo, Novi Pazar/Tutin, and Rozaje in northern Montenegro. All but the last were Albanian-dominated communities. Even within Serbia proper, Kosovar clans outdid host state rivals. The village drug ring of Veliki Trnovac, for instance, famously propelled a narco-boss to political prominence as president of Kosovo's parliament.[46]

The Kosovar diaspora in Europe, furthermore, enabled the ethnocentric separatist mafia to dominate major markets in Germany, Austria, and Switzerland. As early as 1998, the US Drug Enforcement Agency ranked the Kosovar mafia second only to Turkey in Europe's entire heroin market. In 2010, this Western European heroin business was equivalent to the combined GDPs of Kosovo, Albania, and Macedonia.[47] Italy, Germany, Austria, Hungary, the Czech Republic, and Belgium owed 70 percent of their heroin to Albanian providers; in Switzerland and Scandinavia, that figure was 80 percent.[48] This is a breathtaking accomplishment given the modest numbers of Albanian immigrants and fierce competition.

In contrast, South Ossetian cartels within Georgia appear trivial compared to Armenian criminal enterprises in Javakhetia or Chechen armed gangs in the Pankisi Ravine region.[49] The Ossetian leadership (both in North and South Ossetia) has not been associated directly with narco-trafficking. At best, Ossetians strike incidental deals with Russian mafia representatives and KGB remnants. But while the (Kosovo-friendly) Albanian mafia dominated its region's drug trade, the (Ossetian-friendly) Russian mafia was comparatively weak in the Caucasus. Kosovar organized crime is the sole and strongest criminal enterprise rooted in an ethnic minority in Serbia. South Ossetian organized crime is one of many ethnic cartels in Georgia. The Ossetian diaspora, meanwhile, never extended beyond Russia.

Furthermore, South Ossetian drug trafficking is decidedly more multiethnic (Georgian and secondarily Ossetian). It never acquired meaningful independence from bigger mafias in Georgia proper. In the early 2000s, it was Chechen (not Ossetian or Russian) guerrilla groups in the Pankisi Gorge region that stimulated an Ossetian drug ring.[50] After a clash between local narco-gangsters and Chechen rebels led by Ruslan Gelayev, the latter seized control—partly through Gelayev's personal contacts with the host state authorities.

Chechen smugglers made the Pankisi region a "repackaging center" for drugs from Afghanistan, as the merchandise was held in South Ossetia temporarily before moving on. This simply could not be part of an anti-Georgian strategy as it relied on "at least passive cooperation with Georgian authorities," or at most, bribery of border officials and bureaucrats.[51] Ossetian mafias were marginalized by bigger players.

Host state mafias clearly monopolized narcotics. In 2003, two narco-bosses on the Georgian side of the traffic—at the helm of a gang of forty residing in separatist territory—were arrested for heroin possession. Gangsters quickly blocked major roads demanding their leaders' release, with credible threats to "stir up the situation in the conflict zone"; when dealing with insubordinate customers, these drug smugglers "would shoot at or seize the truck or even kill the owner and then blame everything on the Ossetians."[52] Their Ossetian partners—like drug big-timer Alan Dzigoev, who popularized methadone in Georgia—nevertheless remained faithful to those Georgian criminal circles. In sum, Ossetian separatism was, if anything, hindered by the narco-traffic.

THE ARMS TRADE

Arms smuggling differs fundamentally from drug and human trafficking; it is highly sporadic, meets sudden demand surges (i.e., violent conflicts), and provides a nonperishable commodity. Drugs are notoriously fleeting, but guns are purchased rarely and can suffice for decades without replacement. Whereas narco-dealers rely on a continuing market and renewed demand for an expendable good, gunrunners tend to avoid peaceful areas (even militarized ones) until their commodity is in regular use. People are difficult to transport, control, and sustain for labor and sex trafficking; guns are not. Finally, of all contraband, weapons are most readily converted into separatist benefit.

Both Kosovo and South Ossetia had substantial regional opportunities to smuggle weapons from neighboring, contiguous territories. Just as they shared a favorable position in regional drug routes, Serbia and Georgia had excellent geographic channels from the south and north, respectively, for illicit arms. Once again, Kosovo's mafia filtered this opportunity into separatist success— and South Ossetian organized crime did not. In the case of Serbia/Kosovo, a sudden onslaught of illegal arms smuggling from Albania to the separatist region catalyzed the armed conflict of 1998–99, ending in Kosovo's major separatist success. Contrastingly, though South Ossetia had an opportunity for illegal arms imports into a separatist crusade, there were two impediments: first, Russia's dominant role in sustaining the separatist region's military capabilities made arms smuggling unnecessary, and second, the multiethnic, cosmopolitan Ergneti market thwarted any separatist ambitions, even though it had the capacity to make an illegal weapons trade flourish.

The Serbia/Kosovo arms traffic benefited from decades of militarization in Yugoslavia as a whole. Since Josip Broz Tito's schism with Stalin in 1948, the Yugoslav leadership had lived in fear of a Soviet invasion, encouraging accessible weapons across the country. The wars in Bosnia and Croatia generated enormous demand for illicit arms among three terrified ethnic communities. A sizable portion of Yugoslav military arms and munition was looted by civilians and separatist militias alike. In 1992, sanctions on the Milošević regime inspired elaborate methods for circumventing the economic blockade. The emaciated state apparatus could not maintain soldiers at bare existence levels, let alone keep up with munition demands for three wars. To maintain power, the regime relied on gangsters to break the embargo; a major component of the circumvention was the arming of criminal militias whose gun culture was tolerated and encouraged. State-sanctioned gang violence escalated in all major cities. Ordinary citizens sought to purchase weapons, one of the most lucrative contraband in Belgrade, Novi Sad, and other cities' public markets. Regionally, the Balkan gun racket that emerged from Yugoslavia's collapse primarily supplied the separatist republics against Serbia proper, though all were equally forbidden to import armaments. Saudi Arabia, for instance, violated the UN embargo by "smuggling $300 million worth of weapons to the Bosnian government over a three-year period" despite the presence of "UN peacekeeping troops on the ground in Bosnia."[53]

Arms smuggling in Georgia was another matter altogether. For over a decade after the First South Ossetia War (1991–92), there was sustained peace on both sides. By the mid-1990s, the conflict zone had been thoroughly stabilized by peacekeepers, the forced separation of Ossetians from Georgians with checkpoints, and Georgia's preoccupation on other fronts. During 1996–98, the checkpoints were disbanded and a relatively free flow of Russian goods into Georgia commenced.[54] While it was impossible for Georgia to collect customs fees for these de facto imports, South Ossetia levied transit taxes on everything moving through the Roki Tunnel. Unlike in Kosovo, guns were unacceptable contraband. For opposing reasons, both host state Georgia and patron state Russia made illicit arms dealing to separatists extremely difficult. Georgia's Moscow Agreement on a Ceasefire and Separation of Forces in 1994 prohibited the introduction and operation of heavy weapons in the zone of conflict. This Restricted Weapons Zone made the Russian military the sole supplier of arms and training to South Ossetian forces. More than 60 percent of the national budget of South Ossetia comes from Russian funding, and fully 100 percent of the documented arms.[55]

One cannot conclude that Ossetian mafias lacked the capacity, however. On the contrary, the Tedeyev Clan created a veritable mafia masterpiece in the breakaway province. In the late 1990s, the Ergneti market was born on the South Ossetia-Georgia border. This mafia miracle was an administrative area that spontaneously drew around three thousand people daily to trade in a variety of goods—including, marginally, guns. Technically illegal, this site became the leading center of Georgia's gray economy, incorporating local Ossetian as well as Georgian authorities. Dire economic circumstances of host state and separatist communities alike made opportunities for customs-free trade irresistible.[56]

Ergneti soon became a criminal powerhouse. Elements of the Georgian state apparatus tolerated Ergneti because of their own complicity in smuggling rings; others remained passive because they saw the development as a welcome enhancement of the peace process. "Safeguarding Ergneti as a symbol of Georgian-Ossetian friendship, but also as a source of illegal income" became a "top priority" for local officials.[57] Fatefully, this multiethnic "cooperation to maintain smuggling corridors in South Ossetia" was largely premised on their *non*violence. Although the Roki Tunnel—controlled by South Ossetians and backed by Russian troops—smuggled $10 million a month into Georgia without taxes, it also pacified separatist hard-liners. "The Ergneti smuggling market in South Ossetia offered," experts concluded, "an opportunity for interethnic stability that years of confidence building could not deliver"—and mafias knew it.[58] Illicit weapons were both economically and politically disadvantageous.

When Georgia assaulted the Ergneti market, separatist violence returned.[59] It was only *after* the removal of this cosmopolitan organized crime that the separatist movement began—modestly—to benefit from arms trafficking.[60]

WEAPONS IN SEPARATIST TERRITORY

When separatists attain some degree of autonomy from their host states, an occasion arises for mafias to smuggle arms. Both in Serbia and Georgia, such opportunity existed. But while the Kosovar arms trade was unequivocally *predisposed* to aid a separatist insurrection, Ossetian organized crime—through the multiethnic Ergneti market—was not. Whereas Kosovo's arms dealers exploited Serbia's negligence to arm secessionist militants, Ossetian smugglers deliberately curbed the arms trade to preserve nonviolent rackets and partnerships in Georgia.

Though Kosovo was uninvolved in the Yugoslav wars, the 1990s brought the arms trade to this southern province as well. Serbia catalyzed the traffic through a posture of benign neglect toward Kosovar smuggling in general. Drained by efforts in three other breakaway Yugoslav territories, Serbia tolerated organized crime as compensation for its failings toward the Albanian minority. Since "criminal organizations provided all the necessary services," Serbia itself offered "much more indulgence than overtly admitted" in this situation of "mutual gain and convenience."[61] Organized crime in Kosovo became "a basic pillar of the economy."[62]

The Kosovar mafia was up to the task. KLA drug lords established a Swiss foundation (Homeland Calls) as well as a Tirana-based bank (Dardalia Bank), collecting funds from the Albanian diaspora. Donations ranged from a thousand deutsche marks to a thousand Swiss francs. Diaspora gangs also extorted 3 percent from every Kosovar émigré to fill separatist coffers in Priština. In total, roughly a billion deutsche marks were collected in the prewar period under the control of a Kosovo Albanian sympathizer living in Germany. The profit unmistakably poured into separatist armaments. As Serbian aspirations in the territory lost legitimacy, armed action became increasingly popular as righteous resistance. According to Austrian and Italian police reports, "the bulk of the profit [of the KLA in 1998 and 1999] was used to purchase weapons in 'black' markets of Europe."[63]

The first escalation of separatist conflict in Serbia/Kosovo followed in 1998. The timing was not coincidental: in the preceding months, an arms traffic arose due to a fortuitous development in neighboring Albania. In 1997, the collapse of financial pyramid schemes bankrupted thousands in the neighboring country, inducing government collapse.[64] In the ensuing chaos, 40 to 60 percent of the entire armament stockpile of the Republic of Albania tumbled onto the black market. All told, hundreds of thousands of weapons were open for plunder in the smuggling windfall.[65] Ransacking military barracks and police stations throughout the country, gangsters stocked trucks, garages, dugouts, and private warehouses. Between January and March 1997, the following arms and munition vanished: 38,000 handguns, 226,000 AK-47 rifles, 351,000 bolt rifles, 25,000 machine guns, 2,450 grenades, and 770 mortars. Official UN estimates—that 650,000 weapons were stolen—are widely believed to be conservative. In August, Albania offered amnesty for citizens who returned stolen weapons; only 10 percent of the arms and 3 percent of the munition were restored.[66] It remains the largest peacetime arms traffic in post–Cold War Europe.

The remaining loot went—almost in its entirety—into Kosovo.[67] In April 1998, seventeen farm tractors crammed with weaponry and military communication equipment were intercepted. Kosovar mafias also used trucks, vans, cars, horses, and donkeys. An unaccompanied mule would "normally carry 20–30 guns with each crossing."[68] By the summer, enough was trafficked to supply a lethal arm to every single adult in the separatist province. The weapons treasure trove from Albania elevated organized crime in Kosovo to unprecedented authority, as the mafia co-opted no less than the separatist movement itself through the KLA. Violence ensued. By 1998, the number of armed terrorist acts by the KLA rose to fourteen times the entire preceding seven-year period, 1991–97.[69] In March 1999, Serbian repression elicited NATO intervention on behalf of separatist Kosovo, giving the province unprecedented autonomy from the host state.

The sudden onslaught of armed smuggling was not the only cause of separatist confrontation, but there is no doubt that it was a necessary condition of the war. The Kosovar mafias were willing *and* able to inject the contraband weapons into separatist struggle. Even after massive peacekeeping forces entered Kosovo, weapons smuggling proved difficult to curb. Law enforcement weapons paled in comparison to the illicit holdings by 60 to 70 percent of the population, including "organized criminal actors." Smuggled arms continued to be sold in coffee shops and markets.[70] The resilience of arms traffickers was revealed in a 2003 hoax by British journalists. Fully four years after the entrance of peacekeepers, a team of investigators demonstratively purchased fifteen kilograms of Semtex explosives (enough, as they noted, to demolish downtown London) for €15,000 from mafia contacts. The transaction was done simply, almost publicly—near British troops. When the story was published in the Western press, the smuggler who had sold the explosives was murdered in Priština.[71]

South Ossetia likewise had significant regional opportunities, albeit less dramatic and sudden, to import illicit weapons before the 2008 critical juncture. Weapons smuggling existed but was marginal.[72] Ever since June 1992, the entirety of South Ossetia's weapons supply was provided by its northern patron, Russia, whose troops guaranteed its autonomy from Georgia. Though unregulated, the provision of Russian weapons was decidedly a government, not local mafia, affair. Not a single South Ossetian separatist administration has been documented to rely on weapons or profits from the arms trade. Ossetian mafias' gunrunning enterprises remained rudimentary; "[arms trade] organized crime [did] not reach the level of national drug syndicates," themselves modest. While Abkhazia, Georgia's other separatist region, received attention for lethal weapons bartering (including smuggling explicitly aimed at arming anti-Georgian fighters), South Ossetia was conspicuously absent as a significant site in this regard.[73] The market was saturated, but not for long. Georgia's crackdown on the Ergneti market revived the demand for guns— with a vengeance.[74]

In 2004, the newly inaugurated Saakashvili presidency launched an assault on what it considered a symbol of South Ossetian corruption. The first propaganda effort (in 2002) condemned Ergneti as a Russian front supplying weapons to separatists on Georgian soil—a falsehood. The peace process was a farce, Tbilisi insisted, when gangsters are brokers and smugglers are guarantors of interethnic cooperation. Ergneti was said to be a facade for creeping Russian irredentism. The second, more sustained publicity stunt (in 2003) held that South Ossetia was a "criminal problem—a piece of land run by a criminal clan," regardless of ethnic or separatist overtones.[75] Central to this campaign was a scandal regarding the smuggling of (HEU) (chapter 5). Though limited and tangential to separatism, the nefarious criminal episode scandalized the host state, helping to misportray Ergneti as a morass of lethal arms dealing.

Depicted as sinister and violent, smuggling became the central rationale for Georgia's attack on its northern separatist region. Tbilisi willfully hurled into a comprehensive reintegration of South Ossetia: eliminate Ergneti, forcefully disarm the alienated population, and restore sovereignty. Miscalculating, Georgia "tried to drive a wedge between the separatist authorities and the local population of South Ossetia." Sincere or not, the belief that South Ossetians would welcome a Georgian crackdown on smuggling was delusional. Rather, quite sensibly, they perceived the campaign as an existential attack on their ethnic community:

> Ergneti eventually became a self-inflicted problem. Many Ossetians who had no other means of income became dependent on the smuggling operation for their livelihood. When the Georgians eventually closed down Ergneti market in June 2004 this was not perceived by the Ossetian leadership as either a police or an anti-smuggling operation, nor was it widely welcomed by the Ossetian population, as the new Georgian leadership might have expected. Instead, it was perceived as yet another unfriendly act by a belligerent Georgian Government harming the South Ossetian people.[76]

Georgia's crackdown on Ergneti had ironic, unintended effects. The supposed arms trade that motivated the crackdown *created* a market in weapons where there was none. The resulting tensions stimulated gunrunning—by governments, not mafias.

On the formal side, Georgia entered "a period of unprecedented militarisation," with a plan to join NATO in record time, bolstered military budget ("by 2008 the imports of weapons reached USD one billion—an astronomical amount by Georgia's standards"), rejection of peacekeeping operations in separatist regions, and demand for Russian withdrawal from South Ossetia.[77] Tbilisi's offensive weapons purchases skyrocketed, primarily from OSCE countries—supposed mediators in the South Ossetia dispute. In reaction, Russian arms flows to South Ossetian authorities rose, as did Russian military preparedness on the border. In summer 2004, Georgian forces seized nine full trucks of arms and munitions being transported by Russian troops. Though Russians insisted the weapons were their own, Georgia was surely correct that they were intended for Ossetian militias.

On the informal market, private gun purchases rose. The Tedeyev Clan began diverting and supplementing Russian military supplies with black market weapons. By the time that war erupted in 2008, "most able-bodied men in South Ossetia [who] took up arms to protect their homes" were armed by Russian military supplies directly and secondarily by black marketeers. Without its own formal army, South Ossetia organized its fighters into militias (*opolchentsy*), which were asked to arm themselves by any means necessary. In addition, North Ossetian and Russian irregulars crossed the border by the thousands to fight in the conflict, and many of them were criminals importing private gun collections.[78] By 2009, illicit weapons became a staple of the Ossetian household. South Ossetia's ambassador to Russia remarked that "as many as there are people in the population, that's how many weapons there are."[79] Yet the arms traffic remained impartial to the bitter end; most of the weapons (i.e., small guns) "are used mainly in completely criminal circles"— with no import on separatism.[80] Throughout it all, Ossetian mafia capacity for lethal trafficking was not coupled with a willingness to wage separatist war.

Divergent Outcomes

The differences in mafia capacity and predisposition were fateful. Regarding narcotics, the South Ossetian separatist movement did not benefit from drug funds (comparatively miniscule, at that) before *or* after Russian military occupation (2008). Kosovo's drug trade, in contrast, successfully sustained the separatist struggle *preceding* Western military intervention (1999). Whereas the massive drug trade went on for years before the Kosovo War and only escalated thereafter, drug trafficking was a consequence of the South Ossetia war. Ossetian narco-funds were never more than one pillar of separatist strength; Kosovar drug funding, on the other hand, was at the heart of the independence struggle.

Regarding weapons, Kosovo mafias were zealously predisposed to channeling arms directly to armed separatist struggle. But South Ossetian organized crime—though it had the capacity—was opposed to separatist escalation. The KLA took advantage of the deep-rooted arms trade in Serbia and onslaught of weapons from Albania in 1998. South Ossetian militias only turned to violence (and weapons smuggling) after the shutdown of Ergneti. Given Russia's generous supplies to South Ossetia and the prolonged peace between the two Georgian wars, there was no demand for smuggled weapons. Above all, the multiethnic character of organized crime in South Ossetia was diametrically opposite to the ethnocentric, confrontational criminal scene in Kosovo.

Whatever sovereignty that separatist Kosovo enjoys, it owes to the *capacity* and *predisposition* of its mafias to filter both drug and arms flows to the successful 1999 uprising—a narco-funded armed liberation. Directly preceding the 1999 war, Kosovo's separatist fringe monopolized the drug trade and used it to finance an armed insurrection. Fully half of the KLA's finances came from narcotics. In the prelude to the war, the scale of the traffic spiked. In June 1998, sixty Kosovo Albanians were captured by Spanish police for drug trafficking. In July, Greek police seized 1,996.4 kilograms of hashish in two trucks from Albania that had originated in Kosovo; in the same month, Macedonian customs seized 72.3 kilograms of heroin from an Albanian truck, while Czech police arrested three Kosovo Albanians with 30 kilograms of heroin. In August, Austrian police seized three trucks with two tons of marijuana from Kosovo. The profit went almost exclusively to purchasing weapons for guerrilla operations against Serbian forces.[81]

The mafias only grew thereafter. In the postwar period, when Kosovo separatism achieved de facto sovereignty under international military supervision, the scale of the drug trade more than doubled. Up by 120 percent of prewar levels, monthly transit averaged 4.5 to 5 tons. The so-called Italian route, stretching from Kosovo across Albania and the Adriatic directly into Italy, came to the fore after 1999. According to Italian peacekeepers serving in Kosovo, the cartel established close relations with the Italian mafia in the postwar period and established a daily average of 50 kilos of heroin to the Milan market.[82] "Since 2003/2004, the traditional Balkan route from Turkey via . . . Serbia & Montenegro has re-emerged and gained in importance, while trafficking via the more eastern Balkan route (Hungary) has lost in importance."[83] By 2006, there were sixty thousand unresolved cases of drug trafficking in Kosovo.[84]

In contrast, separatists in Georgia enjoyed only postwar benefits—and negligible at that—from the two rackets. The narco-traffic was consistently a minor component of Ergneti smuggling and not a funding source for separatist institutions. The arms traffic had steadily diminished since 1995 in Georgia as a whole, with illegal armament demand saturated both for separatist institutions and civilians.[85] Neither criminal branch meaningfully supported the separatist movement. Furthermore, South Ossetia's separatist escalation in 2008 had, at best, an oblique relation to the drug and arms trade. The Second South Ossetia War was a direct result of Georgian incursion on the Ergneti market—an untaxed haven for a variety of goods, but drugs and arms least among them. Georgia legitimated an antiseparatist crackdown as an antismuggling operation, exaggerating the modest role of narcotics and weapons. It was genuinely a gift to hard-line separatists. In a spectacularly self-fulfilling prophesy, the crackdown on Ergneti *created* an armament opportunity for separatist authorities by terrifying Ossetians into an illicit weapons market.

The 2008 war brought the province greater de facto sovereignty, under tighter Russian control. Whereas Georgia lost control of roughly half the Autonomous Province of South Ossetia in the First South Ossetia War, the 2008 war left it with none. In the ensuing years, drug money simply did not reach separatist coffers. Heroin and opium routes continued to bypass the breakaway territory, while Georgian narco-dealers experimented with Subutex, a pharmaceutical drug, and "Crocodile," a homemade opiod, without separatist implications. Arms trafficking through South Ossetia grew, as Ossetian mafias and renegade Russian peacekeepers fed the newly minted demand for protection. Mostly restricted to pistols and rifles, the smugglers expanded their scope: an Igla antiaircraft system went for a few thousand US dollars on separatist turf.[86] For separatist movement benefits, it was too little, too late.

Filtering Success

Quantifying and measuring transnational organized crime as a single variable has been notoriously elusive.[87] Meanwhile, investigations of transnational smuggling almost never differentiate between host state–specific routes and separatist-specific routes in torn states. Worse still, the differences between trafficked contraband (guns versus drugs) are often left unexplored. These may be serious obstacles to understanding separatist dynamics in torn states. Aggregate levels of transnational smuggling give a distorted picture of what local mafias can or cannot do. Whether separatist territory accounts for none, some, or most of a country's organized crime can yield a radical difference. Finally, not all contraband is as separatist friendly as weapons and narcotics.

Global criminal routes are nothing without *local* mafias administering them. Overall illicit flows across borders were at their highest before Serbia's and Georgia's critical junctures: in the five years preceding 1999 in Kosovo and 2008 in South Ossetia, respectively, smuggling volumes were at a post–Cold War zenith. Customs checkpoints were largely symbolic. Gangsters controlled the import-export economy more than host states did. Black trade far outpaced the formal economy. Yet the two regional opportunities resulted in diametrically opposite effects for separatists: unprecedented success for Kosovo, and obstruction for South Ossetia.

Therein lies mafia agency. Opportunity is nothing without an endogenous criminal "filter." I have argued that two conditions must align for regional opportunities in transnational organized crime to convert to separatist aid: local mafia capacity to meaningfully participate in the regional smuggling must be matched with a predisposition to divert benefits to the separatist movement. Kosovo had both; Ossetia lacked one or the other. The reason is apparent only when we disaggregate the kinds of contraband. Russia-Ossetia border smuggling was nonviolent, arms and drugs were marginal, and the bulk of the market was everyday goods—the key impetus for an interethnic, peace-building mafia enterprise. Kosovo-Albania border smuggling, in contrast, was primarily in arms and drugs—both monopolized by an experienced, ethnocentric mafia. The mafia's capacity coalesced with a predisposition for both traffics, arming a separatist militia that moved from the fringe to mainstream of the separatist movement.

5

Smuggling Kidneys and Uranium

> Head raised high, he smiles and claims that all of this is an unfortunate misunderstanding.
>
> —ORGAN SMUGGLER FATMIR LIMAJ'S REACTION TO ARREST, *KOSOVO*

> [He] played small theatre. Red-faced and trembling [he] turned on his friend, Oleg: "Is it true?! Is it real radioactive materials?! Oh, now my family's ashamed! What have you done?!"
>
> —NUCLEAR SMUGGLER HENRY SUJASHVILI'S REACTION TO ARREST, *100 GRAMS AND COUNTING*

National emancipation is a ruthless endeavor. Realists may object that criminal misdeeds amount to little more than coping mechanisms. Why the puritanical emphasis on the illicit, lawless, and illegal? Separatist movements naturally scramble for resources as best they can, within their means. What is so unique about the mafia, yet another NGO that struggling insurgents rely on? We turn, then, to *real* criminality. The exposure of two nefarious criminal episodes—organ smuggling in Kosovo and HEU smuggling in South Ossetia—tested the resolve, organization, and patriotism of specialized mafias. Caught red-handed, the traffickers tainted separatists' legitimacy as the public scandals provoked repression from international military authorities (in Kosovo) or the host state (in South Ossetia). Damage control was necessary—but only one separatist movement managed it.

Profit, Scandal, and Harm

Justifying profiteering from narcotics, weapons, or people comes effortlessly to the nationalist mind. But even the most fervent separatist hesitates to champion organ harvesting and weapons of mass destruction as a pathway to independence. Whereas most rackets can readily be glorified as emancipatory means, organ and nuclear trafficking carry a universal stigma that makes apologetics after exposure difficult indeed. Separatists routinely rationalize, minimize, or relativize their dealings in cocaine or Kalashnikovs—or even defend them. When caught handling lungs or plutonium, though, denial is the norm.

Under what conditions does nefarious organized crime harm separatists? To be sure, the two episodes in Kosovo and South Ossetia were inflated by tabloids, sensationalist politicians, and opportunistic intelligence services. The scandals elicited an onslaught of bad publicity, threats of sanctions, diplomatic pressure, persecution attempts, and declines in domestic confidence from separatist constituencies. "You give them a bit of independence," the propaganda went, "and look what they do!" In both cases, the nefarious episodes served as rationales for curbing separatism. Priština and Tskhinvali incurred tremendous cost to their credibility and governance, as Serbia and Georgia exploited the exposure to push for reintegration—each within their means. KFOR, the United Nations Interim Administration Mission in Kosovo (UNMIK), and later EULEX sought separatist leadership accountability in Kosovo; Georgia, with NATO and International Atomic Energy Agency support, sought to reintegrate South Ossetia.

But once again, there was a curious divergence. Nefarious crime harmed South Ossetia's separatists more than Kosovo's. The reason was that mafia capacity—its infrastructure, autonomy, and community—was greater in Kosovo, containing the harm. A mafia able to undertake damage control is, we discover, a precious ally indeed.

Despite conspicuous differences, the organ and nuclear traffics have much in common. They are both segments of long transnational chains that transport contraband to desperate people: dying or suffering patients, on the one hand, and violent insurgents, on the other. Both rackets rely on a pool of high-skilled specialists—doctors and medical technicians (organ harvesting), or scientists and engineers (nuclear trafficking)—with the expertise to expedite extraction and recognize quality. Both nefarious enterprises profited individual criminals, not firms or states. There is no evidence that returns were directed to the separatist movements per se, as was the case in preceding chapters.

Both episodes were embedded in other criminal branches. First, both developed *after* the establishment and extension of networks of smuggling in more traditional contraband such as drugs, cars, and persons. Neither created new geographic paths ad hoc, but were encouraged by previous criminal experiences, connections, and means of protection and transportation. Second, both required the patronage of state-affiliated actors who cooperated for profit. Border and customs officers, security service employees, and government officials with information on risks and opportunities appear at every critical step of the two traffics.

In the 1999–2000 Kosovo case, vital organs seem to have been the primary contraband, numbering in the dozens. They were harvested from a subset of documented abductees "taken into central Albania to be murdered before having their kidneys removed in a makeshift operating clinic."[1] "The kidney travels well," able to last up to forty hours in an icebox during transportation; hearts can last four to six hours. Organ trafficking from Kosovo could not have involved procedures as complex as the removal of livers and hearts, but less sensitive organs like kidneys (estimated at $10,000), eyeballs ($1,525 for a pair), spleens ($508), and small intestines ($2,519) were probably harvested. Another possibility is "blood farming," which involves milking victims for blood for extended periods ($25 to $300 a pint)—a less profitable but more reliable method given the difficulties of transportation from Albania's mountainous north.[2]

The organ mafia in 1999–2000 was a pioneer in its region. It achieved profits with inflated prices, and was exceptionally violent in kidnapping and murdering donors in what is usually a voluntary racket.[3] Kidney prices regionally have been documented as high as $150,000 depending on the buyer's urgency, risk of transportation, and whether the organ is purchased from a donor or extracted by force. The profit in Kosovo's organ traffic was especially lucrative for the middlepeople because the suppliers were unpaid abductees. Among the world's most prominent "kidney bazaars" are Pakistan, India, and Turkey. It was to the last of these destinations that Kosovo's traffic was directed.[4]

In the 2006 South Ossetian case, smugglers reported (to law enforcement, unknowingly) that they planned to sell two to three kilograms of the HEU for $30 million. The asking price was $1,000,000 for a hundred grams—or $10,000 per gram.[5] Less than twenty-five kilograms of HEU is required to construct a crude but viable atomic bomb, though a ragtag gang may need up to a year to become a veritable nuclear power. Contrary to popular belief, the dominant concern among experts is not whether terrorists have the capacity to build a bomb but instead whether they can accumulate enough weapons-grade material to fuel it. The known amount of unsecured (loose) nuclear material reached unprecedented heights in the post–Cold War period; "enough highly enriched uranium (HEU) and weapon-grade plutonium remain in the world to build tens of thousands of nuclear weapons."[6] The number of interested, dangerous buyers is even greater—by a factor of at least ten.[7]

The Georgian episode was a landmark case because the HEU was found to be 89 percent enriched (weapons grade), which is fully suitable for military purposes and nuclear weapons. Investigators, the media, and possibly even the smugglers themselves were astounded by the enrichment level when US tests confirmed it. The "realm of nuclear trafficking . . . is littered with rumors and outright scams." Many incidents never amount to more than lies and exaggerations on the part of eager sellers, boastful police officials, or alarmist governments soliciting international aid. Nonetheless, the demand is overwhelming, and the profit is easy to concentrate in a few hands. The "four middle-aged grifters" of South Ossetia who sought to sell to a Turkish buyer "were convinced they were about to become millionaires" instantly.[8]

Contextual Advantage

All circumstances considered, one would have expected that Kosovo suffered more than South Ossetia from these revelations. Remarkably, it was the opposite. The exposure of a nefarious criminal episode imposed far-greater harm on South Ossetian separatism *despite* four contextual reasons that made Kosovar separatism much more vulnerable.

SEPARATIST-CRIMINAL TIES

Plausible deniability is an obvious factor minimizing harm to separatist legitimacy. One would expect the exposure of nefarious organized crime to harm separatism more when gangsters are themselves movement leaders or separatist ideologues. In the case of Kosovo, the criminal-separatist connection was direct and glaring. In the case of South Ossetia, it was obscure and indirect at best.

The organ-smuggling ring was run directly by the separatist movement leadership. The organizers were KLA commanders at the highest level, led by Hashim Thaçi. His accomplices in the traffic—including Ramush Haradinaj, Fatmir Limaj, and Kadri Veseli—constituted more than half the postwar upper echelon of the separatist movement.[9] In contrast, the criminal entrepreneurs in the 2006 HEU case were entirely unaffiliated with separatist institutions and doctrines. The four apprehended culprits had no known ties to the Kokoity oligarchy or preceding, Chibirov one. They had no records of service in Ossetian militias or any positions in the Tskhinvali bureaucracy.

Profit drove both Kosovar and Ossetian smugglers. But while the former were at least draped in separatist liberation, the HEU criminals never even hinted at Ossetian or Russian nationalism. On the contrary, the head smuggler of the HEU gang expressed solidarity with Islamic fundamentalists and other enemies of Ossetia's patron, Russia. (The rest of the gangsters were agnostic.) Their intended customer—in fact, an undercover police officer—fronted as an al-Qa'ida representative. This singular political element was the only documented motivation outside profit. More generally, the "radiological trafficking [in the region] is mainly profit-driven and opportunistic," setting it apart from "terror-crime nexus" groups with explicit ideological motives.[10] There were no proclamations incriminating to the separatist cause whatsoever.

The HEU gangsters had no titles or status to speak of. Oleg Khintsagov, the ringleader and sole Russian, was a forty-nine-year old auto mechanic from North Ossetia. He opened a small trading company in the 1990s to import various goods into Georgia through South Ossetia—an incidental beneficiary of the Ergneti market.[11] Three other gangsters (in their early thirties) were Georgians from around Kazbegi, a secluded town bordering South Ossetia at the base of one of Georgia's highest peaks. These foot soldiers—Vaja Chikhasvili, Henry Sujashvili, and Revaz Kurkumuli—were childhood friends who "had been working together for years in legal and illegal businesses before the HEU trafficking."[12] Khintsagov's connections to the Russian mafia and security apparatus are suspected but undocumented. At most, they are distant.[13] None of the criminals had war-related experiences or ethnic crimes in their biographies.

The organ traffickers were, in contrast, not only seasoned criminals with regional reputations but also outstanding veterans in the separatist liberation struggle credited with "assassinations, detentions, beatings and interrogations in various parts of Kosovo" as well as its southern neighbor "in the context of KLA-led operations on the territory of Albania, between 1998 and 2000." The Drenica Group, named after Kosovo's Drenica Valley and headed by Thaçi, had defeated rivals in turf wars, and "wrested control of most of the illicit criminal enterprises" between Kosovo and Albania.[14] The Drenica Valley was simultaneously a criminal heartland of the separatist territory and the epicenter of resistance to Belgrade's rule.

Nefarious crime in Kosovo was independent of Serbian territory; in Ossetia, it flowed into the host state proper. HEU smugglers relied on Ossetian and Russian ties, but many were unreliable (the first lead that eventually led to persecution "came from South Ossetian criminal contacts run by Georgian intelligence"). They used kinship and clan relations to find customers and advertise prices. The general atmosphere of "reports of nuclear chit-chat in criminal circles in South Ossetia" was symptomatic of a broader pool of mafia accomplices. But the criminals themselves—three of them ethnic Georgians—were hardly in any position to exert leverage through separatist institutions. Indeed, they seemingly infiltrated the host state more than the separatist movement whose reputation they tarnished. Khintsagov relied on his cousin, a former Georgian customs officer, for travel across the Russian-Georgian border.[15] Chikhasvili was a Georgian Ministry of Internal Affairs security guard, enabling transit from Russia. This nefarious crime was just as much a Russian-Georgian affair as it was a Russian-Ossetian one.

In Kosovo, there was no ambiguity. The Council of Europe report dwells on the "collusion between the criminal class and high political and institutional office bearers," with Thaçi as "the most dangerous of the KLA's 'criminal bosses.'" The mafia also enjoyed collaboration with the Albanian secret service through Kadri Veseli, "a kingpin of the Drenica Group." The institutional congruence with the separatist movement could not have been greater: "KLA units and their respective zones of operational command corresponded in an almost perfect mirror image to the structures that controlled the various forms of organised crime."[16]

STIGMA AND RISK

Stealing from beneath human flesh *sounds* worse than peddling metal. A few hundred grams of enriched radioactive material unleashing nuclear apocalypse seems peculiar, almost fantastic. But a kidnapped teenager being mutilated with a scalpel appears personal and dramatic. Gaudy reporting nurtured an awareness (and fear) of organ trafficking disproportionate to its actual prevalence, while the public perception of nuclear smuggling is deemed naive even by nonalarmist experts.[17] The bodily harm and graphic nature of organ harvesting make uranium smuggling appear less gruesome when in fact, given the scale of potential destruction and casualties, the latter is categorically worse. Yet popular intuition and international norms suggest the opposite. Hence organ harvesting is not only riskier and more demanding but is also treated (by public opinion as well as most national laws) to be more egregious than uranium smuggling, inviting harsher penalties and greater stigma.[18]

Organ harvesting appears egregious enough as an assault on human dignity in its usual, voluntary form. But assault on human life itself in abduction-murder cases is far worse. Increasing the stigma, the Kosovo episode involved exclusively involuntary donors. The crimes included kidnapping, imprisonment, human trafficking across an international border (Yugoslavia-Albania), torture, and murder. In contrast, the HEU smugglers were guilty of theft, smuggling, and bribery—nonviolent trifles.[19]

Furthermore, the logistical challenges of organ smuggling were overwhelmingly greater. Exposure—and the repercussions for separatists—were far more likely. Perishable organs require careful but swift transportation across guarded borders, with the risk of expiration measured in hours. Secured deals with trustworthy buyers must precede organ extraction. Timing was essential. The organs had to be carried in a sterilized box with a pump; at minimum, they needed to be in an ice cooler that can sustain the precious cargo en route. Both storage options were conspicuous, requiring bribed customs officers. Enriched uranium, on the other hand, maintains its black market value for years. Indeed, those in illicit possession rarely rush to advertise it, but wait— sometimes over a decade—for suitable buyers or demand to increase with wars. Khintsagov claimed to have bought his commodity in 1999. He "sat on it for five or six years" at least.[20] The smugglers repeatedly rescinded an offer, partner, meeting place or time, or agreed-on method of exchange. Organ traffickers have no such luxury.

Transporting enriched uranium discretely is trivial compared to a kidney. A pocket-size plastic bag of the HEU went from Russia, through South Ossetia, to Kazbegi, and into central Georgia—in a coat compartment and briefcase. It did not pose radiation risks to its carrier, nor did it require protective casing. Simple concealment almost guaranteed discrete transport across customs and administrative checkpoints:

> When the smugglers passed the Russian and Georgian border posts on either side of Kazbegi with 100 grams of highly enriched, weapons-grade uranium, they successfully navigated not only the Russian and Georgian border guards on duty that day, but two sets of US-funded nuclear "portal monitors"—radiation detection sensors installed on either side of the line specifically designed to prevent exactly that.

Though the smugglers did rely on complicit border officials to ensure secure transit, it was a superfluous precaution. The radiation portal monitors installed around the Caucasus—and especially those at the mafia's preferred Kazbegi crossing—were notoriously unreliable. Border officials confessed to tourists "that they hang there broken or inoperative a lot of the time."[21] Incompetence, lack of training, and unpredictable electricity outages made the outdated scanners mere decorations.[22] Detection is so unlikely that the interdiction rate for the HEU is estimated to be less than for narcotics, or below 10 percent.[23] The Ossetian smugglers needed little more than legal travel documents and a pocketed plastic bag—no storage facilities, equipment, urgency, or violence.

The kidney racket could not be more demanding. True, so-called cadaver kidneys are extracted posthumously, eliminating the need for expensive anesthetics. But gangsters required "a state-of-the-art reception centre for the organised crime of organ trafficking," "a makeshift operating clinic," "captives" to have "their kidneys removed against their will," and access to "private overseas clinics" in Istanbul.[24] Surgeons, equipment, Turkish middlepeople, and rehearsed transportation routes were all indispensable. While Ossetian smugglers were free to choose their border crossings, storage, and pace without an additional labor force, their Kosovo counterparts required an entire network of well-coordinated, disciplined accomplices (i.e., potential witnesses). After the initial abductions, traffickers were obliged to transport, restrain, and select their victims.

Four locations were used—Bicaj, Burrel, Rripë, and Fushë-Krujë—as prison camps, where abductees were kept and verified for eligibility. These camps included an abandoned compound along a major road, two privately owned farmhouses whose inhabitants were recruited, and a "'safe house' not only for KLA affiliates, but for other groups of organised criminals involved in smuggling drugs and trafficking in human beings."[25] Not only did the number of witnesses grow with every accomplice, but even "accidental" detection was possible because the traffic overlapped with other, simultaneous criminal enterprises.

While the HEU traffickers traveled freely in populated urban areas, smugglers in Kosovo were restricted to rural mafia hideouts. After "an arduous drive of several hours," some involuntary organ donors were held at a "safe house" owned by a proprietor "who allegedly shared both clan ties and organised criminal connections with members of the 'Drenica Group.'" The victims had to go through a "process of filtering" requiring considerable patience and discipline. The preparation was reminiscent of the Brother Grimms's *Hansel and Gretel*: "The central concern was to maintain the viability of the organ: [prisoners] were initially kept alive, fed well and allowed to sleep, and treated with relative restraint by KLA guards and henchmen who would otherwise have beaten them up indiscriminately." Selected abductees were transported to Fushë-Krujë, chosen for its proximity to the Tirana International Airport. This further increased the exposure dramatically, not least because many captives became aware of their intended fate through rumor, and others figured it out "at the latest when their blood was drawn by syringe for testing" to determine transplantation compatibility (tissue typing) or they were physically examined by people denoted as "doctors."[26] Acts of desperation and escape attempts were constant risks.

After additional stays at the site (requiring alert guards for days and perhaps weeks on end), the final step required the most care and coordination: "As and when the transplant surgeons were confirmed to be in position and ready to operate, the captives were brought out of the 'safe house' individually, summarily executed by a KLA gunman, and their corpses transported swiftly to the operating clinic."[27] Most cases ended with a shot to the head. Even when extraction and transportation were successful, the chores continued; the discrete disposal of corpses and removal of evidence from operating rooms alone exceeded anything required of the HEU smugglers.

REPRESSION

Organ harvesting and HEU-related crimes are typically not exposed by governments alone. The two scandals were discovered through the cooperation of, first, patron states (the United States–European Union and Russia, respectively) with global or regional capacity, and second, NGOs and international nongovernmental organizations (INGO) (the United Nations, OSCE, the International Atomic Energy Agency [IAEA], and Interpol), which supplied information, resources and strategy. Both host states lacked the wherewithal to expose crime on separatist territory. But Kosovo's criminals had a far more repressive set of institutions on their tails than Ossetia's. In Kosovo, enormous international pressure to expose organized crime escalated for twenty years since the organ traffic. In South Ossetia, the HEU episode resulted in a pithy period of international attention followed by total negligence, jurisdictional confusion, and deliberate lawlessness on the part of those with the most capacity—all in only six years.

KFOR and EULEX invested hundreds of millions of dollars, tens of thousands of troops and personnel, and worldwide diplomatic sponsorship into Kosovo's rule of law. Their priority—ahead of economic development or democracy—was "security reconstruction," including police and judicial reforms. Curbing organized crime was a "litmus test" not only for the credibility of US/EU foreign policy but also "determining the success of international organizations in producing enduring peace in post-conflict zones" generally.[28] To that end, overwhelming numbers of police and criminal justice agents were trained in Kosovo, particularly in the five years succeeding the organ trafficking, 1999–2004.[29]

Since 2006, EULEX has administered the separatist territory. The European Union's resolve to restrain and expose organized crime was even more formidable than that of their predecessor. It signified the most comprehensive civilian EU operation in history, with a highly executive mandate that dominated indigenous Kosovar institutions.[30] Not only were European officials, judges, investigators, and prosecutors given unmatched resources and jurisdiction, but separatist institutions were monitored and scrutinized through intrusive administrative oversight. EULEX prosecutors were empowered to investigate, prosecute, and publicize war crimes, crimes against humanity, and organized crime—a jurisdiction that earned them considerable resentment from the population. After the 2008 economic crisis, foreign aid to separatist institutions was more conditional than ever, prompting even greater pressure. The Council of Europe—and the European Union in general—were on a crusade to prove themselves capable of effective peacekeeping in Europe itself.[31]

In contrast, South Ossetia's international NGO scene was vacant. The only multilateral framework was the Joint Control Commission (JCC) and its accompanying JPKF, which included Russian, North Ossetian, and host state and separatist representatives. The European Commission was a mere observer, while Russia dominated the four-way partnership. Moscow resisted every attempt at incorporating meaningful law enforcement possibilities, including OSCE involvement in 2005. Russia, characteristically, preferred military control of a lawless territory to international control of an ordered one. In the 2000s, the JCC "focused primarily on economic issues," partly because consensus on law enforcement was impossible. Whereas KFOR and EULEX had no jurisdictional competition, the JCC was consistently plagued by rivalry between the parties. Ossetians themselves further undermined law enforcement; they "were rather suspicious [even] of NGOs, and were at all events opposed to any activities that they perceived as being in competition with the JCC format" dominated by their patron.[32]

Russia's grip in South Ossetia was thus unequaled. But its capacity to repress organized crime was modest, to say nothing of its willingness. Its commanding role in the JPKF aimed at making South Ossetia as dependent on Russia as possible, conferring minimal support to indigenous institutions. Whereas Kosovo's peacekeepers were "nation building," Russian peacekeepers endeavored to destabilize Georgia and keep South Ossetia under Moscow's heel. The JCC itself was impotent regarding nuclear trafficking. At the time of the HEU episode, there had been a fifteen-year-old multilateral effort by a dozen countries (the United States and Russia included) to curb smuggling and secure unaccounted-for stockpiles of nuclear weapons, with an emphasis on the Caucasus. Over $1 billion had been spent on the crackdown. South Ossetia was isolated from any of the campaign's benefits because "efforts rely too heavily on technology [available only in Georgia proper], rather than old-fashioned police work, to keep nuclear smuggling in check."[33] The per capita numbers of police officers and judges in the separatist territory were miniscule compared to those in Kosovo—by a factor ranging from ten to twenty in the 2000s.[34]

Finally, the nefarious episode in Kosovo had a special court dangling over its head. The International Criminal Tribunal for the Former Yugoslavia (ICTY), created by the United Nations, prosecuted individual criminals in the region. While EULEX's scope was restricted to the territory of Kosovo, the ICTY had jurisdiction over all the former Yugoslav countries as well as Albania, where the organ traffic was centered. No such authority existed in South Ossetia, where immunity was guaranteed. Georgia did lodge two inter-state applications against the Russian Federation with the European Court of Human Rights and International Court of Justice—to no avail. Both prosecute states, and neither could have incorporated individual gangsters.

PRECEDENT

The organ smugglers were entrepreneurial out of necessity. They created a market without organizational precedents in a region detached from the global organ trade. The nuclear traffickers, meanwhile, were surrounded by opportunities, models, and potential partners.

The global organ trade notoriously "flows from poor, underdeveloped countries to rich, developed ones." Buyers predominantly come from the advanced nations, and secondarily, "from wealthy classes from developing countries" in the Middle East.[35] Donors are from the likes of faraway China, India, the Philippines, and Brazil. The only known "hub" for illicit organ donors even remotely near Kosovo is Romania; the only accessible one is Turkey. Otherwise, the Balkans is hardly ideal for organ-harvesting initiatives. In the meantime, nuclear smugglers around South Ossetia enjoyed a flourishing regional market of stolen fissile materials. While organs get smuggled from underdeveloped to rich countries, nuclear smuggling flows between poor states themselves. Instead of wealthy parents with sick children, the buyers are warlords and terrorists who gravitate toward conflict-ridden, impoverished areas.[36] Potential buyers abounded around South Ossetia: Chechen rebels, Kurdish militants, al-Qa'ida cells, and rogue ex-Soviet apparatchiks. Known cases from nearby sites include Azeri, Armenian, and Ukrainian smugglers.[37] The demand is also conveniently high in bordering Turkey, where the greatest number of Georgian nationals smuggling radiological supplies were apprehended.

Above all, South Ossetia's geographic proximity—and political servility—to Russia make it a nuclear-smuggling paradise. After the initial post–Cold War period, the traffic "continues [throughout the 2000s] to be most acute in the regions of the former Soviet Union and, in particular, in the greater Black Sea region."[38] Western Russia is central to the world's nuclear traffic; "most cases of trafficking in weapon-grade nuclear materials [globally] have been related to Russia, which remains [in late 2000s] a major source of unsecured radioactive substances."[39] The IAEA (2006) estimated as many as three hundred sources of "loose" nuclear material recorded in Georgia since independence. At least sixteen incidents of nuclear smuggling have been confirmed between 1993 and 2006—a fraction of the total, undetected traffic.[40] In Serbia/Kosovo and all its neighboring countries, not a single case of organ trading (voluntary or otherwise) was documented before 1999.[41]

Mafia Capacity

Given these four realities, one would expect South Ossetian separatists to bear less harm from exposure than Kosovar separatists. In fact, the opposite transpired. Kosovo's superior mafia capacity—via infrastructure, autonomy, and community—protected the separatist movement from the harmful effects of exposure. South Ossetia's weaker mafia did not—indeed, *could* not—exculpate the separatist cause to that degree.

INFRASTRUCTURE

Both smuggling episodes depended on critical transit points. For the organ smugglers, it was the Kosovo-Albania border: a 115-kilometer stretch with six formal crossings, including the Morine-Vermice with a highway to the capital, Priština. Even before the war, host state monitoring was modest. Criminal gatekeepers (sometimes in uniform) at most crossings would charge travelers and truck drivers. During the war, they levied taxes on refugees. Alongside formal checkpoints, mule riders with Kalashnikovs attached to the animals used informal pathways. Over the years, they secured allies in the Albanian secret service, the Shërbimi Informative Kombëtar, immunizing them from Tirana's law enforcement.[42]

After the war, there was little doubt as to who would inherit jurisdiction. "During this chaotic phase" after June 1999, "the border between Kosovo and Albania effectively ceased to exist": "It was in this context that KLA militia factions moved freely on either side of the border, which . . . had by then become little more than a token dividing line. So it is clear that the KLA held effective control in the region during that critical period [of organ smuggling], both in Kosovo and in the northern part of Albania near the border." Under the KLA umbrella, the organ smugglers could administer all border crossings. KLA officers stood guard at the six checkpoints, but did little more than salute crossing compatriots. Vehicles were uninspected, and documents were not solicited. The Drenica Group thus enjoyed "effectively unfettered control of an expanded territorial area in which to carry out various forms of smuggling and trafficking."[43]

The advantages were threefold. First, smugglers had access to friendly territory far outside host state reach. Albania was also outside the jurisdiction of KFOR and EULEX. Second, the logistics for transporting captives and their organs were already furnished: gatekeepers at crossings, KLA camps and compounds, remote interrogation/recruitment centers where prisoners could be guarded, and rural hamlets with sympathetic Albanian villagers. Third, organ harvesters had access to the Tirana airport. This secured direct flights to Turkey as well as contact with regional mafia branches: "the deeper into Albanian territory a facility's physical location, the less directly it related to the KLA's war effort and the more entrenched its connection proved to be with the underworld of organised crime."[44] While Kosovo itself was entirely peripheral to the global organ trade, Albania was a bridge to Istanbul. By penetrating deep into Albanian territory, the smugglers injected themselves into a major transit hub for the organ market.

The nuclear smugglers likewise had a critical transit point. Having acquired the HEU from the Siberian city of Novosibirsk, the challenge was first to reach South Ossetia and later Georgia proper with minimal risk. The Roki Tunnel is a mountain underpass through the Greater Caucasus range connecting South Ossetia to Russian North Ossetia. It is the sole route into Russia from the separatist territory. At two thousand meters altitude, surrounding stretches of the border are effectively impassable. Although separatist officials levied taxes on their side of the crossing, "the only border control is on the Russian side, and the Russian Customs are hardly a firewall," so it remained a formal interstate crossing. Russian troops, police, peacekeepers, and customs officers never ceded control to criminal gatekeepers. Yet the Roki Tunnel was indispensable. The only two alternative routes between Georgia and Russia were the Gantiadi-Adler crossing (through separatist Abkhazia) and Kazbegi-Verkhni Lars customs checkpoint (through Georgia). Roki was a relatively easy criminal opportunity: it had been outside Georgian control for fifteen years and gave direct terrestrial access—no planes—to the desired Tskhinvali market as well as "the safety of the conflict zone," where they initially sought buyers.[45]

Indicatively, the HEU smugglers did not—and could not—use the Roki Tunnel. The HEU mafia managed to infiltrate the Novosibirsk Chemical Concentrate Plant, "where thefts of enriched radioactive and nuclear material have been recorded." But they lacked the capacity to arrange secure transport or mobilize gatekeeper accomplices at Roki—let alone at six checkpoints simultaneously or an international airport. Instead, they used the regular Georgian border crossing near Kazbegi. Not only was it administered by Georgian officials and US-trained customs officers specifically targeting nuclear materials; the checkpoint was equipped with radiation detectors—a fact the smugglers were fully aware and afraid of. The Russian side was handled by Khintsagov's "cousin who is a former Russian customs officer," while the Georgian side was covered by Chikhasvili as a Ministry of Internal Affairs security guard. Even though three of the smugglers were from Kazbegi, this hapless crossing was detected. In contrast to the organ smugglers' alliance with the Albanian mafia and secret service, the HEU traffickers could not even rely on "their own" Russian mafia or secret service. It was the Russian Federal Security Service that detected the suspicious movement across Kazbegi and shared the evidence with Georgian authorities in an exceptional "brief period of intelligence-sharing on this case."[46]

The lack of control of the Roki Tunnel—and pitiful precautions they took at Kazbegi checkpoint—cost the HEU gang its freedom. Once Georgian undercover police officers enticed them into negotiating, it was too late to retreat to separatist turf:

> The main haggling [between undercover law enforcement and the smugglers] was over the location where they'd meet. According to [the head of the Georgian Unit], the smugglers were pushing for Tskhinvali [the separatist capital,] hardly a place any Turkish middleman in his right mind would bring $1 million cash. It was the . . . middleman, the undercover agent, who suggested Gldani. Thus there was hardly an excuse for things going the way they did.[47]

Worse still, without criminal leverage over the Roki Tunnel, they lacked an exit strategy into Russia.

The Kosovar mafia's comparative infrastructural advantage did not end there. Regarding safe houses and other logistics, the Ossetian smugglers were likewise operating at markedly lesser capacity. Kosovo's gangsters "had virtually exclusive control on the ground" over a variety of sites throughout Kosovo and Albania:

> Factions and splinter groups that had control of distinct areas of Kosovo (villages, stretches of road, sometimes even individual buildings) were able to run organised criminal enterprises almost at will. . . . [Across the border were] six separate detention facilities on the territory of the Republic of Albania, situated across a territory that spans from Cahan at the foot of Mount Pashtrik, almost at the northernmost tip of Albania, to the beachfront road in Durres, on the Mediterranean coast in the west of Albania.[48]

Abductees could be taken to any number of safe houses from "a whole ad hoc network of such facilities" in Cahan, Kukës, Bicaj, Burrel/Rripë, Durres or Fushë-Krujë. Some were prisons and interrogation centers; others had been medical facilities for wartime treatment. Many were remote and secluded. These facilities were administered by Thaçi's mafia well before its ingress into separatist movement staff. The Drenica Group had gradually "built a formidable power base in the organised criminal enterprises that were flourishing in Kosovo and Albania" since the 1990s, well before it ousted Rugova's administration. The mafia enjoyed "firm control over criminal cartels active in municipalities including, but not limited to, Istok, Srbica, Skenderaj, Klina, Prizren and Priština"—before and after the war.[49]

Surgeries were conducted at multiple makeshift hospitals. One witness, a midlevel ranked KLA soldier, was brought in 1998 to a school turned clinic to undergo medical training.[50] Surrounded by pumps, scalpels, vacuums, and plastic bags of "medical liquids," instructors guided trainees through heart, kidney, and lung transplantations with plastic figures. Initially, he recalls, they were told this was to revitalize injured KLA comrades. The innocence soon dissipated as he discovered his true role. Iceboxes on standby, gangsters clasped the victim to hastily harvest organs without anesthesia or sedation, with the donor losing consciousness from pain. (This approach is economical, if the patient survives.) On one occasion, the witness remembers, a captive's rib cage was split with the tip of a Kalashnikov rifle.

The sites were secured by KLA guards, most of whom likely knew nothing. A driver in front was on standby. In the trunk of a Volvo, next to the spare tire, a secret compartment was carved to fit the delicate icebox. Though the witness was told that Tirana was the destination, the parcel was in fact driven to Rinas International Airport, where Albanian military accomplices secured passage onto a private plane with a Turkish flag. How many transplants succeeded and, more important, were commercially gainful is unknown. But the witness described an expanding business: training as many amateur surgeons as possible, minimizing costs of the procedure, and multiplying the number of involuntary donors. In a word, streamlining the process.

The HEU smugglers did not have a single safe house in separatist territory. It was not for a lack of options. South Ossetia was flourishing in criminal hideaways—including training camps for foreign militants, garages for a car-smuggling ring, and "a major transnational counterfeiting operation of American $100 bills ran from a strikingly high-quality printing press." Furthermore, "Tskhinvali and South Ossetia" were "armed to the teeth," offering criminals privacy and protection at low cost.[51]

The gangsters opted for a reckless alternative instead. After at least five trips into South Ossetia in failed search of customers, they reoriented to a neighborhood in Georgia proper. Surrounded by blocks of witnesses, they hid in "a bluish-white, eight-story council house in a low-income suburb called Muthiani, not far from the Gldani Market," where they sought to sell the uranium. On the outskirts of the Georgian capital, the place was completely unguarded, and frequented by casual guests who would visit for a drink and chat. Georgian officers arrested the smugglers at the location, with the HEU in their jacket pocket. Their only logistical task—to transport a "baggie-wrapped, bomb-grade parcel" from North Ossetia—proved too exacting.[52]

AUTONOMY

Kosovo's mafia repeatedly and effectively draped its activities in the cause of separatist ideology. After extracting an organ from a "19–20-year-old" man, one soldier was commended by a "famous senior officer" with the following praise: "Congratulations, you went golden. We need soldiers like that in Kosovo. Only then will we win." Under the banner of fighting traitors, the Drenica Group systematically eliminated witnesses to the organ traffic. One witness, Skender Kuçi, was assassinated with the note, "This is how enemies of the KLA end up."[53] Patriotism also aided in hiding the bodies. When an embarrassing excavation was ordered at a mine shaft where dozens of murdered Serbs were buried (some, it was suspected, after organ harvesting), the mafia terrorized the construction company tasked with the job. But the real obstructionism came from the "local community, which caused considerable delay in carrying out the explorations": "The prevailing attitude among the Kosovar population is to regard as a 'traitor' anyone who provides information regarding mass graves containing Serb victims." Nor were coethnics exempt. "Confirmed dozens—presumed hundreds—of bodies of murdered 'disloyal' Albanians were buried as martyrs to the cause of Kosovo liberation." For many, their true offense was the failure to collaborate with the organ racket. The HEU smugglers, in contrast, had not employed any ideological cover. There is no evidence that any of their actions were made easier by appeals to the separatist cause, they coerced or persuaded accomplices with appeals to ethnic hostility, or local communities were mobilized. The ringleader simply recruited his three accomplices by "promising they'd all get rich."[54]

Serbian antiseparatist propaganda pointing to organ harvesting was belated and quickly dismissed.[55] Meanwhile, the HEU smugglers quickly came to symbolize the cancerous heart of Ossetian separatism: "From the outset, the Georgian government has maintained the uranium smuggling scandal exposes a need for greater international control over separatist South Ossetia."[56] Within hours of the 2006 sting operation, the US Federal Bureau of Investigation (FBI) and Department of Energy nuclear security experts flew into Tbilisi in panic. Their findings were trumpeted and often overstated throughout regional and international news outlets.[57] By the time a pivotal IAEA report came out, the incident was universally presented "as compelling evidence of the international threat posed by South Ossetia's lawlessness."[58] US pressure on Georgia to reintegrate its north escalated.

The propaganda was as persuasive as the separatist connection was weak. Even after it was public that the smugglers were "not known to have brought the goods into the breakaway region itself" and "the materials were not brought into Georgia via South Ossetia," the separatists bore the brunt of the stigma.[59] Russian officials, like the separatist movement, washed their hands of the criminals entirely; they declared the nefarious episode to be a US/Georgian "provocation" designed to humiliate Russia at the July 2006 G-8 summit in Saint Petersburg. South Ossetia's foreign minister "argued that Tbilisi is using the uranium scandal to gain leverage in the ongoing World Trade Organization negotiations between Georgia and Russia."[60] While Georgia insisted that "the incident demonstrates the need to urgently reintegrate the breakaway region of South Ossetia into Georgia," the Ossetians and Russians saw "proof that Georgian leaders are using [the episode] as political leverage."[61] The HEU traffickers therefore could not hope to convince anyone that they were freedom fighters or national liberators—let alone shield their racket under a separatist mantle.

In addition to the weightier ideological cover, Kosovar smugglers enjoyed another, more practical source of immunity. From its origin, the organ traffic bore minimal risk because of protective separatist officeholders. The "mafia structures" of the Drenica Group "evolved from being part of an armed force, the KLA (ostensibly engaged in a war of liberation), into being a conspicuously powerful band of criminal entrepreneurs . . . with designs on a form of 'state capture.'"[62] Many formed political parties and registered legal enterprises such as the Medicus Clinic, a front for organ trafficking. In union with "all political parties in Priština," they "acted as one unanimously denouncing" investigation into the racket.[63] Key protagonists in the traffic assumed the highest offices: Thaçi was a prime minister, deputy prime minister, and foreign minister; Haradinaj was a prime minister; Limaj was a minister of transport and telecommunication; and Veseli was a deputy of the assembly of Kosovo. Gangsters aside, they exercised command over "a large number of former KLA operatives" with no criminal background.[64]

An exemplary case of separatist immunity was Muja, a central figure in the organ traffic—the broker to the Turkish market. True to form, he served as health coordinator for the provisional government of Kosovo, specializing in "the Health portfolio." Based in Albania as a high-level wartime commander, Muja proceeded to become a cabinet member in the separatist government, leading commander of the Kosovo Protection Corps after the war, and an "influential office-holder in the current Kosovo authorities." Beneath an aura of a "humanitarian and progressive practitioner" was

> Muja's central role for more than a decade [before separatist office] in far less laudable international networks, comprising human traffickers, brokers of illicit surgical procedures, and other perpetrators of organised crime. . . . Muja has derived much of his access, his cover and his impunity as an organised criminal from having maintained an apparently legitimate medical "career" in parallel. . . . His profile in organised crime is scarcely known outside of the criminal networks he has worked with and the few investigators who have tracked them.[65]

Investigators who *did* track them collided into the wall of separatist immunity. In November 2008, three German spies were imprisoned in Kosovo on concocted charges of a bombing plot. Against police and laboratory reports that exculpated them, a mafia-infiltrated district court kept the agents imprisoned. It is suspected that this was "revenge," as investigations into organ smuggling "lead to a murky underworld of organized crime and secret service schemes."[66] Only after German diplomatic pressure escalated to a threat did Kosovar authorities release the prisoners. Such "'strong resistance' of separatist authorities" is routine in judicial cases touching on organ harvesting.[67]

The HEU traffickers, on the other hand, were solitary and unshielded. Separatist ministers, parliamentarians, courts, or militias offered no immunity. The Kokoity administration—partly under orders from Moscow, which itself was eager to be exculpated from criminal stigma—restricted itself to low-key corruption, cronyism, and the mismanagement of foreign (i.e., Russian) aid. It took care to avoid any association with nefarious crime. The Russian mafia was likewise reluctant to lend a helping hand: "These professional criminals behaved as rational actors trying to diversify their business interests; any engagement with smuggling in radiological materials would have jeopardized their influence on legal businesses and damaged their links with the upperworld, especially with politicians."[68] Nuclear trafficking "would have jeopardized the protection provided by representatives of the political elite and would have closed doors to the legitimate world."[69] Any cover-ups therefore had to be done by the HEU smugglers themselves.

COMMUNITY

Nothing illustrates the disparity in mafia community better than the contrast between two localities: the "Yellow House" near Burrel, a transit/surgery site for organ harvesting, and the village of Kazbegi, the operational base and origin town of the HEU smugglers.

The Yellow House, a cottage near the Albanian village of Rribe, was the heart of a long-standing criminal community. To the north, the nearby mountainous town of Burrel (with some fifteen thousand inhabitants) was remote and lawless; it was once a prison and torture site during Albania's Communist dictatorship. The reputation persisted: "Burrel was considered synonymous with hell on earth." Organ harvesting took place at a private family residence reachable through a gravel road about fifteen kilometers from Burrel. "Countless memorial plaques line both sides of the road," one traveler noted. "Many of the dead were gangsters. . . . In the late 1990s, Burrel was the most dangerous city in Albania. Three competing Mafia families terrorized the local populace, until the gangs destroyed one another."[70] The Drenica Group mafia built on the tradition; they "ordered and oversaw multiple deliveries of civilian captives to the [Yellow House] over a period of up to a year, from July 1999 until mid-2000." It was a "way station," where abductees underwent " 'processing'/'filtering,' including the testing of their blood and physical condition." After organ extraction, some were unceremoniously disposed of around the village. Witnesses recounted "the burial, disinterment, movement and reburial of the captives' corpses."[71] When an investigative team of the ICTY and UNMIK visited the Yellow House in 2004, they discovered blood stains, syringes, intravenous drip bags, stomach tranquilizers, and suspicious medical instruments.[72]

No sooner had word gotten out than gangsters leapt to expunge the events from memory in a spectacular smoke screen. Villagers around Rribe destroyed evidence, painted the house from conspicuous yellow to white, relocated weapons depots away from the area, threatened neighboring households, vandalized civilians' houses with "traitor" graffiti, spread gossip about the gruesome fate of informants, and declared blood feuds on families believed to be untrustworthy witnesses to the traffic. The family residing in the Yellow House was itself terrified into silence. The panicked household patriarch—a shepherd—gushed incredible tales to investigators. Sitting around him, the family anxiously interjected contradictory alternatives. The syringes and other medical equipment, they vowed, are "perfectly normal for people to administer their own injections in emergencies." First, the blood stains were said to be from child birth, and then from a traditional animal slaughter according to Islamic custom. When investigators uncovered the original yellow paint beneath a fresh layer of white, the father unwaveringly insisted—against eight witnesses who independently described it as yellow—that "it had always been white." (Photographic evidence from UN investigators did little to refresh his memory.) Then his granddaughter "reminded" everyone that they had painted it briefly for a wedding before returning it to white.[73]

Reburying bodies was another errand. The corpses' characteristic mutilations would immediately implicate the traffic, and DNA could in principle be traced to the organs smuggled—even in the organ recipients' bodies. The solution was to rebury them under Albanian names along the gravel road to Rribe itself. When investigators sought to dig up these graves (following testimonies from witnesses who personally drove and entombed victims under false names), villagers objected on all possible grounds—legal, traditional, religious, and pecuniary. The excavation was successfully thwarted. True to mafia custom, villagers were rewarded. The "silence of the inhabitants of Rripe" as to organ-harvesting activities "was obtained by threats, but also by 'pay-offs' including significant sums of money, as well as free access to alcohol, drugs and prostitutes." At the Yellow House, "a large number of trafficked women and girls . . . were exploited for sex not only by the KLA personnel [involved in the traffic], but also by some of the menfolk in the Rripe community."[74]

Finally, new corpses were added to old ones. Forensic expert Jose Pablo Baraybar, former head of the UNMIK Forensics and Missing Persons Office, lamented that his investigation failed to proceed because witnesses were being murdered in Kosovo, engendering a chilling effect: "As soon as that happened, all the sources that could have taken us from the cemetery and shown us exactly where the bodies were buried vanished. Literally vanished! They began hiding and no longer wanted to speak with us. They ran away!"[75] As witnesses "disappeared from the face of the earth," their presumed fate was enough to keep Rribe silent. The remaining informants feared that "any further testimony would be a death sentence for them." After being taken to Italy for their protection, they also disappeared.[76]

By comparison, Kazbegi is a quiet, uneventful place. To be sure, the HEU criminals benefited from kinship ties to the community: "Vaja, Henry and Revaz grew up in the same small town and were close friends, which up in Kazbegi country means a tighter bond than in other parts. 'They were like one family. It was their custom to share money, for example,' . . . 'If one of them became wealthy, then others must be also.'" "Everybody knows everybody in Kazbegi," where the "locals' 'fierce mountain identity'" upheld "a tighter bond than in other parts [of Georgia / South Ossetia]."[77] But this community had nothing like the clan-based discipline and fear of Rribe. Violence was practically unknown in the village, as Georgian investigators readily recruited witnesses. The HEU gang smuggled "low-level contraband" such as wheat, gasoline, and cigarettes—all in modest amounts. One of them was a drug dealer (small time). Gangster kingpin Khintsagov himself survived as a "small time trader," peddling "Turkish chandeliers, dried fish, sausages."[78] He nurtured contacts with the Russian mafia along with unsavory liaisons in Syria and Iraq. Yet neither he nor his minions conducted extortion, bribery, intimidation, or murder around Kazbegi.

The organ traffickers' damage control, meanwhile, extended to Kosovo itself. Potential witnesses were being systematically targeted along with their families, friends, and police officers that they had been in contact with.[79] They were killed in bomb explosions, drive-by shootings, and brazen ambushes in front of dozens of witnesses. On one occasion, when UNMIK-backed police tried to speak to bystanders to one of the assassinations, no less than an anti-tank missile was fired at them in broad daylight. More fortunate villagers received gentler warnings: multiple rounds of "door-to-door campaign[s] of intimidation" in which hooded bandits "were ordered to collect names [of] putative 'collaborators.'"[80] Others received threatening letters and phone calls, gunshots fired into the air in front of homes, the conspicuous trailing of children, and a sniper laser pointed at a witness's wife's face in public.[81] Local and international forces alike were flabbergasted.[82]

The HEU traffickers also nurtured a code of silence, but hardly as effective or systematic. No campaigns of intimidation or violence toward witnesses, accomplices, or law enforcement were recorded, let alone any attack on institutions heading the crackdown. There were no exonerating murders, silencing campaigns, or cover-ups. Instead, the HEU criminals produced a cacophony of contradictory stories about who supported them, where they acquired the HEU, or what they even acquired. Under pain of law, Khintsagov himself equivocated incoherently. Initially he "partially plead guilty" by admitting that he "purchased the material, which he understood to be radioactive, for $10,000 from someone named 'Rashid'" in Novosibirsk. By the time of the trial, he pretended it was "sort of 'typographic oxide' for computer printers" that was collecting dust in his car trunk for years, and then that it was "a common ore readily available in the mines near his village."[83]

Finally, Kosovo and South Ossetia both have strong traditions of tribal codes, clan violence, and blood feuds.[84] While the organ traffickers took full advantage of this conducive, fertile ground, the HEU gang did not. The Drenica Group was a tidily structured mafia whose commanders "establish[ed] protection rackets in the areas where their own clansmen were prevalent in Albania, or where they could find common cause with established organised criminals involved in such activities as human trafficking, sale of stolen motor vehicles, and the sex trade." A strict code of ethics, backed by principles of honor and fear of reprisals for violators, accompanied clan membership: the Kanun.

Relatives or not, the gangsters' blood debt was sacred: "the allegiances they feel towards their criminal 'bosses' are as unbreakable as any family bond." "The Albanian mafia," investigators concluded, "were probably more difficult to penetrate than the Cosa Nostra; even low-level operatives would rather take a jail term of decades, or a conviction for contempt, than turn in their clansmen."[85]

The Georgian/Ossetian criminal milieu, meanwhile, is ethnically diversified. The ecology includes Chechen terrorist cells, Armenian renegades, and Abkhazian smugglers as well as various militias such as the White Legion, Forest Brothers, and Hunter Battalion.[86] These formations compete for lucrative contraband, but—in most permutations—harbor dissimilar ideologies, patronage traditions, religions, and relations to ethnocentric mafias in neighboring states. Armenians, Chechens, and non-Chechen Muslims (of whom there are hundreds of thousands in Georgia) host their own criminal clan communities. The regional nuclear traffic—from Central Asia through Georgia/Ossetia into the Middle East—has also attracted gangs from the Arab world.[87]

Consequently, collaborative criminal efforts are mostly ad hoc and multiethnic—no stable clan relations or codes. Far from clansmen acting out of honor, the HEU criminals were a disoriented gang of opportunists.[88] "None of the men were sophisticated smugglers." Observers marvel at the incompetence of a "smuggler who carries HEU in plastic baggies in his pocket, and who provides his pursuers with an easily traced landline number while chatting on his cell phone after the deal goes sour."[89] Spotting Russian mafia involvement, authorities nevertheless recognize how frail its nuclear racket is: "Investigators frequently refer to the people involved in radioactive materials smuggling as *mochaliche*, a colloquial Georgian term for individuals who are apt, resilient, and resourceful at finding ways to achieve their ends and who are willing to engage in both legal and illegal activities for profit."[90] Hence, three Georgians and a Russian *mochaliche* conspired to sell to anti-Russian Turkish Islamists in anti-Georgian Ossetian territory. In these circumstances, trust was understandably frail, leading to impulsive betrayals among criminals at every step.[91] The organ smugglers were a high-capacity mafia. The nuclear smugglers, to South Ossetia's misfortune, remained an opportunistic gang.

PART III

Three Regions

6

West Africa

Our resources were exhausted and we were tired. The best thing to do was to sell our rebellion at a good price.

—A SEPARATIST FROM THE MOVEMENT OF NIGERIENS FOR JUSTICE (MNJ), *LIBYAN REVOLUTION AND ITS AFTERMATH*

For Belmokhtar, AQIM [al-Qa'ida in the Islamic Magreb] was a tool to make money. He was not interested in the jihad or in building the Caliphate. A true merchant of men, he did not distinguish between smuggling cigarettes or cocaine, and kidnapping foreigners or trafficking migrants. Each of these businesses of trading valuable cargo made him money.

—LORETTA NAPOLEONI ON JIHADI GANGSTER, MOKHTAR BELMOKHTAR, *MERCHANTS OF MEN*

West Africa, alarmists tell us, is "Narco-TrAfrica."[1] But its transnational smuggling enterprises are hardly a novelty—or as menacing as they sound. *Troc*, or barter trade, is a way of life that preceded and survived colonialism. Commerce is known as *al-frud*, from the French *fraude* (fraud), reflecting the World War II–era tradition of regional smuggling. What is new in the globalized period is that mafias in five nations—and just as many budding ones—have played formative roles in regional politics.

Senegal

Senegal hosts the world's singular marijuana-driven separatist movement: Casamance, "where cannabis smuggling has now fueled a low-level Senegalese civil war for thirty years."[2] Casamançais separatism first relied on indigenous and patron state support (1990–99), and then evolved into organized criminal self-sustenance (2000–present) through a Diola cannabis rebel mafia rooted in the Karone Isles.[3] It was organized crime, a force to be reckoned with by both Dakar and the separatist Movement of Democratic Forces of Casamance (MFDC) alike, that has sustained Casamançais autonomy.

A COMPROMISED MOVEMENT

The Casamançais Diola people are traditionally transnational, scattered around a slim landlet between The Gambia and Guinea-Bissau. Their separatist movement initially collected gifts from village elders, sold MFDC membership cards, and organized fundraising dance parties. Patriotic villagers donated rice. The leadership—albeit with "tenuous links with their region"—demanded secession in civil but forceful tones.[4] The movement was native, popular, and unmistakably ethnic: "The Diola-ness of Casamancais separatism explains much of its strength—it is not a shallow, superficial manipulation engineered by a bunch of ambitious political entrepreneurs, but the outcome of a movement whose roots dig deep in a rich social soil."[5] But in the mid-1990s, matters changed. Racketeers replaced activists. Separatist violence began exhibiting a curious pattern: mirroring seasonal variations on harvest and trade, mobilization became wedded to illicit crop production.[6] Though cannabis was critical, timber smuggling and the "political economy of force" were also prominent.[7] Stunning looting campaigns, like the one in the Kolda region that stole several thousand cattle in 2000, were as much pedagogical as economic.[8] Organized crime began to deliver not only livelihoods and rewards but protection as well.

The movement leadership was co-opted by the host state. Dakar rewarded agreeable separatists with funding, recognition, and legitimation in their localities.[9] The government funded loyal separatist elites since the beginning, with some MFDC figureheads going to extraordinary lengths to appear conciliatory. One separatist luminary wrote compromising letters to the Senegalese presidency (the supposed foe of his nationalist movement), whining that his host state subsidies had ceased and begging for all-expenses-paid plane trips.[10] Such elites neglected to build alternative parastate organs in Casamance, with one exception: the only functioning separatist institution became the marijuana taxation branch.[11] As early as 1995, the MFDC extracted millions of dollars in cannabis tax in a single year. This not only "explain[ed] why these several hundred barefoot combatants have acquired increasingly sophisticated weapons over the years" on the black market. It also appeared to explain the exact timing of Casamançais rebellions, which attacked the host state "particularly in the cannabis harvesting season" with increased regularity.[12]

Soon, movement links to mafias divorced militant foot soldiers from their supposed leadership. Guns were bartered for cannabis, and secondarily, for cars, cattle, and cashew nuts.[13] Chronic cross-border raiding during separatist struggle left observers wondering "whether the perpetrators were rebels or opportunistic bandits."[14] To this day, the unofficial taxation of tourists takes the form of "violent robberies on both the trans-Gambian highway and the Bignona-Diouloulou road" to the host state proper.[15] The once-popular separatist cause had metamorphosed significantly. In 1997, gangsters burst into a dance party in the village of Djibanar, which had expressed reservations about the movement. After "reproaching the youth for partying while [we are] fighting for independence," separatists killed nine and injured fifteen.[16] Among the dead were four seven-year-olds, presumably unimpressed by the sermon. The movement transitioned from *organizing* to *raiding* Diola dances. What exactly happened?

THE *MAQUISARDS*

While the host state groomed separatist elites, the movement leadership fragmented.[17] But its base became integrated into organized crime inside Casamance and hence increasingly invested in proactively resisting Dakar encroachment. As some MFDC heads negotiated with the host state, the rank-and-file separatists remained recalcitrant. Initially aided by rogue state elements in neighboring Guinea-Bissau and The Gambia, they subsequently armed themselves independently of any state through gunrunners and domestic racketeering. Eventually, mid- and low-level separatists created an independent mafia.

Known as the maquisards (bush fighters), these ethnocentrically Diola formations overlapped with Casamançais diasporas and refugees, and cooperated with Gambian and Bissau-Guinean gangsters.[18] At first they were sustained from the outside. But the ascent to power—"warlord to drug lord," a biographer called it—of President "Nino" Vieira in Guinea-Bissau disrupted cross-border smuggling and desiccated the funding.[19] At a loss for foreign sponsors, the maquisards tilted to local rackets. In addition to harvesting mangoes, oranges, and other citrus fruits, separatists implemented a regional narco-traffic from the Karone Isles of lower Casamance, which "is difficult to reach by road but offers good access by boat to the river and the sea," ideal for cannabis cultivation. Ever since, "farmers are unwilling to give it up." Weapons-for-weed fishing boats became a staple of Senegalese society.[20] They remain so to this day.[21]

Gradually, economic and ethnic considerations coalesced. On the one hand, large sectors of the separatist community, especially militants, relied on organized crime for their livelihood. "Being a maquisard has become a job," one NGO observer remarked. "You just wait in the bush for your slice of the cake."[22] For many, emerging from the bush was less a matter of emancipatory struggle than of business cycles. On the other hand, this autochthonous mafia was overwhelmingly Diola, symbolizing ethnic perseverance. As Casamançais traditions lack clear political hierarchies, criminal patronage networks naturally filled the void.[23] The mafia also broke separatist dependence on the host state through transnational rackets. Among its allies was Gambian Diola leader Yahya Jammeh, for whom Front Nord gangsters served as bodyguards in the nearby border village of Kanilaye. In exchange, he made it their "supply and trafficking depot" for timber, arms, and cannabis.[24] Brokering ties to the Diola outside Senegal, organized crime sustained not only the economy but Casamançais ethnic pride too.

This emerging rebel mafia was entirely independent of the hapless host state, whose aspiration to co-opt separatists was shattered. Despite rumors of soldiers skimming over the top ("risk indemnities" on top of their salaries), government complicity in mafia activity was in fact minimal, with Senegalese officers serving as a "restraining influence" over sporadic exceptions.[25] Indeed, the organized crime of Senegal proper may have greater entanglements with Bissau than with separatist mafias within its sovereign territory.[26]

Separatist splintering over criminal turf deepened between the Front Nord and Front Sud, respectively north and south of the Casamance River. Both narco-financed, they cultivated in their respective areas, but then converged on the same trade routes through The Gambia, the lower Casamance, and along the West African coast. Despite posturing, *neither* controlled the entire separatist territory. "Those brandishing the weapons," field observers comment, "are today's decision-makers and power within the [separatist] Movement is split between numerous rebel leaders, all of whom command their own individual strongholds."[27] Their only consensus was a united front against the host state.

Over two decades, these strongholds were incubators for specialized gangster fiefdoms. The Front Sud—"more Diola, more Catholic"—turned to "increased reliance on financing from looting," racketeering, extortion, armed robbery, and other involuntary donation drives.[28] Humanitarian aid was also misappropriated. The Front Nord specialized in the drug trade, and secondarily in fishing, timber, and government development aid projects. An implicit nonintervention pact between the host state and separatists was struck. The Front Nord was allowed to settle "in the Bignona region from where it engaged in economic activities largely beyond government control."[29] Accordingly, the Front Nord, which patronizes the Karone Isles mafia, is more reliant than Front Sud on cannabis profits, and thus "may prove to be the most recalcitrant faction of all to demobilize and wean off its timber- and cannabis-trading."[30] United against intrusions, the rival criminal branches remain tied to separatism.

With some justification, the Senegal-Casamance bout has been called the most durable conflict in Africa.[31] Six to nine thousand casualties have accrued over secession. It is an exaggeration to assert that "the conflict in Casamance has lost almost any ideological or political content it may once have had, and has become a pretext for various forms of crime"—but only a slight one.[32] More precisely, the MFDC figureheads represent a movement of mafia-sustained constituencies whose opposition to host state intrusion is critical to their survival. Relevant gangsters pay their dues through kickbacks, bribes, and informal taxations. The separatist movement is structurally constrained by the rebel mafia on which it depends, and that no government (least of all Dakar) is able to dislodge.

Mali

The Sahara-Sahel region boasts rich smuggling traditions that have molded empires for centuries. But an upsurge in transnational organized crime since the early 2000s fueled separatist insurgencies in both Mali (2012) and Niger (2007–9).[33] In the former, where the mafia scene was both ethnocentric and independent of Bamako, organized crime empowered Tuareg separatism in Azawad. Ultimately contained by rival jihadi groups and a French military occupation (2013–14), the separatist movement nevertheless gained unprecedented momentum because of a potent, northern rebel mafia.

The Malian Tuareg are nomadic desert dwellers. Respecting segmentary lineage, their caste structure is highly hierarchical. Overlapping with seven-to-nine tribal confederations across northwest Africa, the Kel Adagh tribal confederation in Kidal and Kel Tademakkat in Timbuktu regulate Tuareg clan relations in northern Mali. An antiagricultural raiding custom was conducive to smuggling and banditry across the centuries. European colonialists concocted elaborate mythologies around the Tuareg, alternatively romanticizing their pastoralism and demonizing their viciousness. The "Targui," Jules Verne wrote, is "a thief by instinct and pirate by nature"—a sentiment that survives in host state characterizations of the Azawad problem.[34]

ENTRENCHMENT IN AZAWAD

Tuareg separatist grievances are numerous and understandable. Government neglect, discrimination, and repression were indeed the norm. In the Azawad movement's early stages, the host state literally poisoned Tuaregs' wells. Droughts and food shortages were chronic. Territorially, the disputed area is almost double the size of the host state proper. But whereas fertile southern Mali enjoys temperate climate, Azawad is half semiarid and half Sahara Desert. Famine, desertification, and the lack of infrastructure were readily imputed to host state cruelty, with or without reason.[35] One in five children in Azawad do not live to see their fifth birthday. Organizing any social movement in this terrain—let alone a secessionist one—was a geographic, demographic, and logistical nightmare.

The Tuareg in northern Mali did periodically stage rebellions short of wars—in 1990–95, and again in 2007–9. But the culmination came in 2012, when separatists executed a coup, ousted the president, and declared independence. Overwhelmed, the host state sought rescue from the French military. The escalation was a spectacular separatist success; "the rapidity with which the secession followed the coup [in 2012] took many Western observers by surprise."[36] The movement vanguard National Movement for the Liberation of Azawad (MNLA) barely numbered three thousand fighters. Yet coordinated and armed, they seized the opportunity of Mali's implosion and occupied Azawad with thousands of automatic rifles, machine guns, grenades, and light antiaircraft artillery—along with as many as six hundred all-terrain vehicles.

How did they do it? Organized crime was a critical ingredient—indeed, a necessary condition—for the unprecedented separatist advance.[37] Unlike previous separatist mobilizations, the 2012 uprising was distinctly gangster led. "Who are these leaders suddenly emerging from Azawad," a journalist wondered, "Taliban by day and smugglers by night?"[38] In fact, a preexisting ethnocentric Tuareg mafia armed and sustained the insurrection, up to and including jihadi co-optation and French invasion—both of which they fought to the bitter end.

Years before they turned to arming rebels, Azawad mafias were rooted in Tuareg clan (*tawshet*) structures. The aforementioned Kel Adagh and Kel Tademekkat—"drum groups," so named after tribal elders who traditionally place drums outside their homes—served as patronage networks across which Azawad smuggling was conducted. The "trafficking in contraband (especially cocaine, hashish, gasoline, and cigarettes)" was a distinctly ethnocentric affair, run "particularly among the nomadic Tuareg."[39] Tuareg and Arab gangs had, to put it mildly, differences of opinion.[40] This ethnic community sanctioned, regulated, and most critical, diverted criminal resources into separatist war coffers. In the process, Azawad mafias rose to prominence as oases in a sea of deprivation.[41] Jean-Pierre Olivier de Sardan (2013, 37–38) recorded how

> cash flows generated by smuggling, drugs and the hostage trade [built] paradoxically in the North of Mali pockets of great wealth. Certainly, this wealth scarcely concerned the vast majority of the population, farmers, herders, small retailers, local civil servants, who, at best, only received a few crumbs. It was concentrated in the hands of what could be called a strange "predatory alliance," which includes various Tuareg or Arab tribal leaders, the leaders of militia groups, fronts and separatist groups. . . . The proceeds were allocated to conventional prestige expenses (in [separatist] Gao, everyone knows the district called the "drug villas"), but also to buy weapons, or 4 × 4 pick-ups (when they were not simply stolen).[42]

Traditional tribal and caste hierarchies were recalibrated as this new criminal class ascended to the top in Kidal, Timbuktu, Gao, and other critical separatist sites. The MNLA relied heavily on precisely this constituency.

SEPARATIST CARGO

By the late 2000s, the restratification of Tuareg communities had prepared them to capitalize on two massive regional smuggling opportunities: arms and cocaine.[43] The first was a product of the six-month NATO bombing of Libya in 2011, which opened the northern gun-trafficking floodgate—a "weapons bonanza" of "man-portable air-defense systems (or, Manpadas), rocket-propelled grenades, SAM-7 missiles, and other sophisticated weaponry."[44] The second, a transnational narcotics route through the Sahel, soared from the late 1990s when US crackdowns on Caribbean cocaine networks reinvigorated alternatives in Africa. Latin American narco-cartel planes began flying across the lower Atlantic. One of them, a Venezuelan Boeing 727 hauling cocaine, crashed into the Malian desert in 2009. Scrambling to destroy the evidence, traffickers took the drugs before burning the jet.[45] By the mid- to late 2000s, upward of fifty tons of cocaine were moving across Mali, Nigeria, Senegal, and neighbors.[46] In addition to these contraband, massive smuggling of food, gasoline, cigarettes, and stolen cars became the only reliable import-export economy of northern Mali.

During the uprising, patriotic gangsters were in the fore. Tuareg exiles and gunrunners from Libya led the charge. Under them were dozens of drivers (*chifor*) well versed in the violent protection of their "cargoes" (*chargement*). Separatist leader Ibrahim ag Bahanga—a top arms supplier to the movement— fought to protect criminal turf as well as Tuareg sovereignty. In 2007, he clashed with host state forces at "the headquarters of his smuggling network" in Tinzaoutene. In 2009, "a group of Tuareg bandits led by Bahanga" hijacked a drug convoy of fifteen vehicles. Releasing the Arab hostages, Bahanga ordered them to spread the word regarding whom future drug shipments belong to.[47] By 2011, his gang was positioned to single-handedly arm a separatist insurrection with "AK47s, grenades, mounted machine-guns, vehicles[,] anti-tank missiles, rocket launchers and MANPADS."[48] Bahanga met his demise in 2011 "in a mysterious desert car crash after clashing with [rival gangs] over control of narcotics smuggling routes in northern Mali."[49] His martyrdom continues to inspire the independence struggle.

On the host state side, Bamako attempted—grudgingly—to patronize Tuareg gangsters. By the time war erupted, mafia capacity had itself become an impediment to centralized rule. "The collapse of the state's control of northern Mali in 2012 has been attributed," Magdalena Tham Lindell and Kim Mattsson (2014, 24) conclude, "to organised criminal activities, mainly cocaine trafficking."[50] Years before the 2012 secession, host state credibility in Azawad plummeted, while "the value and importance of controlling smuggling routes increased substantially." In desperation, President Amadou Toumani (2002–12) sought alliances with northern mafias to curb separatism. He "regarded organised crime as a potential tool in controlling the north," attempting to buy off individual gangsters. The effort backfired miserably:

> President ATT's complicity with organised crime led to an interlinking of the political system with criminal organisations to a degree where legitimate politics were rendered impossible, leading to a loss of state legitimacy and functionality in the north. The administration also regarded the militias that had been established by local drug traffickers and strongmen with interests in the drug trade as a potential resource to use against Tuareg insurgents, and paid little attention to what was happening in the north as long as they could reap the benefits from it both financially and politically.[51]

By June 2012, as the MNLA posed for photographs in front of thirty tanks at separatist-held Gao airport, it was too late. Mali's northern gangsters remained an unwaveringly rebel mafia that empowered Tuareg communities and resisted host state co-optation. The Tuareg dominance of the organized crime scene undermined and briefly defeated the host state by supplying Azawad's separatist movement with guns, funds, and fighters.

Eventually, Azawad separatists were encircled by less-than-secular rivals: the Ansar Dine, Movement for Unity and Jihad in West Africa, and al-Qa'ida in the Islamic Maghreb. Against the (largely foreign) intruders, the indigenous MNLA stood firm. It formed only a loose alliance with Ansar Dine, but refused to dissolve the separatist movement into an Islamist coalition. It was the separatists' alliance with rebel mafias, not Islamists, that midwifed Azawad's secession.[52]

Niger

Like their brethren in Mali, the Nigerien Tuareg have deeply torn their host state. Though never escalating their struggle to sizable war, Agadez separatists have repeated armed rebellions in their contentious repertoire—in 1990–95 (feebly and unproductively), and again in 2007–9 (forcefully and advancing autonomy). These episodes swelled northern Nigerien mafias profiting off the trans-Saharan contraband smuggling market, notably in migrants and narcotics. But a critical difference divides the Tuareg separatist movements in Mali (Azawad) and Niger (Agadez). While the former is fueled by independent, deeply ethnocentric mafias, the latter operates in a *multi*ethnic organized crime scene. Pluralistic and without political agendas, this cosmopolitan mafia significantly undermined both host state and separatist mobilization. Since 2010, after periodic Tuareg uprisings, organized crime in northern Niger has tranquilized state-separatist conflict.

"CHERIF COCAINE'S" COSMOPOLITAN MAFIA

The Nigerien Tuareg, sometimes called the Kel Ayr Tuareg after the "drum group" around the western and southern Aïr Mountains, first staged an insurgency in the early 1990s. The secessionist duet of the Coordination de Résistance Armée and Organisation de Résistance Armée struck a peace settlement with the host state in 1994, with few accomplishments to speak of:

> Considering they were allegedly fighting, at the very least, for greater autonomy, they seem to have settled for very little. Apart from a ceasefire, there were only promises that the National Assembly would approve a decentralisation law, whilst defense, security, the delineation of regions and the division of resources and economic aid were put on one side for further negotiation. Given that the Assembly was dissolved shortly after and the other matters were never negotiated, it seems a poor deal for separatists.[53]

The host state, on the other hand, secured partial disarmament, co-opted many Tuareg fighters into the Nigerien Armed Forces, and imprisoned or killed several separatist political figures. One of them, the Indiana University–educated Mano Dayek, was apparently killed in a plane ride on his way to negotiations with the government. The tourist-heavy city of Agadez, the separatist epicenter, named its airport in his honor.

In the second separatist mobilization, the insurgents radicalized. Dormant for over a decade, the separatist movement reemerged in 2007 as the Tuareg-led MNJ and Toubou-led Revolutionary Armed Forces of the Sahara renounced the 1995 accords, and assaulted government and foreign mining sites. Economic paralysis, land mines, tourist flight, and massive displacement swept the north. The budding secession failed to seize uranium positions or mobilize a sufficiently popular base. But it enjoyed numerous defections from Niger Army ranks and managed to forge significant multiethnic alliances. Tuareg-Toubou unification on the separatist agenda was especially vital because unlike in Mali, the Tuareg are demographically scattered in Niger.

A whirling series of defections, splinters, strategic blunders, and repressive host state overreactions followed until 2009, when the mainstream separatist MNJ fractured and pivoted toward peace accords. The extent to which the host state successfully divided and conquered the separatist movement, as opposed to the latter disintegrating of its own factionalism, remains unclear. The MNJ equivocated greatly in tactics and ideology—a volatility that cost it a coherent ethnic base.[54] On the one hand, soaring declarations of violent resistance were matched by military raids, notably against a base of the French

Areva uranium-mining company. On the other hand, their formal demands were as timid as could be: a fairer share of the uranium wealth, guarantees against displacement, and protection of indigenous lifestyles from ecological destruction. By regional standards, Niamey was fortunate indeed to receive such minimalist demands. It may have been a fiasco for separatism. But the movement's collapse was about to activate one of the most spectacular criminal hubs on the African continent.

From 2010 on, Nigerien mafias burgeoned.[55] The country's regional position in transnational smuggling routes is that of a bridge, not destination, society. Niger is a natural transit hub: massive cocaine, small arms, and migrant traffics traverse northern separatist territory—but almost none of the contraband remains in the country. To be sure, observers noticed "palatial houses being built, and luxury 4×4 vehicles on the streets" in the capital of the impoverished northern region.[56] Unlike in neighboring Mali, however, local gangster leaders did not run militias, trafficked guns did not go to separatist bunkers, and passing migrants were not foreign mercenaries. Agadez organized crime thrived on *bridging* host state and separatist constituencies, not dividing them.

The result was integrative: mafias disincentivized host state repression, undermined separatist allegiances, and made criminal bedfellows across the secessionist divide:

> The central government—which lacks policing resources and therefore relies more on local elites to maintain stability—rarely counters collusion between local officials and criminal networks. Local tribes are intermeshed with criminal groups, and tribal affinities and commercial relationships span post-colonial borders. For example, until his death in 2016, a prominent northern political chief in Agadez, Cherif Ould Abidine, was widely known as Cherif Cocaine. Tuareg networks in Niger, including former prominent rebels who now support the central government, nonetheless maintain relations with rebellious Tuareg networks.[57]

Former rebels were on demand as bodyguards. A booming private security sector involved 150 registered bodyguard companies servicing foreigners, local businesspeople, and government convoys. Thousands of young locals—including hundreds of Tuareg ex-separatists—were employed in these firms.

In Agadez itself, the secessionist capital, rackets are not oriented to local armament or funding insurgents but rather toward gold-mining adventurism, migrant smuggling into Europe, nonmilitant labor trafficking, money laundering through mushrooming new banks, and stolen car trading. The drug trade is vast yet apolitical. One of two major northward cocaine flows in the region goes through the separatist capital on its way to Libya and Europe. Although the host state denounces rebels as drug dealers, there have been—remarkably—no documented cases of narco-funding toward any separatist movement organization.[58]

Since 2014, when people smuggling from Africa into Europe was in demand, the Agadez mafia's migrant racket gained international prominence.[59] Gangsters made millions via fleets of pickup trucks, safe houses, brothels, and intricate desert paths. The slow, gradual trafficking process—it can take up to eighteen months to reach Europe—is lucrative in squeezing every last drop of labor and money from migrants. Many of them were entirely ignorant of where they were going.[60] A group of forty migrants brought $15,000. Then vehicles would be purchased with the money and driven back into Agadez from Libya for additional profit in the local market.[61] Using migrants as cover, gangsters smuggled drugs and arms with them. Truly multiethnic, the Agadez mafia included pimps, prostitutes, drivers, enforcers, and "passers" from Nigeria, Ghana, The Gambia, and other African countries. In Europe, they partnered primarily with the Sicilian mafia.

RELAXING EXTREMISM

Nigerien mafias were equal opportunity traders. They hardly discriminated between Boko Haram, Libyan warlords, Tuareg nationalists, Toubou migrants, or government officials. In the separatist north itself, this multiethnic organized crime tranquilized the country as a "live and let live" informal pact was struck between Niamey and the separatists:

> Revenues from smuggling activity in northern Niger have contributed to establishing some degree of stability in the region. In an area with limited resources and opportunities for formal employment, trafficking of goods and gold prospection bring in much-needed cash. Furthermore, these activities provide a welcome occupation for youth and former [separatist] rebels who have not been reintegrated and who have an excellent knowledge of the terrain and how to handle weapons. Some members of the security forces also benefit from illicit trafficking by extracting bribes or "unofficial taxation," and families and tribes have also set up checkpoints to levy taxes from smugglers passing through their territory.

Government policies toward curbing crime were either avoided or carefully circumvented in implementation due to fears that such "clamp-down is only going to increase insecurity."[62] Host state complicity was a public secret. "François," a midlevel Agadez mafia operator, sought to impress a (female) foreign journalist by bringing her to a family residence of the Nigerien prime minister, where he graciously gave an interview about his criminal operations.[63]

Even intransigent jihadi units from abroad found Agadez's apolitical smuggling irresistible. Since the late 2000s, Niger's separatist territory is a leading sanctuary for jihadi gangsters who lose faith. Contrary to al-Qa'ida's reputation, its enterprise in North and West Africa is hardly itself a narco-mafia; "many jihadists were unwilling to engage directly in the drug trade," dealing with regional gangsters occasionally and tangentially.[64] Rather, what typically transpired was that individual katiba units—consisting of up to a hundred fighters grouped around several pickup trucks with armed rears—would evolve into breakaway mafias in Nigerien localities before forsaking their regional emir leadership.

Breakoff katiba units in the Agadez region repeatedly displayed this cycle. As their commanders resided in caves in the remote Kabylie Mountains, they were sent to spread sharia in Assamaka, Tassara, and other precarious separatist cities in Niger. Immense cash flow surrounded them in the form of drugs, cigarettes, and antiquities. Yielding to temptation, many fighters transfigured into gangsters. Migrants looking for a ride, refugees looking for protection, and angry youngsters looking for a thrill all gravitated to the increasingly secular and ideologically disinterested criminal tycoons. al-Qa'ida's reputation and patronage networks grew. In due course, the funds ceased to go where they were intended: northward to al-Qa'ida superiors. Ultimately the katiba would break off to administer an independent mafia in the locality—sometimes with creative ideological rationalizations. Denouncing the unruly gang as infidels, al-Qa'ida would dispatch a replacement. Soon enough, the substitute would begin the cycle anew.[65]

This phenomenon—christened "criminal jihadism"—signifies the triumph of mafia logic over fundamentalist purity.[66] For these gangsters, profit triumphed over separatism. A prototypical example was the al-Mourabitoun (masked men), a mafia led by the fabled Mokhtar Belmokhtar. The one-eyed smuggling legend was arguably the organized criminal champion of Niger. To avenge his brother's death, he waged a one-person war against the Algerian state. Exiled to the Sahel, he elevated arms trafficking and kidnapping to an art. Not himself Tuareg, he forged smuggling partnerships (including four marriages "expanding his access to Malian commercial networks") and sold protective services to Tuareg tribal communities.[67] Ransom for his Western hostages is estimated to have earned tens of millions of dollars. Declared officially dead a half-dozen times, he dramatically resurfaced as "*le fantome du Sahara*." His cigarette-smuggling ring earned him the epithet "Marlboro Man."[68]

Organizing gangs both within and around Niger, Belmokhtar became a trusted supplier of arms, on-demand negotiator between warring parties, and mediator of hostage releases for both sides of the separatist divide. Beloved by many, he was equally at ease serving Algeria, Mali, and the Tuareg separatists—a true gangster "freelancer."[69] Once al-Qa'ida's southern regional boss, he was a prime organizer of their African network throughout the 1990s. As his mafia grew, he abandoned his umbrella cause in the 2000s and proclaimed the al-Mourabitoun, a battalion that did little else than administer his trafficking enterprises. In response, al-Qa'ida sent (what they hoped was) a devout and loyal replacement, Abdelhamid Abu Zeid. In no time at all, "Abu Zeid smuggled and engaged in other criminal activities just like Belmokhtar" before him.[70] Such is the attraction—but also ethnic pluralism—of organized crime in Niger.

The proposed northern Tenere Republic (alternatively, Agadez Republic or Akal N Tenere) remains untenable for various reasons.[71] Foremost among them is the sustenance of an independent but multiethnic cosmopolitan mafia in the north. Unlike the separatist-minded Azawad mafias in Mali, Nigerien organized crime has pacified both host state crackdowns and separatist agitation.

Nigeria

Popular obsessions over Islam have clouded the understanding of Boko Haram as a *separatist* movement. The roots of the insurgency are not religious; they are socioeconomic.[72] When its leader Abudbakar Shekau boasts of abducting Nigerian schoolgirls, stating "I will sell them in the market, by Allah, I will sell them off," the Western press fixates on the "by Allah" part.[73] In fact, the remainder of the statement better illuminates the nature of this insurgency. Smuggling, extortion, and monopolization of a gang ecology in northern Nigeria explain separatist success. Organized crime—in whatever religious dressing it may appear—was evidently central to the movements' tactics, goals, and administration.[74] Boko Haram would never have succeeded in its stunning secessionist reach without a massive, ethnocentric, and state-independent rebel mafia. In response, Nigeria deployed a modest mafia in uniform comprised of gangs of the Niger Delta.

BORDERS, RACKETS, AND GANGS

Separatism is ubiquitous in Nigerian society. Ethnic categories number in the hundreds in Africa's most populous nation. The great collective trauma of its modern history was the war over secessionist Biafra (1967–70). War casualties (approximately a hundred thousand) were the least of the separatist calamity; up to two million people starved to death through economic blockades. The O'dua People's Congress, Movement for the Actualization of the Sovereign State of Biafra, and Movement for the Emancipation of the Niger Delta are but a few examples of secessionist turmoil. Boko Haram's jihadist sectarianism is thought to distinguish it entirely from such precedents.[75] But this is misleading. While its tactical extremism and cruelty are indisputable,

Boko Haram was fatefully ethnocentric in its Kanuri base.[76] Barely 8 percent of the Nigerian Muslim population, the Kanuris were predominant in Borno State, the central hub of Maiduguri, and surrounding separatist areas in Yobe and Adamawa. Key leaders and benefactors, including Ali Modu Sheriff and Shekau himself, are Kanuri. Put crudely, Caliphate ideals were embedded in Kanuri relations.

Boko Haram's Salafist ideology is, of course, more universalist than its demographic base. But the movement's operational reach was consistently constrained by its ethnotribal patronage network, the "ties that bind."[77] The indispensable smuggling resources that the movement drew on were ethnically concentrated. In earlier phases of separatist mobilization, the Kanuri factor constrained Boko Haram's administrative reach on both sides of Nigeria's borders:

> Kanuri also inhabit regions across the northern border into Niger, and there is evidence to suggest that these tribal relationships facilitate weapons trafficking and other cross-border smuggling transactions, but this is the extent to which Boko Haram's activities go outside Nigeria. While it is very much a locally-oriented movement, the group has not yet attracted a significant following among Nigerians of other tribal or ethnic backgrounds. Further, it has thus far proven difficult for the group to find sympathizers or anyone who would help them facilitate attacks further south, thus the majority of attacks have taken place within the north (and primarily northeastern corner) of the country.[78]

Furthermore, it appears that non-Kanuris are disproportionately offered up as cannon fodder in terrorist actions (notably suicide bombings), discriminated against within Boko Haram, and more likely to be targeted in missions. At the very least, many non-Kanuri separatists are disquieted by the movement's ethnic favoratism.[79]

How, then, could an underequipped and impoverished posse of several hundred ethnocentric gangsters come to control fifty thousand square kilometers? The answer is threefold: smuggling, racketeering, and gangs. First, Boko Haram administered northern Nigerian smuggling. It dominated import-export markets, and created border controls that rivaled and surpassed the government's. Unlike transitory hub Niger, Nigeria is primarily a *destination* society for contraband. Nigeria's terrestrial borders total over four thousand kilometers, nearly half of them along Boko Haram's separatist north. Given jungle and mountainous terrains, the porosity is enormous. The host state controls 84 legal, regular border crossings. Another 1,499 irregular ones operate entirely outside government control.[80] Local communities around these borders—alienated and neglected by the host state—in effect serve as patrollers, customs officers, and border guards. Their allegiance to kinship and tribal networks naturally gravitated to the Kanuri communities of Boko Haram, away from host state forces.

The dominant smuggling branch was arms.[81] Of the total eight million illegal weapons in the West Africa region, 70 percent are in Nigeria.[82] Well before the overthrow of Muammar al-Gaddafi, small- and medium-size weaponry was regularly smuggled southward from Libya. After 2011, the floodgates opened when mercenary gunrunners sold antitank, antiaircraft, and other heavy arms in bulk. True to local custom, they combined modern contraband transport means with traditional commerce "such as the use of specially crafted skin or thatched bags attached to camels, donkeys and cows where arms are concealed and moved across the borders with the aid of nomadic pastoralists or herders."[83] Alternatively, Boko Haram "connived with merchants involved in cross-border trade to help stuff their arms and weapons in goods that are transported via heavy trucks, trailers, and Lorries."[84] Once across the border, ethnic villager networks transported the guns further in sewage tankers, fuel compartments, grain bags, and colorful Kanuri garments. Women and men alike carried explosives and rifles under female veils. Elaborate underground tunneling connected houses to underground bunkers—some of them spacious enough for a hundred people.

Second, Boko Haram ran extortion rackets throughout separatist territory, replacing both tribal and host state mechanisms of extraction. Reputed to be marionettes of Saudi/Qatari Salafists, Boko Haram in fact sustained itself through indigenous fundraising. Before its worldwide renown, it ran a "microcredit system set up by [founder] Yusuf before 2009, when the sect invested in transport, car washing or selling clean water."[85] From 2010 on, the movement advanced to extortion rings. Its original commercial center was a mosque in Maiduguri, the capital of Borno State. Beginning with the Baga fish market and a local motor park, it demonstratively executed traders resisting extortion. Expanding from there, Boko Haram methodically took over the surrounding Borno merchant sites one at time, reaching as far north as Diffa in neighboring Niger. Piracy, abductions, bank robberies, and thefts from government sites followed, spreading like wildfire across northern Nigeria. It was these rackets that established Boko Haram's de facto control over the economy and patronage politics in separatist localities.[86]

Third, the separatist movement organized extant violent gangs across a vast territory—uniting, centralizing, and politicizing them into a rebel mafia. Boko Haram did not invent gangsterism in the Nigerian north. Rather, it consolidated and reanimated preexisting criminal youth groups and hired goons—through "conscription, payment, and proselytization"—toward new, separatist ends.[87] Against the "sudden rupture" thesis, analysts with historical perspective dub Boko Haram "old wine in new bottles."[88] It harnessed the headwind of a preexisting, disorganized criminal scene:

Violent militia groups such as Dan Kaleri in Gombe State and Ecomog in Borno State . . . were used by political godfathers to harass and sometimes assassinate rivals, especially during electoral cycles. As is typical with Nigerian political godfathers, the youth gangs and thugs they use to bulldoze their way to power are often soon afterward discarded because such groups could later threaten the politicians themselves. Used and discarded, such ready-made armies of mayhem often turn the weapons given to them by unscrupulous politicians into other uses, including criminality and antisocial violence. Many members of these groups have become the foot soldiers of Boko Haram.[89]

"Soldier boy" (*sozaboy*) subcultures in northern Nigeria were as potent as any ideology on offer in separatist villages. Saturated with notions of masculinity and empowerment, they gave youths a sense of family, safety, and spiritual meaning. Infusing their "desire to resort to violence as a coping mechanism" with Salafi ideology, Boko Haram appropriated hundreds of male children. The Yan Tauri soldier boys were "economic opportunists, and professional mercenary soldiers, who [were] prepared to offer their services to whoever hires them."[90] Other "street boys" included the Yan Daba, Yan Banga, and Yan Dauka Amarya.[91] Older, no less vicious gangs included Dan Kaleri and Ecomog, hired goons who served various politicians and tribal leaders in the past, and now offered their services to the highest bidder. Boko Haram's virtuosity was in mobilizing gangs under a single separatist banner.

PATRIOTIC GANGSTERS

Apart from the separatist north, Nigeria has a flourishing southern mafia scene based around the Niger Delta. The two mafia ecologies—the separatist north and the south—are detached and ethnocentric. The host state controls neither.[92] Nevertheless, a modest mafia in uniform was temporarily mobilized in the south for antiseparatist purposes.

Nigerian organized crime is the most polycentric and differentiated in the entire region. Otherwise conservative in applying the term "mafia," the World Bank does not hesitate to refer to the "mafia-like criminality of Nigeria."[93] The most conspicuous mafias have nothing to do with either the government or Boko Haram.[94] Narcotics, notably, is almost entirely limited to independent southern mafias. Since the 1970s, Europe-bound cocaine from South America and US-bound heroin from South Asia have transited the Niger Delta. Nigerian narco-traffickers appear to have invented the technique of inserting (orally or anally) drugs into the body within a sealed condom—the so-called mule method.[95] Additionally, southern rackets revolve around oil. Critical fishing and agricultural sectors were battered by ecological destruction from oil mining. In reaction, "a flurry of criminal groups and armed militant gangs often consisting of unemployed youth have engaged in kidnappings, extortion, car bombings, murder," and budding rackets and smuggling operations.[96]

The result was a plethora of vigilante mobs—such as the Egbesu Boys of Africa, Bakassi Boys, and Niger Delta Avengers—marauding and sabotaging the oil industry.[97] A parallel infrastructure emerged of hundreds of makeshift oil refineries, warehouses, and secret bunkers. Tens of millions of barrels of oil were annually smuggled out of Nigeria for upward of $1 billion. The country's leading anticorruption investigator estimated that from independence to 2006, $360 billion had vanished in oil-related theft. Southern gangsters left notable dents on the economy and oil politics regionally.[98] Some Niger Delta mafias have even replaced state provisions with their own governance, such as providing "social services, electricity, fees for students to pay for exams, micro-credit for local businesses, hospital supplies, subsidies for teacher's pay, and so forth."[99] The government has chronically failed to contain, let alone control, this unruly southern crime scene.

The host state, however, did manage to organize a recent mafia in uniform to fight separatism in the early 2010s. In response to Boko Haram gangsters, the host state resorted to its own. Vigilante gangs such as the Bakassi Boys, Oouda People's Congress, Hisbah, and Vigilante Group of Nigeria were folded into Abuja's counterinsurgency. In 2013, an umbrella Civilian Joint Task Force fused them into a combat-ready formation, and "gave them uniforms, cars, identification documents and a stipend." As of September 2017, the record of these hired guns was mixed: a modest contribution to operations against Boko Haram coupled with widespread abuse of power and racketeering in separatist territory. Loyal to the government, they are nonetheless chronically "exploiting their privileged status and relative impunity for criminal purposes, including small-scale drug trafficking and resale of stolen goods."[100]

Boko Haram has succeeded in tearing apart its host state because of extensive Kanuri-based smuggling, racketeering, and the monopolization of gangs in the northern territory. Its rebel mafia continues to be a major obstacle to reintegration of the north. Abuja, for its part, has belatedly instrumentalized a handful of gangs to fight separatism. Whether the government manages to rein in the extortionist tendencies of its mafia in uniform remains to be seen.

Cameroon

Ambazonia is the sole West African separatist movement without any relations to organized crime.[101] The English-speaking Cameroonians from two western provinces are also a rare instance of a nonethnic, nontribal, nonsectarian secessionist movement in Africa. The Anglophones—numbering some six million, or a fifth of the population—seek the reestablishment of the British mandate of Southern Cameroons (1916–61), this time as an independent nation. Among other obstacles, a cosmopolitan mafia contributed to Cameroon's cohesion.

MISSING INGREDIENTS

With deep roots, the anglophone movement was resurgent in 1990, when a manifesto decrying francophone repression mobilized separatist provinces and led to (modest) constitutional concessions on autonomy.[102] A creative "ghost towns" (*ville morte*) campaign in 1991–92 mobilized Ambazonians to fight for separatism by boycotting markets, taxes, and bills, and remaining at home to undermine Cameroon's economy. Initially demanding refederalization, the separatist movement quickly escalated to secessionist demands. "It was only after the persistent refusal of the [host state] to discuss this [federalist] scenario," Piet Konings and Francis Nyamnjoh note, "that secession, which used to be discussed by a limited few, became an overt option with mounting popularity."[103] The government's refusal to even negotiate "was instrumental in turning the separatist movement into a secessionist one."[104]

In the 2000s, the repression intensified. A strike against French language use in schools and courtrooms was crushed, resulting in the death of six people and arrest of hundreds of separatists. Since 2016, escalating violence (responsible for about 420 casualties) has elicited widespread fear over looming separatist war. Cameroon attracted international censure for abusing Ambazonian prisoners. A 2017 anniversary of the region's independence from Britain occasioned massive protests demanding secession. The military again turned on civilians, this time provoking guerrilla attacks. New separatist militias—the Red Dragons, Tigers, and internet-savvy Amba Boys—emerged as supplements to the usual Ambazonian Defense Forces.[105] This recent upsurge in violence is a deviation, however. The overall trajectory of the Ambazonian movement has been steadfastly nonviolent and conciliatory. The separatists' unofficial motto—"the force of argument, not the argument of force," a folk proverb from Buea—captured their moderate tactics well. Formally, the demand was secession; informally, it is believed that most Anglophones did not support it in the 2010s.[106]

For two decades, Ambazonian separatism has lacked two critical ingredients for a more dynamic and successful movement: a patron state and separatist-minded mafias. First, Cameroon's clashes with neighboring Nigeria over the petroleum-rich Bakassi peninsula made Ambazonian separatism extraneous.[107] Flanked by two giants, the anglophone cause was perceived as little more than a distraction. At most, Nigeria occasionally instrumentalized Ambazonian grievances to destabilize Cameroon. But it has refrained from empowering the separatists at the cost of good relations with the host state. Countries like Albania and Jordan allow separatist bases and training camps on their territory to attack neighbors. In contrast, in the middle of escalating repression against Ambazonians in 2018, Nigeria arrested separatist leaders who set foot in Abuja and unceremoniously dumped them back across the border.[108] *That* was the separatist movement's sole regional ally.

Second, Cameroon's organized crime was impartial and unmoved by Ambazonia's plight. Major rackets—in cybercrime, burglary, vehicle theft, illegal logging, and child labor—were steadfastly apolitical.[109] Most smuggling is in innocent everyday goods such as textiles, gasoline, sugar, and soap. Extortionists in separatist territory target primarily the Nigerian minority (whom Anglophones resent for dominating trade routes), but have not demonstrated any anti-Francophone inclinations. Nor is there much potential for anglophone-centric trafficking since the territory is outside transnational smuggling routes. Neither bridge nor destination society, Cameroon's share of West African rackets is peripheral.[110] Intra-Cameroon trafficking rings in domestic work and sexual labor circulate women, children, and other victims across the separatist fault line. Perhaps the most durable mafia is a conglomerate of highway robbery gangs (*coupeurs de route*) operating within both Ambazonia and Cameroon proper, embracing anglophone and francophone gangsters alike.[111] Separatists' attempts to arm themselves—such as the Southern Cameroon Youth League's blundering endeavor to steal explosives from the Razel Company in 1997—revealed the dearth of politically minded criminal partners.

"The main issue for Ambazonian groups," one analyst concluded, "is that they really lack finance. If they had money to buy weapons, train and feed their people, they could raise an army."[112] Alas, as of the first anniversary of the proclaimed Republic of Ambazonia, extant organized crime remained a disobligingly cosmopolitan mafia.

7

Middle East

While we were pretending to fight against terrorism, we were really lining our own pockets.

—HÜSEYIN OĞUZBEY ON THE YÜKSEKOVA GANG'S CRUSADE AGAINST KURDISH SEPARATISM, "SUSURLUK"

We're Palestinians working for the sake of Palestine.

—SMUGGLING TUNNEL LABORER IN EGYPTIAN RAFAH, "GAZA'S TUNNEL PHENOMENON"

On the centenary of the Sykes-Picot Agreement, scholars reminisced about the origins of today's torn countries in the east Mediterranean: a set of "Euro-manufactured instant states born on after-dinner napkins in the hands of Cognac-mellowed British and French colonial officers."[1] It was a sobering aide-mémoire. Indeed, the mystery of the Middle East is not why so many nations are torn by protracted segregation (Turkey and Israel) and civil war (Iraq, Syria, and Yemen). The true mystery is why there are not more torn states. Decades after decolonization, boundary-reconfiguring mafias have proven critical arbiters of lingering nationalist disputes.

Turkey

Turkey and its Kurdish separatist movement regularly accuse each other of mobilizing organized crime to brutalize the other. Both are correct.[2] The host state created the Susurluk mafia; "a special criminal team was established within Emniyet (the Turkish police force) to fight against the PKK [Kurdish Workers' Party]."[3] Profiting on the side, these gangsters nevertheless remained patriotic and indisputably state controlled. Kurdish separatists, meanwhile, marshaled an organized criminal enterprise through the PKK's Kongra-Gel (KGK). The world's largest stateless people may be partitioned by factionalism and the repression of multiple host states. But their movement has successfully organized a significant rebel mafia of its own to counter Turkey's mafia in uniform.[4]

"HONORABLE MEN"

Turkey's mafia ecology is legendary.[5] What oil was to the making of the Gulf states, heroin was to the making of the modern Turkish nation. When Kurdish separatism escalated in the 1990s, organized crime was already in the fore of Turkey's antiseparatist crackdown.[6] Far from a passive observer of mafias, "the state [wa]s spawning criminal gangs" to fight the Kurds.[7] The fortuitous revelation of this "gangs in uniform" (*uniformalı çete*) conspiracy followed a tragic but illuminating car crash.[8]

In 1996, a wrecked bulletproof Mercedes was discovered in the small town of Susurluk, south of Istanbul. Killed in the crash was gangster luminary Abdullah Çatlı—a heroin trafficker and Interpol fugitive wanted for multiple murders. He served prison time in France and Switzerland, but escaped the death penalty in his native Turkey. (In his dim youth, he tried to assassinate the pope). Çatlı kept eclectic company; also dead in the crash were his mistress, a former beauty queen, and a senior police chief with a trail of corruption. The delegation was suspicious enough. But the fourth passenger—and sole survivor—was none other than Sedat Bucak, head of the Siverek Kurdish tribe that "since 1993 had set up a private army of several thousand men, equipped with weapons supplied by the state to combat the PKK."[9] Inside the vehicle were machine guns, ammunition, communication devices, fake state-issued IDs, and a diplomatic passport issued to one of Turkey's leading fugitives. Thread by thread, the state-mafia conspiracy began to unravel.

In exchange for immunity and profitable public tenders, criminals had been recruited to fight the PKK. In the 1980s, a gangster-packed Special Task Force was the government's toughest battering ram against the separatists. When the task force was disbanded, "some became hired guns in the criminal world, specializing in debt collection or intimidation during tenders (kidnapping, threats)," and others became contract killers.[10] In the 1990s, state-hired assassins killed hundreds of Kurdish activists. The chain of command was from the Minister of Interior Mehmet Agar or Chief of Police Korkut Eken to the mafia executors. One intelligence report implicated the prime minister herself, Tansu Çiller, of being "the mother of the guilty ones." A sizable chunk of a $50 million "prime ministerial slush fund to fight the PKK" was unaccounted for, presumably due to its dishonorable recipients. Overall, the host state bankrolled a two-thousand-person mafia "more than $1 million a month to battle Kurdish separatists."[11]

The Turkish mafia—also termed the "deep state" (*derin devlet*)—appeared to be the most stable pillar of the security apparatus, flouting official organizational charts.[12] On their way back from missions against Kurdish terrorists, military helicopters flew heroin. So long as they served Ankara's counterinsurgency, gangsters were permitted to "benefit with all impunity from the niche markets created, notably in drugs and arms trafficking."[13] One deputy prime minister could not contain her enthusiasm for an underworld boss: "Those who shoot or take wounds on behalf of the state are respected by us. For us, they are honorable men."[14]

The Susurluk scandal was ultimately subdued with a handful of minimal repercussions. "While some mafiosi were arrested, an important number of the chief exercises of state power who were alleged to be the [*sic*] part of these gangs survived with little or no penalty."[15] Hundreds of implicated gangsters—with unindicted tens of thousands behind them—remained operational on behest of the state apparatus. While some of his bodyguards received minor penalizations for his murders, Bucak himself enjoyed parliamentary immunity.[16]

By the 2000s, a "new breed of bosses," or *babas*, elevated state-sanctioned gangsterism to iconic status. Gangster kingpins included Sedat Peker, socialite and commander of a contract killer squad, and Alaattin Çakıcı, leader of the Grey Wolves gang, and estranged son-in-law of Turkey's most powerful mob boss. Clouded in intrigue and fear, both men were potent instruments against Kurdish separatism—lead actors in a "large cast of gangsters, politicians, and security personnel who helped to form a series of state-backed gangs (*çetelen*) deployed against the PKK." In their unwavering loyalty to the antiseparatist crackdown, these figures epitomized a "particularly nationalist trend among gangsters" in Turkey.[17]

A tabloid personality, Peker was renowned as an extortionist, sports agent, and seducer of celebrities. As (unofficial) patron of the Turkish Football Association, he rigged matches, blackmailed managers, and beat up players—such as the hapless Rüştü Reçber, the national team's star goalie. While serving a fourteen-year sentence, Peker charmed his defense lawyer into marrying him. In prison, his luxury items included televisions, refrigerators, washing machines, vases, and oil paintings. In court testimonies, Peker not only confessed but endorsed his government patrons' orders to murder Kurdish businesspeople and PKK supporters. An accomplice of his insisted that Peker was a "personal errand boy" and "bag man" of Turkish military intelligence. Another deemed this too modest, insisting that Peker in fact "commanded a death squad" charged with killing mobsters bankrolling the separatist cause.[18] Whatever the precise job position, he steadfastly served his government against the separatist scourge.

Gangster legend Çakıcı was likewise colorful. With neighborhood extortion rackets in Istanbul and Ankara, he created a gambling empire through casinos and hotels. Çakıcı married the daughter of Dündar Kılıç, Turkey's ultimate, if aging, mafia boss (*babaların babası*). After divorcing her, Çakıcı ordered her murder, which was executed in front of her son on Çakıcı's birthday. He was also a patriot from an early age. Çakıcı's tenure in nationalist youth gangs established him as a trusted right-wing militant—and reliable murderer. Recruited for missions against separatists, he served as a loyal state security operative. With direct access to the interior minister, Çakıcı hardly had difficulties evading European, let alone Turkish, law. In 2002, he released himself from prison early. His passport confiscated, he fled by sea to Greece with forged documents, leaving his nephew behind to be arrested. In 2004, he crisscrossed French, Russian, and German cities (changing cars every few hours) to visit his ailing son in an Austrian hospital. He was finally captured with a diplomatic passport issued by the Turkish state apparatus. In custody, he celebrated the anti-Kurdish crusade.

A MAFIA OF OUR OWN

The blow to separatists was considerable. Spokespeople for the Kurdish cause were assassinated by mafia contractors. Kurdish leaders were promised lucrative smuggling profits and tribal authority to desert the cause. State-funded "village guardians" (*korucular*), whose ranks swelled from forty to hundred thousand in separatist areas in the 1990s, were given free reign to create criminal fiefdoms. Heroin traffickers were offered death or desertion of the PKK; most opted for the latter.[19] Numerous Kurdish figures—so-called PKK confessants—were co-opted as antiseparatist gangsters. Underworld figures such as Ali "Drej" Yasak (a Kurd) faithfully served Turkish nationalism. Mafias such as the Soylemez Brothers, ambitious drug and arms dealers, and the Yüsekova Gang, "a uniformed gang of village guards, special team members, and PKK confessants," were used for the "killing and persecution of businessmen and other civilians in the southeast who were suspected of having PKK sympathies."[20]

For all the mafia forces mobilized against them, Kurdish separatists were themselves no strangers to organized crime. Resource mobilization through narco-funding came all too naturally given the PKK's geographic concentration; the mountainous, unpatrolled border areas of southeast Turkey are coincidentally the conduit for the world's greatest heroin route, from Afghanistan to Europe. The PKK's extraordinary forty-year endurance is due to its diversified and logistically adaptible illicit profiteering. From familiar narco-trafficking, human smuggling, and gunrunning, to the more exotic money laundering, document forgery, and blood smuggling, a masterful rebel mafia was embedded in the Kurdish separatist movement.[21]

The PKK is centralized, but with a "hydra-headed" flexibility, like "an octopus that extends its numerous, probing tentacles into neighboring countries and beyond," with "criminal tentacles" in parallel with "guerrilla tentacles." Yet the same "'head' of the octopus structure" managed both, even as they were unaware of each other.[22] Senior separatist Şemdın Sakık did not mince words: "The source of our money was drug trafficking. The PKK and [its leadership] have always gotten a big share from the drug trafficking on the drug route of Turkey-Middle East. We used money generated from drugs to purchase weapons."[23] Among the "tentacles" that accomplished this was the KGK. Nominally a 2003 political "face-lift" of the PKK through the People's Congress of Kurdistan, the branch is in fact the movement's best-documented mafia. Through customs checkpoints for drug trafficking on separatist territory, and elaborate extortion, smuggling, and distribution networks in the European diaspora, the KGK was a spectacular boost to Kurdish separatist coffers.[24]

KGK rackets were fivefold. First, they taxed drug traffickers. One disgruntled heroin peddler recalled the typical routine at separatist checkpoints: "We have to give 1,000 DM to the PKK–KONGRA GEL per kilo of heroin and I was obligated to tribute nearly 1,000,000 DM annually." Second, the KGK engaged in drug cultivation and production, including vast cannabis plantations in the east and southeast Anatolian Mountains as well as mobile heroin laboratories on the Iran and Iraq borders, over which "mafias, feudal paramilitaries, and guerrillas are all in fierce competition to control the profits."[25] Third, they trafficked drugs per se. Separatist figurehead Abdullah "Ado" Öcalan, martyred by Turkish arrest and imprisonment, readily implicated his own brother in "trafficking drugs to Europe." Bemoaning his loss of control over the separatist organization, he swore that he had advised against involvement in the narco-trade.[26]

Fourth, they operated distribution networks in Europe, including the micromanagement of street-level delivery—notably in the Netherlands, Germany, and the United Kingdom in the 1990s. Kurdish gangs in London and Amsterdam staged killing sprees to eliminate rivals in the heroin business. In the Dutch city of Arnhem, five Kurdish crime families dominated the drug trade.[27] The ethnocentric criminal network extends from production in the Middle East to distribution in Western Europe—"a complex vertical business that begins with the morphine base obtained from Pakistan all the way through to sales on the street of Europe."[28]

Finally, the PKK conducted money laundering and extortion. Shakedown rackets took the form of "revolutionary taxes," "voluntary contributions," or "insurance fees" from businesspeople of Turkish-Kurdish origin. In a single year (1993), in a single country (Great Britain), the PKK extorted as much as £2.5 million from the Kurdish diaspora. Beside "big fish" such as wealthy Kurdish entrepreneurs, "cultural centers, doner kebab restaurants, and pizza shops" also paid "solidarity taxes." The profit was then laundered through separatist front organizations. In 2001, the Kurdish Employers Association was founded in Amsterdam to pool extortion funds. A separatist propaganda television station, MED TV, laundered millions of US dollars before being shut down in 1996; $8 million "from drugs, arms, and human smuggling" were uncovered in a Luxembourg bank account.[29] In sum, the PKK's income from organized crime was a stellar $86 million annually in the 1990s. By the late 2000s, estimates ranged from $50 to $100 million, to $500 million, to as much as $615 to $770 million.[30] No separatist movement has ever sustained such a durable mafia enterprise.

The market share and profit obtainable through organized crime in Turkey remains dazing. "The street value of the total volume of drugs passing through Turkey," Martin van Bruinessen (2000, 26) reminds us, was "in the same order of magnitude as Turkey's entire annual government budget." Little wonder that mafias proved precious to both the host state and Kurdish separatists. It is indisputable that the Turkish mafias in uniform dominated overall organized crime vis-à-vis their Kurdish counterparts.[31] Nevertheless, the separatists held their own: within the PKK, an impressive rebel mafia outside Turkish control bolstered separatism for decades.

Israel

While most host states dread the prospect of two separatist insurgencies, Israel has deliberately bifurcated Palestinian separatism between Gaza (Hamas) and the West Bank (Palestinian Authority). Below we focus on Gaza. A rebel mafia based in Sinai-Gaza tribal clans created a spectacular underworld—figuratively *and* literally—that sustained Palestinian autonomy, armed the separatist movement, and restratified Gazan society.

MAFIA "LUNGS"

Like most separatist territories, Gaza remains a clan-based kinship community. Clans (*hamulas*) of families (*a'ilas*)—whose assemblies (*diwans*) pool and distribute critical resources—dictate cultural relations, electoral politics, and informal economies. A pre-Hamas senior police officer bashfully confessed that the clan-based gangster squads were "Gaza's primary security providers." The pyromaniacs, so to speak, were the firefighters. In 2004–5, these "unruly clans also extended involvement in lucrative businesses, such as smuggling, . . . the imposition of safe passage fees on Gaza's roads and the kidnapping of journalists" for ransom. Against a resentful set of "traditional elite families, which derived their power from a combination of status, wealth and position," a realignment of clan hierarchies ensued. Custom was superceded by criminal leverege. The result was the "ascendency of approximately ten clans" with a more pragmatic source of power: "their heavy involvement in the informal economy and ability to amass and deploy weapons." Through traditional *sunduq* funds, males over sixteen would make (semivoluntary) contributions into central clan committees, and the money was in turn channeled into illegal investments. Many Gazans began to specialize in "debt collection, arms-trading, security services, car-jacking," and general banditry.[32]

Concurrently, a generational shift replaced gray-haired, conciliatory patriarchs with young, ambitious gangsters. "It isn't the *mukhtars* who are taking the decisions, but the young thugs who have learned to form networks of family members who are forming their own centres of gravity." Traditional clan mechanisms for arbitration were replaced with vendettas, honor killings, and unmediated clan tusslings. One family—the Abu Hasanains—decided to bring a lioness from a Gaza zoo "when seeking to settle disputes." As Gaza was "atomising into factional and social anarchy," criminal infighting and street politics triumphed over separatist authority. Phone and electricity billing representatives would routinely be robbed and kidnapped. Resolving to see relatives in the hospital, one gangster modified the visiting hours by shooting a police officer in the foot. Gazan neighborhoods became "mini-fiefdoms" with families "barricading their entrances with mounds of sand and palm trunks." Israel (half pleased) "likened the mayhem to warlordism in Somalia and Iraq," while a Palestinian journalist dramatically exclaimed, "The PA [Palestinian Authority] does not exist. The clans have overrun Gaza."[33]

It was into this milieu that Hamas arrived as the national savior. The much-maligned group did not emerge in a vacuum nor a spontaneous delirium of terrorist madness. Hamas—elected democratically—brought a semblance of order and centralization to a diffuse, feuding criminal community. Violently crushing feeble clans while negotiating with tougher ones, Hamas consolidated its territorial control through its militant wing, the Izz ad-Din al-Qassam Brigades (IQB), by "rounding up rapists, car thieves, clandestine liquor merchants, money forgers, the employers of a Sri Lankan maid who has not been paid and dozens of alleged sexual miscreants. Forty drug dealers were incarcerated. Those who resisted were shot." This was their first week. Gradually, "kidnapping, car theft, drug smuggling, racketeering and the hitherto open arms market" were eliminated. Hamas prohibited vendettas, extortion roadblocks, household barricades, and celebratory firing at weddings (a national pastime). Fusing street turf battles and blunt Islamic decrees, the emerging separatist authorities eliminated rivals and subordinated major gangs—one beating at a time. (In the course of taming the unruly Dagmush clan, Hamas even persecuted one hapless romantic couple caught "not in a moral situation.") In organizing *dis*organized crime, Hamas consolidated its position as the mainstream separatist movement elites and Gaza's undisputed authorities.

This crackdown—"widely welcomed by the public"—marked the birth of what would become the most spectacular mafia in Palestinian history.[34]

Separatist tunnels are typically located in remote, isolated terrains away from civilian eyes, such as rural, mountainous, or desert areas. Instead, Palestinian tunnels were unapologetically urban—surrounded by densely populated civilian infrastructure and passing under entire neighborhoods in plain view. Most of them were dug from within civilian living rooms, bathrooms, kitchens, or backyards. Before Hamas came to power, control over the tunnels was concentrated in the hands of a "small group of smugglers" who induced homeowners to "rent their houses to tunnel traders." Initially a modest criminal operation of roughly a dozen dugouts, this budding mafia smuggled jewelry and narcotics (but no weapons) to supplement "normal" trade through Israeli-run terminals toward the West Bank and Israel proper.[35] Israel's blockade of the Gaza Strip was the best thing ever to happen to the tunnelers. Those "who sought to engage in legitimate commerce and trade [were] forced to turn to the underground economy and smuggling just to survive."[36] When Hamas replaced the Israel-preferred Fatah in 2006–7, the economic strangulation intensified. "It's like a meeting with a dietician," a host state spokesperson explained. "We need to make the Palestinians lose weight, but not to starve to death."[37]

The results were that the Palestinians did indeed starve, and organized crime flourished, both in appetite and capacity. Some 60 to 75 percent of Gazans were impoverished, and 40 percent were "food insecure."[38] Fuel shortages brought donkeys and horses back into the streets. Ninety percent of Gaza's factories were closed as unemployment soared. Thirty-four thousand out of thirty-five thousand industrial workers lost their jobs. For most, there was misery; for the aspiring gangsters, opportunity. Smugglers rose to the occasion in the southwest. Gaza borders Egypt (which also severed all ties in 2007) on the Philadelphi Corridor, a narrow strip of land fourteen kilometers long and a hundred meters wide. Rafah, a town divided by the border, is the main crossing site. Around it, criminal entrepreneurs created a spectacular grid of tunnels to smuggle food, weapons, fuel, electronics, and car parts. Dozens of tunnels became scores, and scores swelled to hundreds. In 2005, the smuggling brought in $30 million a year. By 2008, it averaged $36 million *a month*. Tunnel trafficking comprised 60 percent of Gaza's imports, and through the taxation of tunnel users and owners, a fifth of the separatists' income. On a territory where more than half the population lives in poverty, the mafia created a $650 million a year business.[39] Everyone took notice. Externally, Israel, Egypt, and the Palestinian Authority jostled over the Rafah crossing in elaborate diplomatic feuds. Internally, the smugglers were at the center of Hamas's consolidation of power. The tunnels became no less than "the lungs through which Gaza breathes."[40]

FROM CAMELS TO LICENSES

Gaza's great fortune is to border Egypt's Sinai Peninsula, a remarkable mafia zone. Gangsters on the Sinai boasted decades of smuggling experience; they "took it from camels to Land Cruisers and from trusted messengers to sophisticated handheld transceivers used to spy on police signals."[41] Originally agents of Egyptian state security, they "started establishing their own shadowy empires" with "millions of dollars to buy their freedom from the corrupt authorities."[42] Palestinian smugglers seeking partners faced an open door.[43] On the Gazan side, two Palestinian mafias ran most tunnels: the Samhadana and al-Shaer Clans. The latter successfully outmaneuvered the competition through tribal intrigues, innovative digging techniques, and violence.[44] Well before Hamas's ascendance to power, the

> cash-strapped PA [Palestinian Authority] sought to co-opt clans along the border where tunneling was easiest. Sami Abu Samhadana, a senior PA security official and prominent Fatah leader in Gaza, himself from a Bedouin clan straddling the Rafah frontier, oversaw much of the expansion. This fusion of security and business interests, of militia activity and private entrepreneurship, was to become a hallmark of future development.

On the Egyptian side, the smuggling was operated by Egyptians of Palestinian origin and Sinai Bedouins. Three Bedouin clans—the Sawarka, Ramailat, and Tarabin—diverted smuggling funds "not only to erect mansions but also to arm Bedouin defence committees."[45] From their Gazan partners, Egyptian smugglers received lists of required contraband, packaging instructions, and wire transfers through Western Union. For $30,000 to $100,000 per dig out, a tunnel paid for itself in weeks.

The tribal nature of this transnational Egypt-to-Palestine criminal network meant that separatist politics inside Israel were mirroring the Sinai-to-Gaza criminal scene. "If drug dealers and thieves are carrying RPGs in Sinai," an Egyptian specialist observed, "then you can roughly imagine what the Qassam Brigades have in their Gaza bunkers."[46] The Sinai-Gaza mafias completely inverted the hitherto separatist economy. In 1997, 99 percent of Gaza's imports came through Israel and 1 percent from Egypt; by 2007, it was the opposite.[47] Hamas governed smuggling channels through these preexisting gangs. Though "the IQB's domination of the tunnel traffic was undisputed," mafia autonomy was preserved; Hamas "never actually handled the shipments," letting smugglers assume the risk.[48] Hamas merely ordered arms and other goods, and waited for the tunnelers to deliver. In exchange for supplying Hamas with weapons, the smugglers were legitimated and empowered. Investing $80,000 to $200,000 a tunnel, the separatist authorities oversaw the construction while the IQB provided security. Preachers celebrated worker casualties as "martyrs," while Rafah municipal firefighters put out the occasional flame from fuel pumps inside the tunnels.[49] Underground trafficking became drenched in separatist emancipatory meaning: "the Hamas government encouraged residents to smuggle, presenting it as a national struggle against the Israeli blockade." Drugs, alcohol, and cigarettes were supposedly off limits according to official embargoes. But partly in a defiant display of power, the gangsters selected their imports with less piety—including the drug Tramadol, a Gazan youth favorite.[50]

The criminal empire included certifications. The Tunnel Affairs Commission—effectively a smugglers' registration office—regulated taxation, permits, rents, and digging rights. License fees for tunnel operation ran at $2,850. Fuel, cooking gas, cigarettes, and electric generators were the most highly taxed. Security personnel and patrollers on motorcycles guarded entry points, regulated merchants' squabbles, enforced price stabilization (notably of oil), and levied a 14.5 percent value-added tax on all smuggled items. Hamas itself soon acquired "a reputation for profiteering," as leading separatist figures became criminal kingpins. A jihadi purist lamented the transformation as follows: "Before entering government, Hamas acolytes focused on religious sermons and memorizing Qur'an. Now they are mostly interested in money, tunnel business and fraud. Hamas used to talk about paradise, but now they think about buying land, cars and apartments."[51] Though Israel exaggerated the scale and hazard of Sinai arms smuggling, there were undoubtedly many weapons tunneled into separatist hands as well—including Qassam, Grad, and al-Fadjr rockets.[52]

The underground trade was a breathtaking logistical achievement. Winches pulled cargo, if not electric barrels, on rails. Intercom systems allowed gangsters sitting at home to speak with tunnelers manning the merchandise. Many tunnels branched out from Gaza into two or three directions to connect multiple sites and providers on the Egyptian side. A successful smuggler could transfer cages of doves (a popular Gazan pet) in the morning, chocolates (barred by Israel) in the afternoon, and grenade launchers (for Hamas) in the evening. This enabled not only diversification but also discretion. Hamas gunners purchasing ammunition need never know that a tunnel branches out anywhere except to their weapons trafficker. A shipment of construction materials could inconspicuously "hitchhike" on a purchase of narcotics or weapons with multiple patrons who were unaware of each other's shafts. Much of the criminal profiteering therefore discretely paralleled the separatist authorities. While Hamas supposed it was using the mafia, the mafia was correspondingly using Hamas.

The smugglers' resilience surprised everyone. When Egypt began demolishing—and Israel bombing—the tunnels, "owners responded by improving their design and digging to depths of over twenty-five meters," and later, "up to forty meters." Every time a tunnel was closed, Gazans simply dug another beneath it. After Israel's Operation Cast Lead supposedly destroyed five hundred underpasses, the mafia returned stronger: "the new tunnels had increased their shipping capacity more than four times" by mid-2009.[53] When Egyptian State Security Investigations Service officers or Hamas inspectors theatrically staged raids to simulate law and order, smugglers simply bribed them. When the United States and Egypt partnered to insert a much-touted (and costly) steel barrier into the ground (ten kilometers wide and eighteen meters deep), a fifteen-year-old boy pierced through the steel wall with a blow-torch, resuming the smugglers' supply line. The youngster entered urban legend on both sides of Rafah.[54]

After Israeli demolition, it was the mafia economy that rebuilt Gaza. Some 170 metric tons of raw materials and livestock moved every day in 2010 (a ton averaged $1,200, of which $50 covered an entire tunnel worker's shift). Thousands of tons of gravel, steel, and cement were smuggled by 2011 to replace war wreckage. Soon enough, five thousand tunnel owners employed twenty-five thousand workers whose dependents constituted fully 10 percent of Gaza's population.[55] When Egypt finally managed to seal most Gazan tunnels in 2013, Cairo reported an astonishing nineteen hundred of them.[56] The tunnels had forever transformed the Palestinian movement.

The tunneling business tendered incredible social mobility. A "new generation of smugglers" replaced the Israel-oriented traders of northern Gaza. Admittedly "less educated," they "had the benefit of cross-border clan connections": a group of nouveau riche in the Gaza Strip, including tunnel owners, landowners, and tunnel traffickers linked to Hamas. In 2013, the monthly income of tunnel owners reached $50,000.[57] On the Egyptian side, "young men who once picked parsley and arugula in little farms became tunnel owners" earning hundreds of thousands of US dollars monthly.[58] Restaurants, beach cafés, and luxury hotels like the al-Mashtal arose to cater to the "new moneyed elite." The smuggling lifestyle was perilous, however. Hundreds died while countless others were injured or maimed working in the tunnels. Authorities nudged tunnel owners to offer life insurance policies ($9,000, plus another $2,000 for those leaving behind widows) along with funds for the funeral.[59] The smugglers' partners on the Egyptian side likewise transformed the very landscape of their towns. One Sinai gangster-kingpin supplying Gaza "bought a farm in the center of which he built a three-story villa with a brand-new Land Cruised parked outside."[60] One gangster inside Gaza, Abu Nafez, began as a tunnel laborer at seventeen. By age twenty-five, he owned multiple tunnels and managed over a hundred workers. Smuggling "crisps, coffee, cookers, cows, cars," he catapulted himself to the richest layer of Gazan society. From an ostentatious luxury home inside Gaza, the millionaire lamented to a BBC journalist that save for one illegal crawling into Egypt, he had never left Gaza in his life.[61]

Theocratic as it may be, Hamas managed what rival factions within the Palestinian separatist movement failed to. It centralized a chaotic criminal scene and instrumentalized it for separatist purposes. With the aid of a tunnel-smuggling rebel mafia, Gazan authorities sustained their constituency, consolidated their power, and resisted the host state.

Iraq and Syria

Daesh, or IS, was a separatist movement. To be sure, its eschatology and death cult are unusual. But its methods of controlling territory, extracting resources, and mobilizing people are stories of organized crime, not Islam. IS "is not just a terrorist organization," Michael Weiss and Hassan Hassan (2015, xv) demonstrate. "It is a mafia adept at exploiting decades-old transnational gray markets." Evolving from extortion to monopolizing a racket around the oil industry, the IS movement ultimately took the fateful leap from organized crime to state making: "The group's transition from relying on petty crime, to more sophisticated mafia-style protection rackets, to direct involvement in oil production and smuggling reflects the organization's gradual improvement in revenue collection."[62] Its final step—from a rebel mafia into statehood—remained incomplete.

PROPHETS AND PROFITS

Unlike conventional terrorist groups (like al-Qa'ida) that rely on external funding and big state patrons, IS is more akin to classic mafias (like the Sicilian Cosa Nostra) both regarding funding and population control. The most comprehensive study of IS's political economy concluded:

> As it did throughout the period of 2005 and 2010, the Islamic State today [2016] raises money through what can be characterized largely as criminal activities [such as] . . . oil-smuggling, sales of stolen goods, extortion, taxation, sales of looted antiquities, kidnapping for ransom, and even for a time taking a cut of the money that the Iraqi government sent to its employees in Islamic State territory. Donations appear to constitute only a small portion of revenues. And that is the key point: What has characterized the group throughout its history and what appears to characterize the group today is that it places a premium on local fundraising because that gives it maximum control. Local fundraising also allows the group to look more like a state. The group's taxation activities, including road tolls and export and import taxes, resemble what any state might do.[63]

A typical annual budget consisted of $750 million to $1 billion from oil smuggling; $850 million from "taxes, customs, seizures, human trafficking"; and $20 to $45 million from kidnapping and abduction ransoms. On one occasion, the annual income was $2.9 billion. In 2014, IS controlled $2 *trillion* in assets.[64] Who could acquire, let alone administer, such rackets?

In 2015, fully half of IS's fighting force were foreigners. Unlike recruited Iraqi or Syrian locals, these fighters were not paid in wages but rather in food and gasoline. The combatants' salaries were as much as 70 percent of IS's annual budget.[65] With stunning battlefield victories, these fighters were understandably romanticized. But the odd idealists among them may have obscured the emblematic gangsters. Petty theft by foot soldiers, as when a European recruit absconded with $70,000 in the middle of the battle of Sinjar, "significantly reduced ISIS's combat capabilities."[66] A prototypical IS mafia, the Liwa Allah Akbar stationed in the Syrian war, was led by Saddam al-Jamal. His "checkered criminal history as an arms and drugs trafficker" along with the "mentality of a Mafioso" earned him renown among allies and enemies alike. Initially a commander for the Western-backed Free Syrian Army, al-Jamal defected to IS in late 2013 via a stirring YouTube epiphany in which he rediscovered Islam and crowed against "infidels." Ideologically flexible, the men of Liwa Allah Akbar "follow him because they are rewarded with loot, women and cash." Such formations were ubiquitous, often realigning multiple times with several sides of the Syrian Civil War.[67]

IS fighters drew significantly from a network of ex-convicts. In the post-Hussein period, "between 75,000 and 100,000 serious criminals" were released from prisons. "Industrial-strength" criminal gangs, as one political scientist titled them, were available for co-optation in a "culture of lawlessness" and "impunity."[68] As for rank-and-file fighters from abroad, criminal background was a better predictor of European IS recruits than ethnoreligious niceties. "Micro-financing the Caliphate," recruits from Europe have "relied on drug trafficking" insofar as "proceeds garnered from peddling narcotics affords jihadists in Europe the financial flexibility to travel back and forth" to the front lines.[69] Commander ranks included a reputed drug dealer and embezzler who pocketed $5 million worth of cotton. In biography after biography, the typical leader's "gangland past clearly influence[d his] career as a terrorist warlord."[70] This was natural, since IS heads were recruited precisely from such a milieu: "In prisons, where jihadi inmates were not segregated, they were able to socialize and make connections with other people from the underground world like drug traders, weapon traders and smugglers. These contacts also proved useful later when armed groups needed weapons or smuggling services."[71] Alongside fundamentalists and ex-Baathists, "former criminals" (mostly illiterate) in US prisons in Iraq were radicalized by future IS leaders, who were "systematically organizing" them during detention.[72]

Accordingly, at the heart of IS's separatism was its "criminalized war economy and extortion."[73] Millions were extracted through *zakat*, various Islamic customary alms and payments on livestock, precious metals, electronics, crops, and savings. As early as 2006—a decade before its heyday—it accumulated $70 to $200 million yearly through shakedowns. Even before the momentous takeover of Mosul, extortion alone was bringing in $8 million a month "levying taxes on everybody from vegetable sellers in the market to mobile phone and construction companies." Restaurant goers would carefully avoid eateries that had not paid their racket dues, "lest the place be bombed while they were dining."[74] In a single day in 2008 in Mosul, IS extorted $50,000 from a local firm commissioned to pave roads and $100,000 from a contractor implementing a water project. Later that week, it collected the first chunk ($160,000) out of a $200,000 monthly extortion fee from a cell phone operator.[75] In sum, $12 million a month were prized out of this city alone.[76] Bank robbery was the natural progression. Seizing Mosul, IS looted $429 million from the city's Central Bank. By 2013, it withdrew over $1 billion in cash money from bank safes and deposits.[77]

Kidnappings of foreigners (a few dozen in total) were a relatively minor source of IS funding. IS gangsters recognized that European governments' ransom payments were an unreliable source of cash flow.[78] Hostages were a political, not financial, investment.[79] Notwithstanding, even this racket put most separatist treasuries to shame. When refugee movement into Europe escalated in 2015, the taxing of human trafficking into Turkey brought $500,000 daily—exceeding even oil smuggling profits. In a "very, very clever plan" in 2014 to release hostages to European governments (which paid discretely, "without anybody noticing it"), many "ISIS negotiators pocketed large sums of money in total secrecy." The estimated profit was £60 to £100 million.[80]

Finally, significant rackets emerged from the plundering of sites such as the Mosul Museum. Much attention has been paid to the nihilistic destruction of ancient tombs and UNESCO-protected cultural goods, but IS did more than that. It peddled hundreds of millions of US dollars in looted arts and antiquities to Jordanian and Turkish smugglers. It even encouraged civilians to ransack dozens of archaeological sites and sell off artifacts—for a modest 20 percent tax. As it vandalized humanity's oldest tablets and manuscripts in the name of wiping out idolatry, IS also overcame the finer points of its Wahhabism to do exactly what art smugglers in war have always done: profiteer. As if these revenue sources were not enough, IS's most precious racket was in black gold.

OILING MAFIA ORDER

Saddam Hussein's oil-smuggling empire was quite an inheritance.[81] The March 2003 invasion of Iraq "bolstered opportunities not only for the existing mafia but also for new criminal gangs." Fuel smuggling cost Iraq $2.5 to $4 billion in a single year. One Iraqi oil minister warned that the "oil and fuel smuggling networks have grown into a dangerous mafia."[82] The two key provinces were Anbar (with a "historical smuggling economy") and Ninewa (a "strategic hub for smuggling fighters, weapons, money").[83] As it happens, these were the heartland territories of IS separatist jurisdiction.[84] A US intelligence analyst concluded that "the Saddamists who were smuggling the oil in the '90s, to evade UN sanctions, are now doing so for ISIS."[85] Techniques for securing smuggling routes ranged from mining around paths to recruiting local village shepherds as lookouts. Specialists were duly compensated; the most attractive salaries were reserved for engineers operating the oil fields—not fighters or propagandists.[86]

By 2014, IS controlled 13 major oil fields and 300 to 350 oil wells in Iraq alone, enabling the sale of 50,000 to 60,000 barrels of oil a day. In Syria, it controlled another 160 gas and oil fields. Before 2010, oil smuggling brought IS in Iraq an estimated $200 million annually. In mid-2015, the daily oil revenues were $1.3 million, while extortion/taxation revenues were $1 million. When lucky, IS averaged $3 million a day from oil smuggling alone.[87] In a tragically blinkered policy, regional forces did much to strengthen IS smugglers, thinking they could be controlled. Mindlessly supplying arms and other resources to Iraqi and Syrian minions, Saudi Arabia, Turkey, and Jordan came to "be frightened by the Frankenstein's monster they have helped to create." Given the rebel mafia at play, there was "little they c[ould] do to restrain it."[88]

Seizing separatist land is one matter, but sustaining control over a territory the size of the United Kingdom with 2.8 to 5.3 million people is an onerous task. How did IS manage it? Despite its reputation, IS "established a semblance of order in these 'governed' territories." Separatist successes included cleaner streets, cheaper bakeries, effective price controls, repaired electricity lines, fewer checkpoints, newly paved roads, and—the US reader will appreciate—"consumer protection." Above all, many "flocked in large number to join the jihadist group" because "ISIS provided safety and security."[89] Whereas most insurgencies eschew administrative work for civilians, IS "seemed to relish providing services": "When it took control of an area, ISIS wasted no time outfitting police cars, ambulances, and bureaucracies with its ubiquitous black flag emblem. ISIS put traffic cops at intersections; in addition to its law enforcement and consumer protection bureaus, it opened a complaints desk and nursing homes. Its members radiated enthusiasm for those projects."[90]

Furthermore, IS's Sunni base was critical to its meteoric rise—prompting analysts to describe the separatist insurgency as a "new Sunni revolution." For the population under its control, "the ability to live without crime and lawlessness trumps whatever draconian rules ISIS has put into place." After taking a piece of territory, IS "shows zero tolerance for any rivalry or public display of weapons. It immediately disarms the local communities, primarily of heavy weapons." From fratricidal sectarian violence, the "situation changed 180 degrees when ISIS came in."[91] In Syria especially, many Sunni villages welcomed IS as an alternative to "many other rebel groups that are halfway to being bandits." In Iraq, "smuggling, kidnapping, extortion and other criminal activities" that brought the separatist movement its territorial reach "set [IS] at odds with local tribes, pre-existing local militias, and criminal organizations."[92] Its solution was direct: IS "resorted to killing jihadists who didn't join I.S. [in Iraq] to take over [its] operational turf. It was rather like a mafia turf war."[93]

But brute force only went so far. "It would be misleading to argue that ISIS could have secured allegiance by sheer domination," Fawaz Gerges (2016, 196–97) concludes. Equally important was the diversion of funds from "smuggling, looting, drug trading, trafficking in cultural artifacts, corruption at border controls and checkpoints and, of course, oil" toward tribal patronage networks in exchange for their loyalty. Oil revenues purchased considerable devotion. Sometimes, as with the Albu Ezzedine tribe, the offer of a rewarding smuggling deal converted allegiances from rivals like al-Nusra. Another tribal leader, who was co-opted with a share from an oil well, got the proverbial irresistible offer: "They gave him money, they protect him and consult with him on everything. The other option is, they would assassinate him."[94]

Concurrently, IS was a community mediator. With nearly two dozen courts, ten police stations, and twenty-two "sharia institutes," IS successfully reconciled recalcitrant tribes that had been at each other's throats for decades, such as the al-Hassoun and al-Rehabiyeen. Appointing an emir official administrator of "tribal affairs," IS organized meetings among clans, formed arbitration commissions, and entertained envoys' complaints through a ritualized adjudication process. In villages with tribal friction, it sent foreign jihadists as impartial peacekeepers. Indeed, IS branded itself as no less than the "paramount conflict resolver."[95] It was these processes, which Weiss and Hassan (2015, 200–210) memorably termed the "Shakedown of the Sheiks," that sustained IS territorial control—not beheadings, black flags, or cybersermons. "As long as ISIS continues to diversify its criminalized war economy and replenish its coffers," Gerges (2016, 269) noted, "it will strengthen its governance capacity."[96]

IS's state-building ambitions were real. Striving to transition its rebel mafia into a state, it made considerable steps toward governance. Within the jihadi spectrum, IS was the first to enact a separatist vision through the seizure and administration of territory with an emphasis on self-sufficiency through domestic rackets. Unlike al-Qa'ida's vanguard revolutionary utopianism, trying to spark uprising and "awaken the sleeping masses" through terrorism, the separatists "followed the model of a functional—if limited—government."[97]

Yemen

The Arabian Peninsula's only republic descended into a ruinous civil war (2015–present). It came in the aftermath of the withdrawal of President Ali Abdallah Saleh, whose rule over a patrimonial and fractured—but formally unified—Yemen ended in 2012. The al-Houthi rebellion, led by Zaidi Shia Houthis, fought a bitter war against the regime (2004–10), only to ally with Saleh against a Saudi-backed coalition in the 2010s. The Houthi separatists based in the northern city of Sa'dah overwhelmed the unificationist forces, in no small measure because of a state dependent but impartial mafia massively selling arms with little regard for sectarian, tribal, or regionalist causes. Intriguingly unbiased, Yemen's Minderbinder mafia in the north was a formidable force in the country's disintegration.[98]

QAT AND ARMS RACKETS

Saleh ran a patrimonial governance model that addressed every disturbance by co-opting a few disturbers. Yemeni unity depended on oil revenues (three-quarters of the state's operating budget) to purchase loyalty through patronage networks. "For centuries," after all, "tribal politics in Yemen have been driven by one simple concept: loyalty is sold to the highest bidder."[99] The Houthi rebellion made it painfully salient that the host state was no longer the highest bidder. "Salih had tried," to be sure, "his old magic with promises and gifts and flattery and dividing and ruling and compromise, but it had failed."[100] Instead, mafias were able to bid high on loyalty—by dominating two critical rackets.

First, fueling tribal narco-mafias was a national addiction to qat, a shrub leaf stimulant. The average Yemeni household spends 10 percent of its budget on the drug, while 70 percent report at least one user. A staple of the lifestyle, qat "has long been as emblematic of Yemeni culture as the wearing of the *jambiyah* or the *futa*" that Orientalist travelers through the ages found so fetching.[101] The narcotic market is vital for the formal—let alone shadow—economy. Before war, it constituted fully one-third of Yemen's agricultural GDP. A half-million people (one in seven Yemenis) were involved in its cultivation and trade. Qat employed more people than the entire public sector. While the country imported food, mafias smuggled the hardy cash crop into Saudi Arabia and Somalia "using patronage networks that work together to bypass export and import taxes."[102]

As the world's leading net consumer of the drug, Yemen collected $20 to $25 million annually through checkpoint taxes on dealers on their way to markets. But this was a fraction of the total; an (optimistic) finance minister estimated that barely 20 percent of the ostensible qat tax is ever collected. In addition to the legal trade "controlled by syndicates who buy qat from the farmers and then distribute to a network of dealers and middlemen," the illegal (i.e., mafia) market exporting to Saudi Arabia yields untaxed revenues of up to $30 million yearly. If we include Somalia, the other major customer, qat demand fuels a $50 million annual criminal profit.[103] To safeguard this market, tribal gangs grew the suitable violent capacity: "Many of the highland villages, home to some of the most powerful tribes, are now largely dependent on the money generated by the sale of qat. These villages and communities function as mini-states and often possess arsenals worthy of mini-states."[104] Complementing these private armories are folk legends about their owners. Sordid "tales of tribesmen resisting qat taxation in much the same way their forbearers had resisted the Ottomans' tax farmers" have deterred government agents for years. One luckless expedition to establish a checkpoint resulted in six kidnapped soldiers, stolen vehicles, and a humiliated army commander.[105] Conveniently for separatism, the illicit qat imports into Saudi Arabia come from the western districts of the Sa'dah province, the home of the Houthi rebellion.

Qat was not the only locus of mafia autonomy. Among a population of twenty million, Yemen has sixty million guns.[106] Carrying an AK-47 to eateries, dances, weddings, or business meetings is altogether normal. "Just as you have your tie, the Yemeni will carry his gun." Manhood, honor, generosity, and other norms are infused into the gun culture, including training prepubescent boys to use Kalashnikovs. "Just to feel important," businessmen hire entourages brandishing weapons to avoid embarrassment at meetings; twenty gunmen go for $1,000. Traditions regulating mediation and exchange—such as the customary surrender of weapons to a neutral third party when negotiating in good faith or gift of an automatic rifle to solidify a partnership—define familial and tribal autonomies, obligations, and reputations.[107]

As Yemen does not produce small arms, weapons smuggling under the patronage of Saleh created a mafia of "hand-picked strongmen, supplied by obliging dealers, who were motivated by their own entrenched financial interests, operating in close proximity to international black markets." Formally, the government issued gun-import permits (End User Certificates) for official Ministry of Defense purchases. Informally, gangster transporters and distributors struck deals of their own, amassed wealth through kickbacks, and stocked up on weaponry—light and heavy. Saleh's army invented increasingly creative ways to resell guns and military equipment to domestic and foreign arms smugglers; for instance, phony stockpile explosions and spontaneous combustions at arms warehouses concealed massive black market trade.[108]

In due course, the central government began to lose control of the mafias it midwifed, as regional tribal bosses jealously protected their arms trade. The state was understandably "wary enough of [tribal] influence not to attempt radical intervention into tribal arms smuggling." At the turn of the century, it attempted an arms buyback program—to no avail. While the ban on gun toting in major cities was effective in Aden, Taiz, and Sana'a itself, the separatist tribal Marib and al-Hazm remained heavily furnished. Others took the disarmament as an occasion for *re*armament.[109]

The world's greatest gun bazaar arose: the Suq al-Talh. The breezy, jovial marketplace blasted music over hundreds of booths mixing household items with automatic weapons. Popular affordable handguns were only the market staple. For the casual purchaser, there were also hand grenades, AK-47s, and G-3 rifles; for the more discerning customer, there were cannons, rocket-propelled grenade launchers, and antitank mines. Even after its supposed closure, "merchants [in Suq al-Talh] continued to sell to the Huthis just before and in the opening stages of conflict." In Marib, crackdown attempts were farcical. Gunrunners were blocked from bringing cargo into the city. To avenge the insult, they attacked government buildings and checkpoints in clashes that the police could not sustain. The result was another disgraceful compromise: on "some days weapons are permitted past checkpoints while on others the law is enforced."[110] Additional open-air weapons bazaars sprouted up in al-Bayda, al-Jihanah, and the surrounding towns. Around these superstores, in turn, hundreds of small peddlers' shops brandished cheap Kalashnikovs alongside grapes and pomegranates. Though these vendors were only loosely affiliated, their retail providers were a centralized mafia rooted in the Yemeni north.

THE MANA CLAN

The single most important feature of the arms traffic was its *localization* in the northern Sa'dah governorate region. Flanking Saudi Arabia, the province has historically been fertile mafia terrain. Inhabitants of either the same tribes or tribal confederations populate both sides of the border. Residents of the Yemeni-Saudi borderland were allowed to move freely without visas within a twenty-kilometer corridor around the official frontier—a right bestowed by two historic agreements, the Treaty of Ta'if (1934) and Treaty of Jeddah (2000). Smuggling in the province is a way of life. Between a third and a half of the adult population rely on transborder trade ranging from gray (flour, electronics, diesel, and cattle) to black (guns, qat, drugs, and liquor). "Cognitively," Ginny Hill (2017, 191) notes, "there's no demarcation between border communities. They are kith and kin, and they've been trading among themselves for centuries." Smugglers often fight to the death to protect their rackets, staging lethal shooting sprees to avoid the consequence of capture: Saudi Arabia beheads convicted traffickers. Altogether, it is "almost impossible to control the lucrative transfer of contraband across the border"—a fifteen-hundred-kilometer desert frontier.[111]

Adjacent to Saudi Arabia, Sa'dah is geographically endowed to be an organized criminal hub. Its roads and wadis are opportunely positioned to traffic everything from assault rifles and mortars to bullets and knives. There is no shortage of supply either: Yemen and its northern neighbor are among the world's leading arms recipients. In 2001–6, Yemen imported $1.8 billion worth of arms from the United States in 1990 prices; Saudi Arabia imported $17.8 billion worth. In 2017, the United States signed an arms trade deal with the Saudis for $110 billion.[112] Among civilians, by far the greatest concentration of weapons—especially in the hands of sixteen- to forty-four-year-old males—is in Sa'dah, Amran, Jawf, and other separatist "conflict governorates." Strikingly, even arms imports through the port of Aden (in the country's south) do not remain in the south. Rather, they "proceed both through [government] hands into tribal possession and directly into the stocks of tribes in the north."[113] In sum, the north's status as epicenter of Yemeni arms rackets was undisputed.

The arms-smuggling mafia fatefully perpetuated the Sa'ada War (2004–10) between the Houthi insurgency and government.[114] Against the will of both warring sides, indiscriminate weapons smuggling armed both parties, conspicuously prolonging the war. While some partisan sheikhs carefully trafficked weapons to their preferred side, the bulk of the profiteering was at the expense of any progress by *either* Houthi *or* government forces. Mafia operatives within the Yemeni army were major providers of arms and ammunition to Houthi leaders.[115] The military was literally arming its own enemy:

> The most notable feature of the war economy was the role of weapons trafficking inside the military. Army leaders demanded additional weapons from their superiors to fight the insurgents, but diverted a significant proportion to regional markets. . . . Paradoxically, many weapons then ended up in the hands of the rebels they were intended to combat. Saada [the separatists' base] was also a regional smuggling hub where drug mules, arms smugglers and human traffickers plied their lucrative trade across the porous mountain frontier, shifting contraband goods from Yemen to Saudi. Competition to control the border trade was another factor that was said to drive the conflict and lay among the war's unspoken stakes.[116]

Initially, the mafia expected a single, hasty fire sale; "dealers seem to have felt that the confrontation would be short-lived, making it worthwhile to sell weapons early on in great quantities." But they were more fortunate than that. The conflict not only escalated, but the gun-rich stockpiles of the region were in the hands of tribes with fickle allegiances. "Tribes have not remained consistent in their loyalties," so that "regime-friendly tribes" routinely sell and resell weapons the government gives them to "later be used against the [government] when tribes or subgroups switch loyalties."[117] With every switch, the gunrunners rose in power and stature.

What criminal masterminds could run such an extravaganza from within the state? Faris Mana, from a distinguished family with notable figures in politics before and after unification, was raised to be a national dignitary. Instead, he became "one of the most prominent arms dealers in the Middle East," not to mention "by far the most popular member of this family," which boasted intellectual icons, war heroes, and tribal figureheads. He created the Suq al-Talh as a smuggling hub connecting China, Iran, East Africa, and Eastern Europe to the domestic weapons market. In the 1990s, President Saleh sought to incorporate Mana into the government's orbit, commissioning him to equip and arm the Yemeni military. In exchange, the Mana Clan built "a private army of tribal warriors at the state's expense" to safeguard its arms depot in al-Talh and the family's supply lines in the province.[118]

Mana's fully opportunistic, unpatriotic policy was paradigmatic of Yemeni arms traffickers: "supplying both sides in the war."[119] The Mana Clan artfully built enough government bridges to sustain the renegade racket, but kept Mana's network clear of political entanglements: "Faris Mana never belonged to a political party. Indeed, most 'big' traders of the Sa'dah region have tried to maintain more or less neutral positions in times of both peace and war. During the Sa'dah Wars, they apparently made good bargains with all parties to the conflict—hence they were keen in their aftermath to maintain good relations with everyone." Hence the "paradox of Faris Mana": his arm trade having "played an essential role in arming the local population," he then ostensibly "mediated in a war whose weapons he had made available."[120] Houthi rebels as well as the government sought his help during impasses. The host state oscillated between appointing him chair of the Presidential Mediation Commission and blacklisting him for running Chinese arms to rebels—all in a single year. As a (quasi-official) statesman, he negotiated hostage releases and brokered cease-fires. As an (indispensable) gangster, he was furnishing weapons to the combatants he was supposedly pacifying.

Occasionally he went too far. In 2007, the government broke off relations with the Mana Clan when the mafia apparently took money from Gaddafi's Libya to stir rebellion in northern Yemen. In 2010, the United Nations passed a resolution freezing Mana's assets when he was caught arming al-Qa'ida affiliate al-Shabab in Somalia. When he apparently allowed Houthis to raid his main weapons depot and abscond with a substantial stockpile, the government turned its artillery to his private properties in revenge. Arrested in 2010, the gangster was unfathomably resurrected yet again: "he rose from the ashes" to become a separatist statesman in Houthi-controlled Sa'dah.[121] In 2011, he was appointed governor of the Sa'adah governorate. In 2017, he became a prominent minister in the Government of National Salvation. Saleh, Mana's hitherto mortal enemy who imprisoned him for war profiteering with the Houthis, was now in a coalition with him. Yemen's fate aside, at least this remarkable friendship enjoyed "salvation" until Saleh's death in December 2017.

For all its failures, Yemen is an organized criminal nucleus of the South Arabia / Gulf of Aden region.[122] By fueling the Houthi separatist conflict, the impartial Mana Clan's narcotics and arms rackets—deeply rooted in the state apparatus—prolonged war and stifled victory on both sides. An insider captured this Minderbinder mafia best: "a lot of shady deals," Marieke Brandt (2017, 210) marveled. "Someone should make a movie, honestly."

8

Eastern Europe

Everybody has accused me of war profiteering. But who else would have been able to bring these goods into [separatist] Bihać? Who else would have been able to break the blockade? We need to be creative in our fight for freedom. Let's cut deals; it's better than fighting.

—FIKRET ABDIĆ ON HIS RACKET DURING THE BOSNIAN WAR,
"PEACE OPERATIONS AND ILLICIT BUSINESS IN BOSNIA"

Discussing the criminal records of certain people who are my partners now is offensive to me. One should not be reminded of sins committed in youth. . . . Now, they are great statesmen.

—EDWARD SHEVARDNADZE ON GANGSTERS TENGIZ KITOVANI AND DZHABA IOSELIANI BEFORE THEY ATTEMPT TO KILL HIM, *WARLORDS AND COALITION POLITICS IN POST-SOVIET STATES*

The collapses of the USSR and Yugoslavia have produced separatist movements across Eastern Europe. Some secessionists triumphed, others stagnated in "frozen conflicts," and still others descended into protracted bloodshed. The remnant societies that emerged were built not *on* but *with* the ruins of socialism.[1] For states and wannabe states alike, organized crime—with its rogue gallery of gangster brokers, entrepreneurs, and warlords—was integral to making and unmaking nations. "Warfare in postcommunist countries had two main dimensions," scholars observed: "mafia and ethnic conflict."[2] The latter can be overstated.

Bosnia-Herzegovina

The Bosnian War (1992–95) is remembered as a cacophony of ethnochauvinism—a gloomy reminder of the impossibility of Serbian, Croatian, and Bosniak cooperation.[3] But closer analyses portray a surprising alternative: multiethnic organized crime was a critical factor in the conflict, trumping nationalist agendas left and right.[4] The supposed "convulsive surging of ancient hatreds or frenzies whipped up by demagogic politicians" was less exotic on the ground: "small—sometimes very small—bands of opportunistic marauders."[5] Much of the criminality was highly organized, constituting a multiethnic and impartial "Yugo-underground" (*Jugo-podzemlje*) of state dependent smugglers, mercenaries, and war profiteers.[6] This Minderbinder mafia—the Yugo mafia, I will call it—was at the heart of the torn state that emerged as Bosnia-Herzegovina.[7]

FRATERNIZING WITH THE ENEMY

Organized crime did not cause the Bosnian War, but it did profoundly influence its outbreak, duration, outcome, and aftermath.[8] On the territory of Bosnia-Herzegovina, three (Serbian, Croatian, and Bosniak) separate armies (the Army of the Republika Srpska, Croatian Defence Council, and Army of the Republic of Bosnia-Herzegovina) and three distinct police forces (Ministries of Internal Affairs of Republic of Bosnia and Herzegovina, Croatian Community of Herzeg-Bosnia, and Republika Srpska) mingled with a plethora of international peacekeeping units and humanitarian organizations. None were immune from the Yugo mafia.[9] An estimated eighty-three irregular formations, supposedly representing nationalist uprisings of one side or another, amounted to "paramilitary criminal groups" masking their rackets in patriotism. "The interesting element," Sheelagh Brady (2012, 14) notes, "was that many of these feuding groups cooperated across enemy lines." The "mafia economy was built into the conduct of warfare," Mary Kaldor (2013, 56) adds, "creating a self-sustaining logic to the war both to maintain lucrative sources of income and to protect criminals from legal processes which might come into effect in peacetime."[10]

The 1,425-day siege of Sarajevo—three times the duration of the battle of Stalingrad—surprised all parties with its continuation. The stalemate was partly due to figures like Ramiz "Ćelo" Delalić ("former mob boss, racketeer and underworld thug"; a convicted rapist, but an outstanding guerrilla), and Jusuf "Juka" Prazina ("famous for his skilled use of the *čakija*," a traditional knife). On the one hand, by circumventing the weapons embargo to arm Bosniak forces, the gangsters stifled Belgrade's hopes of a quick victory.[11] On the other hand, they drained the Bosniak constituency that they were protecting, undermining "their" side's morale and military prowess.[12] Lording over the formal combatants, Sarajevo gangs were described by a resigned major as follows:

> We have at least 150 mafia guys who drive unregistered Volkswagens. They wear uniforms, carry pistols and the most contemporary weapons, [sun]glasses, walk around, and no one dares engage them. They steal, walk, kill, engage in black market operations, etc. No one dares mobilise them. That's linked to mafia from [surrounding villages], and we all fear them.[13]

The Bosniaks were unexceptional. After underwhelming conscription drives and organizational breakdowns in 1991–92, the Serbian-led Yugoslav army scrambled to form irregular gangster units: "common criminals recruited for the task" with the inviting injunction to "take whatever booty you can."[14] Chronically defying military directives, the paramilitary and parapolice forces were "led mainly by criminals engaging in organized crime" instead of strategic operation.[15]

By one estimate, Serbian "warlord units" were 80 percent "common criminals" and 20 percent "fanatical nationalists"—a ratio that increased as the latter realized that "fanaticism is bad for business." As the war progressed, the idealists reoriented "mainly to rob and pillage, enriching themselves in the process." The gangs ran the gamut from the Spare Ribs—who roamed the town of Bosanski Novi, where they were "a well-known local mafia" that devoured civilian houses in free-range looting—to serious gangster squadrons like Arkan's Tigers.[16] Not to be outdone, Croatia also recruited from the criminal echelons. Gangster turned patriot Siniša "Rambo" Dvorski fought for independent Croatia, but did not revel in it for long. Within a year of independence, he murdered the minister of tourism and returned to jail for a prolonged sentence. Another, nicknamed "Tuta," was a "former protection racketeer" who ran clubs, casinos, and rackets before establishing a convicts battalion.[17] Across ethnic rifts, many gangsters were business partners and friends.

As a UN observer tersely wrote, the war was dictated by "gunslingers, thugs and essentially criminals."[18] To be sure, deploying gangsters instead of drafted soldiers (or even noncriminal mercenaries) was effective at bolstering bandit mystiques and multiplying war crimes.[19] For winning wars, however, it turned out to be disastrous. Bosniak, Serbian, and Croatian authorities alike were paralyzed by defections, duplicities, and sheer waste on the part of the criminal clients they empowered. As frontline gatekeepers, smugglers diverted resources (international humanitarian aid, arms shipments from allies, and fuel supplies from Sarajevo, Belgrade, or Zagreb) away from their intended destinations. Cross-ethnic smuggling, looting, and reselling of war matériel became rampant. Memoirs of commanders on all three sides are saturated with accounts of missions sabotaged by unpatriotic criminals who shamelessly traded with the enemy. Rackets in precious cargo effortlessly transcended ethnic lines:

> Following the price distortion of civil goods and the establishment of enclaves, black markets flourished, and the protagonists cooperated regularly to control lucrative trafficking. Although the Croats blockaded Moslem territory in 1993–1994, racketeers in [Serbian] Banja Luka and Zenica established an exchange of key goods via Mt. Vlasic. Croat entrepreneurs also sent fuel to Serbs in exchange for weapons and the humane treatment of their kin in Central Bosnia. . . . The Sarajevo police chief accused a tri-ethnic mafia of deliberately prolonging the siege to profit from the black market. . . . Disaggregation of communities from April 1993 to February 1994 marked the peak of predatory activity. But uneven economic distribution was a decisive factor in causing ruptures between profiteers and "regular" military units in each community and weakening morale in the Srpska and Bosniak armies.[20]

Some rackets were relatively innocent. The Yugo mafia flogged the commodity on which all wars are sustained: cigarettes (under shelling, they went for as much as a hundred deutsche marks per pack). For five hundred to a thousand deutsche marks, refugees were offered one-way northward trips across Serbia into Europe or boat rides across the Sava River into Croatia.[21] Deserters of all stripes had little difficulty withdrawing from the front lines—especially if they bartered their departure for war booty.

Arms were another matter, though. Nonwarring parties arming each other was to be expected. A patriot could understand that Slovenia, which ended its war for Yugoslav secession early (July 1991), smuggled weapons to Croatia's prolonged liberation struggle.[22] But the intensity of gunrunning *between* warring parties was a sight to behold. Fully 30 percent of the arms supplied by international benefactors to the Bosnian Muslims was diverted to Croatian forces during the bloodshed.[23] The reason was simple: the Yugo mafia was an impartial trader, constantly "sustaining the war by trading with the enemy"—whoever that may have been.[24] The more besieged a given enclave—whether Sarajevo, Bihać, or Srebrenica—the greater the need for interethnic trade. "Those in the right positions," within military structures, "quickly discovered a lucrative opportunity to trade with the enemy, and hundreds of millions of Deutschemarks' worth of weaponry, ammunition, fuel, and goods were exchanged across the front lines."[25]

Ultimately, even the conclusion of warfare was partly induced by the Yugo mafia. Diplomatic options were imposed on all (unwilling) sides by autonomous criminal gangs that had sabotaged further progress on the battlefield. "Contradictions inherent in prosecuting a war on the basis of criminal and predatory economies played a part in forcing the parties towards Dayton," the 1995 peace accord.[26]

"RENT-A-TANK" LIABILITIES

The Yugo mafia was thoroughly embedded in formal military and political institutions. But enemy-of-my-enemy rationales made its arms trade defiantly polycentric and multiethnic. Throughout the war, the notorious Prvi Partizan munitions factory in Užice, Serbia—a state enterprise headed by a Milošević cadre—smuggled over ninety-four tons of munition to Croatian and Bosniak forces.[27] The Bosniak defense minister struck a deal with the Serbian security apparatus to allow shipments through Bosnia to Serbian positions in Croatia, where Serbian forces were fighting a common foe. In return, "the secret service deflected some of the weapons to Bosnian Muslim [*sic*] army-in-the-making." On one occasion, the minister personally intervened to override a police interdiction of three trucks with over a thousand automatic rifles on their way to east Bosnia—in a "misunderstanding."[28] In effect, Serbian forces were arming their own separatist archenemy, while Bosniak forces were sustaining Serbian militias.

On the same principle, four Hawk (*Jastreb*) jets—for a price—took off from the airport of the Serbian separatist Republika Srpska Krajina, on behalf of the Croatian side, to strike at a Bosniak arms factory in Travnjak. With even less nationalist prejudice, Croatian petroleum smugglers sold fuel to a Bosnian Serb assemblyman; he, in turn, sold it to Serbian gangsters fighting Croatian forces; and they, in turn, supplied the original Croatian smugglers—all mortal enemies, all making millions. One senior military figure from the Bosnian Serbian ranks sold heavy artillery to Bosniak forces before retiring to a country home away from the front lines (an ignominy that Serbian nationalists continue to rail about). The Bosnian army, meanwhile, paid Croatian forces to shell Serbs with artillery in a three-way clash in Mostar. The next year, it was vice versa; it gave twenty thousand deutsche marks to Serbian forces to turn their artillery on the Croatians.[29] The Yugo mafia even created a thriving "rent-a-tank" business. For a thousand deutsche marks a day, Croats and Serbs repeatedly leased tanks to and fro to kill each other's outfits. "Whether they had to pay extra for insurance," John Mueller (2000, 58) wryly noted, "is not recorded."

In western Bosnia, smugglers staged a veritable miracle of military history. The Bosnian Fifth Corpus sustained itself—impossibly—for three full years (1992–95) *completely* encircled. On one side was the Republika Srpska army, and on the other, was the Army of Serbian Krajina. Isolated and outnumbered, the Fifth Corpus ought to have been massacred. Instead, the Bosniaks received regular shipments of ammunition, grenades, fuel, and food—all courtesy of the Yugo mafia, not Sarajevo. Tens of millions of deutsche marks were estimated to be made monthly. War profiteers celebrated their "first million" in Knin, Banja Luka, and other Serbian centers of anti-Bosniak operation—the very localities leading the charge against the Fifth Corpus. In a final irony, firsthand observers reported that the United Nations Protection Force, the international presence at the time, was also complicit.[30]

The most successful smuggler of the Bosnian War created nothing less than his own country. Fikret Abdić, a convicted fraudster who was jailed on corruption charges and sought by multiple European governments for embezzlement, operated the most successful mafia in Bosnia-Herzegovina. Based in the western town of Bihać, he founded a short-lived separatist state of his own: the Autonomous Province of Western Bosnia. From September 1993 to August 1995, this separatist enclave—known as the Bihać Pocket—sustained itself cordoned on all sides by overwhelming forces out to overrun it.

The secret to his success? "The survival of Bihać," Andreas (2011, 37) explains, "is inexplicable without taking into account black-market exchanges that transcended ethnic divisions." Not only did Abdić fight his coethnic Bosnian Muslims and resist Bosniak authorities in Sarajevo. He also mastered rackets in food, gasoline, cigarettes, weapons, and humanitarian aid amid Serbian, Croatian, Bosniak, and international partners (many of whom were eager to see him dead—and had the wherewithal to ensure it). Having created "his private fiefdom," Abdić secured "lucrative trade agreements with all sides."[31] To Serbian forces in Croatia, he sold food; to Croatian forces in Bosnia, it was fuel. With contiguous access to Croatia and no oil embargo, Abdić's mafia statelet imported fuel legally under UN auspices before smuggling it onward to various partners in Bosnia.

Colluding with a French UN peacekeeping battalion, he established a black market monopoly for his private company, Agrokomerc, to be the sole provider and distributor of food and other aid into the province. From a modest four hundred tons, his enterprise grew to over twenty-three hundred tons of food supplies a week—"more than three times the amount of aid delivered by the UNHCR [United Nations High Commissioner for Refugees]."[32] Within Bihać, criminal elites around Agrokomerc feathered their nests and legitimated rackets as statecraft. In front of foreign journalists, gangs sported flags, emblems, and other nationalist paraphernalia aimed at convincing the gullible. Abdić's metamorphosis from gangster to statesman called for difficult personnel decisions. For instance, he appointed his most trusted smuggler, a truck driver from Tuscany, as foreign minister—surely the greatest promotion in the annals of trucker history.[33]

Abdić's chief spokesperson was perfectly forthright about the purpose of the Autonomous Province of Western Bosnia: "We see ourselves as the Cayman Islands of the Balkans, we are interested in business, finance, making money."[34] Routinely condemned as a traitor from multiple quarters, this unprejudiced mafia was the lifeline for a separatist enclave in impossible conditions. Its governance, furthermore, managed an improbable impartiality in the midst of ethnic carnage. "Abdić's racket thrived because it was expedient for all concerned," Andreas (2011, 38) noted. "Serbs and Croats got money to buy arms to use on each other (and on Muslims elsewhere in Bosnia), while the UN got a safe area success story."

Bosniak, Serbian, and Croatian ambitions were—for better or worse—structurally constrained by a formidable Minderbinder mafia. Systematic, military-embedded war profiteering in Bosnia-Herzegovina was a paradigmatic case of unbiased organized crime. Michael Pugh (2003, 58) encapsulated the Yugo mafia's impartiality as follows: "Unlike the nationalist politicians, the mafias parody the ideals of multi-ethnicity that have been vaunted by international protectors. The mafias trade with any ethnic group to protect and further their empires." From within state and quasi-state structures, organized crime impaired nationalist projects across the board.

Macedonia

"Macedonia is a nice little country," a US ambassador to Skopje stated, "in a high crime neighborhood."[35] Condescension aside, the remark misses a fundamental asymmetry in the country's domestic organized crime. Namely, though thoroughly corrupt, the host state did not create or instrumentalize mafias, but separatists *did*. A 2001 Albanian insurgency—led by an ethnocentric rebel mafia—extracted constitutional status reforms from Skopje in what remains unmatched separatist movement success. Though it thwarted civil war, the Ohrid Framework Agreement ending the conflict further rived an already-torn host state.[36]

ALBANIAN RULES

Organized crime in Macedonia (where a quarter of the population is Albanian) is a focal point for the "Balkan Golden Triangle" of Albania, Kosovo, and Macedonia. Drugs, arms, and people are smuggled by passenger and freight vehicles, boats across Lakes Ohrid and Prespa, and horses and mules. Across Macedonia's western borders, the unofficial customs authority was the Albanian diaspora.[37] With a shadow economy above 40 percent and toothless anticorruption instruments, the Macedonian state apparatus "allowed the regional mafias to ply their trade unmolested by the authorities."[38] In both politics and economics, predominantly Albanian mafias rose to the occasion. Protection rackets proliferated. Private security firms in Macedonia "largely act as a legalised security force for organised crime," disguising "extortion and racketeering activities." In separatist Struga, for instance, the mayor advised a school director to ruminate on the advantages of commissioning VIP Security, a mafia outfit, "to protect the school from terrorism" and charge parents for the privilege.[39] Small business owners throughout Macedonia endured extortion by neighborhood gangs.[40] Cloaked in traditional clan customs—notably the Kanun honor code regulating blood feuds—the Albanian mafia nurtured a reputation for violence and depravity. One proprietor was shot fifty times for no other offense than being the owner of a bar where a gangster's brother was killed.[41]

Albanian gangs ran globalized black markets in arms, heroin, cigarettes, and sex labor. The Macedonian-born Albanian Daut Kadriovski, a mafia legend, controlled over a dozen crime families, including in New York City, Philadelphia, and Sydney. Based in Turkey, he sustained one of the world's most durable heroin rackets and is credited with rerouting the Balkan narco-traffic through Macedonia, away from the ex-Yugoslav conflict area. Wanted by the FBI, hounded in Hungary, and sentenced to twelve years in absentia in Italy, Kadriovski evaded law enforcement via plastic surgery. He was once caught with ten different passports. He escaped German prison in 1985 (through death threats and bribes) and Albanian prison in 2001 (through death threats, bribes, and a poignant appeal to his poor health).[42]

Locally, five mobster kingpins (including Agim Krasniqi, who would rise to separatist stardom) each led a gang in the 1990s. Collectively, their mafia was known as "the Columbians."[43] Rooted in the separatist west and northwest, the Colombians capitalized on the transnational movement into Kosovo and Albania, where suppliers, partners, and contraband crisscross according to need. With associates in Columbia, Greece, Austria, and Germany, Macedonia's organized crime maintained "cooperation between Turkish and Albanian drug groups," both highly ethnocentric.[44] In Albanian-majority Gostivar, Macedonian-majority Kumanovo, and the capital Skopje, Albanian criminals held facilities for drug storage and repackaging. The separatist narco-traffic survived multiple Macedonian and European police crackdowns. So ethnically embedded was the mafia that Skopje hesitated to arrest prominent gangsters such as Dilivar "Leku" Bojku ("considered untouchable for years") because "any attempt to arrest him or disturb his operations would 'provoke' the Albanian community." Most Albanians, more likely, "wanted to see Leku behind bars."[45]

Ethnic Macedonian criminal entrepreneurs simply could not compete. The government-separatist balance was aptly described as follows: "The Albanian share was control over crime routes in western Macedonia, while the Macedonian share involved the practically unlimited (mis)use of the state apparatus."[46] Albanians were overrepresented in major crime categories inside the host state as well as in transnational rackets extending into Europe from Macedonia.[47] Meanwhile, non-Albanian gangs barely had any regional reach and amounted to *dis*organized crime. The host state's endemic corruption partly incubated Albanian organized crime. High-end graft aside, however, Skopje fell short of sustaining its own mafia against separatist insurgents. The closest that Macedonia came to a mafia in uniform were the Lions, a police unit that repressed, kidnapped, and intimidated Albanians between 2001 and 2004. Splintering from it was a subgroup of ex-Lions, "criminals and thugs who were given arms with very little training." But the gang did not last long and never amplified into a mafia.[48] Organized crime in Macedonia remained an ethnic minority affair.

COALITION

In the 2000s, separatist and mafia interests converged dramatically. Given the "borderless criminal network [that] already operates freely in Macedonia, Albania and Kosovo," secessionist tendencies were conducive to profitable rackets: "Keeping Macedonia at risk allows the contraband trade in drugs, weapons, cigarettes, and humans to flourish unchecked. A destabilized Macedonia is profitable both for criminals and for those who dream of a pure Albanian section of western Macedonia."[49] From February to August 2001, these "intersecting interests of organized criminals and nationalist politicians" led to a near civil war.[50] In the wake of a new Albanian separatist statelet in neighboring Kosovo, the National Liberation Army (NLA) based in Macedonia's northwestern Albanian region staged an insurrection that ended in major host state concessions to separatists.

As much as it was an ethnic rebellion, the insurrection was an act of mafia self-defense.[51] Modeled on its sibling across the border, the KLA, the NLA held two to three thousand fighters, most under thirty.[52] They were armed to the teeth.[53] Beyond advocating greater rights for Albanians in Macedonia, the NLA's demands were improvised, varying, or nonexistent. Its fundraising was comprised of smuggling drugs, arms, people, and cigarettes—leading many observers to classify the entire NLA as a mafia.[54] It began with banditry: car theft, gas station stickups, and armed robberies of pedestrians. Masked gunners replaced vandalized tollbooths (one of them, between Tetovo and Gostivar, was demolished completely). Gangsters improvised checkpoints where passersby could be charged, kidnapped, or stoned. In retrospect, analysts realized the gangs were provoked by "post-2000 Macedonian border patrols' attempt to crack down on cross-border smuggling and weapons trafficking by Albanians."[55] Clashes with government forces ensued in the villages of Tanuševci and Aračinovo—critical mafia hubs for drug trafficking since the 1990s.[56] When the host state recaptured the latter, "long considered a hotbed of Albanian mafia activities, several of the 'commanders' turned out to be the very same local mafia bosses."[57] Skopje had struck the mafia where it mattered—its headquarters—and the NLA escalated to car bombs, kidnappings, and village-by-village ethnic cleansing. Full-scale conflict spread to Tetovo, the unofficial capital of Albanian separatism. As the insurgents fled to regroup in the mountains, observers (not to mention many NLA insiders) wondered what was being fought for. Who were they, and what did they want?

The uprising was a joint mafia-separatist venture. While the Tanuševci branch of the NLA was mafia dominated, the separatists in Kumanovo, Skopje, and Tetovo were only mafia supported. Across the board, organized crime serviced the separatist—never Skopje's—side. Some gangsters were "free riders" fighting private mafia turf wars in nationalist camouflage. They "labelled themselves as 'NLA' while only being indirectly connected." Others were merely supplying the separatist movement from the outside: "traffickers, money launderers and extortionists who form part of the transnational network, but were not part of the military struggle."[58] Still others were movement gunrunners. From Bosnia and Albania, via Kosovo, they transported hundreds of thousands of weapons across mountainous frontiers at a moment of maximal risk (i.e., profit). Donkeys were trained to "move backwards in order to decoy satellite images." On one occasion, a herd of cows was caught trafficking from Kosovo into Macedonia.[59]

Finally, there were sincere nationalists drawing on family mafia ties. The leadership was an assortment of the mercenary and dissidence milieu across Kosovo, Macedonia, and Albania.[60] Ali Ahmeti, an Albanian nationalist from Macedonia, emerged as figurehead. His uncle, Fazli Veliu, was intimate with the Jashari Clan, a major Kosovar mafia. In exchange for securing mafia transit hubs, the clan invested in the NLA financially and logistically. The diaspora likewise contributed. One Albanian mafia boss—"Prince Dobroshi," based in the Czech Republic—channeled millions into separatist coffers to prevent further disruption of his heroin supply.[61]

The NLA was not alone. On the separatist movement fringe was the Albanian National Army (AKSH), a pure mafia contender. Among the AKSH's commanders was Agim Krasniqi, one of the so-called Columbians. The formation was "so deeply involved in criminal activities" that Albanian and Macedonian observers alike styled it "criminals dressed up as patriots."[62] Crowing vague separatist demands (the "fact that no formal demands of independence were advanced appeared to be a matter of political and economic convenience"), gangster deal brokers from the AKSH successfully extorted local authorities in informal negotiations.[63] Most extreme was the Jakupi gang, led by Lirim "the Nazi" Jakupi. The posse was originally under the AKSH umbrella before Jakupi was imprisoned for attempted murder. Absconding from a Kosovar prison, he returned to arms profiteering in Macedonia before a government shoot-out in the separatist northwest killed his minions. Jakupi himself staged another spectacular getaway from the firefight. Macedonia convicted the fugitive in absentia, but he remains—for die-hard "Nazis"—a separatist hero, uncorrupted by Skopje's co-optation.

Having created a crisis, separatist and criminal figures alike were offered propitious agreements to defuse it. Senior NLA figures transformed the paramilitary into a political party, the Democratic Union of Integration (DUI). Ali Ahmeti became the party leader.[64] Commander Fazli Veliu—Ahmeti's uncle and liaison to the Jashari Clan—became vice president. Fatigued and blackmailed, the host state yielded tremendous compromises, including constitutional reform.

The sum effect of the rebel mafia was twofold. First, it was an unprecedented achievement for Albanians delivered by a (hitherto dormant) separatist movement, now spearheaded by the DUI. Second, it resulted in the absolution of criminals-cum-politicians. In one of many scandalous legislative maneuvers, the former gangsters—now with parliamentary immunity—elbowed a law granting amnesty for NLA fighters charged with war crimes. Macedonia remains widely cited as the "clearest example" of "nationalism [a]s a convenient tool which [mafias] are prepared to mobilize if they feel that their business interests are threatened."[65]

Moldova

The separatist Pridnestrovian Moldavian Republic—Transnistria—tore Moldova's industrial heartland out of sovereign control. In March 1992, a brief but intense war between secessionist irregulars and Moldovan troops set a de facto border with the host state on the Dniester River. In the postwar period, the separatist movement built substantive state capacity, including in taxation, law and order, service provision, border control, and promoting ethnonationalist solidarity. With a little help from Russian friends and an indigenous rebel mafia—the Smirnov Clan—Transnistria became one of the most advanced and criminalized separatist movements in Eastern Europe.[66]

GANGSTER SANCTUARY

Organized crime in the host state drew from a deep mire of poverty and lawlessness. A fifth of Moldova's population fled Europe's poorest country—and half of those remaining expressed the desire to do so.[67] Many Moldovans turned to narcotics: local drug use grew by 35 percent on average yearly in the 2000s. Others turned to organ traffickers for sustenance. In one village, thirty-two men donated their kidneys to an entrepreneurial harvester. A third of the country's workforce (about six hundred thousand people) are labor migrants, many subjected to trafficking by "clandestine criminal groups."[68] Moldova is also Europe's top source country for prostitution and sexual trafficking.[69]

To top it all, Transnistria—no small economic loss—defiantly seceded in 1992.[70] As the separatists created a mafia hub, the host state underwent "the rise of its own criminal godfathers" in the early 1990s. Foremost among them was Grigore "the Bulgarian" Caramalac—a distinguished Interpol fugitive who ran Moldova's oil and wine industries. Between 1993 and 2001, six gangs operated under the umbrella of the Soviet-era mafia, the Thieves-in-Law. One gang (led by Vladimir Moscaliciuc) stole and smuggled motor vehicles; another (led by Malhaz Djaparidze) ran drugs and weapons. All six infiltrated the government's thirty-eight districts, appointing criminal supervisors. Mafia assassinations included the head of the Transnistrian Organized Crime Division and president of the Transnistrian Association of Industrialists and Businessmen. For years, "contract killings became ordinary practice" in both business and personal matters.[71] Despite its reputation, the Moldovan government successfully curbed the Thieves-in-Law. In 2001, President Vladimir Voronin's crackdown led to "a restructuring within organized crime where the initiative of conducting illegal business was largely overtaken by economic circles close to the government." Moldovan mafias have remained modest and disorganized ever since: "while organised crime did exist in Moldova, it was very small scale and primitive."[72] Some gangsters turned into businesspeople, and others revisited "street crimes."[73]

But some fled to greener pastures.[74] Thieves-in-Law fugitives naturally gravitated to separatist territory. "By offering a safe haven and service centre, [Transnistria] represents a useful asset for other gangs" escaping law enforcement.[75] From abroad, Russian, Ukrainian, and Moldovan gangsters came to operate in Transnistria. Local criminals traversed the border throughout the 1990s and 2000s to commit crimes and then avoid prosecution. The flight was unstoppable. Out of 150 agreements signed between Moldova and the separatists by 2005, only 2 of them addressed organized crime. Neither was implemented.[76] To this day, judges in Moldovan courts often issue sentences knowing that convicts will simply skip across the Dniester River into sanctuary.

Across the river, an enclave of globalized organized crime matured, sustaining separatism. Much is made of Transnistrians' "siege mentality"; the community supposedly feels isolated, encircled, and alone.[77] Transnistria designed its own flag, currency, and postage stamps—all universally unrecognized. Even patron state Russia refuses to formally acknowledge its independence. Landlocked and internationally stigmatized, Transnistria is derided by visitors as a solitary "museum of communism." In spiteful reaction, the separatists defiantly nurture Leninist iconography and art—attracting further mockery. But the image of Transnistria as a fortress that has raised drawbridges to the outside world could not be more deceptive. On the contrary, the province is one of the most vigorous transnational smuggling hubs in East Europe *because of*, not despite, its disputed borders.

Thousands of tons of goods cross the separatist land (4,163 square kilometers) every year. Alcohol, fuel, and sex rackets filled separatist coffers as well as private criminal interests over two decades. At its heyday, Transnistria imported six thousand times more cigarettes than the host state, including the separatists' trademark fake-brand tobacco—a regional favorite. Indeed, the postwar stalemate was an economic godsend for the separatists. Transnistria averaged $476 million worth of yearly imports; Moldova proper (seven times the size) averaged only $108 million. Contested borders were lucrative borders, and separatists exploited them masterfully. A third of Moldova's frontier with Ukraine is under Tiraspol's administrative control. Chișinău initially rebuked the informal customs posts along the Dniester River. But in 1996, the host state entered negotiations to share official Moldovan custom seals as a quid pro quo for the removal of the renegade checkpoints. The government was duped: as soon as the seal was in their hands, the separatists retracted the agreement. The result was "the de facto legalization of the immense flows of smuggled goods already passing through the Transnistrian region."[78]

The floodgates had opened. By the late 1990s, the Ukraine-to-Transnistria smuggling lane soared in volume and scope. Even as Kiev formally sided with Moldova against the separatists, the Ukrainian ports of Odessa and Ilyichevsk became Europe's greatest criminal conduit. Westward-headed contraband—dead or alive—made pit stops in Transnistria. Counterfeit goods—notably CDs, pharmaceutical knockoffs, and designer clothing (such as Reeboh)—from the separatist territory inundated neighboring countries. Predatory ads lured thousands of Transnistrian women into exploitative gigs (as maids, waitresses, or dancers) operated by sex traffickers in Dubai, Prague, and Moscow. But ordinary goods predominated; "what is smuggled are goods such as frozen chickens, and not drugs and weapons."[79] Transnistria "imports" enough tobacco and poultry for each resident (including newborns) to smoke twelve packs of cigarettes and eat eight kilograms of chicken every week. The discovery inspired a folk witticism: "We *really* like to smoke and eat chicken a lot in Transnistria!" By the mid-2000s, yearly kickbacks into the separatist budget approximated $7 million (Ukraine's loss through the untaxed revenue was $43 million, and Moldova's was $18 million).[80]

SHERIF'S "LAUNDRY"

The arms traffic from Transnistria is clouded in mystery and antiseparatist propaganda.[81] But its benefit in sustaining independence from the host state is undisputed. First, separatists inherited the Soviet-era Kolbasna arsenal, one of Europe's largest during the Cold War. The Russian Fourteenth Army left 24 tanks, 12 combat helicopters, and 120 cannons, along with 40,000 to 50,000 tons of arms and ammunition in Transnistria, for criminal plundering.[82]

Second, manufacturing plants in Tiraspol produced weapons (1995–2000) ranging from machine guns and mortars to rocket and grenade launchers. Exporting them without serial numbers, smugglers supplied regional war zones. Though many accusations of gunrunning remain unsubstantiated, the son of separatist leader Igor Smirnov was apparently arrested in Moscow in 2000 with $1.2 million from weapons sales.[83] Beyond inherited stockpiles and local production, however, the most lucrative aspect of Transnistria was its position as a "weapons laundry"—a site where tax-free contraband is brought in and marked by separatist customs, only to be returned to where it came from for further exporting: "Ukrainian weapons intended for illegal or politically-sensitive markets were transported to [Transnistria] either for airlift to their destinations or, more often, to be shipped from the Ukrainian seaport of Odessa, but now under Transdnistrian custom seals." Transnational traffickers—including Russian gangster Victor Bout, the world's greatest gunrunner—operated in the province. The arms-laundering route from separatist Pervomayskoye to the Black Sea port of Odessa alone raked in $2 billion annually.[84] What kind of separatist regime made this mafia cordon sanitaire, quarantined from all law?

Through familiar post-Soviet crony-privatization schemes, Transnistria had appropriated Moldovan state property through what separatists called "privatization with a human face."[85] "Criminal face" would have been more exact. Smirnov, a Soviet-era factory manager and local city council boss, was Transnistria's founding father. He won presidential "elections" repeatedly (in 1991, 1996, 2001, and 2006) before being ousted in 2011. His greatest asset was his "entrepreneurial zeal to embrace the opportunities offered by today's global underworld."[86] His mafia—the Smirnov Clan—infiltrated major governance organs: the Security Service, Internal Affairs Ministry, and Prosecutor's Office.[87] Transforming political into economic clout, the Smirnov Clan consolidated its grip on Transnistrian institutions through its company, the Sherif Corporation. Founded in 1993, Sherif signed a "mutual cooperation" agreement with separatist authorities (i.e., themselves). Exempt from taxes and duties, Sherif acquired gas stations, shopping malls, car shops, an advertising agency, a cell phone provider, a television station, and a football club recognized by the Union of European Football Association with an ostentatious Sherif Stadium worth $200 million. Political parties Respublika (proregime) and Obnovljenje (nominally oppositional) were both offshoots of Sherif in Transnistria's parliamentary facade.[88]

The Smirnov Clan was a traditional, family mafia. Smirnov's elder son, Vladimir, is an Interpol-sought embezzler and money launderer. He was appointed customs minister. The younger son, Oleg, held senior management positions in Sherif. As a parliamentary deputy, he helped craft the laws that his brother was gainfully flouting. Oleg's wife, Marina Smirnova, was an authority in the local Russian Gazprombank branch, Transnistria's largest bank. Even Russian law enforcement was astounded by the plunder, which included Oleg and Marina diverting Moscow's humanitarian aid to luxury real estate.[89] Observing Sherif machinations, British development officials slated Transnistria "a smuggling company masquerading as a state."[90] In 2002, the European Parliament called Transnistria a "black hole."[91] But the Smirnov Clan went beyond mere corruption. Through murder and extortion, it eliminated all contenders to separatist office.[92] The resulting Karabakh movement became fatefully tied to the Smirnov Clan: "It is best to think of the region as being dominated by a 'clan' of semiautonomous magnates, whose interests often stretch from politics through legitimate business to organised crime. . . . Thus, [Transnistria's] self-proclaimed government, [state security] and organised crime are thoroughly intertwined and often indistinguishable."[93] Kidnappings, shakedowns, and death threats became normal governance techniques. Smirnov's right-hand goon, State Security Minister Vadim Shevtsov, allegedly murdered thirty-six businesspeople. His ministry officials specialized in "extorting money from businessmen," "racketeering the population," and comprehensively "plundering Transnistria." In 2000, a racket extorting money exchangers raised $1 million. By one estimate, "over 200 Transnistrians are missing, presumed dead at the hands of Tiraspol" for crossing the Smirnov Clan.[94]

The separatist security apparatus, "notionally the lead agency in combating organised crime, . . . simply became one more gang in [Transnistria's] rich underworld."[95] Some characterized this as a transition from organized crime to nation building, and others saw it as a shift from the violent Thieves-in-Law rule to "white-collar" organized crime. At a minimum, it is certain that the Smirnov Clan qua mafia sustained Transnistria's secessionist orientation:

> The proceeds from organized criminal activities formed an incentive for the separatist leaders to avoid seeking a resolution to the conflict, even rejecting a proposal of large autonomy after the cease-fire and instead doubling down on their demand for statehood. . . . It is clear that the separatists are increasingly motivated by economic benefits of the organized criminal activities in which they take part.[96]

Transnistria's GDP is $85 million. Sherif's annual budget? $4 *billion*—five times the entire Moldovan economy.[97]

Transnistrian nationalism was not born of criminality.[98] As the separatists drifted from Moldovan control, however, the Smirnov Clan's rackets became indispensable protagonists on the separatist stage. "The growth of organized crime created incentives for the political elites of the separatist region to both become involved in, and provide support to criminal activities."[99] The rebel mafia ultimately co-opted the entire separatist movement and sustained considerable sovereignty outside the host state.

Ukraine

Scholars debate whether post-Euromaidan Ukraine is transitioning from mafia state into a corrupt state, from an oligarchic into a mafia economy, or merely from one mafia state management to another.[100] What is clear is that the "political-criminal-business troika" of post-Soviet nepotism, crony capitalism, and organized crime has towered over the country since independence, culminating in the regime of Viktor Yanukovych (2010–14).[101] In the east, the Donbas War (2014–present) generated two separatist entities, the Donetsk People's Republic (DNR) and Lugansk People's Republic (LNR). Arms smugglers, the Thieves-in-Law, and the Akhmetov Clan left indelible marks on the conflict as Minderbinder mafias.

INTERNATIONALISTS

When separatist war erupted in its industrial east, Ukraine was significantly deprived of its military capacity by rampant, unpatriotic arms trafficking. Engaging Russia militarily in Donbas was daunting enough. But a twenty-five-year smuggling bonanza that only *continued* into the war severely undermined Ukraine's reintegration capacity and its credibility for attracting foreign military assistance. The USSR bequeathed an extensive arms stockpile to Ukraine, which "essentially inherited 30% of the Soviet military-industrial complex." Between 1992 and 1998, $32 billion worth of military assets vanished "through theft, discounted arms sales, and lack of oversight." For every $1 of legal arms exports, $2.40 were illegal. In 1996, at the peak arms outflow, only 20 percent of the weapons export transactions were carried out by legally recognized entities. Low-level larceny by rank-and-file soldiers (who "lost" their weapons) was the least of it. Many commanders "were caught selling off entire military installations."[102]

This was far from a street-level operation. An arms-smuggling mafia was embedded in the state apparatus, from the Ministry of Defense to state-owned export companies. Around the ministry, a web of transporters and brokers congealed. With offshore companies and fleets of vessels and airplanes, "these traffickers sell their connections, their access to fraudulent paperwork and their transportation services to both insurgent groups and embargoed states."[103] The multiethnic gangsters included Russians, Yugoslavs, Africans, Arabs, and Ukrainians (east and west). "Most are multilingual and hold a number of passports."[104] There is no evidence that any criminal's concerns over Ukrainian national security checked the market, as the country became a top-ten global weapons exporter for more than two decades. Tanks, planes, armored vehicles, and artillery were supplied to warring actors in Congo, Sudan, Somalia, Kenya, Nigeria, Croatia, Bosnia, and Sri Lanka—all embargoed. The Black

Sea hub of Odessa and the Crimean port of Sevastopol became epicenters of globalized arms trafficking.[105] How many tens of thousands of tons have been smuggled undetected remains unclear. Serendipitous interdictions—and not government ones at that—offer a glimpse of the scale. One Ukrainian cargo ship, *Faina*, never reached South Sudan because it was intercepted by Somali pirates. Expecting ordinary commercial booty, the hijackers could not believe their luck: $33 million worth of ammunition, grenade launchers, and thirty-three top-notch tanks.[106]

The racket dented the Ukrainian forces considerably. The losses were greater than the combined yearly military expenditures from 2010 to 2017. Underequipped, inexperienced, and devastated by corruption, the host state's military was in no condition for a separatist challenge. Fifteen percent of Ukraine's troops were "battle-worthy," and tens of thousands of them "readily laid down arms before the Russian separatists," in no small part because of weapons shortages.[107] To compensate, there was significant reliance on paramilitaries, many of which were liabilities. "Competition between battalions and public officials for access to the markets of illegal trade and smuggling" hampered reintegration operations as well as tarnished the country's image internationally.[108] Nor did arms smuggling cease with the separatist threat in 2014. On the contrary, it accelerated. A single firm, Techimpex, made twenty-six disreputable deals worth $29.5 million in 2015–16.[109] "These thieves," a Security Services of Ukraine officer complained to the author, "would rather help fucking Assad against terrorists than help us, their own country, to fight *our* [Donbas] terrorists."[110] This may have been an understatement. Sources from the front lines recorded Ukrainian units directly helping "terrorists." In 2015, the Twenty-Eighth Armored Brigade was caught smuggling everything it could get its hands on to the enemy. The entire "brigade, from its commander to soldiers, were engaged in criminal activity."[111] Even the most staunchly patriotic units, such as the Azov Battalion, were not immune to arms trafficking. In 2016, an extremist Frenchman tried smuggling an arsenal of weapons he purchased from Azov contacts. Over a dozen regiment soldiers have been sentenced for gunrunning; many more presumably went unnoticed.[112]

Who were these smugglers that in the middle of the Donbas conflagration, indiscriminately sold off Ukraine's arms? The Thieves-in-Law operating in Ukraine survived Stalinism, the 1990s, and Euromaidan. They would certainly survive—and thrive off—the Donbas War. In December 2014, as the conflict intensified, the mafia held a fateful *skhodka* (council meeting) to devise strategy vis-à-vis the separatist scuffle.[113] The result was an apolitical, all-round smuggling mission aimed at maximizing the profit and market share of arms, fuel, methadone, and especially counterfeit tobacco and alcohol on both sides of the front line. Gangsters were strictly agnostic about Donbas's political future. "While some smugglers in rebel-held territory may be driven by pro-separatist ideology," observers noted, "profit is the likely motivation for most."[114] The world's leading *vory*ologist agreed:

> The gangsters are truly internationalist in their opportunism. Ukraine and Russia may be at virtual war, but their criminals continue to cooperate as before. [According to a Security Services of Ukraine informant], the flow of drugs through Donbas, into Ukraine, and then into Europe simply has not shrunk *by a single percentage point*, even while bullets are flying back and forth across the front line.[115]

The only apparent opponent of the impartial smuggling was the ultranationalist Ukrainian Right Sector (Pravy Sektor), which attempted—in vain—to block what it viewed as a shameful collusion with terrorists.[116]

Meanwhile, the Thieves-in-Law continued regular sit-down *skhodkas*. In October 2018, gangsters congregated in Rostov-on-Don, Russia's nearest city to Donetsk. Fifteen mafia luminaries included representatives of Lugansk (separatist LNR), Dnipro (host state), Gorlovka (separatist DNR), and Russia (Eduard "Edik Osterina" Asatryan, contender for the "boss of all bosses" title). On the agenda were "spheres of influence" and "quotas" in the breakaway territories. Abandoned machine-repairing plants and other enterprises were divvied up. Counterfeit tobacco from the Hamadei factory in the DNR went into Ukraine. Sunflower seeds, salt, and groceries went from the host state into Gorlovka. While the "Rostov side provides transportation, logistics and security," the host state side "provides the work of law enforcement agencies of Ukraine" to look the other way. "One may doubt these things were being discussed at the meeting," an investigative journalist reflected on her informants, "but already a few days later, the entire 'DPR' [DNR] customs were removed from the Gorlovka direction."[117]

FORBES LIST MAFIA

East Ukraine in the 1990s was an extraordinary mafia ecology. Four major clans operated in modern Ukraine, but it was the Donetsk Clan that reigned supreme with national leverage after monopolizing Donbas's political, economic, and criminal scenes.[118] The eastern industrial provinces were national record holders in gangland violence, homicide rates, and prisons. In the 1990s, downtown Donetsk residents would habitually replace their shattered windows after a neighborhood car bomb eliminated yet another businessperson. With the highest proportion of jails of any Ukrainian region, Donetsk boasted a "prison culture" during the Cold War—a "haven for fugitives" from across the USSR. When the jails closed beginning in the 1980s, some seven hundred thousand inmates flooded into "organized crime, the shadow economy, and new business structures." Every third man in Donetsk, a folk quip has it, is in prison, has been in prison, or will be in prison.[119]

Out of the criminal morass, Yanukovych—a twice-convicted violent offender—emerged as governor in 1997 by placing mafia partners into the state apparatus and legal business sector. It was the mafia that "gave them the start-up capital, muscle and patronage networks" to establish oligarchic control over Donbas. By 2001, he consolidated his rule through the Party of Regions by absorbing "his oligarch allies, many of whom had emerged from organized crime." In subsequent years, his "Donetsk clan" co-opted critical government organs, including the State Tax Administration, Ministry of Interior, and Ministry of Finance.[120] The Party of Regions proceeded to win three elections and elevate Yanukovych to Ukrainian president in 2010. His mafia roots were barely cloaked. He "offered no grand narrative, no promise of transcendence, no story about a higher purpose of present suffering," Marci Shore (2018, 29–30) explains. "He was nakedly, unapologetically a gangster." Notwithstanding, the population of Donbas—outraged with nationalist excesses from Kiev—embraced Yanukovych as its defender of regional interests. "He was a bandit, but he was *our* bandit."[121] But if the political head of the Donetsk oligarchy was Yanukovych, its mafia head—who bankrolled his rise to power—was the irrepressible Rinat Akhmetov.

The Akhmetov Clan is arguably the most successful mafia in Eastern European history. Akhmetov's industrial corporation, System Capital Management, dominated the metallurgy, mining, and energy sectors. In 2012, his Donbas Arena hosted the 2012 European Football Championship. Every Valentine's Day, each school-age child in Donetsk received a box of chocolates with felicitations. On each package cover was Akhmetov's grisly visage. In 2013, in the eye of the Donbas War, *Forbes* magazine ranked him the forty-seventh richest person in the world at $15.4 billion—trailing George Soros, but far surpassing Mark Zuckerberg. Where did this éminence grise of Ukrainian politics and economics come from?

The son of a coal miner, Akhmetov was raised in the Oktyabrsky settlement, one of Donetsk's roughest neighborhoods. Killing dozens of opponents, he rose up the ranks through gang feuding, extortion, and backstabbing.[122] The zenith came in 1995, when Akhmetov (allegedly) killed his once-patron Akhat "Alik the Greek" Bragin. The mafia boss and his six bodyguards were blown up in Donetsk's Shakhtar football stadium in a blast so potent that Bragin's Rolex watch was the sole thing remaining intact.[123] After Bragin's murder, his protégé, Akhmetov, inherited the entirety of his assets to become Ukraine's wealthiest citizen and undisputed authority of east Ukraine. His mafia laundered money, extorted businesses, and murdered opponents with impunity. One (former) shopping mall owner, whom the Akhmetov Clan relieved of his business, recalled:

I looked into the eyes of death when representatives of the Donetsk mafia were taking away my property. I was lucky—I survived. But many of the businessmen of Donbas are not alive—those who were shot together with their families in front of their homes, who were beaten to death with screwdrivers and brass knuckles, with baseball bats and axe heads, who were deprived of their lives for the mere reason that they owned one or another business. Today, fifty-five outstanding murders are still unresolved in Donetsk region. [T]he businesses of the murdered people strangely became businesses of Rinat Akhmetov and Boris Kolesnikov [Akhmetov's deputy].[124]

Consolidating most Donbas industries by the early 2000s, Akhmetov transformed from underworld boss to prized oligarch. As his football club—Shaktar—began winning in the European League, his political protégé, Yanukovych, was on his way to the Ukrainian presidency.

The Akhmetov Clan's success is in its pragmatic impartiality. When separatism paid, Akhmetov toed the line; when it jeopardized his business empire, he denounced it. In 2004, the mafia's launching of Yanukovych was thwarted by the Orange Revolution and victory of opponent Viktor Yuschenko. Akhmetov staged mass protests in Donetsk, running "greetings" billboards for Yuschenko that portrayed him in Nazi uniform. Six years later, he achieved success; as soon as the Party of Regions was in power at the national level, all separatist proclivities vanished in favor of expanding business ventures into the host state proper. When Yanukovych was overthrown by Euromaidan and fled to Russia in 2014, the Akhmetov Clan recalibrated. Initially, Akhmetev flirted with the separatist authorities, hoping they or Moscow would anoint him in the upcoming "elections" scheduled for November. Maneuvering to preserve business privileges, he used his publicity as a bargaining chip. On April 8, he ostentatiously stopped a government special forces operation from retaking control of the Donetsk Oblast administration, occupied by separatist protesters. Showing up in person and creating a spectacle, Akhmetov publicly offered to stay inside the building in case of an attack, valiantly urging against bloodshed. (Ukrainian forces canceled the operation.) Separatism had acquired the Akhmetov brand. According to early secessionist leader Pavel Gubarev, the tycoon "paid two thirds of the separatist cost." Residents rumored the DNR to be "Akhmetov's puppet project." In exchange, the authorities refrained from confiscating his major businesses. Prudently eschewing formal alignment, however, the mafia anticipated a mediator's position in whatever arrangement was reached between Donetsk and Kiev. Akhmetov himself was prepared to aid "separatists to reach a deal with either Kyiv *or* Moscow," vacillating wherever the separatist wind blew.[125]

By May 2014, however, separatism "had spiraled out of control."[126] Russian dominance amplified at the expense of the indigenous mafia. In Lugansk, separatist Valery Bolotov, deemed insufficiently sycophantic, was replaced with Igor Plotnitsky. In Donetsk, Alexander Borodai, a "political technologist" from Moscow, was implanted as separatist prime minister. Conspicuously Russian, Boroday was quickly replaced—for appearances—by chicken trader Alexander Zakharchenko, a Donetsk native. Zakharchenko was even Akhmetov's employee before being "offered a bigger boss." As head of the Republic of the DNR, his first act was to hang Vladimir Putin's portrait in his office.[127] Slighted, Akhmetov scrambled behind the Vostok militia, an outgrowth of his personal bodyguard squad, to protect the Clan's property. To no avail. In early June, he fled to the safety of the host state proper—self-exiled into a cozy Kiev suburb. The DNR "nationalized" his property on separatist territory, including two massive metallurgical plants, the Donbas Arena, and the luxurious Donbas Palace Hotel. Akhmetov's net worth in 2017, according to *Forbes*, plummeted to $5.3 billion. The DNR's "independence" cost him, in other words, over $10 billion. Lofty separatist goals receded accordingly. Some of the Akhmetov Clan, like Armen Sarkisian, remained engaged in Donbas as a smuggler working with the Thieves-in-Law. Others integrated into Ukrainian organized crime.

Given NATO/EU blunders and Russian expansionism, conflict in Ukraine may have been inevitable. But the Donbas quagmire was substantially molded by indigenous criminal forces. For a quarter century, a damaging arms-trafficking racket emaciated the host state's military capacity and morale—from within. Multiethnic Thieves-in-Law smuggled any and all contraband (without prejudice) in the DNR, LNR, and Ukraine proper—foiling prospects of reintegration and secession alike. The Akhmetov Clan, after propping the Yanukovych regime's grip on the host state, was only as separatist as its business interests allowed. Geopolitics notwithstanding, these domestic, overlapping Minderbinder mafias undermined both government and separatist ambitions.

Azerbaijan

Nagorno-Karabakh has been praised as the most advanced post-Soviet separatist entity, exceeding both its host state (Azerbaijan) and patron state (Armenia) in governance standards.[128] Separatist violence broke out well before Soviet fragmentation (1980s). Full-scale war followed (1992), killing fifteen to twenty thousand and displacing over a million before a cease-fire (1994). In Azerbaijan proper, a mafia in uniform—the Aliyev Clan—fought Karabakh irredentists and buttressed Baku's patrimonial oil regime. In Karabakh, a rebel mafia—the Babayan Clan—dominated the separatist movement, perpetuating the frozen conflict.[129]

OIL MAFIA STALEMATE

Ex-Communist cadre Illham Aliyev ruled Azerbaijan until the mid-2000s, when his son took over the oil-rich country. In a "contract of the century," Aliyev solidified his power, including leverage against Armenia and Russia, by granting the petroleum fields of the Azeri Caspian basin to ten foreign companies.[130] One of the birthplaces of the oil industry, Azerbaijan gradually depleted its supplies in the post-Soviet period. What remained was a cartelized, "authoritarian oil state" that perpetuated a frozen separatist conflict.[131] Through the Karabakh War (1992–94), the "patrimonial-rentier state" in Baku fused a nationalist legitimacy with regime-based organized crime.[132] Azeri mafia figures were mobilized into private anti-Armenian armies, decorated as military commanders, and in the case of gunrunner Suret Huseynov, made prime minister. Oil revenues significantly funded the host state's failed reintegration campaign. Karabakh was lost, but a "patron family network" of kickbacks, bribery, and racketeering remained. The oil mafia's "*nomenklatura networks*" around the State Oil Company became the bedrock of Aliyev's rule. They cartelized loans, border crossings, import-export licenses, and managerial spots (at approximately $50,000 a position). To protect the oil-related rackets, "government mafias could even engage in their own operations by hiring common criminals as undertakers."[133]

Born of antiseparatist combat, the Aliyev Clan turned in peacetime to self-preservation as an end in itself. But maintaining the mafia status quo required balance. On the one hand, the Azeri political elites could not engage in concessions. "Any leader who tries to make peace [with the separatists] risks losing control."[134] On the other hand, they could not wage war either. Namely, to dissolve the frozen conflict, Azerbaijan needed a formidable army. Yet a strong military may undermine the oil mafia as the epicenter of power. Therefore to preempt the security apparatus from displacing him, Aliyev senior underfunded and ill equipped his armed forces. Following in his father's footsteps, Aliyev junior likewise discovered that a strong army "would be a significant threat to his personal rule."[135] As a result, Karabakh became a singular separatist movement with military capacity superior to its host state's—a unique asymmetry.[136] In effect, Baku abdicated its ability to reintegrate Karabakh by force, indirectly perpetuating separatist stalemate. The oil mafia remained staunchly antiseparatist—but it had other priorities.

Supplementing this debilitating domestic configuration, multiple exogenous pressures constrained Azerbaijan. The brotherly embrace—but sometimes schism—of Armenians from Armenia (*hayastantsi*) and Armenians from Nagorno-Karabakh (*karabakhtsis*) propelled the separatist movement to independence from Baku. Karabakh is often lumped together with regional Russian-propped separatist movements (Abkhazia, South Ossetia, and Transnistria). But the Russian influence among post-Soviet torn states is the least in Karabakh. Armenia donates between a third and 80 percent of the separatist's economic needs through yearly "interstate loans." Unlike in Moldova and Georgia, there are no Russian peacekeepers inside Azerbaijan. Moscow refuses to recognize Nagorno-Karabakh's independence as it did for other client statelets. The Armenian military occupies five Azerbaijani districts around the separatist territory—effectively depriving Baku of any control over its southwest frontiers, including a gainful 130 kilometers piece of the border with Iran. Of 18,500 soldiers in Karabakh, 10,000 are from Armenia—all armed with weapons from Yerevan.

In Nagorno-Karabakh, Armenia—not Russia—was the most consequential. Relative to their total population, Armenians have one of the world's largest diasporas. This ethnic community was the financial lifeline of separatism. "It is difficult to overestimate the role [diaspora] support has played in creating Karabakh in material terms, as well as displacing any urgency for compromise with Azerbaijan."[137] "Among Karabakhians," furthermore, "there is a clear perception that their republic is the darling of the diaspora, more than Armenia" itself. Marinated in nationalist mythology, the separatist movement is credited with transforming Armenians "from victim nation to victorious nation."[138]

At the turn of the century, the patron state infected the separatist movement with a "prevailing environment of illegality" in which "'informal activity'— everything from bribe taking and bank fraud to extortion and assassination for hire—permeate[d] the public and private sectors, from top to bottom."[139] The shadow economy is fully half of Armenia's GDP.[140] The various branches of organized crime constituted "well-defined sectors—the 'bread mafia,' the 'energy mafia,' the 'trade mafia,' [etc.]. There is hardly a single economic domain that unofficial government activity has not come to dominate" in the independence period.[141] Criminal clans known as *akhperutyuns* (brotherhoods) ran transnational rackets stretching from Armenia and Russia into the Middle East and Europe. Armenian mafia branches in the United States, France, Panama, and Lebanon focused on loan sharking, money laundering, and gunrunning. While Azeri smugglers specialized in labor migrants, the ethnocentric "Armenian gangs have specifically targeted their countrywomen in extensive human trafficking tailored to the Russian sex industry."[142]

EXPLOITING FROZEN CONFLICT

During the Karabakh War, Armenian war profiteers coalesced with secessionists. "Some were criminal gangs. Others were fanatics." The typical mélange of "fractions of the Soviet army, volunteer militias and paramilitary groups, and criminal gangs" interbred. Separatist groups such as Dro, associated with the diaspora Armenian Revolutionary Federation, were banned for organizing assassinations and drug trafficking.[143] After the war, however, separatists had additional reason to perpetuate hostilities with the host state.

The greatest gift to Armenian mafias were Turkish-Azeri economic blockades, which effectively sealed 85 percent of Armenia's borders. Criminal suppliers in landlocked Karabakh met the demand accordingly as "well-known warlords established criminal networks and mafia organisations to benefit from the black-market trade across borders created by economic isolations." Safeguarding their rackets, separatist smugglers "strongly oppose[d] the resolution of the Nagorno-Karabakh conflict, because the beneficiaries of the arms deals do not want to lose a source of income."[144] Backtracking on secession became impossible because "they consider peace and normalisation of relations detrimental to their economic and political interests."[145] When Baku and Yerevan agreed to a 1997 Minsk Group peace settlement, separatists mined it. The reason was that "Karabakh would lose its direct access to Iran and the profitable trade that flowed from the south. . . . The proposal therefore risked jeopardizing the personal interests and powerbase of high-ranking Stepanakert officials and would reduce Karabakh's autonomy; it would reduce their access to alternative resources."[146] Entrenched in their separatist position, gangsters steadfastly resisted Azeri encroachment—indeed, any engagement with the government—in peacetime. In the process, many rose from the diaspora's criminal underworld to national political prominence and martyrdom. Fleeing Ukrainian law enforcement, Anushavan Danielian moved from being "a major figure in the Crimean 'mafia scene'" to the prime minister of Nagorno-Karabakh in 1999.[147] Out of the criminal swamp, one mafia emerged as the undisputed Karabakh authority: the Babayan Clan.

Samvel Babayan was chief among the separatist gangsters. The "small, dapper, and neat" kingpin sported a "shiny black mustache"—startling Western journalists as "more like Marcel Proust than a fearsome warlord." Simultaneously the separatist defense minister and commander of the army, he became the "de facto overlord and master of the territory" by heading one of the most sustained organized criminal enterprises in all of post–Cold War Caucasus. Supplementing day jobs as a car washer and busboy, the young Babayan ventured into local gang activity. In 1991, he murdered two brothers in a café in the separatist town of Askeran in a "criminal 'settling of scores.'" The timing was fortuitous. In the nationalistically charged atmosphere, his arrest by the Azeris turned out to be a blessing. He became a separatist "all-Armenian hero" and martyr to the emancipatory cause. Enlisting in a paramilitary, he quickly rose to lead it into strategic battles against the Azerbaijani forces.[148] Between 1991 to 1994, Babayan was the host state's most formidable enemy. Various gangs, irregulars (*fedayeen*), and hunter's groups (*djorads*) congealed into an enduring mafia under his leadership. "Small in build," Thomas Patrick Lowndes de Waal (2013, 227) observes, "this 'little Napoleon' was a creature of the war." Through plunder and racketeering under separatist cloak, he enriched himself by smuggling everything lootable within reach to Iran—from guns, cars, and jewelry, to scrap metal, copper wire, and roof beams. The Artsakh Defense Army, originally integrated into the Armenian military, became increasingly autonomous under Babayan as he appointed criminal minions into the office corps. War profiteering made Babayan one of the wealthiest—and most feared—people in the province.

When the war ended, Babayan emerged as a political icon. He monopolized trades in cigarettes and petroleum, laundering money through infrastructure projects such as the notorious "Babayan Underpass"—Karabakh's bridge to nowhere.[149] "Babayan's rapist propensities" sometimes supplemented his pecuniary ones. One of his extorted victims was asked to bring either of his teenage daughters in lieu of ransom. The minister's liaisons with women left a depraved stamp on Karabakh's culture:

> Young women were afraid to go out in the evenings because Babayan and his friends would crawl the streets in their Mercedes at five miles an hour, in the manner of Stalin's henchman Lavrentiy Beria, looking for female prey. Some parents sent their daughters to Yerevan to escape his rapacity; other young women bore children who were nicknamed "little Samo."[150]

To loyalists, he donated apartments, kiosks, and jobs; to rivals, he sent bullets. In March 2000, he was arrested for the attempted assassination of the president of Nagorno-Karabakh, whose state-building efforts encroached on organized crime.[151] The separatist community has yet to recover from the remnants of Babayan's mafia.[152]

Stemming from post-Soviet collapse and war, the Nagorno-Karabakh polity endures as an unwitting compromise between competing organized criminal interests. On the host state side, a loyal mafia in uniform—the Aliyev Clan—resisted Armenian drift, but not at the expense of regime stability. On the separatist side, a rebel mafia—the Babayan Clan—dominated the movement by sustaining transnational rackets with the patron state and exploiting the postwar stalemate. Known as the "Karabakh syndrome," this commitment to "no war, no peace" for the sake of criminal and political gain is shared by stakeholders in the separatist dispute on three sides.[153] Frozen conflict remains a guarantor of regime stability for Baku, Yerevan, and Stepaneket alike.[154]

9

Conclusion

We routinely distinguish military, political, civic, economic, and cultural processes in torn states. For modern separatism, I have argued, we must become accustomed to discussing organized criminal processes as well. I conclude with five propositions worth deriving from this book for future research.

Proposition 1. The temptation to reduce organized crime to an apolitical, nonagentic, or inconsequential factor has been overindulged. The analytic tools at our disposal for torn states in the globalized world are inadequate to capture the reality of mafia impact. My critique can roughly be reiterated as follows:

- Most studies of separatism neglect to consider organized crime as relevant
- Those (rare) studies that *do* consider organized crime relevant treat it as a mere consequence or symptom—not cause—of more essential phenomena
- Those (even rarer) studies that *do* consider organized crime causal treat it as a catalyst—a minor or proximate cause
- Those (negligibly few) studies that *do* consider organized crime as a major cause assume it to be a force for disintegration and mayhem, not cohesion or stability

In part, the neglect is understandable.[1] Mafia activity—theft, extortion, smuggling, violence, and profiteering—undermines idealizations of free market capitalism. When we conceptualize social contracts, states of nature, veils of ignorance, and other legacies of classical liberalism and romanticism, we rarely imagine rackets. Our cherished concept of the modern state—legitimate, rationalized, and democratic—also appears to exclude mafias. But "states that criminalize racketeering and organized crime," Hirschfeld (2015, 38–48, 13) reminds us, "date back only a few hundred years, and remain quite unevenly distributed around the world. [R]acketeering may have been a much more longstanding and influential force in human history than systems of market exchange." A reinterpretation of separatist dynamics that includes mafias can therefore refresh our understanding of how capital and coercion operate.

On the host state side, relegating organized crime under umbrella categories of warlordism, authoritarianism, and state weakness is simply inadequate. We must not only acknowledge but also distinguish mafias as flexible agents who may ally with the antiseparatist cause (mafias in uniform) or significantly sabotage it (Minderbinder mafias)—both under the government's wing. Scholars rightly emphasize that the criminalization of regimes creates a unique kind of informal political system—a parallel universe of power relations.[2] But they subsume mafias under "corruption," a state-centric concept with a serious selection bias toward developed economies.[3] For instance, Jean-Louis Briquet and Gilles Favarel-Garrigues (2010, 4) address "politico-criminal configurations" between organized crime and states. "Cases of direct reconversion of violent entrepreneurs into political actors are," they find, "fairly rare." In separatist contexts, though, they are anything but rare. They are *normal*. In torn states, gangsters can metamorphose into statesmen all too easily.

On the separatist movement side, a prevailing bias maintans that mafias are too apolitical, conservative, and finance minded to be state makers. The standard view is that organized crime

> does not seek to take over the government—indeed, they don't even pretend to be pursuing this goal. Unlike even the most predatory rebel groups, they do not attempt to disguise their profit-oriented motivations behind a political discourse. If anything, they are mainly interested in preserving the political status quo and co-opting existing political institutions rather than subverting them.[4]

When we consider torn states, all three statements become objectionable. First, it is not at all uncommon for mafias to seize the government apparatus, including for sustained periods of time. Nor is it unheard of that mafias co-opt separatist movements to create brand-new, proto-state institutions (rebel mafias). Second, the "disguise" of their profiteering does indeed assume separatist or antiseparatist political discourse. Instead of understanding this as a deceptive veil, we should appreciate that the degree of mafia *partisanship* is a natural, practical consequence of its profiteering. Third, whether mafias are "mainly interested" in continuity depends on state-separatist dynamics. If a frozen conflict enables massive profitable smuggling across disputed borders, the status quo is maintained (the Ergneti market was a paradigmatic example). If, however, mafias (mis)perceive that there are gains to be had in a new separatist polity, they are prepared not only to "subvert" but to replace existing political institutions (as Kosovo demonstrated). Linguist Max Weinreich (2008a, 362) quipped that a language is a dialect with an army and a navy. Today's budding nation-state, then, is a separatist movement with a loyal mafia.

Proposition 2. Differentiating mafias from governments and insurgents relieves a tired debate about torn states. Namely, is it opportunism or idealism? The answer is, both. Divided heterogeneous societies are full of ethnonational elites whose politics are suspicious. Who are the patriots, driven by nationalism? And who are the pragmatists—profit seeking, resource exploiting, and opportunity seizing? This stale controversy has recurrently divided scholars, not to mention interventionist foreign policy advocates in desperate search of the proper "side" to support in separatist disputes. The most enduring variant of this binary is the immense literature on "greed" versus "grievance"—a gold mine of insights.[5] Exceptions aside, however, both camps mainly attribute motivation to government or the insurgency—a dyadic view. Failing to individuate mafias from their state and movement allies, this vision of torn states is fundamentally blinkered. There is no doubt—certainly not in our three regions—that those who grasp even the slightest power tend to justify it in the name of nation, tribe, clan, or family. We take this for granted. But without a relational, Simmelian view of the state-separatist-mafia triad, we miss a central reason why nationalist politics and criminal greed are wedded. Mafias, I submit, are the missing link that clarifies when as well as how greed and grievance merge.

The reductionist picture of organized crime as apolitical, gluttony-driven profiteering is as misleading today as it was for the classic mafias. Students of organized crime have rightly condemned the "false, misleading and overstated dichotomy": "sharp distinctions between political and economic motivations," Andreas (2004b, 6) says, are "nonsense." For mafias, Williams (2011, 159, 163) notes, "creed and greed are not mutually exclusive," not least because "protection and predation are two sides of the same coin." In the political economy of organized crime, West (2002, 9) insists, "need, greed and creed merge, whether or not this is a conscious choice." Yet there have been no attempts to typologize mafias as pro- and antiseparatist *because* of their opportunism. This book took a preliminary step in that direction, specifying the conditions under which greed and grievance coalesce to tear states apart.

Proposition 3. Mafias' dual capacity to both disintegrate nations and promote state building is a unique feature that differentiates them from related "villainous" categories. Globalization has proliferated fuzzy nonstate actors that muddle our conventional classifications. In the ensuing confusion, mafias' special capacities have been neglected. To be sure, revolutionaries, rebels, warlords, terrorists, and criminals are attracted to each other. This homophily among rogues is ideologically exploitable, but sociologically trivial. They share skill sets, are concentrated in the same regions, and often face the same governments that tend to produce unflattering portrayals of their opponents. Violent lawbreakers need not share ideologies or ethnicities to cooperate. Frequently, "criminal and terrorist groups have an interchangeable membership and recruitment base—essentially posing as terrorists by day and criminals by night."[6] In torn states, this insurgency-crime continuum of hybrid collective actors is especially colorful.[7]

But extant conceptualizations have spread more mystification than insight. A dizzying array of buzzwords has emerged to describe the imbroglio of failed states, terrorists, and mafias as a "nexus"—painting an amalgam of irredeemable evil.[8] In the alarmist tone of Security Studies, the proper Latin plural "nexus" has even given way to "nexuses," amplifying the horror. In most cases, the term designates a vague "tie" or "connection"—leaving the reader to wonder about the exact nature of the relations. Eager to condemn one or another separatist movement, many equate it with organized crime outright. The "term 'nexus' is," in the words of a renowned mafia expert, "politically appealing, analytically appalling."[9]

Worse still, the propagandistic labeling of "criminals" who happen to have a political agenda perpetuates an unfortunate securitization template.[10] "Insurgency," "militancy," and "terrorism" are debased concepts in torn states, deployed to promote a government-centric (i.e., antiseparatist) agenda.[11] The result can be deadly repression. US-backed Mali and Niger, for example, toed the propaganda line "that the Tuareg rebels were merely bandits, criminals and drug dealers, categories which, in Washington parlance, equated with terrorists."[12] "Counterinsurgency" and "counterterrorism," meanwhile, have remained politely underscrutinized for their illegality, futility, and sheer cruelty. As a corrective, I have argued that governments *themselves* can be excellent incubators of mafias in uniform and organized crime can be a societal coping mechanism—sometimes the only possible one.

Finally, mafias are more than engines of war and violence. Recent US excursions into Afghanistan and Iraq inspired a literature on "asymmetrical," "hybrid," and "irregular" warfare, within which organized crime figures prominently. At a loss for words to describe torn states, military practitioners "blended smugglers, militias, insurgents, and criminals within the artificially uniting concept of 'complex irregular activity.'"[13] The term "complex" hardly contributes to our understanding. The assumption that these actors are "irregular" is simply unempirical. Reducing organized crime to an "activity" instead of an agent confuses the sinner for the sin. Nevertheless, the vague recognition that mafias may perpetuate and even cause war is a promising start.[14] Instead of obsessing on deviance and violence, I have argued that mafias in torn states are formative in peacetime—and can be formidable catalysts of peace (cosmopolitan mafias) as well as war. Indeed, transnational smuggling is sometimes the most vigorous peacekeeping force.

When we conflate organized crime with various violent actors, we spread confusion and platitudes. By reorienting our thinking, we avoid two important pitfalls: the propagandistic securitization of mafias, and exoticization of what are in fact normal societal processes in torn states.

Proposition 4. The role of organized crime in a torn state tells us nothing about the legitimacy of the nationalisms at play.[15] *By neglecting to analyze mafia roles out of courtesy, we accept a false political dilemma.* The conflation of studying mafia-separatist dynamics with criticizing separatism is common and cumbersome. When gangsters cling to a national cause as their last rag of decency, the cause becomes repulsive by association. Movements are then dismissed as illegitimate because of their criminal coalitions—exaggerated or not. Quite apart from secessionist ideology, the thought goes, permitting gangster bedfellows indicates wickedness and hypocrisy, disentitling separatists from statehood. But mafia-separatist relations are a global, empirical reality. Studying them does not prejudge which side is righteous, who "started it," or what polity should be permitted to materialize. Rather, whether gangster machinations taint the credibility of governments or their challengers is itself an important empirical question (as chapter 5 explored). We must not sacrifice this research agenda for fear of smearing or exonerating contentious actors.

Consider an analogy. Revisionist historians around the world—from Israel to Bangladesh—have dispelled nationalist fantasies by documenting monstrous "original sins" at the time of the country's creation: expulsions, massacres, and genocides. Against foundation myths, historical documents revealed disquieting cruelties against indigenous populations that paid the price for new nations to form. Does that discredit the demands of Zionism or Bengali nationalism? Not only is that a logical fallacy. It is also hopelessly ahistorical because virtually *all* nations are founded on one or another major crime. They all, furthermore, create elaborate historical mythologies to conceal the fact. If foundational sins were taken to discredit the right to self-determination and statehood, hardly any nation-state would remain on the planet. A similar reductio ad absurdum applies to separatism. If we delegitimate movements on the grounds that they partner with organized crime, practically no separatist movement outside the Organization for Economic Cooperation and Development could ever be justified. Future research on torn states can shed analytic light only if it forgoes this gratuitous normative baggage.

Proposition 5. The fact of mafias' profound impact on torn states is never an apologia for gangsterism. But the potential of organized crime to promote multiethnic integration and state making should inspire creative political action that does not inherently treat mafias as problems. Organized crime emerges from misery, hardship, and deprivation. Preying on insecurity and uncertainty, gangsters often display the depravity of human nature: avarice, cruelty, and unfathomable psychopathy. Global rackets, furthermore, are a humanitarian and ecological catastrophe.[16] Yet without contradiction, organized crime also represents the ingenuity, resilience, and triumph of populations under tremendous stress. A stubborn epistemic blockage prevents most of us (this author included) from comprehending that kind of stress, and what is involved in outliving it. Against economic shortages and political turmoil, globalized mafias "stem from local actors' need to continue doing business. Certainly, in such situations 'criminality' does characterize the predatory practices of violent professionals . . . but it is also part of a population's survival strategy and the way 'civil society' creates its own viable options and seeks to maintain relative stability in a crisis situation that escapes it."[17] In our hopes for democratic governance in torn states, we frequently shun these survival strategies as odious. This is not only empirically misleading but condescending to populations in separatist societies as well. As we saw across three continents, organized crime—for all the havoc it can foist on torn states—also has a mobilizing, cohesive, and pacifistic potential. The significance of mafias is not their illegality, deviance, or criminality.[18] It is their elasticity.

The sole remedy for globalized rackets, experts agree, is multilateralism.[19] But torn states are especially poor at sustaining multilateralism. Inhibited by high costs, diplomatic feuds, and electoral cycles, even high-capacity governments suffer chronic bureaucratic sluggishness, if not paralysis, in multilateral crackdowns. In torn states—plagued by what Olson (1982) called "institutional sclerosis"—international cooperation is even less likely because separatists weaken international credibility, spoil relations with neighboring countries, and preoccupy elites with domestic turbulence. Little wonder that transnational smuggling since the Cold War has been so robust. Successive replacements of mafias ensure continuity of the production, transport, and distribution of contraband. Cyclic state crackdowns only temporarily slow rackets.[20] Law enforcement memoirs are replete with existential soul-searching in the face of immovable structural forces of gangster supply and popular demand. Today's mafias are fast, efficient, and adaptive. Indeed, they are frequently quicker, better coordinated, and more responsive to crises than the governments that seek to repress them. So long as separatism continues to be a bedrock of globalization, so will organized crime.

Whether various rackets should be decriminalized at the national level is a delicate question. Compelling, if unsettling, arguments support decriminalizing soft narcotics, migrant smuggling, and sexual labor.[21] Whatever the balance, future research must reflect on the separatism-specific advantages and pitfalls of such reforms. It is often forgotten that legalization and decriminalization in the advanced democracies has profound ripple effects on peripheral torn states. How an intelligent, systemic global strategy can concurrently address transnational mafias *and* modern separatism remains a mystery—and a challenge.

One thing is certain. The militarization of anticrime policies by governments, the securitization of organized crime by scholars, and the demonization of mafias in popular culture are serious obstacles to systemic solutions. By understanding the diverse roles that mafias can play—good and bad—we secure a more realistic diagnosis.

Below I detail the sources, case selections, and other methodological decisions in part 2 (chapters 3–5) and part 3 (chapters 6–8).

Part II: Kosovo and South Ossetia

Kosovo and South Ossetia are arguably the closest pairing of cases across the three regions, but certainly among the Eastern European ones. Separatist movement milestones were almost simultaneous in the period under examination, 1989–2012. The key difference is in separatist outcome: Kosovo achieved greater sovereignty than South Ossetia.[1] Not only is Kosovo better integrated internationally, recognized by far more nation-states, and able to exercise greater self-government through its provisional institutions (taxation, coercion, and border control); it also has the capacity to exist as an independent political entity. South Ossetia is isolated internationally, recognized by a handful of peripheral countries, has significantly weaker extractive institutions, and is unable to sustain independence without merger with Russia / North Ossetia. The different mafia dynamics in the two cases, as chapters 3–5 suggested, help explain this disparity.

LOGIC OF THE PAIRING

I indicate six similarities between the two cases: forced migrations, Communist legacies, revocations of autonomy, black markets, antiauthoritarian revolutions, and the internationalization of conflict.

First, both societies underwent repeated forced migrations across separatist boundaries. Just as Albanians from Serbia proper fled to Kosovo and Serbs from Kosovo fled to Serbia proper (in 1999, 2004, and 2008), Ossetians from Georgia proper fled to South Ossetia and Georgians to Georgia proper in recurring refugee waves (1991, 1994, and 2004). Despite differences in territorial and population sizes, the "extremely high level of displacement in South Ossetia [in 2008] makes it comparable to—and worse in relative terms than—the large-scale displacement in Kosovo in 1999."[2] Both provinces enjoy territorial contiguity with a patron state: ethnic Ossetians are divided by the border between South Ossetia and Russia's North Ossetian Republic, while

Albanians are divided between Kosovo and the Republic of Albania. Much of the separatist constituency has family, property, and citizenship in the patron state—all facilitating migration.

Second, Serbia and Georgia are both remnants of multinational countries that disintegrated almost simultaneously in the early 1990s: Yugoslavia and the Soviet Union. Both Communist entities sought to preserve ethnic harmony by suppressing nationalist discourse and bestowing provincial autonomy. Despite legacies of bilingualism, the language differences between Serbian and Albanian as well as Georgian and Ossetian were salient symbols of separatist identity. Both Serbia and Georgia inherited robust traditions of political authoritarianism and comprehensive state intervention into economic matters.

Third, Kosovar and South Ossetian separatisms both came to the fore in 1989, aggravated by revocations of autonomy for the two provinces. Serbia reverted Kosovo's status to pre-1974 limits, returning the control of courts, education, and language policy to Belgrade. The Georgian Supreme Council proclaimed Georgian as the principal language. In February 1989, Kosovo Albanian miners engaged in a historic hunger strike, provoking a government crackdown on the province and countermobilization in Serbia proper. In November 1989, the South Ossetian regional council introduced demands for "autonomous republic" status, soliciting clashes with Georgian forces. Both host states escalated further. In 1990, in the wake of losing Slovenia and Croatia, Serbia dissolved the Kosovo assembly and enacted constitutional changes revoking autonomy. The same year, Georgia passed a law banning regional political parties. Following secession from Russia in 1991, Georgia's first president abolished South Ossetia's autonomy.

Fourth, both societies acquired vast black markets in the transition from centralized planning. Georgia's defective commodity distribution network proliferated illegal trade, while Serbia endured a UN sanctions regime. The results were shortages of basic consumer goods, majority unemployment, and the rise of a pervasive shadow economy. Between 1992 and 1995, it was estimated that 60 to 70 percent of the Georgian economy had become "black," with the government collecting only 10 percent of taxes.[3] In the same period, Serbia's illegal economy ranged from 45 to 70 percent, as the country underwent the worst episode of hyperinflation in history.[4]

Fifth, both Serbia and Georgia overthrew authoritarian regimes through popular uprisings based on mass nonviolent protests challenging electoral fraud. Serbia's Bulldozer Revolution (2000), which toppled Slobodan Milošević, and Georgia's Rose Revolution (2003), which toppled Eduard Shevardnadze, are subjects of comparative analyses of origins, outcomes, and the diffusions of revolutionary activism between the two societies.[5]

Finally, both disputes are highly internationalized. The Kosovo conflict widened into a confrontation between Yugoslavia and NATO / European

Union, just as the South Ossetia question widened into a conflict between Georgia and Russia. Both trajectories included episodes of moderate violence—in 1996 in Kosovo, and in 1991–92 in South Ossetia—followed by large-scale wars injecting peacekeepers—in 1999 in Kosovo, with NATO intervention, and in 2008 in South Ossetia, with Russian intervention.[6] Foreign troops from (mostly) NATO countries in Kosovo were as high as fifty thousand—one soldier per thirty-four residents. In South Ossetia, Russian troops numbered thirty-five hundred—one solider for every twenty-nine souls on the ground.[7]

CRITICAL JUNCTURES

Chapter 3 takes the year 1995—when the Yugoslav civil war ended, and Georgian state consolidated after a period of anarchic lawlessness—as a critical juncture in the paired separatist trajectories. It was in 1995 when the role played by organized crime began to diverge between the two cases, with fateful consequences. Chapter 4 treats the 1999 Kosovo War and the 2008 Second South Ossetia War as critical junctures of separatist success. These conflicts solidified the de facto autonomies of both regions.[8] Since the period under examination is brief, and changes in relational configuration sudden and drastic, a "path dependency" framework would be an exaggeration. Furthermore, I do not imply any more sophisticated causal structures such as feedback loops or self-reinforcing/reactive sequences.[9]

WHY NOT ABKHAZIA?

Georgia's second, larger separatist province is the self-proclaimed Republic of Abkhazia.[10] Analyzing South Ossetia and Abkhazia as a single case is common, but the two trajectories have crucial differences. First, while South Ossetia is a relatively recent entity (the South Ossetian Autonomous Region was invented in 1922, severing it from North Ossetia), the wholistic Republic of Abkhazia boasts long-standing traditions of independence (the Principality of Abkhazia began as early as the sixteenth century). Second, though rhetoric in South Ossetia may be more anti-Georgian than in Abkhazia, Ossetians are decidedly more integrated into Georgia. In this sense, Abkhazia is closer to Slovenia than to Kosovo in the context of the former Yugoslavia. Third, while Abkhazia has historically had a well-developed infrastructure and high economic potential (attracting considerable Russian capital), South Ossetia is chronically underdeveloped, with enduring underinvestment and limited self-sustainability—akin to the marginal status and neglect of Kosovo in the former Yugoslavia.

Most important, Abkhazia's ethnic diversity is substantially greater. While Kosovo and South Ossetia share histories of two ethnic groups vying for majority control and fluctuating in relative size, Abkhazia mostly had only a plurality of the titular Abkhaz with at least four sizable minorities in any given period. The first and only census since 1897 that recorded a titular majority was in 2011: 50.7 percent Abkhaz, 19.2 percent Georgian, 17.4 percent Armenian, and 9.1 percent Russian—a dramatically more heterogeneous population than South Ossetia's, whose 2011 estimates stood at 67.1 percent Ossetians, 25 percent Georgians, and not a single other minority above 3 percent. Finally, both Kosovo and South Ossetia underwent historic shifts from one ethnic majority to the other (Serbian to Albanian, and Georgian to Ossetian).

FIELDWORK

With a research fellowship from Harvard's Minda de Ginzburg Center for European Studies in 2013–14, I traveled extensively in Serbia/Kosovo and Georgia/South Ossetia interviewing experts, conducting ethnography, and exploring archives. I spent five and a half months in Serbia, three of which were in Kosovo, and four months in Georgia, four weeks of which were in South Ossetia. In Serbia proper, I have been to Belgrade, Preševo, and Bujanovac; in Kosovo itself, I went to Kosovska Mitrovica, Orahovac, Prizren, Uroševac, and Gnjilane. In Georgia proper, I traveled to Tbilisi, Kutaisi, Gori, and Kazbegi; in South Ossetia, I visited Tskhinvali, Leningor, Kvaisi, and Kurta. Civilian families in northern Mitrovica and Kazbegi fed me, drove me, accepted me as a paying tenant, and helped in finding guides; their kindness and hospitality will stay with me for life. Though the bulk of this work does not reference my ethnographic observations and conversations directly, the discovery and selection of sources that led me to the presented evidence would not have been possible without this fieldwork. I heeded the advice of independent experts, journalists, NGO researchers, government officials, and ordinary residents who directed me toward neglected sources and realities.

BORDERS

I entered Kosovo with a Serbian passport without difficulty—via bus or with a UNHCR crew via car. Invitation letters from Priština offices expedited the movement between Serbian, Kosovar, and international booths—tens of meters apart but technically integrated at some crossings. Contrary to the belief that it is impossible to enter South Ossetia except through Russia, tour guides in Tbilisi provide cheap and guided transportation, along with translation services, for travelers interested in the trip northward. In summers, fixers run small businesses and hiking tours of the breathtaking Ossetian mountains. South Ossetian authorities did not stamp my passport, allowing me to show it to Georgian authorities without raised eyebrows. It may be formally true that the "administrative borders" toward separatist territories are sealed since the

2008 war. But customs guards and soldiers at checkpoints cooperate daily with their friends and cousins to allow for passage without visas, or at a price, even without documents. Via email, I secured a permission letter from the consular section of the Ministry of Foreign Affairs of South Ossetia. Georgian citizens attempting to enter the separatist region from Georgia proper (to visit relatives or conduct commerce) are often harassed for "illegal" crossing.

In north South Ossetia, the Roki Tunnel into Russia is marked by an immense iron gate, which is closed at night. One can only travel during the daytime. Russian peacekeepers control everything that passes on the Trans-Caucasus highway. The tunnel was constructed in 1985, yet was poorly maintained after the Soviets. Repair work had been done in 2004, but the structure is feared crumbling. Avalanches occur every winter (sometimes trapping vehicles and people inside the tunnel). One young Russian soldier reported that some eight hundred vehicles pass through every day—half of them trucks. Boxes of cigarettes are the most reliable "ticket" for civilian travelers without merchandise, although customs guards accept other commodities as well.

LEGACIES OF WAR

In Belgrade and Tbilisi—and even more so in Tskhinvali and Priština—one is immediately struck by how small the communities are. Everyone seems aquainted with everyone else. I encountered the son-in-law of a South Ossetian minister accidentally at a Tskhinvali eatery. He immediately took me on a tour of the main government building (an architectural relic), where separatist officials socialize as much as work. In Priština, I once mentioned a journalist who received mafia death threats (by no means a rarity). My host interrupted me: "Oh, you mean so-and-so. Let me call him. He's right around the corner!"

Everyone's fate is seemingly connected to the wars. Much of the male population consists of forced migrants and/or former fighters, and every family has at least one refugee story. An Albanian acquaintance in Priština fought in the 1995 Bosnian War as well as in 1999 for the KLA. An accidental meeting with a Special Units operative at a Belgrade public pool revealed that he was trained through three wars. Almost every adult male I have met in South Ossetia served in the military. Ossetian and Georgian refugees dominate conversations—both as speakers and subjects. The single most recommended tourist site in Tskhinvali is the monument to victims of the 2008 conflict.

Tskhinvali is among the most hospitable towns I have ever visited. Due to low tourism in the harsh winters (when travel is difficult) and the somewhat arbitrary times when entrance into the province is prohibited without written permission from separatist authorities, Ossetians cherish visitors. Tskhinvali residents are thrilled to see foreigners and reluctant to part with them.

Pensioners invited me into their homes. Small traders enthusiastically introduced me to cousins and drove me through the city. Many felt an obligation to counter hurtful claims that Tskhinvali is an unappealing place to visit. I myself found the ill repute unfounded.

ARCHIVES AND INFORMANTS

I oriented my travels around NGOs, media outlets, university offices, and government archives. In Belgrade, I explored the archives of the Humanitarian Law Centre, Helsinki Committee on Human Rights, daily *Politika*, UNHCR Belgrade office, and Bureau for Coordination of Protection of Human Trafficking Victims. In Tbilisi, I visited the Caucasus Research Resource Center, Terrorism, Transnational Crime, and Corruption Center, United States Agency for International Development branch office, UNHCR Tbilisi office, and International Crisis Group Tbilisi office. Suitably enough, my research into organized crime led me to several government archivists who asked (in no uncertain terms) for bribes and informal "service fees" for dusting off boxes of documents, checking if something was available, and other arduous tasks.

Through snowball sampling, I conducted semistructured expert interviews (n = 43) with policy makers (including three ministers), criminologists and other academic specialists, and people with expert knowledge on mafia machinations: from local firms and children's hospitals to ministries and parliament. In Kosovo, the interviews were often preceded by introductions from friends and acquaintances, who were instrumental in building trust and recruiting informants with colorful biographies. One thirty-six-year-old revealed that he had served time in jail for a blood feud murder of a man who slept with his sister. The victim's family had been disgraced, he told me, so a vendetta was the only suitable response. As the oldest son, he naturally assumed the task. He was nineteen at the time of the murder. This led me to give a second thought to the dimension of Kanun, which I had considered an irrelevant anachronism.

In-depth interviews with gangsters were few (n = 9), pleasant, and perfectly uneventful. I spoke to former Mkhedrioni and National Guard fighters turned smugglers in Tbilisi as well as veterans of the prison system. In Belgrade, I met two Zemun Clan members. I fortuitously identified one of them at a public pool because of a distinctive red rose neck tattoo, a hallmark of the "Red Berets," or Jedinica za Specijalne Operacije (JSO). The man knew Ulemek, the Zemun Clan boss serving prison time for the mafia's assassination of the prime minister. He maintained the whole affair was a setup, the JSO is a misunderstood patriotic organization, and everything it did (including extortion kidnappings, which he gladly admitted to) was for the greater good of "the people." Overall, the gangsters I spoke to were amiable, fiercely loyal, and had vivid imaginations.

In Tbilisi, three guides and translators accompanied me on separate drives through South Ossetia, translating conversations and recommending interviewees. One guide was a veteran of both the First and Second South Ossetia Wars as well as a proud businessman who supported his family throughout the Ergneti period by selling food and electric equipment. Like many Georgian (and even more Ossetian) respondents, he bemoaned the closing of Ergneti. The choice, he repeatedly insisted, was between *trade* (symbolized by Ergneti) and *war* (symbolized by Saakashvili and Kokoity). Through weeks of travel with him, including many nights under the same roof and days in the same car, I grasped the significance of the Roki Tunnel as a strategic site, proximity of Ossetian and Georgian communities in South Ossetia, and widespread dependence on smuggling for survival around the disputed border.

FEAR

In Kosovo and South Ossetia, one is reminded of the Thomas theorem: if people define situations as real, they are real in their consequences. Much of the power that mafias enjoy is not in their objective leverage but rather in the notoriety and terror that they generate in public opinion. In both communities, a steady belief in the existence of a shadowy, unforgiving underworld looms large among ordinary people. Lurid gossip overlaps with criminal realities, magnifying the blanket dread from an amorphous danger "out there" for anyone who crosses "them." A chatty and hospitable restaurant owner in Tbilisi (only kilometers away from a police station) captured it best:

> [The criminals] are everywhere. They take care of each others' backs, and they are connected everywhere. They are only interested in helping each other, and the rest of us better stay out of the way. I don't think there is anybody who can stop them. They have too much money. They have connections. They can make actions together without anyone stopping them. Too many people are scared or take bribes. Politicians are just actors. The real organization is the guys with connections. We just have to swim, save our heads.

For symmetry, consider a similar anecdote from Kosovo. In a downtown Priština cafe, I convened with a television crew from the UNHCR that had come to film a segment on refugee returnees. Seated at the table was our driver, who knew the province well. Midway through our coffee, a noticeable middle-age man walked down the stairs from the locale's upper platform. He was in casts, had visible bruises over his face, and descended insecurely on two crutches. "That guy is the owner of this place," the driver remarked. "He was kidnapped last week." As the youngest and greenest, I was innocent enough to express shock. I asked to confirm if I had heard correctly. "Yeah," the driver nonchalantly retorted, raising his voice and waving his arm as if to check if I might be blind: "You know, they tied him to a radiator or who knows what. It was Haradinaj's people; they do the racket here. Maybe he owed them money or he tried to swindle them, who knows? They do this every few months." The substance was as intriguing as the tone; his surprise was greater than mine, because he could not believe that I should find this unusual.

FREEDOM OF INFORMATION ACT REQUESTS

I filed for Freedom of Information Act requests in both Belgrade and Tbilisi, asking for documents "of public interest" on organized crime and smuggling in the 1989–2012 period. At the suggestion of experts, I tailor formulated both applications referring to already-available but partial data about Kosovo and South Ossetia from the Ministry of Interior websites and National Statistics Bureaus. I took the liberty of insinuating that the heroic anticorruption efforts of the government are a centerpiece of the research.

In Belgrade, my Serbian citizenship allowed me to file the request directly in August 2013. In four months, I picked up hundreds of pages of documents, the most valuable of which was a 1999 Public Safety Bureau report on KLA mafias. I also received the 2001 *White Book* with extensive details about organized criminal clans (notably the Zemun Clan) on a CD. Though segments of this document were already public, it was helpful to receive the unredacted forty-two-page version.

In Tbilisi, the law prohibited noncitizens from filing applications. Through a Princeton connection, I was fortunate to befriend a young, gifted Georgian professional with experience in Saakashvili's administration who later worked at the Finance Ministry in Belgrade. On my behalf, he filed a Freedom of Information Act request in his name. We received a fair assortment of documents electronically within two months of filing in October 2013. Useful documents included statistics and excerpts from the Thieves-in-Law database from the Anti-Organized Crime Unit of the Georgian Ministry of Internal Affairs (1989–2012) and an internal report by the Ministry of Internal Affairs of Georgia (2005) on the first few years of Saakashvili's anticorruption drive.

DATA QUALITY IN TORN STATES

Demographic, census, and electoral records are highly susceptible to bias in separatist areas. Occasionally, the data are so blatantly fraudulent that they become embarrassing to propagate. In the 2011 elections, the Central Electoral Commission of Kosovo announced that the number of registered voters was 1,630,636. The same office added that the proportion of the total population under eighteen years of age was 43 percent. Merging those two data, one could deduce that as many as 2.7 million people live in Kosovo. Yet only months later (April 2012), the population was recorded as 1.7 million—the same as the number of registered voters.

Consider another election-related misconception. Many refer to Kokoity's high popularity in South Ossetia in 2011. It grew astronomically when Georgia attacked in 2008—a familiar cohesion effect under external threat. Much-cited 2011 estimates (ranging from 60 to 90 percent popularity), however, refer to polling and election results later invalidated by the Supreme Court of South Ossetia. Leading opposition candidates had been prevented from even registering in this election cycle. Competitors had been beaten, jailed, and in the case of a senior member of a disqualified political party, *murdered* in North Ossetia. The chilling effect was hardly reflected in the estimates, which are cited widely.

Such fabrications abound and should give fieldworkers pause. I decided to rely on conservative estimates for all figures related to referenda, casualties, public opinion, ethnic distance measurements, political party popularity, population movements, refugee figures, sizes of crowds at major collective actions, numbers of troops and active militia members, and perhaps most important, features of criminal clans.

Chapter 3

Chapter 3 provides a comparative historical analysis of the separatist trajectories of Kosovo and South Ossetia from 1989 to 2012. For chronologies of the Kosovo and Second Ossetian Wars, including details of criminal militia evolution before and after the conflicts, see the multivolume reports of the Independent International Commission on Kosovo (2000) and Independent International Fact-Finding Mission on the Conflict in Georgia (2009). On war and mafia events, organizations, and personalities, I relied on the archives of the Belgrade-based Centre for Humanitarian Law (2003–12) and Tbilisi-based Terrorism, Transnational Crime, and Corruption Center (2004–12) along with the scholarly sources cited in the chapter.

PROCESS TRACING

I process traced the two separatist trajectories regarding three actors: *host state* (the Milošević, Djindjić, Koštunica, and Tadić regimes in Serbia; and the Gamsakhurdia, Shevardnadze, and Saakashvili regimes in Georgia), *separatist movement organizations* (Rugova's "parallel institutions" followed by the Thaçi-led KLA government, and the Kulumbegov-Chibirov-Kokoity Councils in South Ossetia), and *mafias* (the Zemun Clan, JSO, and KLA in Serbia/Kosovo; and the Mkhedrioni, National Guard, and Tedeyev and Chibirov Clans in Georgia / South Ossetia).[11]

The separatist trajectories consist of overlapping processes of state consolidation, separatist mobilization, and criminal co-optation. Dozens of events such as wars, migrations, revolutions, coups, elections, and collective actions indicated these processes. The categories of events included (with selected examples relevant to mafias):

1. *Smuggling episodes* consequential to separatism: arms flow into Kosovo from Albania (1997–98) and the Ergneti market on the Georgia-Ossetia border (1996–2004)
2. *Host state repression campaigns*: the prewar military crackdown on Kosovo (1997–99), seizures of contraband goods (2003), installation of customs booths (2004), and anti-Ossetian "anticorruption" campaign (2004–8)
3. *Major wars*: the NATO war (1999), and First (1991–92) and Second South Ossetia Wars (2008)
4. *Antiseparatist host state mobilization*: Milošević's speech in Gazimestan (1989) and Gamsakhurdia's "March on Tskhinvali" (1989)
5. *Separatist movement mobilization*: the Kosovo protests in 1988, culminating in the miners' strike in 1989, and South Ossetian militias and locally organized civilian barricades in 1989 blocking Georgian protesters from entering the separatist capital
6. *Separatist movement demobilization*: the popularity and membership of Ibrahim Rugova's Democratic Alliance of Kosovo waning in the post-Dayton period, and the South Ossetian parliamentary declaration that provinces would remain in Georgia (1996) if autonomy was formally reinstated

TRIADS

I define each triad as a set of six positions among the host state, separatist movement, and organized crime.

The *rejoicing third*: the separatist movement promotes organized crime indirectly, as an unintended consequence of confronting the host state; organized crime promotes separatism for its own ends, exploiting division; the separatist movement confronts the host state; the host state confronts the separatist movement; the host state does not confront organized crime significantly; and organized crime confronts the host state, exploiting its weakness.

The *divider and ruler*: the separatist movement relies on organized crime for its survival; organized crime co-opts the separatist movement; the separatist movement is incentivized and empowered to confront the host state; the host state confronts the separatist movement; the host state confronts organized crime; and organized crime is incentivized and empowered to confront the host state.

The *mediator*: the separatist movement relies on organized crime as much as the host state does; organized crime does not support the separatist movement; the separatist movement is disincentivized or disabled from confronting the host state; the host state is disincentivized or disabled from confronting the separatist movement; the host state relies on organized crime for its own ends; and organized crime incorporates elements of the host state for its own ends.

Simmel argued that triads have a radically transformative quality over dyads, with their reciprocal effects (*Wechselwirkung*) being an indispensable unit of analysis.[12] Peter Hedström and Richard Swedberg (1998, 5) cite Simmel's *tertius gaudens* as a classic example of a social mechanism, and the triadic form features prominently in network analysis.[13] This Simmelian approach is woefully neglected in comparative historical work.

Chapter 4

Data are extracted primarily from the UNODC's *Transnational Organized Crime Threat Assessment* reports (2006–14) and *World Drug Reports* (1997–2013), EUROPOL's *Serious and Organized Crime Threat Assessment* reports, the European Institute for Crime Prevention and Control annual reports, "National Criminal Justice Profiles" for selected countries (2010–13), and the European Monitoring Center for Drugs and Drug Addiction's "Country Profiles" for Serbia, Georgia, and (separately) Kosovo.

FILTER INDICATORS

Organized criminal "filtering" has two components: regional opportunity, and mafia capacity and predisposition to convert this opportunity into separatist gain. I operationalize *regional opportunity* as shifts in aggregate drug- and arms-smuggling levels in the Balkans and Caucasus that make our two cases potential participants in an international criminal supply chain. By definition, these shifts are not caused by the countries themselves; they are determined by the war in Afghanistan, declaration of independence of Macedonia, state breakdown in Albania, and other geopolitical tremors. Such exogenous opportunity is a precondition for mafia filtering, though insufficient on its own to cause separatist success.

The reaction of the country's organized crime to opportunity is an endogenous development determined by two factors:

1. The *capacity* of organized crime to capitalize on the opportunity. I compare the duration and scope of the smuggling, size and complexity

TABLE 4. Drug Seizures in Serbia and Georgia, 1993–2011

	Cocaine	Cocaine	Heroin	Heroin	Cannabis	Cannabis	Ecstasy	Opium
1993	0.2	NA	159.8	0.2	177.7	NA	0.00	NA
1994	0.8	NA	31.8	NA	143.0	NA	0.00	NA
1995	0.2	NA	30.3	NA	67.1	NA	0.00	NA
1996	3.9	0.000	21.6	0.3	884.2	24.2	0.00	17.60
1997	4.9	0.000	35.6	0.5	1,594.0	NA	0.10	10.30
1998	2.3	0.000	29.2	0.9	1,823.3	NA	0.01	7.50
1999	NA	0.000	NA	2.3	NA	31.9	NA	14.70*
2000	2.4	0.000	57.2	3.9	780.9	NA	0.00	33.50
2001	3.6	0.000	62.5	5.5	1,230.2	32.3	0.09	NA
2002	1.9	NA	43.5	NA	1,729.5	NA	0.08	NA
2003	6.0	0.000	278.8	3.0	1,465.0	42.4	0.06	8.40
2004	15.5	0.000	474.4	0.8	4,111.0	34.1	9,260 u.	1.20
2005	5.3	NA	359.6	NA	1,509.5	NA	7,839 u.	38.00
2006	12.9	0.000	696.6	8.6	1,817.3	25.6	19.00	0.20
2007	16.1	0.001	484.3	16.2	1,625.1	23.6	3.80	0.20
2008	15.1	0.000	207.6	12.1	1,477.8	28.3	0.20	0.10
2009	19.2	0.001	169.2	2.3	1,083.2	4.7	5.40	0.03
2010	7.6	0.010	242.8	1.1	1,352.8	33.3	23.50	0.00
2011	6.0	0.000	64.9	0.5	995.1	32.1	48.70	0.10

* In addition, 83.5 kilograms of opium seed.

Notes: Serbia in white, Georgia in gray. The "u." indicates the units of ecstasy pills when the kilogram value is unavailable.

Source: World Drug Reports, 1999–2012; Ministries of Interior Affairs of the Republic of Serbia and Georgia.

of the mafias, the host state's effectiveness in repressing the traffic, the level of foreign military crackdown on this criminal branch, and the adaptability of traffickers to market fluctuations.

2. The *predisposition* to aid separatists. I compare the ethnocentrism of the mafias associated with the traffic, the separatist share of organized crime vis-à-vis the host state, and financial or other benefits for separatist movement organizations.

SEIZURES

The seizure data are primarily compiled by the National Statistical Offices of Serbia and Georgia, and secondarily, come from Serbian and Kosovar police data. The UNHCR's *World Drug Reports* import data from these domestic sources.[14]

Kosovo-specific drug seizures are the best documented, especially between 2006 and 2012. The seizures range from 14.6 to 94.2 kilograms of heroin, 0.5 to 7.4 kilograms of cocaine, and 67 to 419 kilograms of cannabis. In the chapter, I compare drug possession/abuse charges with drug trafficking charges in 2005–6 because it is a rare opportunity for perfect matching: this two-year period was the first occasion that the UNODC's *World Drug Reports* (2008) compelled countries to standardize their indicators of drug-related crime. The Second South Ossetia War unfortunately made matched comparisons impossible for the subsequent years.

Due to poor data, enduring comparative dilemmas remain.[15] Drug use prevalence, for example, is clearly higher among Georgians than among Serbians. But whether Georgia is more often a destination country for imported drugs, whereas Serbia is more frequently a transit country, remains unclear. The disaggregation of drug seizure and domestic use data in the neighboring countries may further shed light on this difference.

Chapter 5

The two episodes—organ harvesting and HEU trafficking—were the only two exposed nefarious criminal incidents in post–Cold War Serbia and Georgia. Given how unstable and stigmatized these black markets are, the two scandals are the most salient cases we have in Eastern Europe as a whole.[16]

SOURCES

Two in-depth records serve as the main sources: a Council of Europe report on organ smuggling in Kosovo between 1999 and 2000, and a Belfer Center report on nuclear smuggling in South Ossetia and Georgia in 2006. Due to the authors' impartiality, access to witnesses, and duration of the investigation, these documents are the best available expositions of the scope and chronology of the nefarious criminal episodes. These two scandals are otherwise saturated by propaganda and tabloidization.

The Council of Europe report was produced by an investigative team headed by Swiss prosecutor Dick Marty (2010), commissioned by the Parliamentary Assembly of the Council of Europe and adopted in 2011.[17] Marty's team spoke to scores of KLA insiders (from foot soldiers to commanders), INGO and NGO specialists, and officials from all institutions with jurisdiction before and after the recorded period of the traffic: KFOR, the United Nations, the ICTY, the Serbian government and Belgrade-based War Crimes Tribunal, and EULEX. The team also visited sites where organ harvesting took place. Firsthand witnesses included "drivers, bodyguards and other 'fixers' who performed logistical and practical tasks aimed at delivering the human bodies to the operating clinic," in addition to "the 'organisers,' the criminal ringleaders who . . . entered business deals to provide human organs for transplantation purposes in return for handsome financial rewards."[18]

Analogously, the most in-depth and reliable report on nuclear smuggling in South Ossetia was prepared for the Managing the Atom Project at Harvard's Belfer Center in 2008.[19] It was commissioned by the Nuclear Threat Initiative, a credible nonprofit. This detailed account of a 2006 seizure of the HEU by Georgian authorities traces the landmark smuggling operation with rich detail on the perpetrators, their backgrounds, the nature of their criminal infrastructure, and the chronology leading to exposure. For the report, journalist Michael Bronner interviewed dozens of US and Georgian investigators, prosecutors, and law enforcement officials who captured the smugglers; firsthand witnesses to the traffic; interrogators of the gangsters; and NGO specialists covering Georgian organized crime. The report also synthesizes documents and other evidence from the Department of Energy, the FBI's Weapons of Mass Destruction unit, the Russian Federal Security Service, and the IAEA. Bronner personally traveled to major sites related to the traffic. This report covers all institutions with formal jurisdiction over the territory where nuclear smuggling occurred.

Supplementary sources include journalistic, scholarly, and government reports.[20] The most illuminating document on Kosovo is an UNMIK report on a 2004 visit to Rribe (accessed October 18, 2014, www.coe.int/t /dghl/monitoring/minorities/3_FCNMdocs/PDF_1st_Report_Kosovo_en .pdf). An outstanding German Secret Service report ("BND Analyse vom 22.02.2005," Wikileaks.org) details the Kosovar mafia's organizational structure. For the regional nuclear-trafficking context, see the inventory of Black Sea smuggling incidents by Alex Schmid and Charlotte Spencer-Smith (2012) and the Nuclear Trafficking Collection database of the Nuclear Trafficking Initiative (accessed December 15, 2019, www.nti.org/analysis/reports/nis-nuclear -trafficking-database).

RRIBE AND KAZBEGI COMPARISON

These remote, mountainous villages were selected for their clan affinity to the gangsters. Both smuggling rings relied on local villagers' support, shelter, and at least the tacit complicity of kinfolk in stages of the traffic. Furthermore, these sites were the principal locations in which the nefarious episodes were discovered. Were there no investigations at *these* sites, the two mafias would probably never have been exposed. Most important, Rribe's Yellow House and Kazbegi were salient symbolic associations with Kosovar and South Ossetian institutions, respectively. Even though neither of them is on separatist territory, these villages became—in the public eye—the clearest evidence of separatists being caught in *flagrante delicto*. International attention to separatist involvement in the nefarious activities concentrated, likewise, on these localities.

JURISDICTIONS

Serbia lost all law enforcement jurisdiction in Kosovo after the 1999 war. In the years preceding the organ traffic, host state troops withdrew, yielding Kosovo's institutions to international arbitration. Georgia's sovereignty over South Ossetia ended after the First South Ossetia War of 1991–92 and entry of Russian troops. In the years preceding the HEU traffic, Tbilisi began reasserting its territorial control over southern segments of the separatist province, but it never secured oversight of the Ossetian Georgia-Russia border (i.e., the Roki Tunnel). The host states themselves were therefore incapable of combating the mafias. When they attempted to (the Milošević regime in 1998 and Saakashvili regime in 2004), the result was war (in 1999 and 2008, respectively). In both cases, host state strategies toward organized crime in the separatist zones contributed to ethnic polarization and foreign intervention.

International law enforcement, however, was incomparably stronger in Kosovo. KFOR and EULEX were high-capacity administrators and overseers of the separatist region. In South Ossetia, the JCC was "a practical, if not necessarily efficient, conflict-management mechanism" under the dominance of a regional power (Russia) that cared naught for law enforcement.[21] INGO willingness to curb crime in Kosovo was outstanding, even by international standards. A ten-year onslaught of international judges, prosecutors, and police under the auspices of UNMIK was succeeded by an even more aggressive EULEX mandate that ripened the judicial, penal, and police systems of Kosovo. In South Ossetia, the Russian-dominated JCC/JPFK administration remained timid on international supervision, isolating South Ossetia from regional initiatives against nuclear smuggling and deliberately undermining Ossetian law enforcement.

Part III: Three Regions

Chapters 6–8 paint with a broader brush. I examine how *state dependent* and *partisan* mafias in fourteen torn states were (1989–2019) by surveying separatist trajectories: the impact of organized crime on the host state, movement, and evolving dynamic between the two. I idealize the separatist processes of thirty years, decontextualize host state maneuvering from its international relations, and disregard minor variations in organized criminal roles over time. Nevertheless, the mafia typology is based on a careful synthesis of the best available evidence from primary and secondary sources.

SOURCES

The difficulty regarding sources on organized crime in torn states is not scarcity but rather volume. The impact of mafias is well documented in all fourteen cases, yet the facts are often buried in second-order distortions, misinterpretations, and fabrications. For each case, I synthesize a minimum of eight reliable secondary sources—books, articles, documents, scholarly monographs, reports, memoirs, and records—that shed light on the effect of organized crime on separatism from 1989 to 2019. I selected sources based on two criteria: scope and credibility.

Scope: This includes the date of publication, temporal and spatial extent, concreteness of evidence, and extent of separatism-specific data. Regrettably, most publications tend to examine major historical ruptures (wars, regime changes, and migrations) while purportedly "quiet" periods of separatist-mafia dynamics are underdocumented. Many valuable examinations of separatist movements, furthermore, cover mafias superficially, in passing, or not at all. I favored in-depth case-specific studies over broad histories, reports produced prospectively ("in real time") over retroactive inquiries colored by subsequent politics, and works that examine neglected periods over media-frenzied, saturated crises. Above all, I selected sources that produce verifiable, concrete, and direct evidence of mafia impact. In Transnistria, for example, "it is rather difficult to make a clear distinction between businesses and criminal groups involved in trafficking, smuggling, and economic frauds"—an unsatisfying finding.[22] In Turkey, in contrast, a study of Kurdish mafias specifies eleven mafia formations (families), coding them as "B1," "B2," and so on, with accessible references regarding their "European" and "regional" dimensions across a decade—an impressive scope.[23]

Credibility: This involves the quality of the publisher, author expertise, and political/ideological bias. Criminological studies suffer from progovernment favoritism. Others tendentiously overlook one side's criminalization and inflate another's. Voluminous works—without the slightest corroboration—describe fantastic gangster events and personalities that allegedly had fateful consequences on separatist outcomes. Most of these tales are "too good to verify," and are thus perpetuated injudiciously by separatist critics or advocates, depending on the utility of the concocted story. I omitted such literature on separatist mafias. Whenever possible, I gave special preference to evidence provided by sources from whom one would not expect it (e.g., separatist data on separatist-mafia infiltration is preferable to government data on separatist-mafia infiltration). I favored ethnographic and fieldwork-based studies (government, journalistic, and NGO) over secondary sources. Finally, I verified original evidence, when available, behind its second-order citations. In Moldova, for example, an EU Border Assistance Mission of two hundred officials from twenty-two countries produced the best assessments of Transnistrian mafias in multiple reports. Their findings, however, have been propagandized by both sympathizers and opponents of separatism, who selectively lose a sense of proportion when it suits them.

In the main, the selected analysts cautiously differentiate criminals from separatist movements and governments. For instance, "Boko Haram, once a Salafist sect based in Nigeria's north-east, has morphed into something far more deadly and ruthless: a hydra-headed monster further complicated by imitators and criminal gangs who commit violence under the guise of the group." The same book—echoing other sources—records the role of northern gangs such as Ecomog, which "bitter over being abandoned" by its patrons "once elections ended and politicians stopped paying them off," gravitated to Boko Haram.[24] Such nuanced accounts allow for the corroboration of conclusions across sources regarding mafia alliances, oppositions, co-optations, disintegrations, and so forth.

The narrative was written for the skeptical reader, who may doubt the relevance or extent of criminalization in these societies. I adhered to the following rules: when available, important primary sources are consulted and cross-referenced with their secondary regurgitations; when contradictory figures or data are presented across reliable sources, I cited both; when competing interpretations of the same evidence emerged between two equally credible sources, I asked area specialists or an independent expert in the field to adjudicate; between self-serving government estimates and NGO or INGO estimates on the same issue, I opted for the latter; whenever controversial claims are made, I quote specialists' own loaded phrases rather than using my own words to interpret or qualify the nature of state-separatist-mafia entanglements.

The case sources by region are as follows.

Ambazonia: Angwafo 2014; Atanga 2011; Ayim 2010; Dicklitch 2011; Fonchingong 2013; Fossungu 2013; Gros 2003; ICG 2017a; Konings and Nyamnjoh 1997; Mehler 2014; Okereke 2018; Pommerolle and Heungoup 2017. *Azawad*: Bouquet 2013; Doumbi-Fakoly, Ciré, and Boubacar 2012; Gaoukoye (2018); Harmon 2014; Heisbourg 2013; Keenan 2013; Lecocq 2002; Lloyd 2016; Silva 2017; Strazzari 2015. *Agadez*: de Tessières 2018; Felbab-Brown 2017; Guichaoua 2015; Kohl and Fischer 2010; Koré 2010; Nicolaisen and Nicolaisen 1997; Spittler 1999. *Boko Haram*: Adesoji 2011; Comolli 2015; Forrest 2012; Hentz and Solomon 2017; MacEachern 2018; Maszka 2018; Ojochenemi, Asuelime, and Onapajo 2015; Onuoha 2013; Pérouse de Montclos 2014; Smith 2015; Thurston 2018; Uzodike and Maiangwa 2012. *Casamance*: Bassène 2015; de Jong and Gasser 2005; Evans 2003, 2004; Fall 2010; Foucher 2003, 2007, 2011; Gorée Institute 2015; Humphreys and Ag Mohamed 2005; Lambert 1998.

Kurdistan: Beriker-Atiyas 1997; Cengiz 2010; Galeotti 1998; Gingeras 2014; Gunter 1998, 2008, 2016; ICG 2012; Massicard 2010; Pek and Ekıcı 2007; Roth and Sever 2007; van Bruinessen 1996, 2000; White 2015. *Palestine*: Abrahams, Garlasco, and Li 2004; Amir 1998; Finkelstein 2003, 2014; ICG 2007; Pelham 2012, 2015; Roy 2012; Sabry 2015; Yiftachel 2006; Zohar 2015. *Islamic State*: Cockburn 2015; Gerges 2016; Halder 2016; Johnston et al. 2016; Mironova, forthcoming; Napoleoni 2016; Stern and Berger 2015; Weiss and Hassan 2015; Williams 2009, 2011. *Houthis and Southern Movement*: Brandt 2017; Clark 2010; Day 2012; Hill 2017; Lackner 2017; Lewis 2015; Rabi 2015; Salmoni, Loidolt, and Wells 2010.

West Bosnia: Andreas 2004a, 2004b; Corpora 2004; Donais 2003; Ferguson 2015; Hajdinjak 2002; Mueller 2000; Pugh 2003; Smajić 2010. *Greater Albania*: Babanovski 2002; Bellamy 2002; Daskalovski 2004; Finckenauer and Schrock 2004; Gounev 2003; Grillot et al. 2004; Hislope 2002, 2003, 2004; Ilievski 2015; Ilievski and Dobovsek 2013; Todorovski et al. 2018. *Donbas and Crimea*: Hale and Orttung 2016; Katchanovski 2016; Kuzin and Penchuk 2006; Kuzio 2014, 2015, 2016; Shelley 2003; Williams and Picarelli 2001; Yekelchyk 2015. *Transnistria*: Blakkisrud and Kolstø 2011; Bowring 2014; Buttin 2007; Deleu 2005; Galeotti 2004b; Molcean and Verständig 2014; Munteanu and Munteanu 2007; Protsyk 2009, 2012; Sanchez 2009; Tudoroiu 2012. *Nagorno-Karabakh*: Balayev 2013; Bölükbaşı 2011; Chorbajian 2001; Cornell 2011; de Waal 2013; Geukjian 2011; ICG 2005a; Kaldor 2007; Kolstø and Blakkisrud 2012; Krüger 2010, 2014; Özkan 2008; Panossian 2001.

The outstanding regional overviews of organized crime are as follows. *West Africa*: Alemika 2013; Philip de Andrés 2008; Lacher 2012; Mazzitelli 2007; Reno 2011; Shaw, Reitano, and Hunter 2014. *Middle East*: Içduygu and Toktas 2002; Napoleoni 2016; Robins 2002. *Eastern Europe*: Athanassaopolou 2005; Köppel and Székely 2002; Kupatadze 2012; Stojarova 2007; Thachuk 2007, 79–113.

Additional data on mafias were drawn from the following:

- UNODC (www.unodc.org/unodc/en/publications.html)
- Organized Crime and Corruption Reporting Project (www.occrp.org/ en)
- Stockholm International Peace Research Institute (www.sipri.org /databases)
- Global Initiative against Transnational Organized Crime (https:// globalinitiative.net/article_type/publications)
- Council on Foreign Relations' "Conflict Tracker" (www.cfr.org /interactives/global-conflict-tracker)
- International Crisis Group (www.crisisgroup. org/latest-updates/ reports-and-briefings)
- Institute for War and Peace Reporting (https://iwpr.net/)
- Caucasus Analytical Digest (www.css.ethz.ch/en/publications/cad.html)

FOURTEEN CASES

Loosely following Jeff Goodwin's (2001) triregional comparative method, I analyze torn states in three regions to reveal common patterns of organized criminal influence on separatist movement trajectories. Adopting the "contextualized comparisons" approach, I sought "specific sets of cases that exhibit sufficient similarity to be meaningfully compared to one another" without an excessive causal generalization that loses sight of historical contingency.[25] The purpose of the mafia typology—mafias in uniform, Minderbinder mafias, rebel mafias, and cosmopolitan mafias—is to generalize insights hitherto restricted to a handful of countries, underline cross-regional similarities, and reinterpret separatist outcomes in terms of a neglected cause.

This is not an invitation to deny the intra- or interregional diversity of West Africa, the Middle East, and Eastern Europe but rather to reconsider neglected convergences across regions. For instance, Kalyvas (2015, 18), building on Paul Collier's work (2008), contrasts a "bottom billion" African model of "mostly ethnically based and looting-prone insurgencies, in extremely poor and ethnically divided countries," with a Middle Eastern model of "highly ideological rebels in autocratic and religiously divided countries that are closely linked to the geopolitical dynamics of the (unipolar) international system." But chapters 6–7 indicate important similarities between these two models: "looting-prone" elements often come to dominate insurgencies (e.g., Houthis), while ostensibly ideological rebellions (e.g., Boko Haram) are incomprehensible without an analysis of mafias.

Table 5 summarizes all fourteen cases from part 3 (chapters 6–8) as well as three excluded separatist movements (Israel's West Bank, Yemen's Southern Movement, and Ukraine's Crimea), discussed below.

CODING

Area studies specialists will surely—and properly—dispute various categorizations. For our purposes, I have erred on the side of inclusion to produce as comprehensive a set of separatist cases as suitable. Three movements operate across multiple host states: for the Kurdish, I focus on Turkey; for IS, I look primarily at Iraq and secondarily Syria; and for Albanian, I concentrate on Macedonia, having exhausted Serbia/Kosovo in part 2. Formations typically classified as "terrorist" (e.g., Yemen's al-Qa'ida in the Arab Peninsula) are excluded from the set of separatist movements—except Boko Haram and IS, where insurgents came to control sizable territory over prolonged periods, approximating state governance.

Separatist movements call for increased independence, not exclusively outright secession. During the harshest Turkish crackdown of the 1990s, even

TABLE 5. Separatist Movements in Three Regions, 1989–2019

WEST AFRICA

Separatist movement	Host state	Separatist constituency	Political wing	Militant wing	Separatist wars	Transnational smuggling through separatist territory	Foreign troops in separatist territory	Potential to merge with patron state	Mafias
Ambazonia	Cameroon	Anglophones	Southern Cameroons National Council and Ambazonia Governing Council	Ambazonia Defense Force (ADF), and Southern Cameroon Peoples Organization (SCAPO)	None			X	*Coupeurs de route* mafia, Yaounde-based human traffickers, and cybercriminals
Azawad	Mali	Tuareg	Coordination of Azawad Movements	National Movement for the Liberation of Azawad (MNLA)	2012–19	X	X		Bahanga's MTNM, and Kel Adagh–and Kel Tademekkat–based smugglers

	Country	Ethnic group	Governance	Armed groups	Dates				Criminal networks
Tenere Republic / Akal N Tenere (Agadez)	Niger	Tuareg and Toubou	Taniminnak Tidot N Tenere and Tidot Union of Tenere	Movement of Nigeriens for Justice (MNJ) and Revolutionary Armed Forces of the Sahara (FARS)	None		X	X	Agadez smugglers and Al-Mourabitoun
Boko Haram	Nigeria	Kanuri	Shura (executive council)	Armed cells	2009–19		X		Northern gangs and "Street Boys" (Yan Tauri, Dan Kaleri, etc.)
Casamance	Senegal	Diola	Movement of Democratic Forces of Casamance (MFDC)	Attika, Front Nord and Front Sud	None	X	X		Karone Isles narco-traffickers, maquisards gangs, Mouride brotherhood

Continued on next page

TABLE 5. (*continued*)

MIDDLE EAST

Separatist movement	Host state	Separatist constituency	Political wing	Militant wing	Separatist wars	Transnational smuggling through separatist territory	Foreign troops in separatist territory	Potential to merge with patron state	Mafias
Kurdistan	Turkey	Kurds	*Kongra-Gel* (KGK), and Peace and Democracy Party (BDP)	Kurdish Workers' Party (PKK)	1993–99 and 2015–19	X			Susurluk mafia, and European and regional Kurdish mafias
	Iraq		Kurdish Regional Government (KRG)	Peshmerga (*Pêşmerge*)	1991 and 2003–5	X	X		Oil smugglers
	Iran		Democratic Party of Iranian Kurdistan (PDKI)	Kurdistan Free Life Party (PJAK)	None				None
	Syria		Democratic Union Party (PYD)	People's Protection Units (YPG)	2012–present		X		None

Gaza	Israel	Palestinians	Hamas	Izz ad-Din al-Qassam Brigades	2004 and 2008–9		X		Sinai smugglers (Samhadana Clan, Bedouin clans, and Gaza tunnelers)
West Bank			Palestinian Authority (PA)	Palestinian National Security Forces	2000–2005	X	X		None
South Yemen (with Hadhramaut)	Yemen	Adeni Arabs and Hadhrami Arabs	Southern Transitional Council and Council for the Leadership of the Peaceful Revolution of the South	Southern Movement (al-Hirak)	1994		X		None
Houthi rebellion		Zaidi Houthis	Houthi movement (Ansar Allah)	Al-Houthi militia	2004–10		X		Mana Clan
Islamic State (Daesh)	Iraq and Syria	Salafi/Wahabi Sunnis	"Caliph" and Iraq/Syria deputies, and Shura council	ISIL military council	2013–19		X	X	Oil smugglers and Liwa Allah Akbar

Continued on next page

TABLE 5. (*continued*)

EASTERN EUROPE

Separatist movement	Host state	Separatist constituency	Political wing	Militant wing	Separatist wars	Transnational smuggling through separatist territory	Foreign troops in separatist territory	Potential to merge with patron state	Mafias
Nagorno-Karabakh	Azerbaijan	Armenians	Artsakh government	Artsakh Defense Army	1988–94	X	X		Aliyev Clan and Babayan Clan
Transnistria	Moldova	Russians, Moldovans, and Ukrainians	Supreme council	Armed Forces of Pridnestrovian Moldavian Republic	1992	X	X		Thieves-in-Law (*vory-v-zakone*) and Smirnov Clan
Donetsk and Lugansk	Ukraine	Russophones	People's council(s)	Donetsk Armed Forces and Luhansk People's Militia	2014–present	X	X	X	Thieves-in-Law (*vory-v-zakone*) and Akhmetov Clan
Crimea	Russia	Russians	Council of Ministers and state council	None (Russian troops)	None	X	X	X	Thieves-in-Law (*vory-v-zakone*)

Autonomous Province of Western Bosnia	Bosnia-Herzegovina	Bosnian Muslims	Velika Kladuša administration	People's Defense of Western Bosnia (NOZB)	1993–95	X		Yugo-mafia and Abdić Clan
Greater Albania	Macedonia	Albanians	Democratic Union for Integration (DUI)	National Liberation Army (NLA); Albanian National Army (AKSH)	None	X	X	Albanian mafia (the "Columbians," Jashari Clan, NLA's Tanuševci branch, and Jakupi Gang)

Sources: Roth 2015; Beary 2011; Hewitt and Cheetham 2000; Minahan 2002.

the prototypical Kurdish separatists were mainly antisecessionist.[26] On the other hand, uprisings that are not typically classified as separatist—such as those of stateless nomadic people—have the same vacillation between autonomism and secessionism. The Tuareg of Mali and Niger initially had maximalist nationalist demands for full sovereignty before receding to mere autonomy and decentralization, returning to secessionism in the late 2000s.[27] Even the Transnistrian movement—frequently cited as the exemplary Russian lackey—oscillated between demands for independence, integration into Russia, and confederation or even federation with Moldova.[28] The Albanian NLA in Macedonia changed its party line in 2001 from a megalomaniacal Greater Albanian irredentism to a bland human rights reformism almost weekly.[29] In sum, ambivalence and outright contradiction regarding autonomism-separatism-secessionism is all too common—and normal.

The *political* and *military wings* include only the major movement protagonists (e.g., the Tuareg MNLA) around which others gravitate (e.g., the Islamic Movement for the Azawad and Macina Liberation Front). The most contemporary incarnations are listed, unless earlier separatist organizations accounted for movement dynamics discussed in the text. I exclude temporary and tactical coalitions (e.g., Coalition of Southern Cameroons Liberation Movements) as well as minor factions and splinter groups (e.g., Southern Cameroons Youth League) unless they significantly parted from the umbrella organization on organized criminal matters (e.g., the Niger Patriotic Front, a mafia, splintered from the MNJ to maintain its turf). I exclude synonymous designations/titles or replacements (e.g., PKK = Congress for Freedom and Democracy in Kurdistan = Kurdistan People's Congress; All Anglophone Conference = Southern Cameroons People's Conference = Southern Cameroons National Council). Many of these cosmetic retitlings are public relations embellishments seeking to disguise or renounce the criminalization of mainstream movement institutions.[30]

The *separatist wars* reflect civil war literature standards: a minimum of a thousand battlefield deaths in a year, excluding smaller skirmishes (e.g., 2017–19 Cameroon and 2001 Macedonia violence). The First South Ossetia War is thus excluded (at less than a thousand deaths), as is Casamance's prolonged low-intensity warfare (at less than six thousand sporadic deaths from 1982 to 2013).

The *transnational smuggling* codes are for significant, prolonged illegal flows across internationally recognized borders of one or more of the following: small arms / light weapons, heavy arms, opium, heroin, cocaine, marijuana, qat, oil, hostages, labor migrants, sex workers, and refugees. The rough threshold is a quarter ton per year for at least two years, as documented by reliable estimates such as the UNODC. For human smuggling, the rough threshold is a reliable estimate of at least $100,000 profit in a year.

Foreign troops are nonindigenous armed forces or peacekeepers, invited (e.g., US troops in Agadez) or not (e.g., Russian ones in Donetsk), that number a hundred or more, or have military installations on separatist territory.

A *merger with the patron state* includes territorial contiguity, not merely formal irredentist merger without contiguity (e.g., Boko Haram vis-à-vis IS or Nagorno-Karabakh vis-à-vis Armenia).

Mafias are only the most prominent, sizable, or enduring organized criminal groups that at least two independent scholarly or analytic sources identify as such explicitly in distinction to corruption, bandits, militias, insurgents, or separatist parties; have a clear association with the host state or separatist movement organization, or a consequential effect on either's trajectory; and are documented to control major rackets (narcotics, arms, ransom kidnappings, etc.). I conservatively excluded many ambiguous cases that nevertheless meet two of the criteria. I also erred on the side of caution to take separatist rhetoric at its word when movement organizations appear to drift into unadulterated criminality (e.g., the Front de libération de l'Aïr et de l'Azawak, the institutional precursor to the MNJ in Niger, was obviously more oriented toward criminal profiteering than political goals in its early 1990s' raiding of convoys in the Sahara—but I refrain from classifying the MNJ as a mafia).[31]

I have excluded numerous mafias created or used by host states for *non*separatist purposes. The Shabiha, notably, are a Syrian gangster formation (drawn from the Alawite community) used by Damascus to preserve the regime and brutalize the opposition. There is no record of these "ghost thugs" mobilizing for anti-Kurdish or anti-IS purposes, however, but strictly for conventional state repression. Other examples include the *titushki* protecting the Ukrainian regime during Euromaidan and the *balateja* protecting the Yemeni regime during the Arab Spring.[32]

EXCLUDED CASES AND OUTLIERS

Pedantically, one might have divided the Yugoslav (1991–95), Syrian (2011–present), and Yemeni civil wars (2015–present) into as many as six, four, and three separatist movements, respectively. Several other movements in peacetime—in Israel, Yemen, and Ukraine—have also been excluded.

REGIONAL SCOPE

The northern African states are excluded from the Middle East, as are Afghanistan and Pakistan. Iranian Azeris are, by regional standards, tremendously integrated into the host state. Suffice it to estimate that 112 of 170 generals in the Iranian army are Azeri.[33] Despite the exceptional "cockroach cartoon" separatist mobilization of 2006, a sustained Azeri separatist movement is largely absent. "Iran's fifteen-million Azeri population is well integrated into Iranian society and has shown little desire to secede."[34]

Hadhramaut is not treated as a separate movement within Yemen. Although various separatist proposals for Hadrami Arabs have been concocted (South Arabia, Kathiri, Qu'aiti, and Wahidi Balhaf), no coherent or discernible movement has centered around any single one. Al-Qa'ida posturing in the Hadhramaut region also falls short of a separatist movement. Instead, Hadhramaut secessionist tendencies (particularly in the region's south) are best understood as part of the broader Southern Movement (al-Hirak), discussed below.

Restricted to autonomist demands, the Hungarians in Romania (Transylvania) along with the Silesians (Upper Silesia) and Kashubians (Kashubia) in Poland are excluded from Eastern Europe. Successfully reintegrated Ajara (Georgia) and Gagauzia (Moldova) are omitted too. Excluded ex-Soviet cases are Russians in Kazakhstan, Uyghurs in Kyrgyzstan, Karakalpakias in Uzbekistan, and Gorno-Badakhshans in Tajikistan. Excluded ex-Yugoslav cases are the Vojvodinian in Serbia and Serbians in Montenegro.

Bosnia-Herzegovina is treated as host state, even though it was itself not officiated until 1995. Students of Yugoslavia may care to reclassify the Bosniak side as the separatist movement within the Socialist Federal Republic of Yugoslavia as the host state. Then the Bosnian Serb Republika Srpska, Croatian Serb Republika Krajina, and Abdić's Western Bosnia would be separatist cases *within* separatist cases. Azerbaijan, Moldova, and Ukraine are likewise treated as host states, though they were initially secessionist movements within the USSR—and their respective Nagorno-Karabakh, Transnistria, and Donbas were separatist within separatist. For simplicity's sake, I overlook these formalities.

Russia, truly sui generis in its size and state-mafia fusion, is excluded from Eastern Europe. As much as 40 percent of the Russian economy in the 1990s was organized crime.[35] It should be noted, however, that the northern Caucasus—Karachayevo-Cherkesiya, Kabardino-Balkariya, North Ossetia, Ngushetiya, Chechnya, and Dagestan—has extensive organized criminal influence on separatist outcomes. Several within-Russia separatist movements (Chechyna most conspicuously) relied vitally on mafias in their struggle, undergoing processes explored in this book.[36] Russia analysts have produced important insights and conceptualizations of mafia co-optation that are worth comparing to the smaller torn states at hand.[37]

ISRAEL: WEST BANK

Chapter 7 argues that the Gaza-Sinai mafia enabled Hamas's rule. By lining separatist coffers, circumventing Israel and international humanitarian funders, and increasing the population's dependence on Hamas, the tunnelers' black market endowed quasi-state capacity to a hitherto marginal branch of the separatist movement. It was through organized crime that "Hamas transformed itself from a nonstate actor with a social and charitable network, underground movement, and guerrilla force into a governing authority with a well-equipped internal security force, bureaucracy, and economy."[38]

In the West Bank, in contrast, smuggling-oriented organized crime remained rudimentary, consisting mostly of the ordinary peddling of consumer goods to and from Israel.[39] Aside from rackets in stolen cars and fake clothing brands, the mafia scene is trifling in comparison to Gaza's.[40] Arguably the closest thing to organized crime is the massive embezzlement, bribery, and money laundering within separatist Zakat committees.[41]

Mafias in Israel proper, moreover, have not been seminal influences on politics. Modern Israeli organized crime arose with the emigration of a half-million immigrants from the ex-Soviet space to Israel between 1993 and 1998. Russian mafias venturing into document forgery, prostitution, extortion, and drugs partnered with "existing 'native' organized crime groups." The partnerships were punctuated by occasional turf wars. Additionally, the "laundering of money is quite simple and easy," so "Israel is considered a safe haven because of the lack of control on investments in banks."[42] Multiethnic Israeli-Palestinian organized crime periodically appeared as well. Notably, the 1990s marked "the highest rate of car theft in the world" in Israel, as "Israeli and Palestinian mafias made peace in 1993" to create a world-class stolen vehicle racket.[43] But none of these left meaningful marks on the separatist deadlock.

YEMEN: SOUTHERN MOVEMENT

The contemporary Southern Movement (2007–present), al-Hirak, rooted in the southern provinces, and spreading to eastern Hadramaut and al-Mahra, included a brief alliance of convenience with al-Qa'ida in 2009. This case is excluded for two reasons: mafias played no discernible role, and the northern Houthi movement completely overshadowed its southern counterpart. Arms-smuggling mafias—notably the Mana Clan—were formative players in causing, perpetuating, and mediating the Sa'dah War. This conflict, in turn, was an important catalyst reawakening southern secessionism in 2007.

The 1990 unification of Yemen was tragically flawed. Most glaringly, "the northern and southern military units, which had never been merged," clashed in 1994 in a three-month civil war. Supported by Saudi Arabia and Kuwait, the separatist uprising was crushed by the (stronger) northern army and veteran jihadis of the Afghan conflict. This defeat suspended the southern separatist insurgency, but also intensified many grievances that rebounded with a vengeance thirteen years later.[44] The renewed Southern Movement was a peaceful uprising (2007–9), with 623 protests in 2008 without any violent, let alone criminal, dimension. An "increasingly paranoid" President Saleh over-reacted with indiscriminate repression, persecuted movement leaders and journalists, and publicly equated the southern cause with the violent Houthi insurrection in the north. The movement then turned to violent rioting, organized tribal militias, and garnered support from al-Qa'ida to tear Yemen apart again (2009–present).[45] The alliance was tentative and weak; al-Qa'ida quickly resumed attacking the Southern Movement as soon as they jointly expelled Houthi/Saleh forces from Aden.[46]

One leading specialist suggests that the Southern Movement was considered a graver threat by Saleh than the far more violent northern Houthi rebellion: "Salih regarded the southern secessionist movement as the most dangerous snake's head he had to dance on simply because he cherished the 1990 union of the two Yemens as the proudest and most concrete achievement of his thirty years in power."[47]

UKRAINE: CRIMEA

Crimea is excluded as an extreme outlier, being by far the most dependent, patron state–controlled case across three regions. If any separatist movement can be said to lack autonomy—to be a "puppet" of external forces—it is Crimea. Therefore, the relevance of organized crime is difficult, if not impossible, to differentiate from sheer Russian power.

To be sure, mafias were a bedrock of Crimean society. Known as "Ukraine's Sicily" for its criminalization, Crimea hosted the rival Salem and Bashmaki mafias, which staged bloodbaths throughout the 1990s to uphold narco-trafficking and protection rackets. Salem gangs alone conducted dozens of contract killings, including thirty businesspeople, fifteen mafia competitors, two police officers, and a journalist.[48] In total, fifty-two gangs were hierarchically "organized into mafia-style families," while another sixty-eight roamed as disorganized crime. They controlled parliamentarians, mayors, and local town officials. Some seventy gangsters were in office in parliament and local councils, while many political parties were little more than mafia fronts. In 1996, the province accounted for 4 percent of Ukraine's total population, but a fifth (24/120) of all contract killings on Ukrainian territory.[49] Victims included Colonel Mykhailo Zvierev, chief of the Department against Organized Crime.

In 2014, Russia notoriously deployed paramilitaries nicknamed "little green men" to Crimea; many were, in fact, little green criminals. Annexing the peninsula, Russia also installed mafia boss Sergei "Goblin" Aksyonov, formerly of the Salem gang based in Simferopol, as prime minister.[50] All told, if we were to employ the typology, Crimea had an *extremely* partial rebel mafia. But to include it as a case of autonomous organized criminal agency would be misleading.

Chapter 1. Introduction

1. Hewitt and Cheetham 2000. Most new polities emerged from Communist dissolution: USSR (fifteen), Yugoslavia (six), and Czechoslovakia (two). In Africa, Eritrea, Namibia (both in 1990), and South Sudan (2011) declared independence. Belated decolonization brought statehood to East Timor (2002), Palau (1994), Micronesia, and Marshall Islands (both in 1991).

2. Hobsbawm 2000.

3. Hobsbawm 1985, 22. Contemporary cinematic portrayals also muddy the water in this respect; pop psychopathology lessons are often coupled with invitations to the audience to experience vicarious, cathartic release by identifying with gangster antiheros.

4. Caspersen 2017, 11–12, 15.

5. Hill 2003; Siniawer 2011; Galeotti 2002, 2018; Gambetta 1996; Paoli 2004.

6. Chido 2018, 10.

7. Bonikowski 2016.

8. Horowitz 1997, 42.

9. Legal experts are no less divided than scholars. International law cannot tackle "territoriality," let alone "self-determination," without stupefying irregularity: "while 'all peoples' have the right to self-determination, the question of 'who' the people are, continues to defy clarity" (Castellino 2015, 28). By one count, ten out of twenty-one separatist states endured for a modest two to six years (Caspersen and Stansfield 2011, 4).

10. Briquet and Favarel-Garrigues 2010, 4.

11. Mahoney and Rueschemeyer 2003.

12. On external validity and the "small-n problem" of comparative-historical method, see Rueschemeyer 2003.

13. Goldstone 2003, 47.

14. Goldstone 2003, 48–50.

15. Wimmer 2018; Vogt 2019; Cederman, Weidmann, and Gleditsch 2011.

16. To that end, the conclusion lists general insights that may fruitfully be incorporated into alternative methods.

17. For a terminological review, see von Steinsdorff and Fruhstorfer 2012, 118–19. The definitional variety results from analytic verdicts on three sets of distinctions: internal and external legitimacy, formal and informal sovereignty, and—most important—good governance structures that "we" endorse and bad ones "we" deplore. Sometimes scholars categorize according to criminalization, seeking to isolate the "better" separatist movements from contamination by mafia-infested ones (e.g., Vladimir Kolossov and John O'Loughlin [1998] contrast "pseudostates" with the more criminalized "quasi states"). For the tension between "declaratory" and "constitutive" understandings of sovereignty and independence, see Coppieters and Sakwa 2003, 16.

18. For Klaus von Lampe's compilation—mostly of governmental definitions—see www.organized-crime.de/organizedcrimedefinitions.htm.

19. Albanese 2014, 9.

20. Miller 2013, 81–83.

21. On the typical threshold of two years and criterion of "strong indigenous roots" in de facto states, see Caspersen 2017, 11.

22. Calhoun 1997, 97; Hechter 2000, 15–17.

23. Breuilly 1994, 12.

24. On the importance of local criminal agency against geopolitics and a critique of exaggerations of Russian power in torn states, see Driscoll 2015, 81–84. On the unreliability of patron states, see Bartkus 1999, 166. South Ossetians, for example, were hardly Russian puppets when they democratically elected a local teacher, Alla Dzhioyeva, against Moscow's stooge candidate in 2011. When the Kremlin annulled the vote, protesters took to Tskhinvali's streets—a courageous revolt against the patron state (Waters 2014, 178).

25. Secession, allegedly, "is a group-led movement. Irredentism, on the other hand, is state initiated, although groups of course, lobby the retrieving state to take irredentist action" (Horowitz 1997, 423). More accurately, *both* secession and irredentism are strategic outlooks of separatist movements. After movement "initiation," demands change dramatically, not least because the patron—"retrieving state"—vacillates between resistance, tacit or overt support for secession, and irredentist hospitality toward separatists. In addition to this empirical matter, there is a normative difficulty with Donald Horowitz's dichotomy: the groupist categorization of "group-led movements" implies a division between "authentic," presumably more democratic cases, and those initiated by patron states, presumably less homegrown and thus "artificial."

26. Horowitz 1985.

27. O'Leary 2001, 62–63.

28. John Breuilly's (1994, 9) state-centered approach begins with the "relationship between the nationalist movement and the state which it either opposes or controls," deducing a three-part classification: "separation," "reform," and "unification."

29. Host states frequently come to regret their failure to deal with the pacifistic wings of separatist movements. After disillusionment and radicalization, militant factions take over and compromise becomes impossible. When Cameroon slights the nonsecessionist Cameroon Anglophone Movement in 1992, it gets the pugnacious Southern Cameroons Youth League in 1995. When Nigeria kills Boko Haram's founder Mohammed Yusuf (who, it is forgotten, headed a nonviolent group), he is replaced by Abubakar Shekau—hardly an improvement. Mafias, for their part, prefer to deal with hard-liners. These separatists are more likely to require weapons, fighters, and other lucrative contraband. They are also more likely than their moderate colleagues to entertain criminal personnel, channels of distribution, and methods of dealing with opponents.

30. Following Katherine Hirschfeld (2015, 26), the "racket"—nonautonomous economic transactions induced by coercion—is taken to be the central feature of organized crime. Students of separatism regularly encounter rackets premised on protection from the protectors themselves. Jesse Driscoll (2015, 51) insightfully noted that gangster warlords "encourage their followers to go out, take things, hurt people, and then . . . sell protection against the anarchy that they could unleash."

31. Hirschfeld 2015, 76–79.

32. Hastings 2010, 151. On the whole, the smuggling component of rackets is not as labor intensive as service provision (e.g., protection in Gaza) and goods production (e.g., cannabis in Casamance), both of which are localized. Insofar as labor intensity of rackets swells mafia size, therefore, the need for workforce growth and gangster hiring is primarily met locally.

33. Fieldworkers struggle to replace "smuggler" terminology with the likes of "state trafficking" to emphasize government corruption (ICG 2002, 3).

34. On the need to shed the term's ethnic connotations and the obsession with the Sicilian model, see Hirschfeld 2015, 23. On labeling dilemmas for multiethnic, polygloth gangsters of the

Russian *mafiya*, the world's most globalized, see Galeotti 2004a, 67n2. On the relation to disorganized crime, I follow Elijah Anderson's (1997, 35) lead: "the essential characteristic of a mafia that differentiates it from other groups engaged in violent or criminal activity is corruption or substantial influence in at least some agencies or bureaux of the legitimate government. It is *this relationship* that warrants the use of the term mafia around the world" (emphasis added). In torn states, the possibilities for state and quasi-state penetration are, by definition, greater. Anderson's defense of the term "mafia" is therefore even more forceful for this book's cases.

35. Capital *C* Clans will refer to mafias (e.g., Yemen's Mana Clan and Moldova's Smirnov Clan) in a nonethnic sense. Lowercase *c* clans (e.g., Tuareg clans in Mali and Dagmush clans in Palestine) will denote ethnic, tribal, or familial kinship, understood loosely. Small *c* clans across the three regions are intimidatingly diverse and complex, so the term implies no convergence or homogeneity of kinship systems. I presume nothing about whether clan lineage, descent, familial ties, and so on, are actual or fictive.

36. Briquet and Favarel-Garrigues 2010, 3; Albanese 2015, 69–84.

37. Briquet and Favarel-Garrigues 2010, 3.

38. Anderson 1997.

39. ICG 2002, 3.

40. Berdal and Serrano 2002.

41. For a concise debunking of the myths of criminal globalization, see Briquet and Favarel-Garrigues 2010, 2–3. On what the globalization of mafias does *not* mean, see Serrano 2002, 25–26; Andreas 2002, 47–48. On three key transformations that have globalized organized crime (migration, modern border customs, and the global war on drugs), see Andreas 2002, 40; Berdal and Serrano 2002, 197–98; van der Veen 2003.

Chapter 2. Normal Bedfellows

1. See, respectively, Bartkus 1999; Bélanger, Duchesne, and Paquin 2005; Spencer 1998; Dos Santos 2007; O'Leary, Lustick, and Callaghy 2001; Hale 2008; Cabestan and Pavković 2013; Riegl and Doboš 2017. These works are rich in scope and conceptual variety, each deserving a thorough forensic analysis of how they ignore organized crime. Here I can only sketch the contours of such a critique. Viva Ona Bartkus's (1999) emphasis on the costs and benefits of remaining inside the host state fails to recognize that organized crime can change secession's appeal. Louis Bélanger, Érick Duchesne, and Jonathan Paquin (2005) neglect formative mafias in cases scattered on both sides of their binary, the democracies (India, Israel, Moldova, Russia, and Turkey) as well as the autocracies (Azerbaijan, Georgia, Indonesia, Iraq, Senegal, and Sudan), even though many of the stipulated mechanisms of patron state support (443) occurred precisely via organized criminal smuggling in the 1990–92 period. Metta Spencer (1998) once mentions organized crime (22), petty smuggling (123), and gangsters (221) in a volume full of cases of mafia-separatist coalitions. Anne Noronha Dos Santos (2007) does not entertain the possibility of criminal autonomy, even when arms smugglers feature prominently (111, 113, 116). Bruno Coppieters and Richard Sakwa's volume (2003) evaluates just cause, right intentions, and other ethics of separatism without reference to organized crime (for two exceptions, see "bandit's revolt the likes of which has rarely been seen before" [164], and when the "criminal and political worlds formally merge[d]" as "Chechyna's leading mafia figures" entered separatist politics [172]. This is mentioned in passing, as formative Chechen and Russian mafia influence is glossed over). Brendan O'Leary, Ian S. Lustick, and Thomas Callaghy (2001) treat organized crime incidentally (212–14, 246) or not at all—though "gangster regimes without formal secession" are correctly prophesied in one case (130). Henry E. Hale (2008, 25–30) dismisses a strawman argument for mafia relevance under "ethnicity-as-epiphenomenal theories." Jean-Pierre Cabestan and Aleksandar Pavković (2013) ignore mafias entirely, focusing on dyadic analyses of host state (concilliatory versus confrontational) and

separatist (successful versus modest) strategies; contributors to their volume neglect obvious differences between mafia-free movements (Scotland, Tibet, and Taiwan) and notorious cases of criminal resource mobilization (Kosovo, Chechyna, and Sri Lanka). Martin Riegl and Bohumil Doboš (2017), partly in an effort to resist reductionist exaggerations of separatist criminality (11), go too far in the opposite direction by relativizing (12), skimming over (46–47, 145), or simply forgetting mafias.

2. Lynch 2004; Caspersen 2012.

3. Reno 1999; Forrest 2004.

4. Lehning 2005; Moore 1998; Wellman 2005.

5. See also O'Leary, Lustick, and Callaghy 2001.

6. Sambanis, Germann, and Schädel 2018.

7. In Christopher Hewitt and Tom Cheetham's (2000) encyclopedia of separatism, 34 out of 132 are in the advanced democracies. In Brian Beary's (2011) catalog of separatist movements, it is 17 out of 59. Except for the Basques, not a single one of these movements has a militant wing. Three of them—the Inuit, Saami, and Greenlanders—represent populations under 100,000.

8. Dion 1996.

9. Sambanis, Germann, and Schädel 2018, 665.

10. Beary 2011, 13.

11. Sambanis, Germann, and Schädel 2018, 682n12.

12. Jones 2018.

13. Among separatists, there are two exceptions: the Irish Republican Army (Wang 2010, 15) and French Corsican cases (Briquet and Favarel-Garrigues 2010, 8). Among host states, the only Western criminalized case was Spain; in the 1980s, Madrid routinely "hired thugs with criminal backgrounds to complement the police and intelligence officers' mission to eradicate Basque radical nationalism" (Guild, Bigo, and Gibney 2018, 202).

14. For a critique, see Malešević 2010, 61–62.

15. Fearon 1995; Wintrobe 2006; Laitin 1995, 2007.

16. Laitin 2007, 22; Hechter 1992, 467.

17. Hechter 1992, 467.

18. Gagnon 2006; Mueller 2000.

19. Gellner 1983; Hechter 2000.

20. King 2010, 103–33.

21. Taras Kuzio (2001) criticized Brubaker's "nationalizing states" as a concept implicitly rooted in an obsolete distinction between a civic West and ethnic East, advocating a return to "nation-building" as a superior umbrella concept (cf. Brubaker 2011).

22. Hirschfeld 2015, 113–17.

23. Huszka 2013.

24. Fearon 2004.

25. Brubaker 2004; Wimmer 2013.

26. Horowitz 1997.

27. O'Leary, Lustick, and Callaghy 2001.

28. Horowitz 1997, 433.

29. Zolberg, Suhrke, and Aguayo 1992.

30. Mann 2005.

31. Bakić 2011.

32. Brubaker 1994; Hale 2008; Roeder 2009; Motyl 2001.

33. de Vries, Englebart, and Schomerus 2019; Owen 2013; Reno 1999.

34. For a genealogy of the principle, from the Enlightenment to decolonization, see Bartkus 1999, 104–14. Max Kampelman (1993) traces the concept of self-determination to Aristotle, the first separatist icon. On legal standards, see Walter, von Ungern-Sternberg, and Abushov 2014.

For survey of instruments of international law used by separatist elites, see Beary 2011, 343–50. On two vital flaws of the self-determination principle after the Cold War, see Fabry 2010, 179–219.

35. Calhoun 1997, 103.

36. On "nation builders" versus "nation splitters," see Hobsbawm 1990, 163–65. The traditional moral attitude toward nationalism was that it was legitimate "when it tends to unite, in a compact whole, scattered groups of population," while separatism was "illegitimate when it tends to divide a state" (33). Partly for this reason, coalition building, which is normal for other social movements, is burdensome for separatists: "Separatist movements find it much more difficult to widen their coalitions than revolutionary [or reformist] movements" (Licklider 1993, 320).

37. Falk 2011.

38. Licklider 1993, 320.

39. Wellman 2005.

40. Kahneman, Knetsch, and Thaler 1991; Quattrone and Tversky 1988.

41. McDermott 2004; Masters 2004.

42. Separatist elites are often unconstrained by the risk of economic catastrophe. In 1968, the head of the failed separatist Republic of Biafra observed, "In the question of independence and self-determination, viability is usually given a very, very low priority" (Bartkus 1999, 53).

43. Jović 2017.

44. Sekelj 1993, 277.

45. Hobsbawm and Ranger 1983.

46. Simmel 2010, 98; Malešević 2010, 185.

47. Brubaker 1996.

48. Zolberg, Suhrke and Aguayo 1986; Heraclides 2004; Horowitz 1985.

49. Dos Santos 2007; Thomas 2003.

50. Driscoll 2015, 7.

51. On the "hornets' nest of inconsistency" of applying secessionist right to republics and not nationalities in pre-Dayton Yugoslavia, but then reversing criteria in the case of Kosovo, see Detrez 2003; Oeter 2014.

52. For a compelling reductionist view, see Mearsheimer 2014. On the inadequacies, see Gleditsch 2009.

53. See also Matsuzato 2008.

54. Shain and Sherman 1998; Shain 2007; Demmers 2007.

55. Wahlbeck 2002; Carment and James 1995.

56. Cizre 2001, 243.

57. Soule 2004.

58. Baker 2001, 80.

59. Beissinger 2002.

60. Ayres and Saideman 2000.

61. Berdal and Serrano 2002; Galeotti 2014; Hirschfeld 2015; Albanese and Reichel 2013; Bridenthal 2013; Roth 2017.

62. Gambetta 1996, 100–102.

63. Anderson 1997, 38.

64. Albanese 2015, 130.

65. Block, Bovenkerk, and Siegel (2003); Berdal and Serrano 2002.

66. Anderson 1997, 40.

67. van de Bunt, Siegel, and Zaitch 2014.

68. Chido 2018, 16.

69. Offshore "shadow states" like Belize, for instance, have become empty shells in which "criminal transnational networks" dictate economic affairs (Duffy 2010). The internet has undoubtedly re-created and empowered mafias in fascinating ways (Glenny 2011; Clarke and

Knake 2014), but cybercrime (estimated at $2 trillion a year) has inspired exaggerations of discontinuity from traditional organized crime. Cybertechnology empowers *dis*organized crime at the expense of "geographically [and] genetically fixed mafia entities" (Roth 2017, 475, 471–96), but it does not eliminate the latter. On the contrary, continuities regarding organization, violence, and law enforcement dynamics are striking in the transition from off-line to online mafias.

70. On congruence of "stationary banditry" with Lynch's separatism-specific concept of "racketeer state," see Blakkisrud and Kolstø (2011, 180–81.).

71. Bovenkerk, Siegel, and Zaitch 2003.

72. Hastings 2010, 39.

73. Perusing 2000–2018 maps of global smuggling routes of narcotics (United Nations Office on Drugs and Crime [UNODC]) and people (Migration Data Portal), we see that most separatist movements are in bridge societies for at least one traffic. For the two sets of maps, see, respectively, www.unodc.org/wdr2018/en/maps-and-graphs.html; https://migrationdataportal.org/themes/smuggling-migrants.

74. Trzciński 2004, 212.

75. Bayart, Ellis, and Hibou 1999; Skaperdas 2001; Cockayne 2016.

76. Collins 2011; Albanese 2015, 130. Fatefully theorized by Weber, patrimonialism is a form of traditional political domination in which a private household exercises arbitrary power. In such a system, administration and coercive force are under the direct, personal control of the ruler. Today's mafias can be understood as anachronisms: they maintain premodern patrimonial governance in those pockets where rationalized, bureaucratized modernity is in retreat.

77. Anderson 1997, 34.

78. On the centrality of "extralegal governance," see Varese 2011, 5–6. On mafias as "autonomous ruling regimes," see Stephenson 2015, 21. On Calabrian mafia's territorial control, see Sciarrone 2010. On how clandestine transnational organizations—mafias and separatists included—tend to have clear territorial ambitions backed by administrative clout in Southeast Asia, see Hastings 2010, 20–21. On the road to gangster states, or the "evolutionary progression from gangster to kleptocrat (and back again)" (Hastings 2010, 83) from a Darwinian perspective, see Hirschfeld 2015.

79. For a review of the debate between scholars of transnational organized crime that emphasize its international trafficking component arising from prohibition (mafias as *smugglers*) and those who stress its local, protection component arising from insecurity (mafias as *racketeers*), see Serrano 2002, 16–20, 32n7.

80. Guichaoua 2015, 325.

81. Briquet and Favarel-Garrigues 2010, 2. On "mafias of the moment," see Roth 2017, 475.

82. Stephenson 2015, 154, 245–46.

83. Roth 2017, 49–53; Hazen and Rodgers 2014.

84. Knox, Etter, and Smith 2018, 25. Microlevel solidarity and socialization are also indispensable foundations of violence (Collins 2008; Malešević 2010), further preserving mafia rootedness in highly localized clans, gangs, and families.

85. Hirschfeld 2015, 126.

86. Cockayne and Lupel 2011, 7–9; Serrano 2002, 21. The hasty terminological borrowing from biology—reminiscent of social Darwinism—is also unfortunate because technically, parasitism is a kind of symbiosis.

87. Hislope and Mughan 2012, 270.

88. See, respectively, Gayer 2010; Bertrand 2010; Cribb 2008; Siniawer 2011; Campbell 1977.

89. Anderson 1997, 37, 35–36.

90. Andreas 2004b, 6.

91. Hirschfeld 2015, 20; Jung 2003, 21.

92. Tilly 1985, 170. For a survey of "wartime political orders," see Staniland 2012. This approach recognizes that "smugglers may be key brokers in putting together and maintaining

[state-insurgent relationships] and their interests could shape the political objectives of contending actors beyond simply providing resources" (254), but stops short of incorporating these "key brokers" who wield such considerable power into the typology.

93. Clarke 2012, 658.

94. West 2002, 5.

95. McCoy 2010.

96. A prototypical case is Kosovo, where the escalation of the international presence conspicuously correlated with flourishing prostitution (Friesendorf 2007, 382–91; Strazzari 2003, 148, 159n8). In peacekeeping contexts, foreigners may account for the bulk of profits. In Bosnia, for instance, nonlocals contribute 70 percent of the brothel profits, but are only 30 percent of the customers (Andreas 2004b, 8). On the sex-trafficking conspiracy among UN and military contractors in Yugoslavia, see Bolkovac and Lynn 2011.

97. Nine studies were particularly inspirational. On modern mafia governance in the Middle East and Latin America, see Felbab-Brown, Trinkunas, and Hamid 2018. For reinterpretation of criminal strategy with attention to "mafia separatism," see Cockayne 2016. On the globalization of mafias as Clandestine Transnational Organizations with territorial ambitions in Southeast Asia, see Hastings 2010, 146–72. For a game-theoretical model of the gangster-statesmen dynamic in Georgia and Tajikistan, see Driscoll (2015). For examination of de facto mergers of states and mafias in nine cases, see Briquet and Favarel-Garrigues 2010. On the role of globalized mafia state-making and state-contraction, see Jung 2003. On the natural bonding of international forces—including humanitarian—with organized crime in torn states, see Cockayne and Lupel 2011. On criminal profitability of Eurasian separatist stalemates, see King 2010, 103–33. On how globalization is embedded in kinship politics and the smuggling culture of Sahara/Sahel mafias, see Scheele 2012. In my view, these works have generated theoretical insights beyond what their authors' claim.

98. Driscoll 2015, 52, 86, 174, 192.

99. Wolff 1950, 157.

100. Wolff 1950, 146–47, 154–69.

101. Massicard 2010, 54.

102. Roth and Sever 2007, 915.

Chapter 3. The Third Man

1. On Serbian host state organized crime, see Strazzari 2003, 150–55. A criminologist described this mafia in uniform as follows: "The police have been largely responsible for the existence of organized crime in [Serbia] since 1992. State security, to be precise. They invited prominent underworld bosses to be their associates in the battle for Serbian national interests in Bosnia, Croatia, [and so on]. The secret police was through them involved in plundering, war crimes and war profiteering. They enabled every prominent criminal to have a [state security] identity card." The resulting "overlap of the secret service, the underworld and the police" further congealed as one war followed another (Berry et al. 2003, 86). With cosmetic word substitutions, the quote applies to Georgia.

2. Novaković 2013, 2014.

3. Nielsen 2012b.

4. Stewart 2008, 46, 69.

5. Stewart 2008, 76–78, 207.

6. Čolović 2000; Cohen 2005.

7. Serbian military intelligence had no illusions about the loose cannon they had commissioned. It "viewed Arkan as an essentially criminal phenomenon, whose primary interests were to increase his own popularity among Serbs and amass large quantities of wealth through theft, smuggling and the sale of 'ranks' to politicians and businessmen" (Nielsen 2012a, 51).

8. Kaltcheva 2009; Djurić 1998.

9. Mijalkovski and Damjanov 2002, 89.

10. Mijalkovski and Damjanov 2002, 75–76, 61.

11. Baev 2003, 127.

12. On the genealogy of early criminal warlords and militias ("not even bothering to hide their ties to organized criminal groups"), including extraordinary testimonials from recruits, see Driscoll 2015, 62–70. The number of militias in Tbilisi alone peaked at fourteen during the civil war, dropping to five or less in 1995 (91); nearly four-fifths of sampled recruits switched militias at least once (99). There were "dozens of self-financing militia factions within the Mkhedrioni and the National Guards" (131).

13. ICG 2004, 7.

14. Slade 2013, 127.

15. Sörensen 2003, 62.

16. Kaliterna 2005, 32.

17. Sörensen 2006, 328.

18. Brock 2005, 273.

19. Ljepojević 2006, 34–36.

20. Like in post-Soviet economies, fraud and embezzlement were legacies of centralized planning. One Kosovo precedent involved the systematic diverting of Tito-era World Bank development funds to purchases of Serbian property to be resold to Albanians (Trifković 1998, 53). Real estate fortunes were made, creating a ring of entrepreneurs with nationalist credentials.

21. Mijalkovski and Damjanov 2002, 90–91.

22. Driscoll 2015, 64.

23. Jones 2015, 77.

24. Jones 2015, 83.

25. Slade 2013, 126–27.

26. Driscoll 2015, 133–46.

27. Zürcher, Baev, and Koehler 2005, 271.

28. Nilsson 2014, 116.

29. George 2009, 111.

30. Anastasijević 2010, 154–58.

31. I owe the term "thugs for hire" to Lynette Ong's (2018) investigation of privatized coercion in China.

32. On the role of football in recruiting nationalist criminals, see Čolović 2000. On the contemporary legacy of sports and hooligan-related organized crime, including its use by the Serbian government in antiseparatist protests, see the three-part series *Nemoć Države* by B92's "Insajder" investigative journalists, broadcast in November–December 2009.

33. Novaković 2013.

34. George 2009, 109.

35. Political and ideological camouflage served to conceal that their coup was of a "greed-driven nature," "need[ed] to secure their monopoly on the extortion racket" (Collier and Sambanis 2005, 272). One estimate found that 40 percent of Georgian criminal militia recruits were "opportunistic joiners" who got involved after the violent conflict ended (Driscoll 2015, 59).

36. Baev 2003.

37. Souleimanov 2013, 92.

38. Souleimanov 2013, 156.

39. Collier and Sambanis 2005, 267.

40. Slade 2013, 126–27.

41. Jones 2015, 97, 90.

42. Shelley, Scott, and Latta 2007, 53.

43. Anastasijević 2010, 154.

44. Grubać 2009, 703.

45. Stewart 2008; Novaković 2014.

46. The Montenegrin branch (specialized in cigarette and oil smuggling) strayed from its mafia superiors in the capital. As early as 1993, separatist Montenegro served as a "safe haven, if not a veritable pirate colony, for Italian *mafiosi* of various affiliations," 450 of whom would seek refuge from the law there. Over $1 billion worth of cigarette smuggling crossed Montenegro in this period, employing some 26,000 people for the mafia enterprise (Strazzari 2003, 154). Kinship connections between Montenegrin and Serbian gangsters turned into blood feuds. Disputes between Milošević supporters, "possibly on the division of the assets from areas in Croatia and Bosnia," further split Belgrade from Montenegro, Yugoslavia's only access to sea smuggling (Sörensen 2006, 328).

47. Bujošević and Radovanović 2000, 24–29.

48. Protić 2005; Vasić 2005.

49. Bujošević and Radovanović 2000, 179, 124–26, 56–61, 167–69.

50. Sekelj 2001.

51. Korać 2003.

52. See transcript of "Atentat: Naša Privatna Stvar," *Peščanik*, https://pescanik.net/atentat -nasa-privatna-stvar-3/. The exchange between Djindjić and Sreten Lukić is recalled by witness Žarko Korać (2003), later head of the commision investigating flaws in Djindjić's security.

53. The mafia continued high-level kidnappings and assassinations, including defiantly public ones. In successive media spectacles, the Clan kidnapped a white-collar swindler, business tycoon, and eight-year-old son of a celebrity tennis player and folk singer. Extracting tens of millions of euros in days, it issued lofty patriotic proclamations after each abduction.

54. Regarding the sickening report of Spanish forensic experts, see Vukosavljević 2012.

55. Kaliterna 2005, 37.

56. Vasić 2005.

57. Public Safety Bureau 1999, 25–27.

58. Pean 2013, 194.

59. Public Safety Bureau 1999, 6. At least nine sites (Bayram Curi, Tropol, Krumë, Kukës, Peshkopi, Elbasan, Diat, Durrës, and Labino) were drilling and equipping Kosovars. In the leading camp, Bayram Curi, former Yugoslav officers of Albanian nationality were trainers; many had fought in wars in Croatia, Slovenia, and Bosnia (Public Safety Bureau 1999, 6).

60. Public Safety Bureau 1999, 8–11, 16, 20–21.

61. Marty 2010, 13.

62. Chossudovsky 1999.

63. Public Safety Bureau 1999, 8.

64. Leading North Atlantic Treaty Organization (NATO) states, along with UN resolution 1160, designated the KLA a "terrorist organization." The US Department of State and France later removed the group from the terrorist list.

65. A Western observer marveled in real time at the "installation in Kosovo of a paramilitary regime with links to organized crime. . . . Much of the KLA is criminalised, with war criminals, common murderers and drug traders forming an 'interim administration'" (Pilger 2000). For a subsequent discussion of the "mafia state," see Naím 2012.

66. Ljepojević 2006, 98. The reports subsequently become available through Wikileaks.org under "UNMIK Reports into Corruption at Priština Airport." Although the odd airport accomplice had to be murdered, air transport tremendously decreased cost and risk.

67. Pean 2013. In an exemplary case, Skender Kuçi, an Albanian witness against Haradinaj, was slaughtered with the note, "This is how enemies of the KLA end up" (Pean 2013, 237). The Hague's chief prosecutor first publicized the trend in her memoir (Del Ponte 2008).

68. Ljepojević 2006, 95.

69. United Nations Interim Administration Mission in Kosovo (UNMIK) chief Søren Jessen-Petersen would himself be faulted for corruption in 2006 by the United Nations. Such accusations are as plausible or staged as any number of criminal schemes rumored weekly in the Kosovo press, courtrooms, and nongovernmental organization (NGO) reports.

70. Marty 2010.

71. On "cover-up" murders, see Trotter 2012. See also UNMIK's police annual reports from the 2000s. On popular support for the KLA leadership compared to support for Rugova and his Democratic League of Kosovo in the immediate postwar period, see Hudson 2003, 136.

72. Anastasijević 2010, 159.

73. Jones 2015, 104.

74. Tchantouridzé 2013, 685.

75. Jones 2015, 164.

76. Scott 2007, 18–19.

77. Jones 2015, 165, 197.

78. Shelley 2007, 5.

79. From June 1992 until the outbreak of the Second South Ossetia War in 2008, a mixed contingent of peacekeepers remained deployed in the province. Though Russian dominated, it was at least formally committed to the pretense of multilateralism and impartiality. This allowed South Ossetian smuggling to develop independently of Russian mafia operations.

80. King 2010, 121. See also Jones 2015, 258.

81. Logistical dependence on Russia was enormous. Georgia signed a formal agreement in 1995 (the Russian-Georgian Agreement on the Stationing of Military Bases) consenting to Russian military installations on its territory. Ossetian leaders essentially leased their land through a forty-nine-year defense agreement. Georgia joined the Commonwealth of Independent States and even supported Russian intervention in Chechnya, further emboldening South Ossetia's own collaboration with Russian peacekeepers.

82. While the separatist government's annual budget was a shy $1 million, an OSCE official estimated the value of smuggled goods across its northern border at $60 to $70 million (Jones 2015, 258). Since "South Ossetia did not receive sustained support from Russia" before 2000, smuggling was a necessity for the survival of the separatist cause for more than a decade (Caspersen 2012, 59). Russian goods and capital were reserved for a handful of South Ossetian Russophiles, including former KGB officers and ethnic Russians serving in low-level administrative positions. Even at the height of pre-2008 Russian aid, smuggling accounted for more than half of the South Ossetian apparatus.

83. George 2009, 135.

84. A Russian pipeline through North Ossetia (intended to bypass Chechnya) and the construction of the corollary Dzuarikau-Tskhinvali pipeline fastened South Ossetians to North Ossetians. Just like Albania for Kosovo, North Ossetia became South Ossetia's lifeline. Unlike in Kosovo, however, this illegal economy inhibited separatist agitation.

85. "Safeguarding Ergneti as a symbol of Georgian-Ossetian friendship, but also as a source of illegal income" became a "top priority" for local officials. Across the nationalistic spectrum, the emergence of Ergneti was hailed as a "confidence-building measure" and veritable part of the "peace process" (Independent International Fact-Finding Mission 2009, 104). Despite post-2004 excuses for the assault on Ergneti, the fact is that Tbilisi was initially passive and tacitly in agreement with this nonviolent stalemate. Often-cited arguments against Ergneti—untaxed revenues being lost, Ergneti's threat to markets in Georgia proper (including bread prices), the host state's tarnished international image, and the predominance of Russian goods in the smuggling—are largely retrospective, post-factum rationalizations. On the well-documented "backfire" of Georgia's anti-Ergneti campaign, see George 2009; Kupatadze 2005; Freese 2005; Gotsiridze 2004.

86. Nilsson 2014, 111.

87. In 1999, the quadrilateral Joint Control Commission (JCC) concluded in a report that the "crimes and incidents taking place [in South Ossetia] did not have an ethnic character" (ICG 2004, 10, 23). They identify drug dealing and car theft as major smuggling branches.

88. While Georgian aid was nonexistent in the 1990s, in the 2000s it rose to miniscule. It was restricted to Georgian villages in the province. Ossetians receiving Georgian aid were—like all Ossetian villagers—forced to rely *more* on organized crime while their Georgian neighbors had an alternative lifeline, however miserly. Pressuring Ossetian aid recipients only increased their dependence. See George 2009, 179–80.

89. Jones 2015, 258.

90. Many emigrants paid extravagant figures to illegal travel liaisons with secret-compartment trucks and acquaintances at checkpoints. Across intimidating Ossetian mountains, pompous "Security Consultant Firms" made fortunes off weary first-time smugglers.

91. On the remaining "elite corruption," see Kukhianidze 2009. Saakashvili installed techno-cratic, pro-Western professionals who purged the judiciary, state financial apparatus, and most important, police force (Machavariani 2007). On results in border controls, human trafficking, and bribery, see Kukhianidze 2009, 227. A turning point came in March 2006, when violence broke out in Ortachala Prison 5 in the capital. Making an example of the mavericks, Saakashvili ordered special units into the prison, tranquilizing the riot and killing seven inmates (Slade 2014, 90). Though unrelated to Ergneti, this sent shivers down the spines of its architects. One smuggler—now a tour agent—canceled thirty trucks of deliveries on hearing the news.

92. Kukhianidze 2009, 225.

93. Ironically, Saakashvili became the first Georgian president to offer autonomy for South Ossetia. But the receptive Chibirov was no longer there to accept it. His successor, Eduard Kokoity, returned the separatist government to an irredentist position. Saakashvili even sought to groom a separatist leader to his liking. Dmitri Sanakoev, South Ossetian prime minister under Chibirov, was supported in his anti-Kokoity stance, and lured financially and diplomatically to establish a parallel South Ossetian government in the northern city of Kurta.

94. George 2009, 174.

95. ICG 2004.

96. George 2009, 6.

97. For a summary of each international actor's involvement—the United Nations, European Union, Organization for Economic Cooperation and Development, Russia, and the United States—see Wolff, n.d.

98. ICG 2004, 13.

99. Caspersen 2012, 142.

100. Jones 2015, 241.

101. Most casualties were Ossetian civilians killed by indiscriminate Georgian artillery attacks on Tskhinvali and its suburbs. Russian troops engaged in ethnic cleansing in Georgian villages, as did renegade Ossetian militias. See International Independent Fact-Finding Mission 2009, 223–25.

102. George 2009, 7, 11.

103. For an amusing example, see February 2013 discussions in the Georgian press regarding the wisdom of reopening the Ergneti market. Some of the most zealous spokespeople for crushing Ergneti in 2004 later appeared as expert witnesses to its miraculous, healing effects.

Chapter 4. Mafia Filter

1. In Georgia, two episodes of separatist escalation are notable, with a stable period of multi-ethnic cooperation between them. The first was in 1991–92, when Russia entered South Ossetia (the First South Ossetia War); the second was in 2008, a repeat of the first episode, pitting Russia directly against Georgia (the Second South Ossetia War).

2. Mafias in both cases, incidentally, were well versed in kidnapping and escorting. They were fully capable of handling human smuggling opportunities—but to no avail. Kosovo and South Ossetia could not have had human trafficking benefits (e.g., profits, mercenaries, hostages, and drug mules) because the regional supply-demand dynamics were unfavorable before 1999 and 2008, respectively. For reasons that foreign interventionism promoted human trafficking in Kosovo and elsewhere, see Smith and Smith 2010.

3. Pugh, Cooper, and Goodhand 2004.

4. The citations of the UNODC's annual *World Drug Report* are hitherto abbreviated as *WDR*. See the appendix.

5. Robins 2008; Chatwin 2003.

6. McCoy 2010; Asad and Harris 2019.

7. *WDR* 1999, 34.

8. Glonti 2001, 389.

9. Georgian law enforcement was more efficient. It managed more shutdowns of domestic production, better border controls, and a successful police reform in the early 2000s that became the envy of Eastern Europe (Kakachia and O'Shea 2012). As early as 1998, Georgia shut down a heroin lab. Serbia failed to seize a comparable site of production of *any* kind of narcotic until 2003 (a modest amphetamine lab). The United Nations repeatedly found that Georgia was a leading country globally in curbing the cannabis racket: in 2000, Georgia confiscated 31.9 kilograms, or 1 percent of the total world seizures—remarkable for such a miniscule country (*WDR* 2001).

10. *WDR* 2011, 53.

11. *WDR* 2000–3, 2005.

12. *WDR* 2004, 420.

13. *WDR* 2011.

14. Data on injecting drug users registered as AIDS patients—a rough indicator of drug prevalence—went through fluctuations for Serbia, but remained stubbornly stable for Georgia from 1994 to 2003 (*WDR* 2005, 151). Whereas Serbia was regionally unexceptional, Georgia was unique in its consistency of prevalence indicators among Commonwealth of Independent States countries. While the likes of Belarus and Kazakhstan had enormous fluctuations, drug use remained stable only in Georgia, Azerbaijan, and Tajikistan.

15. Data from the National Statistical Offices of Serbia and Georgia. Serbia's trafficking-specific crime count is astronomical compared to Georgia's. In 2005, Serbia prosecuted 4,968 drug traffickers, while Georgia prosecuted 94. In 2006, Serbia prosecuted 4,839 traffickers, and Georgia only 61.

16. For all recorded drug seizures, see table 4 in the appendix.

17. Public Safety Bureau 1999, 23.

18. *WDR* 2010, 2011; Curtis 2002.

19. *WDR* 2008, 48.

20. *WDR* 2008, 44, 27.

21. *WDR* 2004, 107.

22. *WDR* 2001.

23. *WDR* 2003, 95.

24. *WDR* 2006, 134.

25. *WDR* 2006, 82.

26. *WDR* 2004, 49. The increasing concentration of the drug trade in Kosovo at the expense of Serbia proper included a shift toward production in addition to mere transit. Experts on the ground held informed suspicions that heroin laboratories as well as cannabis and opium poppy plantations were operative on Kosovar territory—"possibly protected by landmines" (Friesendorf 2011, 49). Georgia not only had modest criminal domestic production but there is also no evidence that the country's narco-traffic ever adapted by significantly diverting or rerouting from host state to separatist territory.

27. Vickers 1998, 225.

28. Strazzari 2003, 141–42; Provvisionato 2000, 96.

29. Cornell 2006, 50.

30. Cohen 2002.

31. Glonti 2005, 73.

32. Kukhianidze, Kupatadze, and Gotsiridze 2007, 75–76.

33. EMCDDA 2014a, 2014b.

34. Macedonian police reports complain that it is more expensive for Skopje to oversee its mountainous border than it is for Kosovo to divert drug flows away from roads to mountains. On ineffective and sometimes farcical law enforcement against organized crime inside Kosovo, see Friesendorf 2011.

35. Nevala and Aromaa 2003, 93.

36. The author conducted an informal survey of over a dozen tour guides, most of them seasoned smugglers, in Tskhinvali in October 2013. One of them, seemingly insulted by the insinuation that he cannot handle narcotics, insisted, "It's not out of pride. I can smuggle you anything, anything in the world. I'll sell poison, I don't care! There's just no tradition here. It goes through Tbilisi."

37. Public Safety Bureau 1999, 24.

38. Each of these indicators is at least three orders of magnitude greater than for the entirety of Georgia in *any period*. In 2008 alone, 2.6 kilograms of cocaine and 42.1 kilograms of heroin were seized in Kosovo; in comparison, the total Georgian seizures (including South Ossetian) were 12.1 kilograms of heroin and no cocaine at all in the same year.

39. EMCDDA 2012, 17.

40. Mafia capacity in regard to the Montenegro border was due to rackets of great longevity. As early as 1993–94, some two hundred boats were crossing Lake Skadar between Montenegro and Kosovo (both still within Yugoslavia). Oil, fuel, arms, and narcotics were floated for $1,000,000 *daily* (Strazzari 2003, 145). The 2007 shift away from Serbia to Kosovo built on this precedent. South Ossetia, bordering only Russia, lacks such alternatives.

41. *WDR* 2004, 71; Friesendorf 2011, 49.

42. Profit from the drug trade, with the assistance of the Albanian diaspora, financed Kosovo's parallel institutions since the early 1990s (Southeast European Legal Development Initiative 2002, 13). In the mid-1990s, "numerous specialized foreign services against trafficking of narcotics, as well as Interpol, emphasize the connection of the Albanian narco-mafia to leaders of the [separatist] KLA, as well as to Thaçi, its leader" (Public Safety Bureau 1999, 23).

43. On the *pax mafiosa* struck between lead Serbian gangster Željko Ražnatović and Enver Hajin, "a prominent figure among the Albanian criminal bosses operating around the [Skadar] lake," see Strazzari 2003, 145. Both were killed. Had this alliance blossomed, perhaps the Serb-Kosovar analogy to the Georgian-Ossetian Ergneti market might have arisen around Lake Skadar. This counterfactual may have been the missed opportunity for a peace-building mafia.

44. Public Safety Bureau 1999, 22.

45. *WDR* 2004, 58.

46. Ljepojević 2006, 98.

47. *WDR* 2010, 59.

48. Sörensen 2006, 336.

49. Glonti 2005, 73.

50. This route through Georgia proper had "decreased in influence due to the introduction of a Train and Equip Programme and anti-terrorist operations. It has become too risky for drug smugglers to use the Pankisi Gorge" (Nevala and Aromaa 2003, 92). Yet even after the Chechen drug ring was terminated by force, Ossetian criminal entrepreneurs failed to seize this opportunity by filling the market void or replacing the severed route.

51. Curtis 2002, 3–9; Berry et al. 2003, 59; Bureau for International Narcotics and Law Enforcement Affairs 2001.

52. Kukhianidze, Kupatadze, and Gotsiridze 2007, 81–82.

53. Brock 2005, 206. For a comparison of the protectorates of Kosovo and Bosnia as peacetime mafia statelets, including the international peacekeepers' and administrators' complicity, see Pugh 2003. "It is not so much a case of foreign carpetbaggers replacing home-grown mafias," Michael Pugh (2003, 55) notes, "as the prospect of coexistence in which the population is squeezed from two directions."

54. Francis 2011, 75, 98.

55. Lemay-Hebert 2005.

56. Sakashvili would later claim that Georgia will be free only when the Roki Tunnel connecting South Ossetia to Russia is under host state control. This was due to the misperception that "smuggling kept the separatist government functioning" (Freese 2005, 107; Cornell 2006, 62). In reality, while the pre-2004 smuggling economy between Georgian and Ossetian regimes hindered reintegration, it also prevented further South Ossetian drift (Kolstø and Blakkisrud 2008). Thus the "sudden close [of Ergneti] resulted in the polarisation of the situation and in a 'rally-round-the-flag' effect in South Ossetia" (Francis 2011, 286).

57. Independent International Fact-Finding Mission 2009, 104.

58. Kukhianidze 2009, 224.

59. George 2009, 138; Cornell 2006, 49. See also Freese 2005.

60. An analogous closure was of the Sadakhlo market on the Georgia-Armenia border. It functioned like the Ergneti market for the Nagorno-Karabakh separatist dispute. Sadakhlo was the largest market in the Caucasus, bringing together Armenians and Azerbaijanis in bottom-up peace building through barter. Its closure (a "short-sighted move") likewise restoked nationalist bitterness (de Waal 2013, 280). In Bosnia-Herzegovina, comparably, it was the Arizona market that promoted "peace through illicit trade" (Andreas 2011, 43).

61. della Rocca 1999, 64.

62. Mutschke 2000; Barnett 2002; Khakee and Florquin 2003.

63. Strazzari 2003, 147; Public Safety Bureau 1999, 24.

64. Kosovar mafia pyramid schemes were world class. A single Kosovar from the diaspora, the Swiss-based Hajdin Sajdia, assembled $40 million from Albanian peasants and workers through extortion and theft (Strazzari 2003, 147). Intra-Albanian criminal collisions and predatory over-stretch resulted in the collapse, while separatist mafias were an important contributor to Albania's 1997 subsequent descent into chaos.

65. For a complete inventory, see Public Safety Bureau 1999, 24–25. Serbian seizures included not only conventional weapons but also arms banned under international law, massive amounts of emergency medical equipment, and a surgery set worth half-million deutsche marks. Some of this equipment proved useful in the organ traffic that will be examined in chapter 5.

66. Stijković 2007, 66–68.

67. It was after this arms traffic that Albanian criminal enterprises acquired the aforementioned monopoly on various rackets in Western Europe (including a 40 percent share of the heroin trade). Mafias' arms and narco-traffic reinforced each other, strengthening their overall capacity.

68. Khakee and Florquin 2003, 25, 29.

69. Public Safety Bureau 1999, 2.

70. Khakee and Florquin 2003, 30, 41.

71. Ljepojević 2006, 100.

72. Darchiashvili 2003.

73. Darchiashvili 2003, 32; Kukhianidze 2009.

74. Nor did the closure of Ergneti eliminate smuggling entirely. It merely increased costs, pushing gangsters underground from plain view (Cornell 2006, 63). This strengthened the role

of mafias at the expense of small-time peddlers, shopkeepers, wheeler-dealers, and other disorganized criminals.

75. Independent International Fact-Finding Mission 2009, 92.

76. Independent International Fact-Finding Mission 2009, 13, 104.

77. Independent International Fact-Finding Mission 2009, 107.

78. Independent International Fact-Finding Mission 2009, 193, 352.

79. Ellen 2009.

80. Darchiashvili 2003, 32.

81. Public Safety Bureau 1999, 20–25.

82. Jamieson 2001, 382–83. On Kosovar mafias' stunning European reach and cooperation with the Italian *ndgrangheta*, see Strazzari 2003, 145–47. The Sicilian mafia established connections with the separatist mafias as well, effectively creating a criminal duopoly on the Balkan route.

83. *WDR* 2006, 65.

84. Human Rights Watch 2006, 396.

85. Darchiashvili 2003, 43.

86. Darchiashvili 2003, 27, 32.

87. van Dijk 2007.

Chapter 5. Smuggling Kidneys and Uranium

1. Marty 2010, 24–25.

2. Scheper-Hughes 2003; Flottau 2008. The estimated black market prices are averaged from *Havocscope—Information about the Global Black Market* (accessed April 13, 2016, www.havocscope .com). The estimates of annual profits of the organ market globally range from $600 million to $1.2 billion. The bulk is from kidneys, which alone account for between $500 million and $1 billion yearly, and 5–10 percent of the kidney transplantations worldwide are trafficking related (Haken 2011, 21).

3. A World Health Organization estimate in 2007 found that the bulk of the kidney market involved voluntary donations (Budiani-Saberi and Delmonico 2008).

4. Jafar 2009.

5. Bronner 2008, 2.

6. Kupatadze 2010, 219.

7. Schmid and Wesley 2006.

8. Bronner 2008, 1–2.

9. Marty 2010, 20.

10. Kupatadze 2010, 220.

11. Khintsagov was certainly unaffiliated with the Tedeyev Clan, Ossetia's principal mafia.

12. Kupatadze 2010, 225.

13. Bronner 2008, 19–20.

14. Marty 2010, 16, 14.

15. Bronner 2008, 8, 10.

16. Marty 2010, 10, 15, 19, 14.

17. Meyer 2006; Frost 2005.

18. For an overview of international organ smuggling, see Shimazono 2007; Budiani-Saberi and Delmonico 2008. For legal frameworks, see Delmonico 2009. For an "undercover ethnography" of the illicit organ trade, see Scheper-Hughes 2004. For an overview of uranium smuggling, see Zaitseva and Hand 2003. For the practical and legal ramifications, see Cochran and McKinzie 2008.

19. The Belfer Center report assumes an alarmist tone (Bronner 2008, i–ii) in part because these may appear trivial, victimless crimes. At best, the charge of directly aiding terrorism is applicable in principle, but is nearly impossible to prove in practice.

20. Bronner 2008, 17.

21. Bronner 2008, i, 12, 9.

22. Power outages were a notable problem because the equipment requires rebooting every time power is cut. "Under the old [government] system, I mean, we lost power here a lot. Every day, ten times a day or more. . . . At some point, people just said, 'The hell with turning—I mean, we gotta walk 100 meters to turn it back on.' So they didn't. In other cases, people were not motivated to use the equipment" (Bronner 2008, 9).

23. Sheets 2008.

24. Marty 2010, 22.

25. Marty 2010, 24.

26. Marty 2010, 25, 24.

27. Marty 2010, 25.

28. Dursun-Ozkanca 2009.

29. Wilson 2006.

30. Spernbauer 2010.

31. Brosig 2011.

32. Independent International Fact-Finding Mission 2009, 103, 112.

33. Bronner 2008, 4.

34. On the JCC and JPKF, see Mackinlay et al. 2003. On Kosovo's international presence, see KFOR and EULEX press releases; Kosovo Statistical Office.

35. Haken 2011, 22.

36. Langewiesche 2007.

37. Kupatadze 2010, 222.

38. Schmid and Spencer-Smith 2012, 1.

39. Kupatadze 2010, 219. The regional demand for nuclear contraband was so diverse that fake suppliers selling ordinary metal became a black market in their own right. "According to Georgian law enforcement officers, for every bona fide smuggler who has access to radiological materials and the ability and intention to sell them, there are approximately three or four minor swindlers who might pretend to have access to radiological materials in order to perpetrate a scam" (Kupatadze 2010, 227).

40. IAEA 2007. The Georgian Ministry of Environment cited 270 sources since the end of the Cold War (Traughber 2007).

41. On Kosovo precedent in regional context, see Bowden 2013, 462–65; Ambagtsheer et al. 2013.

42. Marty 2010, 14. Thaçi personally secured support "from Albania's secret services, and from the formidable Albanian mafia" (Marty 2010, 14). See also Human Rights Watch 2008.

43. Marty 2010, 7, 17.

44. Marty 2010, 20.

45. Bronner 2008, 7, 11.

46. Bronner 2008, 17, i, 10.

47. Bronner 2008, 2.

48. Marty 2010, 17–18.

49. Marty 2010, 22, 14.

50. Deputy War Crimes Prosecutor Bruno Vekarić first publicized the case in "Anatomy of a Crime," broadcast October 9, 2012, on Radio Televizija Srbija. Doubts have been raised about the exaggerations of the witness (particularly regarding a heart transplant he was to perform on a prisoner). He has been deemed credible by the tribunal, and his testimony was included in the work of the 2011 Special Investigative Task Force dealing with the traffic. In 2018, an international court—the Kosovo Specialist Chambers and Specialist Prosecutor's Office—has bolstered the dim prospects for prosecutions.

51. Bronner 2008, 7, 2.

52. Bronner 2008, 12, 10.

53. Pean 2013, 13, 237.

54. Marty 2010, 9, 21, 6.

55. Schmidle 2013.

56. Corso 2007, 1.

57. Kupatadze 2010.

58. Sheets 2008, 4, 9.

59. Corso 2007, 1. Pre-2006 NGO reports emphasizing the "trafficking of nuclear materials . . . being transferred by non-Georgians" are frequently circulated in this context, even though they have no connection to the later episode (Shelley, Scott, and Latta 2007, 51).

60. Blagov 2006, 1.

61. Sokova, Potter, and Chuen 2007, 1.

62. Marty 2010, 18.

63. Noutcheva 2012, 186.

64. Marty 2010, 13.

65. Marty 2010, 16–17.

66. Lachmann 2008, 1.

67. Marty 2010, 9.

68. Kupatadze 2010, 230. Russian criminal groups were found to have "a clear awareness on the part of senior [crime] figures that the dangers in such activities far outweigh the potential gains" (Kupatadze 2010, 230).

69. Kupatadze 2010.

70. Flottau 2008, n.p.

71. Marty 2010, 23.

72. Grange and Frydenlund 2004.

73. Flottau 2008, n.p.

74. Marty 2010, 23.

75. Baraybar's quotation appears on an uncredited website dedicated to the Yellow House, accessed May 5, 2020, http://thebloodyellowhouse.wordpress.com/jose-pablo-baraybar. (Notably, the website also presents untrustworthy sources and unsubstantiated claims alongside its compilation of documents.) The Council of Europe report reached the same conclusion: "[The organ smugglers] have succeeded in eliminating, or intimidating into silence, the majority of the potential and actual witnesses against them (both enemies and erstwhile allies), using violence, threats, blackmail, and protection rackets [while] accru[ing] personal wealth totally out of proportion with their declared [patriotic] activities" (Marty 2010, 15).

76. Flottau 2008, n.p.

77. Bronner 2008, 5–6.

78. Sheets 2008.

79. Pean 2013, 221–22.

80. Marty 2010, 17.

81. Pean 2013, 226.

82. Not only were local forces (KFOR, UNMIK, EULEX, and the Kosovo police) made impotent, so was the ICTY. The Hague court brought war crimes charges against Haradinaj, a key figure in the traffic. After securing thirty-four witnesses, prosecutors were forced to issue warrants for eighteen who changed their minds despite guarantees of safety and anonymity. Two more appeared voluntarily but refused to testify (one was too frightened to enter the courtroom for fear of running into a familiar face). Thirteen obeyed the issued warrants but tempered their testimonies. Others reneged on their testimonies weeks after giving them. One witness even withdrew midway through his verbal exposition in a panic attack fearing for his life. In sum, after nine

mafia assassinations of witnesses, and the rest intimidated into silence or withdrawal, Haradinaj was exonerated in April 2008 (Pean 2013, 236–38).

83. Bronner 2008, 17. His mafia superordinate may have inspired the fear. Khintsagov "was apparently so afraid of his nuclear suppliers that after he was arrested, he refused to give even their first names. He could have just invented some generic Russian names—Oleg, Dmitry. But he didn't even do that. . . . He was evidently terrified, possibly for his relatives, and possibly because when his jail sentence in Georgia is up, he knows he will be deported back to Russia" (Sheet 2008, 3).

84. For Kosovo, see Kaltcheva 2009. For South Ossetia and mountainous Georgia proper, see Immigration and Refugee Board of Canada 2015.

85. Marty 2010, 15, 14, 26, 11.

86. Arasli 2007, 7.

87. Traughber 2007.

88. The regional Thieves-in-Law—analogous to the Albanian mafia in Kosovo—were unrelated to the HEU traffic: "Significantly, none of the above cases [including the 2006 episode] involved anyone from the professional criminal organizations that were dominant in the former Soviet Union, namely the vory-v-zakone. . . . Georgian law enforcement and intelligence agencies are not aware of any evidence that would indicate that the vory were involved in radiological trafficking" (Kupatadze 2010, 229).

89. Bronner 2008, 5–6, i.

90. Kupatadze 2010, 224.

91. Bronner 2008, 16–18.

Chapter 6. West Africa

1. Warner 2010. On scholars' ideological coloring of West African smuggling, see Meagher 2014.

2. Bybee 2012, 79.

3. Faye 2006.

4. Englebert 2005, 48.

5. Foucher 2011, 91.

6. Faye 2006, 53.

7. Evans 2003, 15–16.

8. Evans 2000, 652.

9. Englebert 2005, 46–51. Wagane Faye (2006, 64) summarized the co-optation: "In exchange for their willingness to cooperate, the Senegalese government provides the civilian leaders of both MFDC factions with [sic] monthly payments. The MFDC civilian leaders use these transfers to reinforce their local power. In effect, the flow of resources from the state enhances the separatists' local control and gives them credibility as local patrons. Thus, the conflict remains a vehicle for the different MFDC civilian leaders to achieve elite status and benefit from state resources."

10. Faye 2006, 81.

11. Directorate General for Development 2003, 77.

12. Labrousse 2003, 28.

13. Evans 2004, 7–8. Gangsters' wealth was underwhelming, however: "While some people may have gained part of their living from the 'war economy,'" Evans (2004, 12) notes, "no one has got rich exploiting the low-value resources available." There are no "narco-villas" in Casamance as there are in separatist territories such as Azawad and Kosovo. The narco-traffic is a matter of making ends meet for the separatist community.

14. Evans 2000, 655.

15. Beary 2011, 33.

16. Evans 2004, 9.

17. Foucher 2011, 83. Two notable MFDC splinter groups are the Movement for Liberation of People of the Casamance and the Revolutionary Front for Social Equilibrium in Senegal, while the militant Attika has three competing currents: the Baraka Mandioka, Cassolol, and Diakaye (Fall 2010, 18).

18. On MFDC's ethnocentric composition, see Foucher 2019, 287.

19. Vigh 2017.

20. Faye 2006, 53–55.

21. The Karone Isles mafia has the distinction of being the only narco-traffic in West Africa that serviced the region itself. Casamançais separatists were the only ones with a transnational drug flow that did not aim—as heroin and cocaine routes do—for Europe and the United States (UNODC 2005, 40).

22. Evans 2004, 12. On the resulting "war economy with low profits," with "guerrillas mov[ing] between the bush and civilian life," see Foucher 2019, 285.

23. Much has been made of Casamance's "acephalous" political culture. Pierre Englebert (2005, 47) emphasizes an impenetrable patronage community run by independent-minded patriarchs, with "very little hierarchy in political relations altogether": "Casamance separatist leaders are not therefore local authority figures pushing for cultural recognition. They are, by and large, modernized (educated) would-be elites who have been kept off local positions of administrative authority by Dakar's policy of direct rule." However decentralized the culture, it sustained a mafia organized enough to cultivate, crop, package, and smuggle West Africa's biggest (and possibly oldest) marijuana racket.

24. Evans 2000, 655. See also Foucher 2011, 85, 88.

25. Evans 2003, 14. Government antimafia measures, furthermore, are comparatively excellent. With Nigeria, Senegal tops the region in drug seizures. Of twenty-four hundred members of crime groups prosecuted in 2000–2003 by Senegalese law enforcement, fifteen hundred were charged with armed robbery, six hundred with cattle rustling, and three hundred with smuggling (Ezeanyika and Ubah 2012, 17).

26. Shaw 2015. Specialists speculated that enterpreneurs in the cannabis racket "did much to convince the MFDC to establish a base in the area, to keep the Senegalese security forces at bay" (Foucher 2019, 285n54).

27. Directorate General for Development 2003, 78.

28. Englebert 2005, 39; Fall 2010, 18–19; Faye 2006, 56–57. On the myth of Catholic prevalence in the separatist community, see Foucher 2019, 270n14.

29. Englebert 2005, 39.

30. Evans 2004, 14. "Cannabis may be more important for the *Front Nord*, which has some control over its trafficking to The Gambia and also 'taxes' other contraband flows across the border where it can (typically Casamance primary produce goes in one direction, and manufactured goods that can be obtained more cheaply in Gambian markets in the other)" (Evans 2004, 10–11). On the narco-distribution method, see Evans 2004, 18n21.

31. Foucher 2011, 82.

32. Ezeanyika and Ubah 2012, 4.

33. For an overview of Tuareg nationalism in the region, see Lecocq and Klute 2019. Unlike Kurdish or Albanian nationalisms, Tuareg separatist movements remain compartmentalized, without a proposed "Greater Azawad" or "Greater Azawaq" across multiple host states.

34. Quoted in Chivvis 2016, 59n36.

35. On the last item, see Benjaminsen 2008.

36. Trumbull and George 2012, 30; Chivvis 2016, 56.

37. Heisbourg 2013, 9; Trumbull and George 2012, 32–33; Brown 2013, 18; Lloyd 2016, 135–37. At minimum, state-centered explanations concede that the northern mafias were instrumental in Mali's collapse (Chivvis 2016, 54–56), which in turn enabled the Tuareg rebellion. In an

exculpatory qualification, Jeremy Keenan (2013, 108) argues that the Tuareg uprisings in Mali and Niger had no "involvement with drug traffickers or Islamists" at "the outset of the rebellions"; rather, they partnered with them belatedly when forced to. His analysis is more persuasive regarding the "Islamist" than the narco-trafficking convergence.

38. Bouquet 2013, 1.

39. Larémont 2013, 6; Harmon 2014, 150. Judith Scheele (2009, 82n13, 91), the leading anthropologist on "mafias" (liberally defined) in the region, cautions against a crude view of "tribalism" in northern Mali, stressing the complex ethnocultural and familial embeddedness of organized crime: "Agents of the state and smugglers, who consider themselves autonomous, coexist in networks that oscillate between tribal logics and pseudo-state mafias" (author translation from French).

40. The ethnocentrism of the cocaine mafia was on display in the "Battle of Bouraissa," where Tuareg gangsters stood their ground violently: "One group, reportedly led by Halid (Klalid) ag Mohamed, consisted exclusively of Kel Iforas (Ifoghas) Tuareg, originally from Kidal region, who traditionally fell under the supreme religious authority of the Kounta family of Baba Ould Sidi El Moctar. The second group comprised Berabich Arabs from the adjoining Tilemsi valley area, the people of Baba Ould Sheikh," a drug smuggler commissioned by "the highest levels of Malian state" (Keenan 2013, 167–68). The Tuareg triumphed, seizing all the cocaine and extorting €300,000. Fighting both host state and rival mafias, the Tuareg narco-gangs served a twofold agenda: they stood for the autonomy of Azawad and the Tuareg cocaine racket.

41. On trans-Saharan smugglers' "vast dynamic moral economy requiring careful maintenance," see Guichaoua 2015, 325.

42. The Gao neighborhood referred to here is known by locals as "Cocaine Town" (*Cocainebougou*).

43. The mafia expansion was catalyzed by the US-led "war on terror" in 2003. "This has not only fueled bitterness and anger but forced hundreds of young men to find alternative 'employment' in the burgeoning smuggling and trafficking businesses" (Keenan 2007, 47). The Tuaregs' nomadic lifestyle (itself exaggerated, since many villages are firmly sedentary) has been confused for their mafias' primitive criminal tactics. In reality, they used GPS and satellite photography to construct sophisticated desert narco-paths (Lindell and Matsson 2014, 22).

44. Zoubir 2012. The piece also notes that the effects were entirely predictable at the time: "Algeria, Mauritania, and Niger, w[ere] always uneasy about Libya's civil war. Many feared that it would pry the lid off Tripoli's sizeable weapons cache and lead to the dispersal of arms across the region. It turns out that they were right to be worried." It was precisely "criminal activities" that gave "sufficient financial resource to recruit in large numbers; it allowed them to capitalise on the poverty and lack of economic opportunities in Northern Mali, where affiliations of ethnicity and religious affiliations were outweighed by the attraction of money and status" (Brown 2013, 18).

45. Napoleoni 2016, 10. On the gangsters behind the "Air Cocaine" incident and its aftermath, see Keenan 2013, 160–61; Harmon 2014, 153. No outlier, the incident was indicative of a thriving racket: "The 'Air Cocaine' incident is, of course, only the tip of the iceberg. Many other planeloads of cocaine . . . made it through the desert to be met with convoys of 4×4s and young men to transfer the cargo" (Harmon 2014, 154).

46. UNODC 2013. The peak year was 2007, after which annual volume steadied to approximately twenty tons of cocaine annually across West Africa, most of it through Mali; the estimated $1.25 billion that this racket is worth is "more than most regional defense budgets" (Harmon 2014, 148).

47. Keenan 2013, 163. Stephen Harmon (2014, 106) identifies two characteristics of the late 2000s' uprising that distinguish it from prior episodes of separatist mobilization, both mafia related. First, "it is around 2006 when organized crime began to take hold in northern Mali as different criminal networks strove to control smuggling routes in order to impose transit fees." Second, "the smuggling of cocaine . . . began to comprise a significant part of the smuggling trade

across northern Mali around 2007," and consequently, "the lucrative cocaine trade, as opposed to contraband traffic in cigarettes and commodities, is what attracted outside organized crime networks, called 'mafias' in Algeria, to norther Mali in the first place."

48. Guichaoua 2015, 333.

49. McGregor 2017, n.p. Bahanga's mafia, the Mouvement Touareg du Nord Mali, would later merge into the separatist MNLA as its criminal wing. The gangsters' allegiance to racketeering was sometimes so conspicuous that they were hard put to even articulate a coherent separatist message: "The failure of Bahanga and [partner-in-crime] Fagaga to elucidate any kind of political basis for their rebellion . . . led to suspicions that the real motive for the revolt was to drive away security forces interfering with Bahanga's lucrative smuggling trade" (McGregor 2017, n.p.). See also Harmon 2014, 175–76.

50. See also Harmon 2014, 187–88.

51. Lindell and Mattsson 2014, 25, 23–24. Proposals that conflict resolution should take the form of *replacing* the illicit contraband economy fell on deaf ears (Larémont 2013, 6–7). Meanwhile, the "high concentration of disputes over the control of narco-trafficking from West Africa through Mali to the Mediterranean coast made [separatist] northern Mali particularly vulnerable to resumption of violence" (Guichaoua 2015, 332).

52. It is highly misleading to treat Azawad separatists as "nationalists-turned-jihadists" (Richemond-Barak 2018)—a platitude among security experts whose focus on Islamic terrorism clouds their vision of nationalism. The Islamic insurgents coinciding with the separatists were not even indigenous: "leaders of all the Islamist groups in Azawad are agents, operatives, or associates of Algeria's [state security]" (Keenan 2013, 268).

53. Baker 2001, 78.

54. Lecocq and Klute 2019, 40.

55. On the Agadez mafia, see Politzer and Kassie 2016. On their origin, see Brachet 2018. The Algerian smuggling economy (*trabendo*) was a vital contextual cause. A notable pioneer of organized crime in the region was Hadj Bettu, founder of the trans-Saharan arms traffic in the 1980s. Paradigmatically multiethnic, he served as the "Algerian mafia state's representative in the extreme south" (Keenan 2013, 186–87), peddling arms to the highest bidders across Africa—without prejudice.

56. de Tessières 2018, 71.

57. Felbab-Brown 2017, n.p. Alain Deschamps (2000, 17) traces Niamey's reliance on questionable deputies in separatist localities to the 1990s: "When [Niger] had some actions and exactions, it preferred for a long time to attribute them to *bandits*" (author translation from French; emphasis in original).

58. On the perception of Agadez mafia by the local population, including its stunning reach as well as relation to deprivation and unemployment, see McCullough et al. 2017. The way the authors repeatedly encounter *organized crime* when searching for violent extremism is symptomatic (6–7, 14, 19, 35).

59. Politzer and Kassie 2016; Harmon 2014, 154–58.

60. Molenaar and El Kamouni-Janssen 2017, 47–48.

61. de Tessières 2018, 72.

62. de Tessières 2018, 71n140.

63. Politzer and Kassie 2016.

64. Chivvis 2016, 29.

65. On mafia factions splintering from jihadi insurgent hierarchies, see Chivvis 2016, 27–30.

66. Napoleoni 2016.

67. Harmon 2014, 184n53.

68. The nickname is possibly deceptive. According to some sources, he interfered in the tobacco traffic by burning cargoes with stern admonitions that the vice was "haram" for Muslims

(Boeke 2016, 927). But most analysts dismiss his public pieties: "Belmokhtar is a savvy business-man who manipulatively leverages purported jihadist ideology to inspire supporters and solicit ransom payments by governments and private organizations" (Bøås 2014, 8, 10). On the evolution of his abduction/kidnapping racket into a full-blown mafia, see Napoleoni 2016, 13–14, 40. For a curious testimony from UN envoys kidnapped by Belmokhtar, reflecting on his gentlemanly chivalry toward female prisoners, see Napoleoni 2016, 37–38.

69. Keenan 2013, 245.

70. Chivvis 2016, 30.

71. Among other factors, Western "antiterror" operations in the region were instrumental in creating insurgencies fueled by organized crime (Keenan 2007, 2013). The French experienced firsthand local mafias' sabotage of their military aims, as "Nigerien authorities face[d] pressure from those bothered by Western military presence, starting with illicit traffickers and especially drug traffickers who have strong connections in the highest echelons of the state apparatus" (Pellerin 2014, 83). In 2016, the United States began construction of a $100 million drone base in Agadez. How Nigerien organized crime and Agadez separatism will adapt remains to be seen.

72. Ojochenemi, Asuelime, and Onapajo 2015; MacEachern 2018.

73. The BBC (2004) aptly called Shekau "part-theologian, part-gangster," but reporting typically fixates on the former. On overlooked, noncaptive women in the separatist movement, including "Boko Haram wives," see MacEachern 2018, 168–70.

74. For an exaggerated reduction of Boko Haram in its entirety to "organized crime, a non-ideological enterprise using religion to mask its profiteering orientation," see Alozieuwa 2016, 192. The case is overstated, but the critique of reductionistic creed-centered accounts of Boko Haram is apposite.

75. Pérouse de Montclos 2014, 6. Even this expert, however, documents how Boko Haram "became increasingly criminalized over a period of years" (7).

76. MacEachern 2018, 159–60; Weeraratne 2017, 622; Forrest 2012, 1; Zenn and Pieri 2017; cf. Baca 2015.

77. Zenn and Pietri 2017, 51–53.

78. Forrest 2012, 1.

79. Weeraratne 2017, 622.

80. Onouha 2013, 4.

81. The main route was the "Salvador pass" connecting Libya to Niger, where "most of the arms smuggled out of Libya during the 2011 civil war entered . . . to be sold in Agadez" (Guichaoua 2015, 324). Alongside arms, cigarettes, contraband logging, and fishing, tens of millions of dollars were brought in annually by toxic dumping, theft of humanitarian aid, and antimalarial drugs. To a lesser degree, local gangsters also smuggled women for sexual trafficking in Europe (Forrest 2012, 50–51).

82. Onuoha 2013, 4.

83. Onuoha 2013, 5. "Smuggling is at the heart of this war," a historian accentuated, because "Boko Haram is also a for-profit criminal enterprise which incorporates many smugglers, and which depends on crime and violence that generate signficiant income in an environment of socio-economic distress" (cited in MacEachern 2018, 172).

84. Onuoha 2013, 5.

85. Pérouse de Montclos 2014, 12.

86. Pérouse de Montclos 2014, 12. See also Onuoha and Ezirim 2013, 6. Marc-Antoine Pérouse de Montclos (2014, 27) also notes the absurdity of UN sanctions, which are "symbolic because Boko Haram does not currently appear to need to rely on foreign funding. It still resorts to armed robberies and racketeering, extortion money from local businessmen and traders."

87. Thurston 2018, 49, 246.

88. Aghedo 2014. Scott MacEachern (2018, 129, 167–69) traces direct continuity from decades-old communities of "stuntmen" (*cascadeurs*) and moto-taxi drivers (*achabas*)—akin to biker gangs such as the Hell's Angels—to Boko Haram.

89. Aghedo 2014, 243.

90. Adesoji 2011, 113.

91. On gangs in the separatist north, see Dawha 1996; Adesoji 2011, 133. On Nigerian government's white paper documenting Boko Haram's appropriation of local gangs, see Smith 2015, 84–85. Many of these mafia remnants will surely outlive the besieged Boko Haram. A 2009 amnesty-for-militants drive left "tens of thousands of weapons . . . in the hands of small gangs who are either engaging in low-level criminal activity or adopting a 'wait and see' attitude," anticipating future opportunities (Forrest 2012, 109).

92. On Nigeria proper, Stephen Ellis's (2016) work is unmatched. An amusing illustration is the "copy-cat gangsters" in south Nigeria. Unrelated to Boko Haram, and far outside its breakaway territory, Nigerian Christian criminal syndicates "sent threatening messages to businesses and foreign embassies in the name of Boko Haram," while "criminal gangs posing as Boko Haram militants have colluded with bank officials to stage robberies" across the country (Weerantne 2017, 622).

93. Dechery and Ralston 2015, 17.

94. The country's cybercrime is notorious (Glenny 2011, 31–38) because 419 scams are conspicuous to Western readers. They need only open their emails to observe gangsters at work. But this cybermafia is regional; specialists note that the notorious "Nigerian Letter" is more accurately described as the "West African Letter" (Shaw, Reitano, and Hunter 2014, 12).

95. Watts 2007, 50.

96. Forrest 2012, 45.

97. Maszka 2018, 117–50; Ellis 2016, 201–5.

98. Smith 2015, 71; Watts 2007.

99. Forrest 2012, 52.

100. ICG 2017b, 17, 19.

101. Separatist organizations mushroomed after the Cold War, including the All Anglophones Conference, Southern Cameroons People's Organization, Southern Cameroons Youth League, Southern Cameroons Defense Force, Southern Cameroons Independence Restoration Council, Southern Cameroons Restoration Government, Ambazonia Liberation Party, and maximalist Ambazonia Movement. Not a single one has documented stakes in organized crime.

102. Konings and Nyamnjoh 2019; Awasom 1998.

103. Konings and Nyamnjoh 1997, 229.

104. Baker 2001, 76.

105. Mysterious and possibly fleeting, these formations are the most likely focal points for a future merger of mafia-separatist activities (ICG 2017a). As of January 2019, however, there is no evidence of mafia ties. See also Chothia 2018; Browne 2019.

106. Dicklitch 2011, 57; Beary 2011, 58.

107. Baye 2010; Mbuh 2004.

108. When Nigeria was itself under separatist siege from Biafra in the late 1960s, Cameroon curbed the separatists' access to precious smuggling channels across the border. "The Nigerian federal government was only too grateful that Cameroon prevented the flow of war material to the secessionists" (Cornwell 2006, 51). Over fifty years later, Nigeria returned the favor by blocking Ambazonian access to its markets.

109. Albanese and Reichel 2013, 107; Angwafo 2014, 102–4; Mazzitelli 2007, 1077–78, 1083.

110. Philip de Andrés 2008, 5–7.

111. Anwafo 2014, 106–8. Beyond Cameroon, the *coupers de route* are ubiquitous around the Lake Chad Basin (MacEachern 2018, 129–36).

112. ICG senior researcher Hans De Maire Heungoup quoted in "Separatists Declare War in Cameroon," 2018.

Chapter 7. Middle East

1. Khouri 2016, n.p.

2. On symmetrical scapegoating, see Eccarius-Kelly 2012, 247. Notable agents of *im*plausible deniability on the separatist side are Kurdistan Workers' Party (PKK) bloggers, and on the host state side, Turkish intelligence agents. "Interestingly, Turkish political circles have vacillated between denying Turkey's role as a major heroin transshipment country and blaming the Kurdish insurgency for the rise of the drug trade" (Eccarius-Kelly 2012, 247). Both self-serving theses are hopelessly untenable.

3. Selçuk 2011, 286.

4. Below I focus only on Kurdish separatism in Turkey. More than half the Kurdish population of the Middle East is in Turkey. On Kurds in Syria, see Gunter 2016, 87–133. On those in Iran, see Gunter 2016, 133–51. Most neglected in the subsequent analysis will be the Iraqi Kurds (Gunter 2016, 61–87). Two facts are worth mentioning in passing: the Kurdish community in Iraq boasts by far the most successful organized crime in the service of Kurdish nationalism in general, and Kurdish reliance on the organized criminal smuggling of oil, catalyzed in part by international mismanagement, allowed Kurdish mafias in northern Iraq to achieve profits unheard of in Turkish Kurdish areas. For evidence on these two claims, see UNODC 2003; Weiss and Hassan 2015, 42–43; Hickok 2003, especially 78, 84–85, 87–89; Natali 2001, 282–84; ICG 2012, 7, 11.

5. Gingeras 2014.

6. For manageable summaries of the Susurluk revelations, see Human Rights Foundation of Turkey 2000, 39–85; Gunter 1998; Massicard 2010, 43–45. The related Ergenekon conspiracy (Gingeras 2014, 240–44) has compelled scores of gangsters to publicly testify since 2008. These two episodes, and the accompanying record (around ten thousand pages), make Turkish and Kurdish organized crime the best-documented cases featured in this book.

7. Gunter 1998, 125.

8. On the Cold War Operation Gladio origins of anti-PKK Turkish mafia, see Gunter 1998, 129, 132; Ganser 2005, 240–44; Beyerle 2014, 238. For a network analysis of the reincarnation of Gladio in Ergenekon in the 2000s, see Demiroz and Kaupcu 2012.

9. Massicard 2010, 44.

10. Massicard 2010, 53.

11. Selçuk 2011, 286; Gunter 1998, 121, 124–25.

12. Gingeras 2014, 243–70.

13. Selçuk 2011, 287; Gunter 1998, 120.

14. Massicard 2010, 44–45; Gingeras 2014, 249–50. For an inventory of gangs and their members, see Massicard 2010, 69n71.

15. Selçuk 2011, 287.

16. For a catalog of leading figures, see Massicard 2010, 60, 63. The collaboration was arguably better for the gangsters than for the host state's antiseparatist crusade. "The Bucak family were not much engaged in military action against the PKK but instead used their salaries and the weapons they acquired to reinforce their position in the [*korucu*] tribe" (Massicard 2010, 55).

17. Gingeras 2014, 241, 247, 250. On the erosion of traditional Turkish mafia ties and transition to the young babas, see Galeotti 2012.

18. Gingeras 2014, 252–53; 256–57.

19. As a result, narcotics began flying on Turkish military helicopters as separatists were deprived of a much-needed source of funds. Alongside the Turkish-Kurdish war was a conflict over the heroin monopoly; fifteen officers were assassinated and over a hundred were kidnapped

in turf scuffles (Massicard 2010, 59). In the 1990s, two thousand unresolved assassinations were recorded—many of them presumed to be mafia related (Massicard 2010, 70).

20. Gunter 1998, 127, 132.

21. Eccarius-Kelly 2012, 239; Roth and Sever 2007; Curtis and Karacan 2002, 18–21; Shelley and Melzer 2008. For a critique of criminological bias in studies of the PKK, see Casier and Jongerden 2012. For an (overly) sympathetic portrayal of the PKK, with not a solitary mention of Kurdish narco-trafficking, while the government-mafia links are duly noted, see White 2015, 109–10.

22. Eccarius-Kelly 2012, 238, 246.

23. Pek and Ekıcı 2007, 148; Roth and Sever 2007, 909.

24. PKK camps in the Kandil Mountains are important sanctuaries and trading hubs. The UNODC (2010, 123) has (diplomatically) noted that "ethnic Kurdish groups" in the Iran-Iraq-Turkey route "may be responsible for border crossings in those regions."

25. Per and Ekıcı 2007, 143, 145.

26. Roth and Sever 2007, 908–9.

27. Fijnaut 1998, 86.

28. Pek and Ekıcı 2007, 149; Roth and Sever 2007, 913–14; Cengiz 2010, 269–79.

29. Roth and Sever 2007, 908, 910; Pek and Ekıcı 2007, 151; Eccarius-Kelly 2012, 241.

30. Roth and Sever 2007, 906; Eccarius-Kelly 2012, 241; Unal 2012, 13.

31. The separatists controlled 30 percent of heroin laboratories, "whereas the Turkish mafia controls the rest" (Hutchinson and O'Malley 2007, 1098). On the modesty of Kurdish organized crime compared to the host state's, see Massicard 2010, 52. On Hüseyin Baybaşin, the "Pablo Escobar of heroin," as an illustration of how proseparatist gangsters fare in Turkey, see Gingeras 2014, 254–56.

32. ICG 2007, 11, 4, 7. On the Hamas election context, see Finkelstein 2014, 2–3, 104.

33. ICG 2007, 4–6, 10–11.

34. ICG 2007, 15, 1

35. Abrahams, Garlasco, and Li 2004, 46; Sabry 2015, 86–87.

36. Sullivan and Jones 2008, 118.

37. Sabry 2015, 88. The blockade of the Gaza Strip began in 1991 during the first Palestinian Intifada and persists to this day with variation in the severity. For evidence that Israeli repression in Gaza incentivized arms smugglers (including an intriguing testimony from Hamid, an early tunnel-smuggling entrepreneur), see Sabry 2015, 87. On the counterproductive humanitarian aid politics, see Roy 2012; Qarmout and Béland 2012.

38. Roy 2005, 65–66.

39. Richemond-Barak 2018, 22; Sabry 2015, 97.

40. Pelham 2012, 9–10; Zohar 2015, 448.

41. Sabry 2015, 60.

42. Sabry 2015, 63.

43. Under Hosni Mubarak, Egypt crafted a notable mafia to carry out the regime's repressive and unlawful chores. Branching into the Sinai, the El-Adly Cartel recruited "criminal networks of born-and-bred bandits" from the region. But the organized crime took on increasing independence from the state apparatus, spawning the likes of the al-Menaei Clan, "the largest arms smuggling network in Sinai," which earned its wealth and notoriety by running guns to Palestinians (Sabry 2015, 56, 71).

44. Their principal rivals are the Dagmush Clan, which founded in 2006 the Army of Islam, a major intraseparatist challenger to Hamas in Gaza. On the remarkable gangster figure of Mumtaz Dughmush, who "auctioned services to the highest bidder" for decades, see ICG 2007, 11. The clan apparently undermined the Fatah-Hamas reconciliation attempt (Mecca Agreement) because "reconciliation was bad for business" (ICG 2007, 12).

45. Pelham 2012, 7, 21.

46. Sabry 2015, 81.

47. Pelham 2012, 12. The world's premier Gaza specialist, Sara Roy, recommends moderate skepticism about Nicolas Pelham's estimates of the tunnel economy (author interview, March 5, 2019, Cambridge, MA).

48. Pelham 2012, 10; Sabry 2015, 73.

49. Pelham 2012, 9.

50. Zohar 2015, 148; Shay 2016, 1.

51. Pelham 2012, 23.

52. SIPRI 2009. On the host state's cynical use of Gaza smuggling as pretext for a punishing naval blockade, see Finkelstein 2014, 110–14.

53. Pelham 2012, 13, 14; Sabry 2015, 103.

54. Sabry 2015, 105–6.

55. Pelham 2012, 10, 14, 16, 19; Sabry 2015, 96.

56. Daphné Richemond-Barak (2018, 24) cites the figure of 1,370. Shaul Shay (2016, 1) records 1,900 tunnels between January 2011 and December 2015. Human Rights Watch documented how Israel exaggerated the number (by conflating shafts with tunnels, for instance) to validate Gazan house demolitions (Abrahams, Garlasco, and Li 2004).

57. Pelham 2012, 20; Zohar 2015, 449.

58. Sabry 2015, 92.

59. Pelham 2012, 19, 27n8.

60. Sabry 2015, 94.

61. Dennison 2018.

62. Johnston et al. 2016, 257.

63. Johnston et al. 2016, xxiv.

64. Crabtree 2016, 22; Johnston et al. 2016, xxiv; Gerges 2016, 267.

65. Halder 2016, 48; Gerges 2016, 269.

66. Cockburn 2015, 145; Weiss and Hassan 2015, 165; Mironova, forthcoming, 153.

67. In 2013, European intelligence documented four separate battalions that shifted allegiances from the Free Syrian Army to the Turkish-backed al-Nusra, and yet again to IS, seemingly for criminal purposes (Dettmer 2013).

68. Williams 2011, 157.

69. Reitano, Clarke, and Adal 2017.

70. Weiss and Hassan 2015, 57.

71. Mironova, forthcoming, 249.

72. Stern and Berger 2015, 33–39. On the comparison of jihadi leaders with US gangster Whitey Bulger, for whom "prison was his university," see Weiss and Hassan 2015, 10.

73. Gerges 2016, 269. Unlike peer separatist movements, IS has a pitiable stake in narco-traffic (Crabtree 2016, 2). The single exception is trafficking in Captagon, a cancer opioid and major contraband in the Syrian war. In Afghanistan, ISIS/ISIL "support zones" control under three thousand hectares of opium/poppy cultivation, or just 1.4 percent of the total drug market. The Taliban, by contrast, control 85 percent (UNODC 2017, 36; Crabtree 2016, 23).

74. Cockburn 2015, 49.

75. Johnston et al. 2016, 198.

76. Halder 2016, 53.

77. Halder 2016, 50.

78. Napoleoni 2016, 113, 138.

79. Williams 2011, 165.

80. Napoleoni 2016, 211, 233; Halder 2016, 52.

81. Bypassing the United Nations' oil-for-food program (devastating to the population, but not to its regime), Iraq smuggled nine hundred million barrels of oil from 1991 to 2002. In the

last seven years of Hussein's rule, oil smuggling brought him $8 billion; the "smuggling network was huge, involving thousands of vessels, vehicles, and trucks." In 2000, a metric ton of smuggled Persian Gulf oil went for $205. Of that, an admirable $60 went to nonstate smugglers (Wahab 2006). These gangsters fatefully transferred to IS in later years.

82. Wahab 2006, 56. On the "oil-smuggling mafia" succeeding Hussein, see Williams 2011, 159.

83. Johnston et al. 2016, 27.

84. Another strategic "transit-point for an ISIS oil-smuggling operation" was Kirkuk, where Albanian, Russian, and regional ISIS fighters clashed over checkpoint controls (Mironova, forthcoming, 153). In Syria, the struggle over the porous Turkey-Syria frontier (833 kilometers) was largely about smuggling; "many of the intra-rebel battles have been fought over the control of border crossings that can be used to move men and weapons, and to provide a source of revenue" (Cockburn 2015, 91).

85. Weiss and Hassan 2015, 234.

86. Mironova, forthcoming, 168; Stern and Berger 2015, 88.

87. Johnston et al. 2016, 255–56; Halder 2016, 51; Gerges 2016, 267.

88. Cockburn 2015, 7.

89. Gerges 2016, 265; Weiss and Hassan 2015, 224.

90. Stern and Berger 2015, 114.

91. Weiss and Hassan 2015, 165, 226–27.

92. Cockburn 2015, xviii; Johnston et al. 2016, 60.

93. Weiss and Hassan 2015, 64.

94. Gerges 2016, 196–97; Weiss and Hassan 2015, 206.

95. Felbab-Brown, Trinkunas, and Hamid 2018, 65; Gerges 2016, 231.

96. Gerges 2016, 269.

97. Stern and Berger 2015, 55, 71. To draw an analogy between 1900s' socialism and contemporary jihadism, if al-Qa'ida was the Spartacus League, IS was the Bolsheviks.

98. On the separatist ambivalence of the Houthi uprising's creators, see Rabi 2015, 165–66.

99. Mardini 2010, 4.

100. Clark 2010, 237.

101. Hill 2017, xiii; Clark 2010, 22.

102. Lewis 2015, 105:

103. Clark 2010, 267; Lewis 2015, 105.

104. Mardini 2010, 219, 221.

105. Clark 2010, 267.

106. For more conservative estimates, see Hill 2017, 70–71; Salmoni, Loidolt, and Wells 2010, 37.

107. Salmoni, Loidolt, and Wells 2010, 61; Hill 2017, 72.

108. Hill 2017, 85.

109. Mardini 2010, 4, 77.

110. Salmoni, Loidolt, and Wells 2010, 197; Mardini 2010, 76.

111. Brandt 2017, 69.

112. Lackner 2017, 34, 54; Salmoni, Loidolt, and Wells 2010, 124–27.

113. Salmoni, Loidolt, and Wells 2010, 38–39.

114. The Sa'dah War is partitioned by purists into six separate Sa'dah Wars (in 2004, 2005, 2005–6, 2007, and 2008), underlining the cyclic nature of the conflict. For our purposes, the pauses inspiring the division are worth considering because they are the respites during which gunrunners rearmed, reconfigured, and reinvigorated warring cliques. For a detailed, phase-by-phase trajectory of the Sa'dah War, see Salmoni, Loidolt, and Wells 2010, 129–57. For a local fable—not entirely fanciful—that the war was in fact a turf-defense attempt by "people who used to make lucrative livings by smuggling goods and weapons to and fro," see Clark 2010, 248.

115. Salmoni, Loidolt, and Wells 2010, 197.

116. Hill 2017, 191. For ease, quotation marks have been removed from Hill's passage, which synthesizes several authoritative sources on the issue. For the same conclusion—that smugglers perpetuated war—see ICG 2009.

117. Salmoni, Loidolt, and Wells 2010, 198–99.

118. Brandt 2017, 69–72, 313.

119. Brandt 2017, 315. For context, see Samuel Perlo-Freeman's (2019) précis on the arms suppliers of the Yemen war.

120. Brandt 2017, 71.

121. Brandt 2017, 316–37.

122. Lewis 2015.

Chapter 8. Eastern Europe

1. Eyal, Szelenyi, and Townsley 1997, 68.

2. Hale and Orttung 2016, 215.

3. Kaplan 2005.

4. Andreas 2004a; Mueller 2000; Gagnon 2006.

5. Mueller 2000, 42.

6. Smajić 2010.

7. One corruption specialist fumed that "nothing in Bosnia-Herzegovina—not one segment of human life, including the economy, industry, sports and culture—is more organized than organized crime" (Smajić 2010, 212). The hyperbole is not entirely groundless. On postwar organized crime and "mafia welfare" in Bosnia, see Donais 2003; Pugh 2004. On the symbiosis between peacekeepers and gangsters in Bosnia, see Andreas 2011. One might add that nothing in Bosnia-Herzegovina is more *multiethnic* than organized crime.

8. In English, Andreas (2004a, 2004b) has documented the criminal effects and interethnic collusion most extensively.

9. Ferguson 2015, 134–69.

10. See also Donais 2003, 363.

11. Mueller 2000, 51; Bakić 2011, 489, 546.

12. "Juka's men, who had defended the city from the Serbs in 1992, soon began plaguing the defended without regard to ethnicity. They stole automobiles; extorted money and valuables; abducted, abused, and raped civilians; and looted the city's warehouses and shops, making off with 20,000 pairs of shoes in one venture. In addition, they monopolized the black market that made up the city's only trade, earning fortunes in a city where many people spent their days scavenging for water and bread" (Mueller 2000, 57).

13. Ferguson 2015, 146.

14. Mueller 2000, 49.

15. Smajić 2010, 208. The irregular unit ecology was not entirely criminal, of course, and varied across war phases and ethnic sides (Ferguson 2015). For a comparison of organized crime in Sarajevo with related besieged cities like Bihać, Srebrenica, and Mostar (a "mafia-like fiefdom"), see Andreas 2011, 34–41.

16. Mueller 2000, 50, 52.

17. Mann 2005, 421. Much of Croatian organized crime was a thorn in the side of Zagreb's nationalist cause in Bosnia: "On the eve of the war, illegal activities appeared to become vital for the maintenance of the new separatist entities. In particular, the Croat Herzegovinan mafia clans [in Bosnia] began to demand a policy of non-interference in their illicit activities" (Strazzari 2003, 143–44). To Zagreb's chagrin, one British adventurer serving as a Croatian mercenary boasted to the BBC that he "liberated" two television sets (Ferguson 2015, 157).

18. Mueller 2000, 55.

19. War crimes and atrocities were primarily "committed by men with long criminal records" (Mueller 2000, 52), to say nothing of the gangsters' battlefield ineptitude.

20. Pugh 2003, 52.

21. Hozić 2004, 37; Hajdinjak 2002, 24.

22. Šurc and Zgaga 2013.

23. Pugh 2003, 52.

24. Andreas 2004a, 40–42.

25. Mueller 2000, 58.

26. Pugh 2003, 52.

27. Tmušiš 2002.

28. Hadjinjak 2002, 10.

29. Andreas 2011, 45n44.

30. War journalist Davor Lukač, who covered the conflict extensively, discusses the wartime mafia in *Da Možda Ne: Zločini pred kamerom—Slučaj Atifa Dudakovića*, broadcast on Radio Televizija Srbija on March 24, 2018.

31. Andreas 2011, 38. For his memoir, see Abdić 2016. The self-panegyric is titled "From Idol to War Criminal and Back" (author translation).

32. Andreas 2011, 38.

33. Strazzari 2003, 143.

34. Quoted in Andreas 2011, 38.

35. Hislope 2003, 129.

36. Bellamy 2002.

37. Raufer and Quere 2006; Grillot et al. 2004, 39.

38. Hislope 2004, 23; Bellamy 2002, 126.

39. Vangelovski 2017, 281.

40. One of them was a café owner subjected to extortion and violence within months of opening her bar. In subsequent years, she became (in retaliation?) a leading academic specialist on Albanian organized crime (Arsovska 2015). An analogous stroke of luck for scholarship was the fate of Boris Penchuk, former owner of the Bely Lebed (White Swan) mall in Donetsk, Ukraine. When the Akhmetov Clan appropriated his business, he fled to Kiev and funded the writing of *Donetsk Mafia* (Kuzin and Penchuk 2006), the most detailed study of organized crime in east Ukraine.

41. Arsovska 2015, 215.

42. Raufer 2007, 402.

43. Arsovska 2015, 2.

44. Todorovski et al. 2018, 66.

45. Vangelovski 2017, 182n80.

46. Hislope 2004, 23.

47. This does not absolve the widespread anti-Albanian prejudice (much of it racist) in Macedonian public opinion "that Albanians are criminals and thieves" (Hislope 2003, 133, 139).

48. Grillot et al. 2004, 12; Vangelovski 2017, 185.

49. ICG 2001, 6.

50. Hislope 2004, 19.

51. The debate ranges from those who reduce the entire separatist insurgency to organized criminal dynamics (the mafia's "active conspiracy to start a war") to those who assert that the mafia merely determined the outbreak, timing, scale, or outcome of the conflict (on the "two schools," see ICG 2002, 24–28). The argument for mafia reductionism is made most forcefully by French criminologist Xavier Raufer (Raufer and Quere 2006). For milder, mafia-determinist conclusions, see Babanovski 2002; Bellamy 2002; Gounev 2003; Hislope 2002; Tomovska 2008. Much of the disagreement is normative/political, not technical. All agree that Albanian organized

crime was a major cause of the separatist uprising. None dispute the ethnocentric nature of the mafia (Arnovska 2015).

52. For the best figures, see Grillot et al. 2004, 20–21. An inflated estimate is six thousand (Hislope 2004, 21), but this appears to count Kosovo-based affiliates. On the "spillover effect from Kosovo," see Hislope 2003, 130, 140–45. For an analysis emphasizing Albania, not Kosovo, as the center of criminal gravity ("Albania is at the centre of a 'narco-terrorist' ring that ferments instability in Macedonia"), see Bellamy 2002, 119.

53. Stefanova 2004, 268–69. On the smuggled arsenal, see Grillot et al. 2004, 21–22.

54. Babanovski 2002; cf. Grillot et al. 2004, 21. Less plausibly, "some observers have speculated that [Hashim] Thaçi's monopoly of the Macedonian export market to Kosovo so irritated Kosovo mafia groups that they, in turn, unleashed the NLA insurgency" (Hislope 2004, 26n44). In this interpretation, "the NLA may have been given a push from patrons eager to see the [Macedonian Albanian leadership] put in its place"—"an intra-Albanian feud" between "powerful groups in Kosovo" and Albanian leaders inside Macedonia (ICG 2002, 25).

55. Daskalovski 2004, 41, 47.

56. Arnovska 2015, 54; Bellamy 2002, 134.

57. Hislope 2002, 39.

58. Bellamy 2002, 140, 131–32.

59. Arsovska and Kostakos 2008, 363; Ilievski 2015, 41.

60. Daskalovski 2004, 41; Hislope 2004, 25n33.

61. Hislope 2002, 39. "Some of the rebels' funding," Ahmeti divulged to MSNBC, "might come from narcotics trafficking and a flourishing sex slave trade in the region." With less understatement, another commander confessed purchasing "weapons from organized criminal gangs and various gun dealers" (quoted in Grillot et al. 2004, 21–22).

62. A witness in real-time reporting for the *Economist* insisted that the militia was no more than "50–70 cigarette smugglers" who were "prompted by their desire to stop Macedonia's police from shutting down their smuggling routes" (Grillot et al. 2004, 25).

63. Hislope 2004, 24; Strazzari 2003, 150.

64. A postmortem of the conflict by the ICG (2002, 25) reminds us that "Ahmeti did not emerge as public leader of the NLA until the conflict had already broken out." On Ahmeti as an ex post facto nationalist spokesman for what was initially an ambiguous criminal uprising, see Bellamy 2002, 132. There were many intraseparatist machinations between militants and politicians, and Ahmeti's ascendency was as much a result of skilled backroom dealings as of operational merit.

65. Glenny 2004, 251.

66. Blakkisrud and Kolstø 2011; Protsyk 2012.

67. It held this distinction for the longest stretch of time in the post–Cold War period (Tudoroiu 2012, 138–39), overtaken only recently by Ukraine (2015).

68. Molcean and Verständig 2014, 142–43.

69. Galeotti 2004b, 400; Sanchez 2009, 156. Whereas women from the host state proper are predominantly trafficked into Europe, Transnistrian sex workers tend to go to Turkey and the United Arab Emirates. Inside Transnistria, the "prostitute networks operate with the acceptance, probably even cooperation, of Smirnov" (Sanchez 2009, 169).

70. At the moment of secession, Transnistria accounted for 33 percent of industrial goods, 56 percent of consumption goods, and 88 percent of the electricity of host state Moldova (Buttin 2007, 15n5).

71. Galeotti 2004b, 400; Molcean and Verständig 2014, 138.

72. Galeotti 2004b, 402.

73. Molcean and Verständig 2014, 139.

74. On the coalescing of Transnistrian and Moldovan organized crime until there was "little difference between the two," see Galeotti 2004b, 400. The author implies that the separatist mafia

overshadows criminals in the host state proper: Moldovan organized crime is an "'infection' from TDMR-based gangs," with the host state being "poisoned" by separatist crime (Galeotti 2004b, 400, 403).

75. Galeotti 2004b, 401.

76. Molcean and Verständig 2014, 147.

77. Protsyk 2012, 177; Tudoroiu 2012, 144.

78. Molcean and Verständig 2014, 140.

79. Blakkisrud and Kolstø 2011, 187.

80. Smuggling declined after 2005, when an EU Border Assistance Mission introduced a semblance of control on the Transnistrian-Ukrainian border (410 kilometers). In 2006, an EU-brokered deal on customs stamps between Moldova and Ukraine forced over four hundred Transnistrian companies to register in Moldova, further curbing illegal flows (Peterka-Benton 2012, 78). Tiraspol natives jokingly divulged to the author what the Pridnestrovian Moldavian Republic's acronym *really* stands for: "Papina i Moia Respublika," or "My Papa's and My Republic" in reference to the Smirnov family.

81. Peterka-Benton 2012. A 2005 scandal—partly fabricated—publicized the prospect of Alazan rockets equipped with nuclear warheads being peddled in Transnistria. Nuclear smuggling in separatist territory has been under intense Moldovan and international scrutiny since then, though the extent of smuggling remains unclear (Molcean and Verständig 2014, 143–44). For a fetching insider's account of the Transnistrian arms traffic by a French journalist, see Deleu 2005.

82. Sanchez 2009, 163; Molcean and Verständig 2014, 141.

83. Blakkisrud and Kolstø 2011, 188; Molcean and Verständig 2014, 141.

84. Galeotti 2004b, 402.

85. Munteanu and Munteanu 2007, 52.

86. Galeotti 2004b, 398.

87. Kolstø and Malgin 1998, 111.

88. Blakkisrud and Kolstø 2011, 202; cf. Protsyk 2009.

89. Molcean and Verständig 2014, 145–46.

90. Buttin 2007, 22.

91. On "consensus among most international observers that the allegations of Transnistria being a 'black hole' are overblown," see Blakkisrud and Kolstø 2011, 187. Notwithstanding, "smuggling activities have been protected and controlled by a few clans, all of them connected and dependent on the secessionist authorities" (Popescu 2006, 6).

92. Blakkisrud and Kolstø 2011, 190n36.

93. Galeotti 2004b, 399.

94. Galeotti 2004b, 399–400; Buttin 2007, 22; Sanchez 2009, 169.

95. Galeotti 2004b, 399.

96. Blakkisrud and Kolstø 2011; Molcean and Verständig 2014, 130, 149.

97. Buttin 2007, 23; Munteanu and Munteanu 2007, 53.

98. "There seems to be no evidence that the separatists were involved in organized criminal activities at the onset of the conflict. Thus, while economic incentives may have played a role, gains from organized criminal activities did not serve as a major goal during the early stages of the separatist movement" (Molcean and Verständig 2014, 148). For the argument that mafia roots of Transnistrian secessionism evolved into nation building, see Blakkisrud and Kolstø 2011. The authors note that Moldova's unusually pithy separatist war meant that criminal warlords had shorter longevity than in Georgia and Azerbaijan, which gave Transnistria an advantage in state making. Transnistria successfully disbanded or absorbed wartime militias such as Cossack irregulars and the *gvardeitsi* (guards), consolidating a seventy-five-hundred-strong army. The host state—six times as populous—has only six thousand soldiers (Blakkisrud and Kolstø 2011, 185–86).

99. Molcean and Verständig 2014, 148.

100. Kuzio 2015, 358.

101. Williams and Picarelli 2001, 110.

102. Williams and Picarelli 2001, 112; SIPRI 2003, 63, 46n96; UNODC 2010, 142, 145, 292n39.

103. SIPRI 2011, 7–8; UNODC 2010, 144; Williams and Picarelli 2001, 112–13; Kuzio 2015, 471.

104. UNODC 2010, 144.

105. Williams and Picarelli 2001, 121–24; SIPRI 2011.

106. UNODC 2010, 144.

107. Ministry of Defence of Ukraine 2011, 2013, 2014; Malyarenko and Galbreath 2016, 119; Kinstler 2014.

108. Malyarenko and Galbreath 2016, 124; Yekelchyk 2015, 146–47.

109. Stack 2017.

110. Interview in Kiev, December 2017. See also Losh 2016b; Karmanau 2016; Prentice and Zverev 2016; Woords 2016; Nemtsova 2016.

111. Malyarenko and Galbreath 2016, 133n15, 133n17.

112. Burdyha 2018.

113. Galeotti 2018, 248–49.

114. Losh 2016a.

115. Galeotti 2018, 186 (emphasis added). On the "major smuggling operation—of coal, scrap, weapons and probably drugs—that is enriching officials on both sides of the line," see ICG 2016, 8. Frontline journalists made the same discovery: "The conflict in eastern Ukraine has done little to dent the coffers of the country's criminal underworld. Smugglers are profiting from the war as an economic blockade of separatist territories spawns a black-market trade in food, fuel, and medicine" (Losh 2016a).

116. ICG 2016, 8.

117. Polukhina 2018. In this context, a personal anecdote may be excusable. The author was smuggled into Donetsk through the Maryinka checkpoint with a box of asbestos rope, crates of champagne, and food-order deliveries for on-duty guards—Ukrainian and DNR alike. The first of these items was suspicious, compelling my chauffer-smuggler to slip (another) two hundred hryvnia note into the Passport jacket pocket handed to Ukrainian authorities. The driver is part of a coordinated operation of a dozen vehicles that cross daily. The head smuggler—an acquaintance—described his effort as "baby games" compared to the competition.

118. Kuzio 2016, 185–86.

119. Kuzio 2015, 411–12.

120. Kuzio 2016, 193–94, 190; Kuzio 2015, 417.

121. Kuzio 2015, 416.

122. On the 1990s' mafia bloodbath preceding Akhmetov's triumph, see Kuzio 2014, 196–97.

123. Kuzio 2014, 206; 2015, 420.

124. Kuzin and Penchuk 2006, 4–5. Author translation from Russian.

125. Kuzio 2015, 424.

126. Kuzio 2015, 424.

127. The friction between Donbas separatists and patron state Russia is constant. In Lugansk, Cossack commanders who were supposed to do Moscow's anti-Ukrainian bidding were unreliable: "Many challenged the Russian decreed leadership, either because of their own hubris or over lucrative illicit rackets" (Bowen 2017, 19). In Donetsk, Russia is presumed to have killed several autochthonous leaders for failing to toe Moscow's line. The two most prominent were Arseny "Motorla" Pavlov, a separatist warlord who was killed in an elevator, and DNR head Zakharchenko, who was blown up in a restaurant fittingly called Separ (separatist).

128. The Helsinki Human Rights Group's conclusion that "Karabakh today is an oasis of good governance, respect for law and decency compared with most of the rest of the post–Soviet

Union" is deemed an "exaggeration" even by analysts sympathetic to the separatist movement. Indicatively, one of the main qualifications is how "extremely attractive for criminal and other shady businesses" the territory is (Kolstø and Blakkisrud 2012, 149, 144). In the main, judgments on Karabakh's criminalization range from assessing it a "racketeer state" (Lynch 2002; cf. Kolstø and Blakkisrud 2012) to the more reserved view that it is merely "a haven for organised crime" (Kaldor 2007, 157).

129. For an indictment of overethnicization of the separatist dispute, see Özkan 2008. With nationalist reductionism, the role of mafias is lost. Karabakh's "patronage networks, clan interests, and black market profiteering" are neglected in favor of abstract ethnonational "'ancient hatred' paradigm[s] and grand geopolitical schemes" (Özkan 2008, 574).

130. Sierra 2011, 241.

131. Kaldor 2007, 157–58, 166.

132. On the four stages of Karabakh War, see Geukjian 2011, 189–205. On Azeri mafia contributions during the conflict, see Kaldor 2007, 163; Sanamyan 2016, 39. On organized crime in Baku, see Goltz 1998, 9, 309.

133. Kaldor 2007, 163, 170–71; Özkan 2008, 591; Bölükbaşı 2011, 216.

134. Kaldor 2007, 179.

135. Özkan 2008, 591.

136. The separatist army had 316 tanks, almost as many as patron state Armenia (102) and host state Azerbaijan (220) *combined*. Karabakh also outnumbered Azeri forces in artillery pieces (322 versus 282) and nontank armored vehicles (324 versus 135). See Kaldor 2007, 171.

137. Lynch 2002, 847. On role of the diaspora and how the ambivalence of Armenia's irredentism is mirrored in Nagorno-Karabagh's separatist movement, see Chorbajian 2001, 160.

138. Kolstø and Blakkisrud 2012, 144.

139. Chorbajian 2001, 191.

140. Kaldor 2007, 178.

141. Welt and Bremmer 1997, 83.

142. Giragosian 2009, 4.

143. Kaldor 2007, 159, 162.

144. Özkan 2008, 586; Mammadov 2017, 99.

145. Özkan 2008, 587.

146. Caspersen 2008, 368.

147. Panossian 2001, 162n18.

148. de Waal 2013, 317, 241.

149. On his front company Jupiter and assets that made him "unimaginably wealthy" by Karabakh standards, see de Waal 2013, 253.

150. de Waal 2013, 254.

151. de Waal 2013, 239, 252–55, 360n6; ICG 2005b, 12; Lynch 2002, 840–42.

152. On Karabakh's exceptional success in curbing narco-trafficking, however, see Beglarian 2004.

153. Saroyan 1990.

154. Özkan 2008, 592.

Chapter 9. Conclusion

1. Even in landmark classics, the neglect is almost a casual reflex. Surveying considerable evidence for the role of organized crime in the Yugoslav wars, for example, Michael Mann (2005, 421–43) oddly dismisses multiple authorities on the question, who allegedly "all exaggerate the role of criminal thugs"—an unfounded charge.

2. Scott 1972; Philp 2017.

3. The "term 'corruption' suggests that these regimes aspire to be democratic but have somehow been led astray by malevolent forces, such as greed or rent-seeking behavior on the part of public officials. Gangster-states, however, are not Westphalian states that have become corrupted by bad actors. Economic predation, territorial expansion and wealth extraction are the organizing principles of their existence. Governance in the interest of citizens is an afterthought, if it is considered at all" (Hirschfeld 2015, 16).

4. Kalyvas 2015, 4.

5. Collier and Hoeffler 2002; Cederman, Gleditsch, and Buhaug 2013.

6. Makarenko 2005, 136.

7. Hastings (2010, 35, 147) insightfully noted two crucial differences between transnational organized crime and transnational terrorists. First, mafias, focused as they are on smuggling, tend to "create their own distribution networks," if not entire market institutions. Terrorists do not. Second, terrorists, focused as they are on fighting, tend to train their rank and file systematically. Mafias do not.

8. West 2002; Irrera 2015; Carrapico, Irrera, and Tupman 2017.

9. Williams 2012. Even the most overstated variants of the "convergence thesis" that mafia and social movement are indistinguishable ultimately acknowledge that in fact, it is a marriage of convenience between separate groups. Debunking a globalized *pax mafiosa* or "global criminal conspiracy," Williams (2002, 69) offers instead a typology of mafia relationships ranging from strategic alliances to short-term barter agreements—all short of convergence. This book built on these insights for separatist contexts, but future research may fruitfully explore variants of our mafia typology in nontorn states.

10. On the defects of securitization frameworks of organized crime, see Serrano 2002, 27–31. Despairing of the prevailing state-centric orthodoxy, the author describes her critique as "hurling caveats at the wind."

11. Romaniuk and Webb 2015. The malignant role of foreign actors in promoting counterinsurgency have been especially overlooked (Zolberg, Suhrke, and Aguayo 1986). Scholars tend to aknowledge only the "potential for perverse incentives created by international interventions" (Felbab-Brown, Trinkunas, and Hamid 2018, 8), but not direct or willful injury.

12. Keenan 2013, 84, 90–91.

13. Malis 2012, 187.

14. Malis 2012, 64–65, 346, 370.

15. For review of the moral philosophy of separatism from John Stuart Mill onward, see Bartkus 1999, 15–18.

16. Shelley 2018.

17. Briquet and Favarel-Garrigues 2010, 9.

18. Classic presuppositions about the supposedly peerless status of deviance as criterion for what is criminal (long abandoned by criminology) are ironically resurfacing in current mafia scholarship. Battersby (2014, 209), notably, locates the essence of transnational organized crime in "the systemic nature of transgression, or *unlawfulness* [emphasis in original]," implying that "amorality" is the underlying principle.

19. Berdal and Seranno 2002, 199–201.

20. The widely fictionalized saga of Pablo Escobar—the world's "King of Cocaine"—was ended by a US-Colombian operation in 1993. The celebratory frenzy had barely finished when an even deadlier, greater North Valley Cartel effortlessly replaced the Cali and Medellin Cartels. When the Northern Valley Cartel was, in turn, repressed in 2012, a dozen successors renewed and restored the traffic within mere months. These dynamics are also typical of Prohibition in the United States (Andreas 2013) and the Golden Triangle in Southeast Asia (McCoy 1991). Creative, multilateral solutions remain elusive.

21. See, respectively, Jenner 2011; Tinti and Reitano 2017; Weitzer 2012.

Appendix

1. On legalisms, see Summers 2014 (on Kosovo); Waters 2014 (on South Ossetia).

2. Stepanova 2008, 2.

3. Mishra 2008.

4. Sörensen 2006.

5. Beissinger 2007.

6. For a contextual comparison of these two cases in relation to other 1990s' cases, see Baev 1999, 26.

7. Lavrov 2010.

8. On critical junctures, see Mahoney 2000, 2004; Mahoney, Kimball, and Koivu 2009; Capoccia and Keleman 2007.

9. Katznelson 2003, 290–92.

10. Mirzayev 2014; Coppieters and Sakwa 2003, 187–212.

11. On process-tracing methods and causal mechanisms in comparative historical research, see Mahoney 2003, 363–65. For classic approaches to sequence analyses, see Moore 1966; Abbott and DeViney 1992; Mahoney and Rueschemeyer 2003, 146n10. On the Weberian tradition of causal analysis via comparative historical method, see Kalberg 2012.

12. For the theoretical basis of triadic forms, see Wolff 1950, 146–47, 154–62, 162–69.

13. Burt 2009.

14. See also Friesendorf 2011.

15. On the standards for interpreting seizure statistics, see UNODC 2015, 14–16.

16. Shimazono 2007; Zaitseva and Hand 2003.

17. For his spellbinding memoir, see Marty 2019.

18. Marty 2010, 25.

19. Bronner 2008.

20. Sheets 2008; Sokova, Potter, and Chuen 2007; Schmidle 2013.

21. Independent International Fact-Finding Mission 2009, 108.

22. Molcean and Verständig 2014, 145.

23. Pek and Ekıcı 2007, 142.

24. Smith 2015, 5, 84.

25. Locke and Thelen 1995; Ragin 1987; Mahoney and Rueschemeyer 2003, 8–15.

26. Cizre 2001, 222–24.

27. Lecocq 2004.

28. Kosienkowski 2013.

29. Daskalovski 2004, 41–45.

30. For the pedantry and politics of IS = ISIL = ISIS = Daesh titles, see Siniver and Lucas 2016. On the uniformity of IS throughout the moniker changes, see Gerges 2016.

31. Nicolaisen and Nicolaisen 1997, 292.

32. On the latter, "Saleh-loving thugs," see Kasinof 2014, 78.

33. Beary 2011, 197.

34. Croissant 1998, 61.

35. Satter 2004, 131; Hirschfeld 2015, 10–11; McCauley 2001.

36. Tishkov 2004.

37. Volkov 2002; Favarel-Garrigues 2010; Stephenson 2015.

38. Pelham 2012, 22.

39. Natsheh and Parizot 2015.

40. Natsheh and Parizot 2015, 123–26.

41. Lundblad 2007; Schäublin 2009.

42. Amir 1998, 134–35.

43. Robins 2002, 151.

44. Day 2012, 56–85; Mardini 2010, 176.

45. Day 2012, 230–39.

46. On separatist grievances in the 1990s, see Day 2012, 117–28, 130–59. On separatist griev-ances in the 2000s, see Day 2012, 227–36, 241–49. For a sampling of secessionist arguments within the movement, see Rabi 2015, 141–54. For an unsympathetic analysis of the Southern Movement, see Lackner 2017, 167–89.

47. Clark 2010, 237.

48. Kuzio 2015, 360.

49. Williams and Picarelli 2001, 125–27; Kuzio 2015, 360.

50. Kuzio 2016, 195.

REFERENCES

Abbott, A., and S. DeViney. 1992. "The Welfare State as Transnational Event: Evidence from Sequences of Policy Adoption." *Social Science History* 16 (2): 245–74.

Abdić, F. 2016. *Od idola do ratnog zločina i natrag*. Zagreb: Kvarner.

Abrahams, F., M. Garlasco, and D. Li. 2004. *Razing Rafah: Mass Home Demolitions in the Gaza Strip*. New York: Human Rights Watch.

Adesoji, A. O. 2011. "Between Maitatsine and Boko Haram: Islamic Fundamentalism and the Response of the Nigerian State." *Africa Today* 57 (4): 98–119.

Aghedo, I. 2014. "Old Wine in a New Bottle: Ideological and Operational Linkages between Maitatsine and Boko Haram Revolts in Nigeria." *African Security* 7 (4): 229–50.

Albanese, J. 2014. "North American Organised Crime." In *Global Crime Today: The Changing Face of Organised Crime*, edited by M. Galeotti, 8–18. London: Routledge.

———. 2015. *Organized Crime: From the Mob to Transnational Organized Crime*. Abingdon, UK: Routledge.

Albanese, J., and P. Reichel, eds. 2013. *Transnational Organized Crime: An Overview from Six Continents*. Los Angeles: Sage Publications.

Alemika, E.E.O., ed. 2013. *The Impact of Organised Crime on Governance in West Africa*. Abuja, Nigeria: Friedrich-Ebert-Stiftung.

Alozieuwa, S. H. 2016. "Political Economy of War and Violence: The Boko Haram in the Lake Chad Basin." *African Renaissance* 13 (1–2): 165–98.

Ambagtsheer, F., D. Zaitch, and W. Weimar. 2013. "The Battle for Human Organs: Organ Trafficking and Transplant Tourism in a Global Context." *Global Crime* 14 (1): 1–26.

Amir, M. 1998. "Organized Crime in Israel." In *Crime and Criminal Justice in Israel: Assessing the Knowledge Base toward the Twenty-First Century*, edited by R. R. Friedman, 121–38. New York: SUNY Press.

Anastasijević, D. 2010. "Getting Better?: A Map of Organized Crime in the Western Balkans." In *Transnational Terrorism, Organized Crime, and Peace-Building*, edited by W. Benedek, C. Daase, V. Dimitrijevic, and P. van Duyne, 149–68. New York: Palgrave Macmillan.

Anderson, A. 1997. "Organised Crime, Mafia, and Governments." In *The Economics of Organised Crime*, edited by G. Fiorentini and S. Peltzman, 33–53. Cambridge: Cambridge University Press.

Andreas, P. 2002. "Transnational Crime and Economic Globalization." In *Transnational Organized Crime and International Security: Business as Usual*, edited by M. R. Berdal and M. Serrano, 37–52. Boulder, CO: Lynne Rienner Publishers.

———. 2004a "The Clandestine Political Economy of War and Peace in Bosnia." *International Studies Quarterly* 48 (1): 29–51.

———. 2004b. "Criminalized Legacies of War: The Clandestine Political Economy of the Western Balkans." *Problems of Post-Communism* 51 (3): 3–9.

———. 2011. "Peace Operations and Illicit Business in Bosnia." In *Peace Operations and Organized Crime: Enemies or Allies?*, edited by J. Cockayne and A. Lupel, 33–46. London: Routledge.

———. 2013. *Smuggler Nation: How Illicit Trade Made America*. Oxford: Oxford University Press.

Angwafo, P. T. 2014. *Cameroon's Predicaments*. Bamenda, Cameroon: Langaa Research and Publishing.

Arasli, J. 2007. "The Rising Wind: Is the Caucasus Emerging as a Hub for Terrorism, Smuggling, and Trafficking?" *Connections: The Quarterly Journal* 6:5–26.

Arsovska, J. 2015. *Decoding Albanian Organized Crime: Culture, Politics, and Globalization*. Berkeley: University of California Press.

Arsovska, J., and P. A. Kostakos. 2008. "Illicit Arms Trafficking and the Limits of Rational Choice Theory: The Case of the Balkans." *Trends in Organized Crime* 11 (4): 352–78.

Asad, A. Z., and R. Harris. 2019. *The Politics and Economics of Drug Production on the Pakistan-Afghanistan Border*. Abingdon, UK: Routledge.

Atanga, M. 2011. *The Anglophone Cameroon Predicament*. Bamenda, Cameroon: Langaa Research and Publishing.

Athanassaopolou, E., ed. 2005. *Organized Crime in Southeast Europe*. London: Routledge.

Awasom, N. F. 1998. "Colonial Background to the Development of Autonomist Tendencies in Anglophone Cameroon, 1946–1961." *Journal of Third World Studies* 15 (1): 163–83.

Ayim, M. A. 2010. *Former British Southern Cameroons Journey towards Complete Decolonization, Independence, and Sovereignty: A Comprehensive Compilation of Efforts, Vol One*. Bloomington, IN: AuthorHouse.

Ayres, R. W., and S. Saideman. 2000. "Is Separatism as Contagious as the Common Cold or Cancer?: Testing International and Domestic Explanations." *Nationalism and Ethnic Politics* 6 (3): 91–113.

Babanovski, I. 2002. *ONA: Teroristička paravojska vo Makedonija*. Skopje, Macedonia: Veda.

Baca, M. 2015. "Boko Haram and the Kanuri Factor." *African Arguments*. Accessed June 3, 2019, https://africanarguments.org/2015/02/16/boko-haram-and-the-kanuri-factor-by-michael -baca/.

Baev, P. 1999. "External Interventions in Secessionist Conflicts in Europe in the 1990s." *European Security* 8 (2): 22–51.

———. 2003. "Civil Wars in Georgia: Corruption Breeds Violence." In *Potentials of Disorder*, edited by J. Koehler and C. Zürcher, 127–44. Manchester: Manchester University Press.

Baker, B. 2001. "Separating the Sheep from the Goats among Africa's Separatist Movements." *Terrorism and Political Violence* 13 (1): 66–86.

Bakić, J. 2011. *Jugoslavija: Razaranje i njegovi tumači*. Belgrade: Službeni Glasnik.

Balayev, B. 2013. *Right to Self-Determination in the South Caucasus: Nagorno Karabakh in Context*. Lanham, MD: Lexington Books.

Barnett, N. 2002. "The Criminal Threat to Stability in the Balkans." *Janes Intelligence Review* 14 (4): 30–32.

Bartkus, V. O. 1999. *The Dynamic of Secession*. Cambridge: Cambridge University Press.

Bassène, R. C. 2015. *Casamance: Récits d'un conflit oublié (1982–2014)*. Paris: L'Harmattan.

Battersby, P. 2014. *The Unlawful Society: Global Crime and Security in a Complex World*. Basingstoke, UK: Palgrave Macmillan.

Bayart, J. F., S. Ellis, and B. Hibou. 1999. *The Criminalization of the State in Africa*. Bloomington: Indiana University Press.

Baye, F. M. 2010. "Implications of the Bakassi Conflict Resolution for Cameroon." *African Journal on Conflict Resolution* 10 (1): 9–34.

BBC. 2004. "Nigeria's Boko Haram Leader Abubakar Shekau in Profile." *BBC News*, May 9. Accessed April 21, 2020, https://www.bbc.com/news/world-africa-18020349.

Beary, B. 2011. *Separatist Movements: A Global Reference*. Washington, DC: CQ Press.

Beglarian, A. 2004. "*Karabakh Rejects Drug Claims*." *CRS* 223, March 18. London: Institute for War and Peace Reporting.

Beissinger, M. R. 2002. *Nationalist Mobilization and the Collapse of the Soviet State*. Cambridge: Cambridge University Press.

———. 2007. "Structure and Example in Modular Political Phenomena: The Diffusion of Bulldozer/Rose/Orange/Tulip Revolutions." *Perspectives on Politics* 5 (2): 259–76.

Bélanger, L., É. Duchesne, and J. Paquin. 2005 "Foreign Interventions and Secessionist Movements: The Democratic Factor." *Canadian Journal of Political Science / Revue canadienne de science politique* 38 (2): 435–62.

Bellamy, A. J. 2002. "The New Wolves at the Door: Conflict in Macedonia." *Civil Wars* 5 (1): 117–44.

Benjaminsen, T. A. 2008. "Does Supply-Induced Scarcity Drive Violent Conflicts in the African Sahel?: The Case of the Tuareg Rebellion in Northern Mali." *Journal of Peace Research* 45 (6): 819–36.

Berdal, M. R., and M. Serrano. 2002. *Transnational Organized Crime and International Security: Business as Usual?* Boulder, CO: Lynne Rienner Publishers.

Beriker-Atiyas, N. 1997. "The Kurdish Conflict in Turkey: Issues, Parties, and Prospects." *Security Dialogue* 28 (4): 439–52.

Berry, L. V., G. E. Curtis, J. N. Gibbs, R. A. Hudson, T. Karacan, N. Kollars, and R. Miró. 2003. *Nations Hospitable to Organized Crime and Terrorism*. Washington, DC: Library of Congress, Defense Technical Information Center.

Bertrand, R. 2010 "Governor Sutiyoso's 'Wars on Vice': Criminal Enterprises, Islamist Militias, and Political Power in Jakarta." In *Organized Crime and States: The Hidden Face of Politics*, edited by J. Briquet and G. Favarel-Garrigues, 73–97. New York: Palgrave Macmillan.

Beyerle, S. 2014. *Curtailing Corruption: People Power for Accountability and Justice*. Boulder, CO: Lynne Rienner.

Blagov, S. 2006. "Putin to Tbilisi: Our Peacekeepers Are Staying Put." *Eurasia.net*. Accessed April 19, 2020, https://reliefweb.int/report/georgia/georgia-putin-tbilisi-our-peacekeepers-are-staying-put.

Blakkisrud, H., and P. Kolstø. 2011. "From Secessionist Conflict toward a Functioning State: Processes of State- and Nation-Building in Transnistria." *Post-Soviet Affairs* 27 (2): 178–210.

Block, A., F. Bovenkerk, and D. Siegel, eds. 2003. *Global Organized Crime: Trends and Developments*. Dordrecht: Springer Netherlands.

Bøås, M. 2014. "Guns, Money, and Prayers: AQIM's Blueprint for Securing Control of Northern Mali." *CTC Sentinel* 7 (4): 1–7.

Boeke, S. 2016. "Al Qaeda in the Islamic Maghreb: Terrorism, Insurgency, or Organized Crime?" *Small Wars and Insurgencies* 27 (5): 914–36.

Bolkovac, K., and C. Lynn. 2011. *The Whistleblower: Sex Trafficking, Military Contractors, and One Woman's Fight for Justice*. New York: Palgrave Macmilan.

Bölükbaşı, S. 2011. *Azerbaijan: A Political History*. New York: I. B. Tauris.

Bonikowski, B. 2016. "Nationalism in Settled Times." *Annual Review of Sociology* 42:427–49.

Bouquet, C. 2013. "Between Ideological Gloss and Organized Crime: Are Warlords Operating in the Region of the Sahel and the Sahara? *Afrique contemporaine* 1:85–97.

Bovenkerk, F., D. Siegel, and D. Zaitch. 2003. "Organized Crime and Ethnic Reputation Manipulation." *Crime, Law, and Social Change* 39 (1): 23–38.

Bowden, J. 2013. "Feeling Empty: Organ Trafficking and Trade: The Black Market for Human Organs." *Intercultural Human Rights Law Review* 8: 451–95.

Bowen, A. 2017. "Coercive Diplomacy and the Donbas: Explaining Russian Strategy in Eastern Ukraine." *Journal of Strategic Studies* 42 (3–4): 1–32.

Bowring, B. 2014. "Transnistria." In *Determination and Secession in International Law*, edited by C. Walter, A. von Ungern-Sternberg, and K. Abushov, 157–74. Oxford: Oxford University Press.

Brachet, J. 2018 "Manufacturing Smugglers: From Irregular to Clandestine Mobility in the Sahara." *ANNALS of the American Academy of Political and Social Science* 676 (1): 16–35.

Brady, S. 2012. *Organised Crime in Bosnia and Herzegovina: A Silent War Fought by an Ambush of Toothless Tigers or a War Not Yet Fought.* Accessed April 23, 2020, https://www.occrp.org/documents/OC_in_BH_ENG.pdf.

Brandt, M. 2017. *Tribes and Politics in Yemen: A History of the Houthi Conflict.* Oxford: Oxford University Press.

Breuilly, J. 1994. *Nationalism and the State: 2nd Edition.* Chicago: University of Chicago Press.

Bridenthal, R., ed. 2013. *The Hidden History of Crime, Corruption, and States.* New York: Berghahn Books.

Briquet, J., and G. Favarel-Garrigues, eds. 2010. *Organized Crime and States: The Hidden Face of Politics.* New York: Palgrave Macmillan.

Brock, P. 2005. *Media Cleansing, Dirty Reporting: Journalism and Tragedy in Yugoslavia.* Los Angeles: GM Books.

Bronner, M. 2008. *100 Grams (and Counting . . .): Notes from the Nuclear Underworld.* Cambridge, MA: Belfer Center for Science and International Affairs.

Brosig, M. 2011. "The Interplay of International Institutions in Kosovo between Convergence, Confusion, and Niche Capabilities." *European Security* 20 (2): 185–204.

Brown, T. 2013. "The Tuareg Puzzle in Mali." In Cornish, M. (Ed.), *Managing Conflict in the Developing World*, edited by M. Cornish, 15–24. Adelaide, Australia: University of Adelaide.

Browne, G. 2019. "Cameroon's Separatist Movement Is Going International." *Foreign Affairs*, May 13. Accessed April 21, 2020, https://foreignpolicy.com/2019/05/13/cameroons-separatist-movement-is-going-international-ambazonia-military-forces-amf-anglophone-crisis/.

Brubaker, R. 1994. "Nationhood and the National Question in the Soviet Union and Post-Soviet Eurasia: An Institutionalist Account. *Theory and Society* 23 (1): 47–78.

———. 1996. "Nationalizing States in the Old 'New Europe'—and the New." *Ethnic and Racial Studies* 19 (2): 411–37.

———. 1998. "Myths and Misconceptions in the Study of Nationalism." In *National Self-Determination and Secession*, edited by M. Moore, 272–306. Oxford: Oxford University Press.

———. 2004. *Ethnicity without Groups.* Cambridge, MA: Harvard University Press.

———. 2011. "Nationalizing States Revisited: Projects and Processes of Nationalization in Post-Soviet States." *Ethnic and Racial Studies* 34 (11): 1785–814.

Budiani-Saberi, D. A., and F. L. Delmonico. 2008. "Organ Trafficking and Transplant Tourism: A Commentary on the Global Realities." *American Journal of Transplantation* 8 (5): 925–29.

Bujošević, D., and I. Radovanović. 2000. *5. Oktobar: Dvadeset četiri sata prevrata.* Belgrade: Medija Centar.

Burdyha, I. 2018. "A Hello to Arms: Is There a Black Market for Guns in Ukraine?" *Hromadske*, May 23. Accessed April 25, 2020, https://en.hromadske.ua/posts/a-hello-to-arms-is-there-a-black-market-for-guns-in-ukraine.

Bureau for International Narcotics and Law Enforcement Affairs. 2001. *International Narcotics Control Strategy Report 2011: US State Department Publication.* Washington, DC: US State Department.

Burt, R. S. 2009. *Structural Holes: The Social Structure of Competition.* Cambridge, MA: Harvard University Press.

Buttin, F. 2007. "A Human Security Perspective on Transnistria." *Revue de la Sécurité Humaine* 3:13–28.

Bybee, A. N. 2012. "The Twenty-First Century Expansion of the Transnational Drug Trade in Africa." *Journal of International Affairs* 66 (1): 69–84.

Cabestan, J. P., and A. Pavković, eds. 2013. *Secessionism and Separatism in Europe and Asia: To Have a State of One's Own.* New York: Routledge.

Calhoun, C. 1997. *Nationalism.* Minneapolis: University of Minnesota Press.

Campbell, R. 1977. *The Luciano Project: The Secret Wartime Collaboration of the Mafia and te US Navy*. New York: McGraw-Hill Companies.

Capoccia, G., and R. D. Kelemen. 2007. "The Study of Critical Junctures: Theory, Narrative, and Counterfactuals in Historical Institutionalism." *World Politics* 59 (3): 341–69.

Carment, D., and P. James. 1995. "Internal Constraints and Interstate Ethnic Conflict toward a Crisis-Based Assessment of Irredentism." *Journal of Conflict Resolution* 39 (1): 82–109.

Carrapico, H., D. Irrera, and B. Tupman, eds. 2017. *Criminals and Terrorists in Partnership: Unholy Alliance*. London: Routledge.

Casier, M., and J. P. Jongerden. 2012. "Understanding Today's Kurdish Movement: Leftist Heritage, Martyrdom, Democracy, and Gender." *European Journal of Turkish Studies* 14. Accessed April 21, 2020, https://journals.openedition.org/ejts/4656.

Caspersen, N. 2008. "Between Puppets and Independent Actors: Kin-State Involvement in the Conflicts in Bosnia, Croatia, and Nagorno-Karabakh." *Ethnopolitics* 7 (4): 357–72.

———. 2012. *Unrecognized States: The Struggle for Sovereignty in the Modern International System*. Cambridge, UK: Polity Press.

———. 2017. "Making Peace with De Facto States." In *Unrecognized States and Secession in the 21st Century*, edited by M. Riegl and B. Doboš, 11–22. Cham, Switzerland: Springer.

Caspersen, N., and G. R. Stansfield, eds. 2011. *Unrecognized States in the International System*. New York: Routledge.

Castellino, J. 2015. "International Law and Self-Determination: People, Indigenous Peoples, and Minorities." In *Self-Determination and Secession in International Law*, edited by C. Walter, A. von Ungern-Sternberg, and K. Abushov, 27–44. Oxford: Oxford University Press.

Cederman, L. E., K. S. Gleditsch, and H. Buhaug. 2013. *Inequality, Grievances, and Civil War*. Cambridge: Cambridge University Press.

Cederman, L. E., N. B. Weidmann, and K. S. Gleditsch. 2011. "Horizontal Inequalities and Ethnonationalist Civil War: A Global Comparison." *American Political Science Review* 105 (3): 478–95.

Cengiz, M. 2010. "*The Globalization of Turkish Organized Crime and the Policy Response*." PhD diss., George Mason University.

Chatwin, C. 2003. "Drug Policy Developments within the European Union: The Destabilizing Effects of Dutch and Swedish Drug Policies." *British Journal of Criminology* 43 (3): 567–82.

Chido, D. 2018. *Intelligence Sharing, Transnational Organized Crime, and Multinational Peacekeeping*. Cham, Switzerland: Springer International Publishing.

Chivvis, C. S. 2016. *The French War on Al Qa'ida in Africa*. Cambridge: Cambridge University Press.

Chorbajian, L. 2001. *The Making of Nagorno-Karabagh: From Secession to Republic*. Basingstoke, UK: Palgrave Macmillan.

Chossudovsky, M. 1999. "Kosovo 'Freedom Fighters' Financed by Organized Crime." *Peace Research* 31 (2): 29–42.

Chothia, F. 2018. "Cameroon's Anglophone Crisis: Red Dragons and Tigers—the Rebels Fighting for Independence." *BBC News*, October 4. Accessed April 21, 2020, https://www.bbc.com/news/world-africa-45723211.

Cizre, Ü. 2001. "Turkey's Kurdish Problem: Borders, Identity, and Hegemony." In *Right-Sizing the State: The Politics of Moving Borders*, edited by B. O'Leary, I. S. Lustick, and T. Callaghy, 222–52. New York: Oxford University Press.

Clark, V. 2010. *Yemen: Dancing on the Heads of Snakes*. New Haven, CT: Yale University Press.

Clarke, M. 2012. "Does War Have a Future?" In *The Oxford Handbook of War*, edited by Y. Boyer and J. Lindley-French, 647–63. Oxford: Oxford University Press.

Clarke, R. A., and R. K. Knake. 2014. *Cyber War: The Next Threat to National Security and What to Do about It*. Old Saybrook, CT: Tantor Media, Inc.

Cochran, T. B., and M. G. McKinzie. 2008. "Detecting Nuclear Smuggling." *Scientific American* 298 (4): 98–104.

Cockayne, J. 2016. *Hidden Power: The Strategic Logic of Organized Crime*. Oxford: Oxford University Press.

Cockayne, J., and A. Lupel, eds. 2011. *Peace Operations and Organized Crime: Enemies or Allies?* London: Routledge.

Cockburn, P. 2015. *The Rise of Islamic State: ISIS and the New Sunni Revolution*. London: Verso.

Cohen, A. 2002. "Moscow, Washington, and Tbilisi Wrestle with Instability in the Pankisi Gorge." *Eurasia Net, February 19. Accessed April 17, 2020,* https://eurasianet.org/search ?keywords=Moscow%2C+Washington+and+Tbilisi+Wrestle+with+instability+in+the+Pankisi+Gorge.

Cohen, L. J. 2005. "Political Violence and Organized Crime in Serbia." In *Democratic Development and Political Terrorism: The Global Perspective*, edited by W. Crotty, 396–420. Boston: Northeastern University Press.

Cole, P., and B. McQuinn, eds. 2015. *The Libyan Revolution and Its Aftermath*. Oxford University Press.

Collier, P. 2008. *The Bottom Billion: Why the Poorest Countries Are Failing and What Can Be Done about It*. Oxford: Oxford University Press.

Collier, P., and A. Hoeffler. 2002. *Greed and Grievance in Civil War*. Oxford: Oxford University Press.

Collier, P., and N. Sambanis, eds. 2005. *Understanding Civil War: Evidence and Analysis, Volume 1: Africa*. Washington, DC: World Bank.

Collins, R. 2008. *Violence: A Micro-Sociological Theory*. Princeton, NJ: Princeton University Press.

———. 2011. "Patrimonial Alliances and Failures of State Penetration: A Historical Dynamic of Crime, Corruption, Gangs, and Mafias." *ANNALS of the American Academy of Political and Social Science* 636 (1): 16–31.

Čolović, I. 2000. "Football, Hooligans, and War." In *The Road to War in Serbia: Trauma and Catharsis*, edited by N. Popov and D. Gojković, 373–98. Budapest: Central European University Press.

Comolli, V. 2015. *Boko Haram: Nigeria's Islamist Insurgency*. Oxford: Oxford University Press.

Coppieters, B., and R. Sakwa, eds. 2003. *Contextualizing Secession: Normative Studies in Comparative Perspective*. Oxford: Oxford University Press.

Cornell, S. 2006. "The Narcotics Threat in Greater Central Asia: From Crime-Terror Nexus to State Infiltration?" *China and Eurasia Forum Quarterl* 4 (1): 37–67.

———. 2011. *Azerbaijan since Independence*. Studies of Central Asia and the Caucasus. Armonk, NY: M. E. Sharpe

Cornwell, R. 2006. "Nigeria and Camerron: Diplomacy in the Delta." *African Security Studies* 15 (4): 48–55.

Corpora, C. A. 2004. "The Untouchables: Former Yugoslavia's Clandestine Political Economy." *Problems of Post-Communism* 51 (3): 61–68.

Corso, M. 2007. "Georgia: Uranium Smuggling Highlights Border Security Concerns." Accessed April 2020, https://eurasianet.org/georgia-uranium-smuggling-highlights-border-security-concerns.

Crabtree, B. 2016. *The Nexus of Conflict and Illicit Drug Trafficking: Syria and the Wider Region*. November. Geneva: Global Initiative against Transnational Organized Crime.

Cribb, R. 2008. *Gangsters and Revolutionaries: The Jakarta People's Militia and the Indonesian Revolution, 1945–1949*. Singapore: Equinox Publishing.

Croissant, M. P. 1998. *The Armenia-Azerbaijan Conflict Causes and Implications*. Westport, CT: Praeger.

Curtis, G. E. 2002. *Involvement of Russian Organized Crime Syndicates, Criminal Elements in the Russian Military, and Regional Terrorist Groups in Narcotics Trafficking in Central Asia, the Caucasus, and Chechnya*. Washington, DC: Library of Congress.

Curtis, G. E., and T. Karacan. 2002. "The Nexus among Terrorists, Narcotics Traffickers, Weapons Proliferators, and Organized Crime Networks in Western Europe." Washington, DC: Federal Research Division, Library of Congress.

Darchiashvili, D. 2003. "Georgia: A Hostage to Arms." In *The Caucasus: Armed and Divided: Small Arms and Light Weapons Proliferation and Humanitarian Consequences in the Caucasus*, edited by A. Matveeva and D. Hiscock, 76–78. London: Saferworld.

Daskalovski, Ž. 2004. "The Macedonian Conflict of 2001: Between Successful Diplomacy, Rhetoric, and Terror." *Institute for East West Studies*, 1–53.

Dawha, E. 1996. *'Yan Daba, 'Yan Banga, and 'Yan Daukar Amarya: A Study of Criminal Gangs in Northern Nigeria*. Institut français de recherche en Afrique. Ibadan, Nigeria: IFRA African Book Builders.

Day, S. 2012. *Regionalism and Rebellion in Yemen: A Troubled National Union*. Cambridge: Cambridge University Press.

Dechery, C., and L. Ralston. 2015. *Trafficking and Fragility in West Africa*. No. 22475. Washington, DC: World Bank.

de Jong, F., and G. Gasser. 2005. "Contested Casamance: Introduction." *Canadian Journal of African Studies / La Revue canadienne des études africaines* 39 (2): 213–29.

Deleu, X. 2005. *Transnistrie: La poudrière de l'Europe*. Paris: Hugo et Compagnie.

della Rocca, M. 1999. *Kosovo: La guerra in Europa*. Milan: Guerini e associati.

Delmonico, F. L. 2009. "The Implications of Istanbul Declaration on Organ Trafficking and Transplant Tourism." *Current Opinion in Organ Transplantation* 14 (2): 116–19.

Del Ponte, C. 2008. *Madame Prosecutor: Confrontations with Humanity's Worth Criminals and the Culture of Impunity: A Memoir*. Milan: Feltrinelli Editore.

Demiroz, F., and N. Kapucu. 2012. "Anatomy of a Dark Network: The Case of the Turkish Ergenekon Terrorist Organization." *Trends in Organized Crime* 15 (4): 271–95.

Demmers, J. 2007. "New Wars and Diasporas: Suggestions for Reserach and Policy." *Peace, Conflict, and Development* 11:1–26.

Dennison, J. 2018. "Gaza's Smuggling-Tunnel Millionaire." BBC News. Accessed April 21, 2020, http://news.bbc.co.uk/2/hi/programmes/from_our_own_correspondent/8805418.stm.

de Sardan, J.P.O. 2013. "The 'Tuareg Question' in Mali Today." *Mapinduzi Journal* 3:25–38.

Deschamps, A. 2000. *Niger 1995 Révolte touarègue: Du cessez-le-feu provisoire à la "paix définitive."* Paris: L'Harmattan.

de Tessières, S. 2018. *At the Crossroads of Sahelian Conflicts: Insecurity, Terrorism, and Arms Trafficking in Niger*. Geneva: Small Arms Survey.

Detrez, R. 2003. "The Right to Self-Determination and Secession in Yugoslavia: A Hornets' Nest of Inconsistencies." In *Contextualizing Secession: Normative Studies in Comparative Perspective*, edited by B. Coppieters and R. Sakwa, 112–32. Oxford: Oxford University Press.

Dettmer, J. 2013. "Syria's Jihadists Linked to Organized Crime." *Daily Beast*, December 10. Accessed April 21, 2020, https://www.thedailybeast.com/syrias-jihadists-linked-to-organized-crime.

de Vries, L., P. Englebert, and M. Schomerus, eds. 2019. *Secessionism in African Politics: Aspiration, Grievance, Performance, Disenchantment*. London: Palgrave Macmillan.

de Waal, T. 2013. *Black Garden: Armenia and Azerbaijan through Peace and War*. New York: NYU Press.

Dicklitch, S. 2011. "The Southern Cameroons and Minority Rights in Cameroon." *Journal of Contemporary African Studies* 29 (1): 49–62.

Dion, S. 1996. "Why Is Secession Difficult in Well-Established Democracies?: Lessons from Quebec." *British Journal of Political Science* 26 (2): 269–83.

Directorate General for Development. 2003. "Country Report: Senegal." *Courier: The Magazine of ACP-EU Development Cooperation* 196 (January–February).

Djurić, S. S. 1998. *Osveta i kazna: Sociološko istraživanje krvne osvete na Kosovu i Metohiji*. Belgrade Prosveta.

Donais, T. 2003. "The Political Economy of Stalemate: Organised Crime, Corruption, and Economic Deformation in Post-Dayton Bosnia. *Conflict, Security, and Development* (3): 359–82.

Dos Santos, A. N. 2007. *Military Intervention and Secession in South Asia: The Cases of Bangladesh, Sri Lanka, Kashmir, and Punjab*. Westport, CT: Praeger.

Doumbi-Fakoly, H. M., B. Ciré, and D. Boubacar. *L'occupation du nord du Mali*. Paris: France: L'Harmattan.

Doyle, D. H., ed. 2010. *Secession as an International Phenomenon: From America's Civil War to Contemporary Separatist Movements*. Athens: University of Georgia Press.

Driscoll, J. 2015. *Warlords and Coalition Politics in Post-Soviet States*. Cambridge: Cambridge University Press.

Duffy, R. 2010. "Shadow States: Globalization, Criminalization, and Environmental Change." In *Organized Crime and States: The Hidden Face of Politics*, edited by J. Briquet and G. Favarel-Garrigues, 97–117. New York: Palgrave Macmillan.

Dursun-Ozkanca, O. 2009. "Rebuilding Kosovo: Cooperation or Competition between the EU and NATO?" Unpublished paper.

Eccarius-Kelly, V. 2012. "Surreptitious Lifelines: A Structural Analysis of the FARC and the PKK." *Terrorism and Political Violence* 24 (2): 235–58.

Ellen, B. 2009. "With Russian Guarantees of Security, South Ossetia Tries to Disarm Its Citizens." *New York Times*, August 14, A4.

Ellis, S. 2016. *This Present Darkness: A History of Nigerian Organised Crime*. London: Hurst and Company.

Englebert, P. 2005. "Compliance and Defiance to National Integration in Barotseland and Casamance." *Africa Spectrum* 40 (1): 29–59.

European Monitoring Centre for Drugs and Drug Addiction (EMCDDA). 2012. *Annual Report on Kosovo*. Brussels: Publications Office of the European Union.

———. 2014a. *National Report: Kosovo*. Brussels: Publications Office of the European Union.

———. 2014b. *National Report: Serbia*. Brussels: Publications Office of the European Union.

Evans, M. 2000. "Briefing: Senegal: Wade and the Casamance Dossier." *African Affairs* 99 (397): 649–58.

———. 2003. *Ni paix ni guerre: The Political Economy of Low-Level Conflict in the Casamance*. Humanitarian Policy Group Report 13. London: Overseas Development Institute.

———. 2004. *Senegal: Mouvement des forces démocratiques de la Casamance (MFDC)*. AFP BP 04/02. London: Royal Institute of International Affairs.

Eyal, G., I. Szelenyi, and E. Townsley. 1997. "The Theory of Post-Communist Managerialism." *New Left Review* 1 (222): 60–92.

Ezeanyika, S., and C. Ubah. 2012. "Towards Understanding Africa's International Criminal Organizations as an Emerging Industry in a Globalizing World." *African Journal of Criminology and Justice Studie* 6 (1–2): 1.

Fabry, M. 2010. *Recognizing States: International Society and the Establishment of New States since 1776*. Oxford: Oxford University Press.

Falk, R. 2011. "The Kosovo Advisory Opinion: Conflict Resolution and Precedent. *American Journal of International Law* 105 (5): 50–60.

Fall, A. 2010. *Understanding the Casamance Conflict: A Background*. Accra, Ghana: Kofi Annan International Peacekeeping Training Centre.

Favarel-Garrigues, G. 2010. "Mafia Violence and Political Power in Russia." In *Organized Crime and States: The Hidden Face of Politics*, edited by J. Briquet, G. Favarel-Garrigues, and R. Leverdier, 147–71. New York: Palgrave Macmillan.

Faye, W. 2006. *"The Casamance Separatism from Independence Claim to Resource Logic."* PhD diss., Naval Postgraduate School.

Fearon, J. D. 1995. "Rationalist Explanations for War." *International Organization* 49 (3): 379–414.

———. 2004. "Separatist Wars, Partition, and World Order." *Security Studies* 13 (4): 394–415.

Felbab-Brown, V. 2017. *In the Eye of the Storm: Niger and Its Unstable Neighbors.* Brookings Institution Press. Accessed April 20, 2020, http://search.proquest.com/docview/1909000814/.

Felbab-Brown, V., H. Trinkunas, and S. Hamid. 2018.*Militants, Criminals, and Warlords: The Challenge of Local Governance in an Age of Disorder.* Washington, DC: Brookings Institution Press.

Ferguson, K. 2015. *"An Investigation into the Irregular Military Dynamics in Yugoslavia, 1992–1995."* PhD diss., University of East Anglia.

Fijnaut, C. 1998. *Organized Crime in the Netherlands.* Boston: Kluwer Law International.

Finckenauer, J. O., and J. L. Schrock, eds. 2003. *The Prediction and Control of Organized Crime: The Experience of Post-Soviet Ukraine.* London: Routledge.

Finkelstein, N. G. 2003. *Image and Reality of the Israel-Palestine Conflict.* London: Verso.

———. 2014. *Method and Madness: The Hidden Story of Israel's Assaults on Gaza.* New York: OR Books.

Flottau, R. 2008. "Albania's House at the End of the World: Family Denies Organ Harvesting Allegations." *Spiegel*, September 22. Accessed April 19, 2020, https://www.spiegel.de/international/europe/albania-s-house-at-the-end-of-the-world-family-denies-organ-harvesting-allegations-a-580422.html.

Fonchingong, T. 2013. "The Quest for Autonomy: The Case of Anglophone Cameroon." *African Journal of Political Science and International Relations* 7 (5): 224–36.

Forrest, J. B. 2004. *Subnationalism in Africa: Ethnicity, Alliances, and Politics.* Boulder, CO: Lynne Rienner Publishers.

———. 2012. *Confronting the Terrorism of Boko Haram in Nigeria.* No. JSOU-12-5. MacDill, FL: Joint Special Operations University.

Fossungu, P.A.A. 2013. *Democracy and Human Rights in Africa: The Politics of Collective Participation and Governance in Cameroon.* Bamenda, Cameroon: Langaa Research and Publishing.

Foucher, V. 2003. "Pas d'alternance en Casamance?" *Politique africaine* 3 (91): 101–19.

———. 2007. "Senegal: The Resilient Weakness of Casamançais Separatists." In *African Guerrillas: Raging against the Machine*, edited M. Bøås and K. C. Dunn, 171–97. Boulder, CO: Lynne Rienner Publishers.

———. 2011. "On the Matter (and Materiality) of the Nation: Interpreting Casamance's Unresolved Separatist Struggle." *Studies in Ethnicity and Nationalism* 11 (1): 82–103.

———. 2019 "The Mouvement des Forces Démocratiques de Casamance: The Illusion of Separatism in Senegal?" In *Secessionism in African Politics: Aspiration, Grievance, Performance, Disenchantment*, edited by L. de Vries, P. Englebert, and M. Schomerus, 265–92. London: Palgrave Macmillan.

Francis, C. 2011. *Conflict Resolution and Status: The Case of Georgia and Abkhazia (1989–2008).* Brussels: Brussels University Press.

Freese, T. 2005. "A Report from the Field: Georgia's War against Contraband and the Struggle for Territorial Integrity." *SAIS Review of International Affairs* 25 (1): 107–21.

Friesendorf, C. 2007. "Pathologies of Security Governance: Efforts against Human Trafficking in Europe." *Security Dialogue* 38 (3): 379–402.

———. 2011. "Problems of Crime-Fighting by 'Internationals' in Kosovo." In *Peace Operations and Organized Crime: Enemies or Allies?*, edited by J. Cockayne and A. Lupel, 47–67. London: Routledge.

Frost, R. M. 2005. "The Nuclear Black Market." *Adelphi Papers* 45 (378): 11–24.

Gagnon, V. P. 2006. *The Myth of Ethnic War: Serbia and Croatia in the 1990s.* Ithaca, NY: Cornell University Press.

Galeotti, M. 1998. "Turkish Organized Crime: Where State, Crime, and Rebellion Conspire." *Transnational Organized Crime* 4 (1): 25–42.

———, ed. 2002. *Russian and Post-Soviet Organized Crime*. London: Dartmouth Publishing Company.

———. 2004a. "The Russian 'Mafiya': Consolidation and Globalisation." *Global Crime* 6 (1): 54–69.

———. 2004b. "The Transdnistrian Connection: Big Problems from a Small Pseudo-State." *Global Crime* 6 (3–4): 398–405.

———. 2012. "Turkish Organised Crime: From Tradition to Business." In *Traditional Organized Crime in the Modern World: Responses to Socioeconomic Change*, edited by D. Siegel and H. van de Bunt, 49–64. Boston: Springer.

———. 2014. *Global Crime Today: The Changing Face of Organised Crime*. Abingdon, UK: Routledge.

———. 2018. *Vory: Russia's Super Mafia*. New Haven, CT: Yale University Press.

Gambetta, D. 1996. *The Sicilian Mafia: The Business of Private Protection*. Cambridge, MA: Harvard University Press.

Ganser, D. 2005. *NATO's Secret Armies: Operation Gladio and Terrorism in Western Europe*. London: Routledge.

Gaoukoye, A. 2018. *Conspiration au Mali et au Sahel*. Paris: L'Harmattan.

Gayer, L. 2010. "The Pakistan Rangers: From Border Defense to Internal 'Protection.'" In *Organized Crime and States: The Hidden Face of Politics*, edited by J. Briquet and G. Favarel-Garrigues, 15–41. New York: Palgrave Macmillan.

Gellner, E. 1983. *Nations and Nationalism*. Ithaca, NY: Cornell University Press.

George, J. A. 2009. *The Politics of Ethnic Separatism in Russia and Georgia*. New York: Palgrave Macmillan.

Gerges, F. 2016. *ISIS: A History*. Princeton, NJ: Princeton University Press.

Geukjian, O. 2011. *Ethnicity, Nationalism, and Conflict in the South Caucasus: Nagorno-Karabakh and the Legacy of Soviet Nationalities Policy*. Burlington, VT: Ashgate.

Gingeras, R. 2014. *Heroin, Organized Crime, and the Making of Modern Turkey*. Oxford: Oxford University Press.

Giragosian, Y. 2009. "Networks of Crime and Corruption in the South Caucasus." *Caucasus Analystical Digest* 9 (9): 2–4.

Gleditsch, K. S. 2009. *All International Politics Is Local: The Diffusion of Conflict, Integration, and Democratization*. Ann Arbor: University of Michigan Press.

Glenny, M. 2004. "Migration Policies of Western European Governments and the Fight against Organised Crime in SEE." *Southeast European and Black Sea Studies* 4 (2): 250–56.

———. 2011. *DarkMarket: Cyber Thieves, Cyber Cops, and You*. New York: Alfred A. Knopf.

Glonti, G. 2001. "Trafficking in Human Beings in Georgia and the CIS." *Demokratizatsiya* 9 (3): 382–98.

———. 2005. "Problems Associated with Organized Crime in Georgia." *Trends in Organized Crime* 9 (2): 68–77.

Goldstone, J. A. 2003. "Comparative Historical Analysis and Knowledge Accumulation in the Study of Revolutions." In *Comparative Historical Analysis in the Social Sciences*, edited by J. Mahoney and D. Rueschemeyer, 41–90. Cambridge: Cambridge University Press.

Goltz, T. 1998. *Azerbaijan Diary: A Rogue Reporter's Adventures in an Oil-Rich, War-Torn, Post-Soviet Republic*. New York: M. E. Sharpe

Goodwin, J. 2001. *No Other Way Out: States and Revolutionary Movements, 1945–1991*. Cambridge: Cambridge University Press.

Gorée Institute. 2015. *Conflit et paix en Casamance: Dynamiques locales et transfrontalières*. Île de Gorée, Senegal: Gorée Institute.

Gotsiridze, R. 2004 "Georgia: Conflict Regions and the Economy." *Central Asia and the Caucasus* 1 (25).

Gounev, P. 2003. "Stabilizing Macedonia: Conflict Prevention, Development, and Organized Crime." *Journal of International Affairs* 57 (1): 229–40.

Grange, T., and H. Frydenlund. 2004. "Forensic Examination and Assessment in Albania." In *UNMIK Publications*. Priština, Kosovo: Kosovo Office on Missing Persons and Forensics.

Grillot, S. R., W. C. Paes, H. Risser, and S. O. Stoneman. 2004. *A Fragile Peace: Guns and Security in Post-Conflict Macedonia*. Geneva: UN Development Programme and Small Arms Survey.

Gros, J. G. 2003. *Cameroon: Politics and Society in Critical Perspectives*. Lanham, MD: University Press of America.

Grubač, M. 2009. "Organizovani kriminal u Srbiji." *Zbornik radova Pravnog fakulteta u Splitu* 46 (4): 701–9.

Guichaoua, Y. 2015. "Tuareg Militancy and Sahelian Shockwaves of the Lybian Revolution." In *The Libyan Revolution and Its Aftermath*, edited by P. Cole and B. McQuinn, 321–37. London: Hurst and Company.

Guild, E., D. Bigo, and M. Gibney, eds. 2018. *Extraordinary Rendition: Addressing the Challenges of Accountability*. London: Routledge.

Gunter, M. 1998. "Susurluk: The Connection between Turkey's Intelligence Community and Organized Crime." *International Journal of Intelligence and Counter Intelligence* 11 (2): 119–41.

———. 2008. "Taming Turkey's Deep State." In *The Kurds Ascending*, edited by M. Gunter, 107–30. New York: Palgrave Macmillan.

———. 2016. *The Kurds: A Modern History*. Princeton, NJ: Markus Wiener.

Hajdinjak, M. 2002. *Smuggling in Southeast Europe: The Yugoslav Wars and the Development of Regional Criminal Networks in the Balkans*. Sofia, Bulgaria: Center for Study of Democracy.

Haken, J. 2011. "Transnational Crime in the Developing World." Global Financial Integrity report, February. Washington, DC: Center for International Policy.

Halder, S. 2016. *Islamic State: Emergence, Ideology, and Funding*. Dhaka, Bangladesh: Muktochinta.

Hale, H. E. 2008. *The Foundations of Ethnic Politics: Separatism of States and Nations in Eurasia and the World*. Cambridge: Cambridge University Press.

Hale, H. E., and R. W. Orttung, eds. 2016. *Beyond the Euromaidan: Comparative Perspectives on Advancing Reform in Ukraine*. Stanford, CA: Stanford University Press.

Harmon, S. A. 2014. *Terror and Insurgency in the Sahara-Sahel Region: Corruption, Contraband, Jihad, and the Mali War of 2012–2013*. New York: Routledge.

Hastings, J. V. 2010. *No Man's Land: Globalization, Territory, and Clandestine Groups in Southeast Asia*. Ithaca, NY: Cornell University Press.

Hazen, J. M., and D. Rodgers, eds. 2014.*Global Gangs: Street Violence across the World*. Minneapolis: University of Minnesota Press.

Hechter, M. 1992. "The Dynamics of Secession." *Acta Sociologica* 35 (4): 267–83.

———. 2000. *Containing Nationalism*. Oxford: Oxford University Press.

Hedström, P., and R. Swedberg, eds. 1998. *Social Mechanisms: An Analytical Approach to Social Theory*. Cambridge: Cambridge University Press.

Heisbourg, F. 2013. "A Surprising Little War: First Lessons of Mali." *Survival* 55 (2): 7–18.

Hentz, J., and H.Solomon. 2017. *Understanding Boko Haram: Terrorism and Insurgency in Africa*. New York: Routledge.

Heraclides, A. 2004. "Ethnicity, Secessionist Conflict and the International Society: Towards Normative Paradigm Shift." *Nations and Nationalism* 3 (4): 493–520.

Hewitt, C., and T. Cheetham. 2000. *Encyclopedia of Modern Separatist Movements*. Santa Barbara, CA: ABC-CLIO.

Hickok, M. R. 2003. "Suspended rReality: Historical Perspectives on the Political Economy of Northern Iraq." In *Shadow Globalization, Ethnic Conflicts, and New Wars: A Political Economy of Intra-State War*, edited by D. Jung, 70–92. London: Routledge.

Hill, G. 2017. *Yemen Endures: Civil War, Saudi Adventurism, and the Future of Arabia*. Oxford: Oxford University Press.

Hill, P. B. 2003. *The Japanese Mafia: Yakuza, Law, and the State*. Oxford: Oxford University Press.

Hirschfeld, K. 2015. *Gangster States: Organized Crime, Kleptocracy, and Political Collapse*. New York: Palgrave Macmillan.

Hirschman, A. O. 1970. *Exit, Voice, and Loyalty: Responses to Decline in Firms, Organizations, and States*. Cambridge, MA: Harvard University Press.

Hislope, R. 2002. "Organized Crime in a Disorganized State: How Corruption Contributed to Macedonia's Mini-War." *Problems of Post-Communism* 49 (3): 33–41.

———. 2003. "Between a Bad Peace and a Good War: Insights and Lessons from the Almost-War in Macedonia." *Ethnic and Racial Studies* 26 (1): 129–51.

———. 2004. "Crime and Honor in a Weak State: Paramilitary Forces and Violence in Macedonia." *Problems of Post-Communism* 51 (3): 18–26.

Hislope, R., and A. Mughan. 2012. *Introduction to Comparative Politics: The State and Its Challenges*. Cambridge: Cambridge University Press.

Hobsbawm, E. 1985. *Primitive Rebels: Studies in Archaic Forms of Social Movement in the 19th and 20th Centuries*. Manchester: Manchester University Press.

———. 1990. *Nations and Nationalism since 1780: Programme, Myth, Reality*. Cambridge: Cambridge University Press.

———. 2000. *Bandits*. New York: New Press.

Hobsbawm, E., and T. Ranger, eds. 1983. *The Invention of Tradition*. Cambridge: Cambridge University Press.

Horowitz, D. 1985. *Ethnic Groups in Conflict*. Berkeley: University of California Press.

———. 1997. "Self-Determination: Politics, Philosophy, and Law." *Nomos* 39:421–63.

Hozić, A. A. 2004. "Between the Cracks: Balkan Cigarette Smuggling." *Problems of Post-Communism* 51 (3): 35–44.

Huband, M. 2003. *The Skull Beneath the Skin: Africa after the Cold War*. Boulder, CO: Westview Press.

Hudson, K. 2003. *Breaking the South Slav Dream: The Rise and Fall of Yugoslavia*. Sterling, VA: Pluto Press.

Human Rights Foundation of Turkey. 2000. *1998 Human Rights Report*. Ankara: HRFT Documentation Center.

Human Rights Watch. 2008. "Kosovo/Albania: Investigate Postwar Abductions, Transfers to Albania." Human Rights Watch. Retrieved May 5, 2020, https://www.hrw.org/news/2008/05/04/kosovo/albania-investigate-postwar-abductions-transfers-albania.

Humphreys, M., and H. Ag Mohamed. 2005. "Senegal and Mali." In *Understanding Civil War: Africa*, edited by P. Collier and N. Sambanis, 1:247–302. Washington, DC: World Bank Publications.

Huszka, B. 2013. *Secessionist Movements and Ethnic Conflict: Debate-Framing and Rhetoric in Independence Campaigns*. London: Routledge.

Hutchinson, S., and P. O'Malley. 2007. "A Crime-Terror Nexus?: Thinking on Some of the Links between Terrorism and Criminality." *Studies in Conflict Terrorism* 30 (12): 1095–107.

İçduygu, A., and S. Toktas. 2002. "How Do Smuggling and Trafficking Operate via Irregular Border Crossings in the Middle East?: Evidence from Fieldwork in Turkey." *International Migration* 40 (6): 25–54.

Ilievski, A. 2015. *Operation of the Albanian Mafia: Macedonian Case*. Saarbrücken, Germany: Lambert Academic Publishing.

Ilievski, A., and B. Dobovsek. 2013. "Operation of the Albanian Mafia in the Republic of Macedonia." *Varstvoslovje* 15 (2): 190.

Immigration and Refugee Board of Canada. 2011. *Georgia: Blood Feuds, Including Definitions, Statistics, State Protection, Mediation, and Relocation (2002–2011).* January 26. Accessed February 6, 2015, http://www.refworld.org/docid/51dd0ef84.html.

Independent International Fact-Finding Mission on the Conflict in Georgia 2009. *Report to the Council of the European Union: Volumes 1–3.* Vienna: Organization for Security and Cooperation in Europe.

International Atomic Energy Agency (IAEA). 2006. "Radioactive Sources Recovered in Georgia." Accessed April 19, 2020, https://www.iaea.org/newscenter/news/radioactive-sources -recovered-georgia.

———. 2007. "Georgian Authorities Report Seized Illicit Nuclear Material." Accessed April 19, 2020, https://www.iaea.org/newscenter/news/georgian-authorities-report-seized-illicit -nuclear-material.

International Crisis Group (ICG). 2001. *Macedonia: Last Chance for Peace.* Balkans Report 113. Brussels: ICG.

———. 2002. *Macedonia's Public Secret: How Corruption Drags the Country Down.* Balkans Report 133. Brussels: ICG.

———. 2004. *Avoiding War with South Ossetia.* Europert 159. Brussels: ICG.

———. 2005a. *Kosovo after Haradinaj.* Europe Report 163. Brussels: ICG.

———. 2005b. *Nagorno-Karabakh: Viewing the Conflict from the Ground.* Europe Report 166. Brussels: ICG.

———. 2007. *Inside Gaza: The Challenge of Clans and Families.* Middle East Report 71. Brussels: ICG.

———. 2009. *Yemen: Defusing the Saada Time Bomb.* Middle East Report 86. Brussels: ICG.

———. 2012. *Iraq and the Kurds: The High-Stakes Hydrocarbons Gambit Crisis Group.* Middle East Report 120. Brussels: ICG.

———. 2016. *Ukraine: The Line.* Europe and Central Asia Briefing 81. Brussels: ICG.

———. 2017a. *Cameroon's Anglophone Crisis at the Crossroads.* Africa Report 250. Brussels: ICG.

———. 2017b. *Double-Edged Sword: Vigilantes in African Counter-Insurgencies.* Africa Report 251. Brussels: ICG.

Irrera, D. 2015. "The Crime–Terror–Insurgency 'Nexus': Implications for Global Security." In *Insurgency and Counterinsurgency in Modern War*, edited by S. Romaniuk and S. Webb, 62–75. Boca Raton, FL: CRC Press.

Jafar, T. H. 2009. "Organ Trafficking: Global Solutions for a Global Problem." *American Journal of Kidney Diseases* 54 (6): 114557.

Jamieson, A. 2001. "Transnational Organized Crime: A European Perspective." *Studies in Conflict and Terrorism* 24 (5): 377–87.

Jenner, M. S. 2011. "International Drug Trafficking: A Global Problem with a Domestic Solution." *Indiana Journal of Global Legal Studies* 18 (2): 901–27.

Jennings, I. 2011. *The Approach to Self-Government.* New York: Cambridge University Press.

Johnston, P., J. N. Shapiro, H. J. Shatz, B. Bahney, D. F. Jung, P. Ryan, and J. Wallace. 2016. *Foundations of the Islamic State: Management, Money, and Terror in Iraq, 2005–2010.* Santa Monica, CA: RAND Corporation.

Jones, S. 2018. "'We Are Truly Sorry': ETA Apologises for Four Decades of Deadly Violence." *Guardian*, April 20. Accessed April 28, 2020, https://www.theguardian.com/world/2018/apr /20/eta-apologises-basque-separatists-deadly-violence.

Jones, S. F. 2015. *Georgia: A Political History since Independence.* London: I. B. Tauris.

Jović, D. 2017. *Rat i mit: Politika identiteta u suvremenoj Hrvatskoj.* Zagreb: Fraktura.

Jung, D., ed. 2003. *Shadow Globalization, Ethnic Conflicts, and New Wars: A Political Economy of Intra-State War*. London: Routledge.

Kahneman, D., J. L. Knetsch, and R. H. Thaler. 1991. "Anomalies: The Endowment Effect, Loss Aversion, and Status Quo Bias." *Journal of Economic Perspectives* 5 (1): 193–206.

Kakachia, K., and L. O'Shea. 2012. "Why Does Police Reform Appear to Have Been More Successful in Georgia than in Kyrgyzstan or Russia?" *Journal of Power Institutions in Post-Soviet Societies* 13. Accessed March 16, 2020, http://journals.openedition.org/pipss/3964.

Kalberg, S. 2012. *Max Weber's Comparative-Historical Sociology Today*. Burlington, VT: Ashgate.

Kaldor, M. 2007. "Oil and Conflict: The Case of Nagorno-Karabakh." In *Oil Wars*, edited by M. Kaldor, T. L. Karl, and Y. Said, 157–83. London: Pluto.

———. 2013. *New and Old Wars: Organised Violence in a Global Era*. Oxford: Polity Press.

Kaliterna, T. 2005. "Od početka na početku." In *Država, moć sistema*, edited by L. Caracciolo, 31–43. Belgrade: Hesperia.

Kaltcheva, T. 2009. "Kosovo's Post-Independence Inter-Clan Conflict." *Human Security Journal* 2:113–24.

Kalyvas, S. 2006. *The Logic of Violence in Civil War*. Cambridge: Cambridge University Press.

———. 2015. "How Civil Wars Help Explain Organized Crime—and How They Do Not." *Journal of Conflict Resolution* 59 (8): 1517–40.

Kampelman, M. M. 1993. "Secession and the Right of Self-Determination: An Urgent Need to Harmonize Principle with Pragmatism." *Washington Quarterly* 16 (3): 5–12.

Kaplan, R. D. 2005. *Balkan Ghosts: A Journey through History*. New York: Picador.

Karmanau, Y. 2016. "War Turns Ukraine into 'Supermarket' for Illegal Weapons." AP, August 6. Accessed April 25, 2020, https://apnews.com/16ffe979bc2947ce9373079264232406/war-turns-ukraine-supermarket-illegal-weapons.

Kasinof, L. 2014. *Don't Be Afraid of the Bullets*. New York: Arcade Publishing.

Katchanovski, I. 2016. "The Separatist War in Donbas: A Violent Break-Up of Ukraine?" *European Politics and Society* 17 (4): 473–89.

Katznelson, I. 2003. "Periodization and Preferences: Reflections on Purposive Action in Comparative Historical Social Science." In *Comparative Historical Analysis in the Social Sciences*, edited by J. Mahoney and D. Rueschemeyer, 270–301. Cambridge: Cambridge University Press.

Keenan, J. 2007. "The Banana Theory of Terrorism: Alternative Truths and the Collapse of the 'Second' (Saharan) Front in the War on Terror." *Journal of Contemporary African Studies* 25 (1): 31–58.

———. 2013. *The Dying Sahara: US Imperialism and Terror in Africa*. London: Pluto Press.

Khakee, A., and N. Florquin. 2003. *Kosovo and the Gun: A Baseline Assessment of Small Arms and Light Weapons in Kosovo*. Geneva: Small Arms Survey.

Khouri, R. 2016. "Yes, Let Us Honestly Assess Sykes-Picot's Ugly Century." *Agence Global*, May 11. Accessed April 21, 2020, https://middle-east-online.com/en/yes-let-us-honestly-assess-sykes-picot's-ugly-century.

King, C. 2010. *Extreme Politics: Nationalism, Violence, and the End of Eastern Europe*. Oxford: Oxford University Press.

Kinstler, L. 2014. "Why Is Ukraine's Army So Appallingly Bad?" *New Republic*, May 9.

Knox, G. W., G. Etter, and C. F. Smith. 2018 *Gangs and Organized Crime*. Abingdon, UK: Routledge.

Kohl, I., and A. Fischer, eds. 2010. *Tuareg Society within a Globalized World: Saharan Life in Transition*. London: I. B. Tauris

Kolossov, V., and J. O'Loughlin. 1998. "Pseudo-States as Harbingers of a New Geopolitics: The Example of the Trans-Dniester Moldovan Republic (TMR)." *Geopolitics* 3 (1): 151–76.

Kolstø, P., and H. Blakkisrud. 2012. "De Facto States and Democracy: The Case of Nagorno-Karabakh." *Communist and Post-Communist Studies* 45 (1–2): 141–51.

Kolstø, P., and A. Malgin. 1998. "The Transnistrian Republic: A Case of Politicized Regionalism." *Nationalities Papers* 26 (1): 103–27.

Konings, P. 2009. *Neoliberal Bandwagonism: Civil Society and the Politics of Belonging in Anglophone Cameroon.* Bamenda, Cameroon: Langaa Research and Publishing.

Konings, P., and F. B. Nyamnjoh. 1997. "The Anglophone Problem in Cameroon." *Journal of Modern African Studies* 35 (2): 207–29.

———. 2019. "Anglophone Secessionist Movements in Cameroon." In *Secessionism in African Politics: Aspiration, Grievance, Performance, Disenchantment,* edited by L. de Vries, P. Englebert, and M. Schomerus, 59–89. London: Palgrave Macmillan.

Köppel, T., and A. Székely. 2002. "Transnational Organized Crime and Conflict in the Balkans." In *Transnational Organized Crime and International Security: Business as Usual,* edited by M. R. Berdal and M. Serrano, 129–40. Boulder, CO: Lynne Rienner Publishers.

Korać, Ž. 2003. *Izveštaj o uredjivanju, organizovanju i funkcionisanju obezbedjenja predsednika vlade Republike Srbije Dr. Zorana Djindjića, s predlogom mera.* DT 72 Broj: 00–002/2003–86. 13. avgust. Belgrade: Komisija za ispitivanje sistema obezbeđenja predsednika Vlade Republike Srbije.

Koré, L. C. 2010. *La rébellion touareg au Niger: Raisons de persistance et tentatives de solution.* Paris: L'Harmattan.

Kosienkowski, M. 2013. "Is Internationally Recognised Independence the Goal of Quasi-States?: The Case of Transnistria." In *Moldova: In Search of Its Own Place in Europe,* edited by N. Cwiinskaja and P. Oleksy, 55–65. Bydgoszcz, Poland: Oficyna Wydawnicza Epigram.

Krüger, H. 2010. *The Nagorno-Karabakh Conflict: A Legal Analysis.* New York: Springer.

———. 2014. "Nagorno-Karabakh." In *Self-Determination and Secession in International Law,* edited by C. Walter, A. von Ungern-Sternberg, and K. Abushov, 214–235. Oxford: Oxford University Press.

Kukhianidze, A. 2009. "Corruption and Organized Crime in Georgia before and after the 'Rose Revolution.'" *Central Asian Survey* 28 (2): 215–34.

Kukhianidze, A., A. Kupatadze, and R. Gotsiridze. 2007. "Smuggling through Abkhazia and Tskhinvali Region of Georgia." In *Organized Crime and Corruption in Georgia,* edited by L. Shelley, E. R. Scott, and A. Latta, 69–92. London: Routledge.

Kupatadze, A. 2005. "The Impact of the Rose Revolution on Smuggling through Abkhazia and South Ossetia." *Insight Turkey,* 67–76.

———. 2010. "Organized Crime and the Trafficking of Radiological Materials: The Case of Georgia." *Nonproliferation Review* 17 (2): 219–34.

———. 2012. *Organized Crime, Political Transitions, and State Formation in Post-Soviet Eurasia.* Basingstoke, UK: Palgrave Macmillan

Kuzin, S., and B. Penchuk. 2006. *Donetskaya mafia.* Kiev: Fond Antikoruptsiya.

Kuzio, T. 2001. "'Nationalising States' or Nation-Building?: A Critical Review of the Theoretical Literature and Empirical Evidence." *Nations and Nationalism* 7 (2): 135–54.

———. 2014. "Crime, Politics, and Business in 1990s Ukraine." *Communist and Post-Communist Studies* 47 (2): 195–210.

———. 2015. *Ukraine: Democratization, Corruption, and the New Russian Imperialism.* Santa Barbara, CA: ABC-CLIO.

———. 2016. "Oligarchs, the Partial Reform Equilibrium, and the Euromaidan Revolution." In *Beyond the Euromaidan: Comparative Perspectives on Advancing Reform in Ukraine,* edited by H. E. Hale and R. W. Orttung, 181–204. Stanford, CA: Stanford University Press.

Labrousse, A. 2003. "The War against Drugs and the Interests of Governments." In *Global Organized Crime: Trends and Developments,* edited by A. Block, F. Bovenkerk, and D. Siegel, 25–31. Dordrecht: Springer Netherlands.

Lacher, W. 2012. *Organized Crime and Conflict in the Sahel-Sahara Region*. Vol. 1. Washington, DC: Carnegie Endowment.

Lachmann, G. 2008. "German Spy Affair Might Have Been Revenge." *Die Welt Online*, November 30. Accessed April 20, 2020, https://www.welt.de/english-news/article2806537/German-spy-affair-might-have-been-revenge.html.

Lackner, H. 1995. "National Revivals and Violence." *European Journal of Sociology* 36 (1): 3–43.

———. 2017. *Yemen in Crisis: Autocracy, Neoliberalism, and the Disintegration of the State*. London: Saqi Books.

Laitin, D. 1995. "National Revivals and Violence." *European Journal of Sociology / Archives Européennes de Sociologie* 36 (1): 3–43.

———. 2007. *Nations, States, and Violence*. New York: Oxford University Press.

Lambert, M. C. 1998. "Violence and the War of Words: Ethnicity v. Nationalism in the Casamance." *Africa* 68 (4): 585–602.

Langewiesche, W. 2007. *The Atomic Bazaar: The Rise of the Nuclear Poor*. New York: Farrar, Straus and Giroux.

Larémont, R. 2013. "After the Fall of Qaddafi: Political, Economic, and Security Consequences for Libya, Mali, Niger, and Algeria." *Stability: International Journal of Security and Development* 2 (2): Art. 29.

Lavrov, A. 2010. "Post-War Deployment of Russian Forces in Abkhazia and South Ossetia." In *The Tanks of August*, edited by R. Pukhov, 115–29. Moscow: Center for Analysis of Strategies and Technologies.

Lecocq, B. 2002. "'That Desert Is Our Country': Tuareg Rebellions and Competing Nationalisms in Contemporary Mali (1946–1996)." PhD diss., Universiteit van Amsterdam.

———. 2004. "Unemployed Intellectuals in the Sahara: The Teshumara Nationalist Movement and the Revolutions in Tuareg Society." *International Review of Social History* 49 (S12): 87–109.

Lecocq, B., and G. Klute. 2019. "Tuareg Separatism in Mali and Niger." In *Secessionism in African Politics: Aspiration, Grievance, Performance, Disenchantment*, edited by L. de Vries, P. Englebert, and M. Schomerus, 23–57. London: Palgrave Macmillan.

Lehning, P. B., ed. 2005. *Theories of Secession*. New York: Taylor and Francis.

Lemay-Hebert, N. 2008. "Zone of Conflict: Clash of Paradigms in South Ossetia." *Orta Asya ve Kafkasya Araştırmaları* 5:57–70.

Lewis, A. 2015. *Security, Clans, and Tribes: Unstable Governance in Somaliland, Yemen, and the Gulf of Aden*. Basingstoke, UK: Palgrave Macmillan.

Licklider, R. 1993. *Stopping the Killing: How Civil Wars End*. New York: NYU Press.

Lindell, M. T., and K. Mattsson. 2014. *Transnational Threats to Peace and Security in the Sahel*. Stockholm: FOI Swedish Defense Research Agency.

Ljepojević, S. 2006. *Kosovo i Metohija: Realnost, ekonomija i zablude*. Belgrade: Tanjug.

Lloyd, R. B. 2016. "Ungoverned Spaces and Regional Insecurity: The Case of Mali." *SAIS Review of International Affairs* 36 (1): 133–41.

Locke, R., and K. Thelen. 1995. "Apples and Oranges Revisited: Contextualized Comparisons and the Study of Comparative Labor Politics." *Politics and Society* 23 (3): 337–68.

Losh, J. 2016a. "How Ukraine's War Became Big Business for the Underworld." *Vice News*, February 22. Accessed April 25, 2020, https://news.vice.com/en_us/article/ywjqny/how-ukraines-war-became-big-business-for-the-underworld.

———. 2016b. "War in Ukraine Helps Smugglers in the Black Market Get Richer." Washington Post, October 11. Accessed April 25, 2020, https://www.washingtonpost.com/news/worldviews/wp/2016/10/11/rebel-ukraine-turns-to-smuggling-for-income/.

Lundblad, L. G. 2007. "Islamic Welfare, Discourse, and Practise: The Institutionalization of Zakat in Palestine." In *Interpreting Welfare and Relief in the Middle East*, edited by N. Naguib and I. Okkenhaug, 195–216. Leiden, Netherlands: Brill.

Lustick, I. S. 1993. *Unsettled States, Disputed Lands: Britain and Ireland, France and Algeria, Israel and the West Bank-Gaza*. Ithaca, NY: Cornell University Press.

Lynch, D. 2002. "Separatist States and Post-Soviet Conflicts." *International Affairs* 78 (4): 831–48.

———. 2004. *Engaging Eurasia's Separatist States: Unresolved Conflicts and De Facto States*. Washington, DC: US Institute of Peace Press.

MacEachern, S. 2018. *Searching for Boko Haram: A History of Violence in Central Africa*. Oxford: Oxford University Press.

Machavariani, S. 2007. "Overcoming Economic Crime in Georgia through Public Service Reform." In *Organized Crime and Corruption in Georgia*, edited by L. Shelley, E. R. Scott, and A. Latta, 37–49. London: Routledge.

Mackinlay, J., P. Cross, F. H. Fleitz Jr., H. Langholtz, B. Kondoch, A. Wells, and P. C. Wood. 2003. *Regional Peacekeepers: The Paradox of Russian Peacekeeping*. New York: United Nations University Press.

Mahoney, J. 2000. "Path Dependence in Historical Sociology." *Theory and Society* 29 (4): 507–48.

———. 2003. "Strategies of Causal Assessment in Comparative Historical Analysis." In *Comparative Historical Analysis in the Social Sciences*, edited by J. Mahoney and D. Rueschemeyer, 337–72. Cambridge: Cambridge University Press.

———. 2004. "Comparative-Historical Methodology." *Annual Review of Sociology* 30:81–101.

Mahoney, J., E. Kimball, and K. L. Koivu. 2009. "The Logic of Historical Explanation in the Social Sciences." *Comparative Political Studies* 42 (1): 11446.

Mahoney, J., and D. Rueschemeyer, eds. 2003. *Comparative Historical Analysis in the Social Sciences*. Cambridge: Cambridge University Press.

Makarenko, T. 2005. "The Crime-Terror Continuum: Tracing the Interplay between Transnational Organised Crime and Terrorism." *Global Crime* 6 (1): 129–45.

Malešević, S. 2010. *The Sociology of War and Violence*. Cambridge: Cambridge University Press.

Malis, C. 2012. "Unconventional Forms of War." In *The Oxford Handbook of War*, edited by Y. Boyer and J. Lindsey-French, 185–99. Oxford: Oxford University Press.

Malyarenko, T., and D. J. Galbreath. 2016. "Paramilitary Motivation in Ukraine: Beyond Integration and Abolition." *Southeast European and Black Sea Studies* 16 (1): 113–38.

Mammadov, F. 2017. "Foreign Policy Postures and Priorities of Azerbaijan." In In *The South Caucasus–Security, Energy, and Europeanization*, edited by M. Altunışık and O. Tanrisever, 95–110. London: Routledge.

Mann, M. 2005. *The Dark Side of Democracy: Explaining Ethnic Cleansing*. Cambridge, MA: Cambridge University Press.

Mardini, R., ed. 2010. *The Battle for Yemen: Al-Qaeda and the Struggle for Stability*. Washington, DC: Jamestown Foundation.

Marty, D. 2010. *Inhuman Treatment of People and Illicit Trafficking in Human Organs in Kosovo*. Strasbourg: Council of Europe, Committee on Legal Affairs and Human Rights.

———. 2019. *Izvesna Predstava o Pravdi*. Belgrade: Metella.

Massicard, E. 2010. "'Gangs in Uniform' in Turkey: Politics at the Articulation between Security Institutions and the Criminal World." In *Organized Crime and States: The Hidden Face of Politics*, edited by J. Briquet and G. Favarel-Garrigues, 41–71. New York: Palgrave Macmillan.

Masters, D. 2004. "Support and Nonsupport for Nationalist Rebellion: A Prospect Theory Approach." *Political Psychology* 25 (5): 703–26.

Maszka, J. 2018. *Al-Shabaab and Boko Haram*. London: World Scientific Publishing.

Matsuzato, K. 2008. "From Belligerent to Multi-Ethnic Democracy: Domestic Politics in Unrecognized States after the Ceasefires." *Eurasian Review* 1:95–119.

Mazzitelli, A. L. 2007. "Transnational Organized Crime in West Africa: The Additional Challenge." *International Affairs* 83 (6): 1071–90.

Mbuh, M. 2004. *International Law and Conflict: Resolving Border and Sovereignty Disputes in Africa*. New York: iUniverse.

McCauley, M. 2001. *Bandits, Gangsters, and the Mafia: Russia, the Baltic States, and the CIS since 1991*. Harlow, UK: Longman.

McCoy, A. W. 1991. *The Politics of Heroin*. New York: Lawrence Hill Books.

———. 2010. "Can Anyone Pacify the World's Number One Narco-State?: The Opium Wars in Afghanistan." *Asia-Pacific Journal* 4 (14): 1–10.

McCullough, A., M. Schomerus, A. Harouna, Z. Maikorema, K. Abdouramane, Z. Dingarey, I.M.M. Noura, H. Rhissa, and R. Rhissa. 2017. *Understanding Trajectories of Radicalisation in Agadez*. London: Overseas Development Institute.

McDermott, R. 2004. "Prospect Theory in Political Science: Gains and Losses from the First Decade." *Political Psychology* 25 (2): 289–312.

McGarry, J. 1998. "'Orphans of Secession': National Pluralism in Secessionist Regions and Post-Secession States." In *National Self-Determination and Secession*, edited by M. Moore, 215–32. Oxford: Oxford University Press.

McGregor, A. 2017. "The Carousel of Rebellion and Reintegration: A Profile of Northern Mali's Colonel Hassan ag Fagaga." *Jamestown Foundation's Militant Leadership Monitor* 8 (6).

Meagher, K. 2014. "Smuggling Ideologies: From Criminalization to Hybrid Governance in African Clandestine Economies." *African Affairs* 113 (453): 497–517.

Mearsheimer, J. J. 2014. "Why the Ukraine Crisis Is the West's Fault: The Liberal Delusions That Provoked Putin." *Foreign Affairs* 93 (5): 77–89.

Mehler, A. 2014. "Why Federalism Did Not Lead to Secession in Cameroon." *Ethnopolitics* 13 (1): 48–66.

Meyer, S. 2006. "Trafficking in Human Organs in Europe." *European Journal of Crime, Criminal Law, and Criminal Justice* 14 (2): 208–29.

Mijalkovski, M., and P. Damjanov. 2002. *Terorizam Albanskih ekstremista*. Belgrade: Novinsko Izdavački Centar Vojska.

Miller, B. 2013. "The State-to-Nation Balance and War." In *Nationalism and War*, edited by J. A. Hall and S. Malešević, 73–97. Cambridge: Cambridge University Press.

Minahan, J. B. 2002. *Encyclopedia of Stateless Nations: Ethnic and National Groups around the World*. Santa Barbara, CA: Greenwood Press.

Ministry of Defence of Ukraine. 2011. *White Book 2011: Armed Forced of Ukraine*. Accessed May 5, 2020, https://www.files.ethz.ch/isn/167335/WB_Eng_final_2011.pdf.

———. 2013. *White Book 2013: Armed Forces of Ukraine*. Accessed April 24, 2020, http://www.mil.gov.ua/content/files/whitebook/WB_2013_eng.pdf.

———. 2014. *White Book 2014: Armed Forces of Ukraine*. Accessed May 5, 2020, https://www.mil.gov.ua/content/files/whitebook/WB_2014_eng.pdf.

Mironova, V. Forthcoming. *From Freedom Fighters to Jihadists*. Oxford: Oxford University Press.

Mirzayev, F. 2014. "Abkhazia." In *Self-Determination and Secession in International Law*, edited by C. Walter, A. von Ungern-Sternberg, and K. Abushov, 191–214. Oxford: Oxford University Press.

Mishra, P. P., ed. 2008. *Organized Crime: From Trafficking to Terrorism, Vol. 1*. Santa Barbara, CA: ABC-CLIO.

Molcean, A., and N. Verständig. 2014. "Moldova: The Transnistrian Conflict." In *Conflict, Crime, and the State in Postcommunist Eurasia*, edited by S. Cornell and M. Johnson, 129–50. Philadelphia: University of Pennsylvania Press.

Molenaar, F., and F. El Kamouni-Janssen. 2017. *Turning the Tide*. CRU Policy File Report. Amsterdam: Netherland Institute of International Relations.

Moore, B. 1966. *Social Origins of Dictatorship and Democracy: Lord and Peasant in the Making of the Modern World*. Boston: Beacon Press.

Moore, M. 1998. *National Self-Determination and Secession*. Oxford: Oxford University Press.

Motyl, A. 2001. "Reifying Boundaries, Fetishizing the Nation: Soviet Legacies and Elite Legitimacy in the Post-Soviet States." In *Right-Sizing the State: The Politics of Moving Borders*, edited by B. O'Leary, I. S. Lustick, and T. Callaghy, 201–18. New York : Oxford University Press.

Mueller, J. 2000. "The Banality of 'Ethnic War.'" *International Security* 25 (1): 42–70.

Munteanu, A., and I. Munteanu. 2007. "Transnistria: A Paradise for Vested Interests." *SEER– South-East Europe Review for Labour and Social Affair* 4:51–66.

Mutschke, R. 2000. "Links between Organized Crime and 'Traditional' Terrorist Groups." *Testimony Transcript*, December 13. Washington, DC: US House of Representatives Judiciary Committee.

Naím, M. 2012. "Mafia States: Organized Crime Takes Office." *Foreign Affairs* 91 (3): 100–111.

Napoleoni, L. 2016. *Merchants of Men: How Jihadists and ISIS Turned Kidnapping and Refugee Trafficking into a Multi-Billion Dollar Business*. Crows Nest, Australia: Allen and Unwin.

Natali, D. 2001. "Manufacturing Identity and Managing Kurds in Iraq." In *Right-Sizing the State: The Politics of Moving Borders*, edited by B. O'Leary, I. S. Lustick, and T. Callaghy, 253–85. New York: Oxford University Press.

Natsheh, B., and C. Parizot. 2015. "From Chocolate Bars to Motor Cars: Separation and Goods Trafficking between Israel and the West Bank (2007–2010)." In *Israelis and Palestinians in the Shadows of the Wall*, edited by S. Abdallah and S. Parizot, 109–27. Farnham, UK: Ashgate.

Nemtsova, A. 2016. "Ukraine's Out of Control Arms Bazaar in Europe's Backyard." *Daily Beast*, June 9. Accessed April 25, 2020, https://www.thedailybeast.com/ukraines-out-of-control -arms-bazaar-in-europes-backyard.

Nevala, S., and K. Aromaa. 2003. "Organised Crime, Trafficking, Drugs." *Selected Papers Presented at the Annual Conference of the European Society of Criminology Helsinki 2003*. Helsinki: European Institute for Crime Prevention and Control.

Nicolaisen, J., and I. Nicolaisen. 1997. *The Pastoral Tuareg: Ecology, Culture, and Society*. Copenhagen: Rhodos.

Nielsen, C. 2012a. *Policing and Internal Affairs in the Serb-Controlled Entities in Croatia 1990–3. Research Report for Hadžić Case (IT-04–05)*. The Hague: International Criminal Tribunal in the Hague.

———. 2012b. "The Symbiosis of War Crimes and Organized Crime in the Former Yugoslavia." *Südosteuropa Mitteilungen* 52 (3): 6–17.

Nilsson, N. 2014. "Georgia's Conflicts: Abkhazia and South Ossetia." In *Conflict, Crime and State in Post-Communist Eurasia*, edited by S. Cornell and M. Jonsson, 103–29. Philadelphia: University of Pennsylvania Press.

Noutcheva, G. 2012. *European Foreign Policy and the Challenges of Balkan Accession: Conditionality, Legitimacy, and Compliance*. Abingdon, UK: Taylor and Francis.

Novaković, M. 2013. *Otmice Zemunskog klana*. Belgrade: Novosti.

———. 2014. *Državo, ruke uvis*. Belgrade: Vukotić Media.

Oeter, S. 2014. "The Role of Recognition and Non-Recognition with Regard to Secession." In *Self-Determination and Secession in International Law*, edited by C. Walter, A. Ungern-Sternberg, and K. Abushov, 45–68. Oxford: Oxford University Press.

Ojochenemi, D. J., L. E. Asuelime, and H. Onapajo. 2015. *Boko Haram: The Socio-economic Drivers*. Cham, Switzerland: Springer International Publishing.

Okereke, C.N.E. 2018. "Analysing Cameroon's Anglophone Crisis." *Counter Terrorist Trends and Analyses* 10 (3): 8–12.

O'Leary, B. 2001. "The Elements of Right-Sizing and Right-Peopling the State." In *Right-Sizing the State: The Politics of Moving Borders*, edited by B. O'Leary, I. S. Lustick, and T. Callaghy, 15–68. New York: Oxford University Press.

O'Leary, B., I. S. Lustick, and T. Callaghy, eds. 2001. *Right-Sizing the State: The Politics of Moving Borders.* New York: Oxford University Press.

Olson, M. 1982. *The Rise and Decline of Nations.* New Haven, CT: Yale University Press.

———. 2000. *Power and Prosperity: Outgrowing Communist and Capitalist Dictatorships.* Oxford: Oxford University Press.

Ong, L. H. 2018. "'Thugs-for-Hire': Subcontracting of State Coercion and State Capacity in China." *Perspectives on Politics* 16 (3): 680–95.

Onuoha, F. C. 2013. "Porous Borders and Boko Haram's Arms Smuggling Operations in Nigeria." Al Jazeera Center for Studies. Accessed April 21, 2020, http://studies.aljazeera.net/en/reports/2013/09/201398104245877469.html.

Onuoha, F. C., and G. E. Ezirim. 2013. "Terrorism and Transnational Organized Crime in West Africa. Al Jazeera Centre for Studies. Accessed April 21, 2020, http://studies.aljazeera.net/en/reports/2013/06/2013624102946689517.html.

Owen, R. 2013. *State, Power, and Politics in the Making of the Modern Middle East.* London: Routledge.

Özkan, B. 2008. "Who Gains from the 'No War No Peace' Situation?: A Critical Analysis of the Nagorno-Karabakh Conflict." *Geopolitics* 13 (3): 572–99.

Panossian, R. 2001. "The Irony of Nagorno-Karabakh: Formal Institutions versus Informal Politics." *Regional ad Federal Studies* 11 (3): 143–64.

Paoli, L. 2004. "Italian Organised Crime: Mafia Associations and Criminal Enterprises." *Global Crime* 6 (1): 19–31.

Pean, P. 2013. *Kosovo: "Pravedni" rat za mafijašku državu.* Belgrade: Službeni Glasnik.

Pek, A., and B. Ekıcı. 2007. "Narcoterrorism in Turkey: The Financing of PKK-KONGRA GEL from Illicit Drug Business." In *NATO Security through Science Series: Human and Societal Dynamcs,* edited by O. Nikbay and S. Hancerli, 140–52. Amsterdam: IOS Press.

Pelham, N. 2012. "Gaza's Tunnel Phenomenon: The Unintended Dynamics of Israel's Siege." *Journal of Palestine Studies* 41 (4): 6–31.

———. 2015. "The Rise and Fall of Gaza's Tunnel Economy (2007–2014)." In *Israelis and Palestinians in the Shadows of the Wall,* edited S. L. Abdullah and C. Parizot, 129–45. Burlington, VT: Ashgate.

Pellerin, M. 2014. "Geopolitical Disruptions in the Sahel: An Opportunity for Global Cooperation?" In *Transatlantic Security from the Sahel to the Horn of Africa,* edited by R. Alvaro and N. Pirozzi, 71–85. Rome: Edizioni Nuova Cultura.

Perlo-Freeman, S. 2019. "Who Is Arming the Yemen War?" An Update." Reinventing Peace: World Peace Foundation. March 19. Accessed April 22, 2020, https://sites.tufts.edu/reinventingpeace/2019/03/19/who-is-arming-the-yemen-war-an-update.

Pérouse de Montclos, M. A. 2014. *Nigeria's Interminable Insurgency?: Addressing the Boko Haram Crisis.* Chatham House Resarch Paper 2014. London: Royal Institute of International Affairs.

Peščanik. 2000. *Peščanik 21 Emisija.* September 13. Accessed May 8, 2020, https://pescanik.net/21-emisija/.

———. 2016. *Peščanik: Veronika Surroi intervju.* September 6. Accessed May 8, 2020, https://pescanik.net/veton-surroi-intervju/.

Peterka-Benton, D. 2012. "Arms Trafficking in Transnistria: A European Security Threat?" *Journal of Applied Security Research* 7 (171–92.

Philip de Andrés, A. 2008. "West Africa under Attack: Drugs, Organized Crime, and Terrorism as the New Threats to Global Security." *UNISCI Discussion Papers* 16: 203–28.

Philp, M. 2017. "Conceptualizing Political Corruption." In *Political Corruption: Concepts and Contexts,* 41–58. New York: Routledge.

Pilger, J. 2000. "Kosovo, Close to Being a Mafia State, Is Littered with Unexploded Bombs. That's the Result of Ethical Blairism." *New Statesmen,* January 24.

Politzer, M., and E. Kassie. 2016. "The 21st Century Gold Rush: How the Refugee Crisis Is Changing the War." *Huffington Post*, December 21. Accessed April 20, 2020, https://highline .huffingtonpost.com/articles/en/the-21st-century-gold-rush-refugees/#/niger.

Polukhina, Y. 2018. "Скажи мне, кто твой куратор." *Novaya Gazeta*, October 7. Accessed April 25, 2020, https://www.novayagazeta.ru/articles/2018/10/08/78106-skazhi-mne-kto -tvoy-kurator.

Pommerolle, M. E., and H.D.M. Heungoup. 2017. "The 'Anglophone Crisis': A Tale of the Cameroonian Postcolony." *African Affairs* 116 (464): 526–38.

Popescu, N. 2006. *Democracy in Secessionism: Transnistria and Abkhazia's Domestic Policies*. Budapest: Open Society Institute.

Prentice, A., and A. Zverev. 2016. "Ukraine, After War, Becomes a Trove for Black Market Arms Trade." Reuters, July 25. Accessed April 25, 2020, https://www.reuters.com/article/us -ukraine-crisis-arms-insight-idUSKCN1050ZE.

Protić, M. St. 2005. *Izneverena revolucija: 5. oktobar 2000*. Belgrade: Čigoja Štampa.

Protsyk, O. 2009. "Representation and Democracy in Eurasia's Unrecognized States: The Case of Transnistria." *Post-Soviet Affairs* 25 (3): 257–81.

———. 2012. "Secession and Hybrid Regime Politics in Transnistria." *Communist and Post-Communist Studies* 45 (1–2): 175–82.

Provvisionato, S. 2000. *Uck: L'armata Dell'ombra: L'Esercito Di Liberazione Del Kosovo: Una Guerra Tra Mafia, Politica e Terrorismo*. Rome: Gamberetti.

Public Safety Bureau. 1999. *Terorizam Albanskih separatista na Kosovu i Metohiji i metod njihovog delovanja*. Belgrade: Resor Javne Bezbednosti, Serbian Ministry of Internal Affairs.

Pugh, M. 2003. "Protectorates and Spoils of Peace: Political Economy in South-East Europe." In *Shadow Globalization, Ethnic Conflicts, and New Wars*, edited by D. Jung, 47–70. London: Routledge.

———. 2004. "Rubbing Salt into War Wounds: Shadow Economies and Peacebuilding in Bosnia and Kosovo." *Problems of Post-Communism* 51 (3): 53–60.

Pugh, M., N. Cooper, and J. Goodhand. 2004. *War Economies in a Regional Context: Challenges of Transformation*. Boulder, CO: Lynne Rienner Publishers.

Qarmout, T., and D. Béland. 2012. "The Politics of International Aid to the Gaza Strip." *Journal of Palestine Studies* 41 (4): 32–47.

Quattrone, G. A., and A. Tversky. 1988. "Contrasting Rational and Psychological Analyses of Political Choice." *American Political Science Review* 82 (3): 719–36.

Rabi, U. 2015. *Yemen: Revolution, Civil War, and Unification*. London: I. B. Tauris.

Radio Free Europe. 2008. "South Ossetia Crisis could be Russia's Chance to Defeat Siloviki." Radio Free Europe, August 8. Accessed May 1, 2020, https://www.rferl.org/a/South_Ossetia_Crisis _Could_Be_Russian_Chance_To_Defeat_Siloviki/1189525.html

Ragin, C. C. 1987. *The Comparative Method: Moving beyond Qualitative and Quantitative Strategies*. Berkeley: University of California Press.

Raufer, X. 2007. "Albanian Organized Crime." In *Long March to the West: Twenty-First Century Migration in Europe and the Greater Mediterranean Area*, edited by M. Korinman and J. Laughland, 397–406 Ilford, UK: Vallentine Mitchell.

Raufer, X., and S. Quere. 2006. *Zakana za Evropa, Albanska mafija*. Skopje, Macedonia: Di-eM.

Reitano, T., C. Clarke, and L. Adal. 2017. "Examining the Nexus between Organised Crime and Terrorism and Its Implications for EU Programming." CT Morse. Accessed April 22, 2020, http://ct-morse.eu/wp-content/uploads/2017/04/OC-Terror-Nexus-_-Think-Piece.pdf.

Reno, W. 1999. *Warlord Politics and African States*. Boulder, CO: Lynne Rienner Publishers.

———. 2011. "Understanding Criminality in West-African Conflicts." In *Peace Operations and Organized Crime*, edited by J. Cockayne and A. Lupel, 68–83. London: Routledge.

Richemond-Barak, D. 2018. *Underground Warfare*. Oxford: Oxford University Press.

Riegl, M., and B. Doboš, eds. 2017. *Unrecognized States and Secession in the 21st Century*. Cham, Switzerland: Springer.

Robins, P. 2002. "From Small-Time Smuggling to Big-Time Racketeering: Turkey and the Middle East." In *Transnational Organized Crime and International Security: Business as Usual*, edited by M. R. Berdal and M. Serrano, 141–54. Boulder, CO: Lynne Rienner Publishers.

———. 2008. "Back from the Brink: Turkey's Ambivalent Approaches to the Hard Drugs Issue." *Middle East Journal* 62 (4): 630–50.

Roby, Y. 2004. *Franco-Americans of New England: Dreams and Realities*. Sillery, Quebec: Septentrion.

Roeder, P. G. 2009. "Ethnofederalism and the Mismanagement of Conflicting Nationalisms." *Regional and Federal Studies* 19 (2): 203–19.

Romaniuk, S. N., and S. T. Webb, eds. 2015. *Insurgency and Counterinsurgency in Modern War*. Boca Raton, FL: CRC Press.

Roth, C. F. 2015. *Let's Split: A Complete Guide to Separatist Movements and Aspirant Nations, from Abkhazia to Zanzibar*. Sacramento, CA: Litwin Books.

Roth, M. P. 2017. *Global Organized Crime: A 21st Century Approach*. London: Routledge.

Roth, M. P., and M. Sever. 2007. "The Kurdish Workers Party (PKK) as Criminal Syndicate: Funding Terrorism through Organized Crime, a Case Study." *Studies in Conflict and Terrorism* 30 (10): 901–20.

Roy, S. 2005. "Praying with Their Eyes Closed: Reflections on the Disengagement from Gaza." *Journal of Palestine Studies* 34 (4): 64–74.

———. 2012. "Reconceptualizing the Israeli-Palestinian Conflict: Key Paradigm Shifts." *Journal of Palestine Studies* 41 (3): 71–91.

Rueschemeyer, D. 2003. "Can One or a Few Cases Yield Theoretical Gains?" In *Comparative Historical Analysis in the Social Sciences*, edited by J. Mahoney and D. Rueschemeyer, 305–36. Cambridge: Cambridge University Press.

Sabry, M. 2015. *Sinai: Egypt's Linchpin, Gaza's Lifeline, Israel's Nightmare*. Oxford: Oxford University Press.

Salmoni, B. A., B. Loidolt, and M. Wells. 2010. *Regime and Periphery in Northern Yemen: The Huthi Phenomenon*. Washington, DC: Rand Corporation.

Sambanis, N., M. Germann, and A. Schädel. 2018. "SDM: A New Data Set on Self-Determination Movements with an Application to the Reputational Theory of Conflict. *Journal of Conflict Resolution* 62 (3): 656–86.

Sanamyan, E. 2016. "*The Logic of Occupation in the Nagorno-Karabakh War: The Cases of Agdam and Shaumyan*." PhD diss., Virginia Tech.

Sanchez, W. A. 2009. "The 'Frozen' Southeast: How the Moldova-Transnistria Question Has Become a European Geo-Security Issue." *Journal of Slavic Military Studies* 22 (2): 153–76.

Saroyan, M. 1990. "The 'Karabakh Syndrome' and Azerbaijani Politics." *Problems of Communism* 39 (5): 14.

Satter, D. 2004. *Darkness at Dawn: The Rise of the Russian Criminal State*. New Haven, CT: Yale University Press.

Schäublin, E. 2009. *The West Bank Zakat Committees (1977–2009) in the Local Context*. Geneva: Graduate Institute.

Scheele, J. 2009. "Tribus, États et fraude: la région frontalière algéro-malienne. *Études rurales* 184:79–94.

———. 2012. *Smugglers and Saints of the Sahara: Regional Connectivity in the Twentieth Century*. Cambridge: Cambridge University Press.

Scheper-Hughes, N. 2003. "Keeping an Eye on the Global Traffic in Human Organs." *Lancet* 361 (9369): 1645–48.

———. 2004. "Parts Unknown: Undercover Ethnography of the Organs-Trafficking Under-world." *Ethnography* 5 (1): 29–73.

Schmid, A., and C. Spencer-Smith. 2012. "Illicit Radiological and Nuclear Trafficking, Smuggling, and Security Incidents in the Black Sea Region since the Fall of the Iron Curtain—an Open Source Inventory. *Perspectives on Terrorism* 6 (2): 117–57.

Schmid, A., and R. Wesley. 2006. "Possible Causes and Motives of Nuclear and Radiological Terrorism in the Light of Empirical Data on Smuggling Incidents of Nuclear Materials." In *Tangled Roots: Social and Psychological Factors in the Genesis of Terrorism*, edited by J. Victoroff, 357–94. Amsterdam: IOS Press.

Schmidle, N. 2013. "Bringing Up the Bodies." *New Yorker*, April.

Sciarrone, R. 2010. "Mafia and Civil Society: Economico-Criminal Collusion and Territorial Control in Calabria." In *Organized Crime and States: The Hidden Face of Politics*, edited by J. Briquet and G. Favarel-Garrigues, 173–96. New York: Palgrave Macmillan.

Scott, E. R. 2007. "Georgia's Anti-Corruption Revolution." In *Organized Crime and Corruption in Georgia*, edited by L. Shelley, E. R. Scott, and A. Latta, 17–37. London: Routledge.

Scott, J. C. 1972. *Comparative Political Corruption*. Englewood Cliffs, NJ: Prentice Hall.

———. 1998. *Seeing Like a State: How Certain Schemes to Improve the Human Condition Have fFailed*. New Haven, CT: Yale University Press.

Sekelj, L. 1993. *Yugoslavia: The Process of Disintegration*. New York: Columbia University Press.

———. 2001. "Forced Democratization of a Criminalized State." In *Revolution and Order: Serbia after October 2000*, edited by I. Spasić and M. Subotić, 95–109. Belgrade: Institute for Philosophy and Social Theory.

Selçuk, F. Ü. 2011. "The Rising Mafioso Capitalists, Opportunities, and the Case of Turkey." *Capital and Class* 35 (2): 275–93.

"Separatists Declare War in Cameroon." 2018. eNCA, February 17. Accessed April 21, 2020, https://www.enca.com/africa/separatists-declare-war-in-cameroon.

Serrano, M. 2002. "Transnational Organized Crime and International Security: Business as Usual?" In *Transnational Organized Crime and International Security: Business as Usual*, edited by M. R. Berdal and M. Serrano, 13–36. Boulder, CO: Lynne Rienner Publishers.

Shain, Y. 2007. *Kinship and Diasporas in International Affairs*. Ann Arbor: University of Michigan Press.

Shain, Y., and M. Sherman. 1998. "Dynamics of Disintegration: Diaspora, Secession, and the Paradox of Nation-states." *Nations and Nationalism* 4 (3): 321–46.

Shaw, M. 2015. "Drug Trafficking in Guinea-Bissau, 1998–2014: The Evolution of an Elite Protection Network." *Journal of Modern African Studies* 53 (3): 339–64.

Shaw, M., T. Reitano, and M. Hunter. 2014. *Comprehensive Assessment of Drug Trafficking and Organised Crime in West and Central Africa*. African Union Report, January. Addis Ababa, Ethiopia: African Union.

Shay, S. 2016. *Egypt's War against the Tunnels between Sinai and Gaza Strip*. Herzliya, Israel: Institute for Policy and Strategy Publications, Lauder School of Government.

Sheets, L. S. 2008. "A Smuggler's Story." *Atlantic Monthly* 301 (3). Accessed April 19, 2020, https://www.theatlantic.com/magazine/archive/2008/04/a-smuggler-s-story/306736/.

Shelley, L. 2003. "Russia and Ukraine: Transition or Tragedy?" In *Menace to Society: Political-Criminal Collaboration around the World*, edited by R. Godson, 199–230. Brunswick, NJ: Routledge.

———. 2007. "Introduction. In *Organized Crime and Corruption in Georgia*, edited by L. Shelley, E. R. Scott, and A. Latta, 1–17. London: Routledge.

———. 2018. *Dark Commerce: How a New Illicit Economy Is Threatening Our Future*. Princeton, NJ: Princeton University Press.

Shelley, L., and S. A. Melzer. 2008. "The Nexus of Organized Crime and Terrorism: Two Case Studies in Cigarette Smuggling." *International Journal of Comparative and Applied Criminal Justice* 32 (1): 43–63.

Shelley, L., E. R. Scott, and A. Latta. 2007. *Organized Crime and Corruption in Georgia.* London: Routledge.

Shimazono, Y. 2007. "The State of the International Organ Trade: A Provisional Picture Based on Integration of Available Information." *Bulletin of the World Health Organization* 85 (12): 955–62.

Shore, M. 2018. *The Ukrainian Night: An Intimate History of Revolution.* New Haven, NJ: Yale University Press.

Sierra, O.B.P. 2011. "No Man's Land?: A Comparative Analysis of the EU and Russia's Influence in the Southern Caucasus." *Communist and Post-Communist Studies* 44 (3): 233–43.

Silva, A. F. 2017. "The Forgotten of the Desert: Tuareg Resistances in Azawad." *PAX et Bellum Journal* 4 (Spring): 3–18.

Simmel, G. 2010. *Conflict and the Web of Group Affiliations.* New York: Simon and Schuster.

Siniawer, E. M. 2011. "Befitting Bedfellows: Yakuza and the State in Modern Japan." *Journal of Social History* 45 (3): 623–41.

Siniver, A., and S. Lucas. 2016 "The Islamic State Lexical Battleground: US Foreign Policy and the Abstraction of Threat." *International Affairs* 92 (1): 63–79.

Siroky, D. S., and J. Cuffe. 2015. "Lost Autonomy, Nationalism, and Separatism." *Comparative Political Studies* 48 (1): 3–34.

Skaperdas, S. 2001. "The Political Economy of Organized Crime: Providing Protection When the State Does Not." *Economics of Governance* 2 (3): 173–202.

Skrbiš, Z. 1999. *Long-Distance Nationalism: Diasporas, Homelands, and Identities.* Brookfield, VT: Ashgate.

Slade, G. 2013. *Reorganizing Crime: Mafia and Anti-Mafia in Post-Soviet Georgia.* Oxford: Oxford University Press.

Smajić, M. 2010. "Organizovani kriminal u Bosni i Hercegovini—Tranzicijske dileme." *Pregled— Časopis Za Društvena Pitanja LI* 2:203–25.

Smith, A. 1979. *Nationalism in the Twentieth Century.* New York: NYU Press.

Smith, M. 2015. *Boko Haram: Inside Nigeria's Unholy War.* London: I. B. Tauris.

Smith, C. A., and H. M. Smith. 2011. "Human Trafficking: The Unintended Effects of United Nations Intervention." *International Political Science Review* 32 (2): 125–45.

Sokova, E., W. C. Potter, and C. Chuen. 2007. *Recent Weapons Grade Uranium Smuggling Case: Nuclear Materials Are Still on the Loose.* Monterey, CA: Center for Nonproliferation Studies.

Sörensen, J. S. 2003. "War as Social Transformation: Wealth, Class, Power, and an Illiberal Economy in Serbia." *Civil Wars* 6 (4): 55–82.

———. 2006. "The Shadow Economy, War, and State Building: Social Transformation and Re-Stratification in an Illiberal Economy (Serbia and Kosovo)." *Journal of Contemporary European Studies* 14 (3): 317–51.

Soule, S. A. 2004. "Diffusion Processes within and across Movements." In *The Blackwell Companion to Social Movements,* edited by D. Snow, S. A. Soule, and H. Kriesi, 294–310. Malden, MA: Blackwell.

Souleimanov, E. 2013. *Understanding Ethnopolitical Conflict: Karabakh, South Ossetia, and Abkhazia Wars Reconsidered.* New York: Palgrave Macmillan.

Southeast European Legal Development Initiative. 2002. *Anti-Corruption in Southeast Europe: First Steps and Policies.* Sofia: Center for the Study of Democracy.

Spencer, M. 1998. *Separatism: Democracy and Disintegration.* Lanham, MD: Rowman and Littlefield.

Spernbauer, M. 2010." "EULEX Kosovo: The Difficult Deployment and Challenging Implementation of the Most Comprehensive Civilian EU Operation to Date." *German Law Journal* 11 (7): 769–802.

Spittler, G. 1999. "Stress, Crisis, and Catastrophe: Communication and Survival Strategies of Tuareg Nomads during a Famine." In *Food Security and Nutrition: The Global Challenge*, edited by U. Kracht and M. Schulz, 157–68. New York: St. Martin's Press.

Stack, G. 2017. "Arms Washing: Ukraine Network Moves Embargoed European Arms to Africa and the Middle East." Organized Crime and Corruption Reporting Project. Accessed April 29, 2020, https://www.occrp.org/en/investigations/7037-arms-washing-ukraine-network-moves-embargoed-european-arms-to-africa-and-the-middle-east.

Staniland, P. 2012. "States, Insurgents, and Wartime Political Orders." *Perspectives on Politics* 10 (2): 243–64.

Stefanova, R. 2004. "Fighting Organized Crime in a UN Protectorate: Difficult, Possible, Necessary." *Southeast European and Black Sea Studies* 4 (2): 257–79.

Stepanova, E. 2008. *South Ossetia and Abkhazia: Placing the Conflict in Context*. SIPRI background paper, November. Stockholm: SIPRI.

Stephenson, S. 2015. *Gangs of Russia: From the Streets to the Corridors of Power*. Ithaca, NY: Cornell University Press.

Stern, J., and J. Berger. 2015. *ISIS: The State of Terror*. New York: Ecco Press.

Stewart, C. S. 2008. *Hunting the Tiger: The Fast Life and Violent Death of the Balkans' Most Dangerous Man*. New York: St. Martin's Press.Stijković, Z. 2007. *Kosmet—Moje svedočenje*. Belgrade: Zoran Stijković (self-published).

Stockholm International Peace Reseach Institute (SIPRI). 2003. *Relics of Cold War: Europe's Challenge, Ukraine's Experience*. Policy paper 6. Stockholm: SIPRI.

———. 2009. *Arms Transfers to the Middle East*. Background paper, July. Stockholm: SIPRI.

———. 2011. *Ukrainian Arms Supplies to sub-Saharan Africa*. Background paper, February. Stockholm: SIPRI.

Stojarova, V. 2007. "Organized Crime in the Western Balkans." *HUMSEC Journal* 1 (1): 91–114.

Strazzari, F. 2003. "Between Ethnic Collision and Mafia Collusion: The 'Balkan Route' to State-Making." In *Shadow Globalization, Ethnic Conflicts, and New Wars: A Political Economy of Intra-State War*, edited by D. Jung, 140–83. London: Routledge.

———. 2015. *Azawad and the Rights of Passage: The Role of Illicit Trade in the Logic of Armed Group Formation in Northern Mali*. Oslo: Norwegian Peacebuilding Resource Centre.

Sullivan, D., and K. Jones. 2008. *Global Security Watch-Egypt: A Reference Handbook*. Westport, CT: Praeger Security International.

Summers, J. 2014. "Kosovo." In *Self-Determination and Secession in International Law*, edited by C. Walter, A. von Ungern-Sternberg, and K. Abushov, 235–55. Oxford: Oxford University Press.

Šurc, M., and B. Zgaga. 2013. *U ime države: Prodaja*. Zagreb: Jesenski i Turk.

Tchantouridzé, L. 2013. "Georgia: A Political History since Independence." *Nationalities Papers* 41 (4): 684–86.

Thachuk, K. L., ed. 2007. *Transnational Threats: Smuggling and Trafficking in Arms, Drugs, and Human Life*. Santa Barbara, CA: Greenwood Publishing Group.

Thomas, R. G., ed. 2003. *Yugoslavia Unraveled: Sovereignty, Self-Determination, Intervention*. Lanham, MD: Lexington Books.

Thurston, A. 2018. *Boko Haram: The History of an African Jihadist Movement*. Princeton, NJ: Princeton University Press.

Tilly, C. 1985. "War Making and State Making as Organized Crime." In *Bringing the State Back In*, edited by P. B. Evans, D. Rueschemeyer, and T. Skocpol, 169–86. Cambridge: Cambridge University Press.

Tinti, P., and T. Reitano. 2017. *Migrant, Refugee, Smuggler, Savior*. Oxford: Oxford University Press.

Tishkov, V. 2004. *Chechnya: Life in a War-Torn Society*. Berkeley: University of California Press.

Tmušiš, Z. 2002. "Užička municija za Alijine Bošnjake." *Alternativna Informativna Mreža (9 February)*. Sarajevo: AIM Press.

Todorovski, L., I. Ilijevski, Z. Dimovski, and K. Babanoski. 2018. "Operational Aspects of Revealed International Channels of Illicit Drug Trafficking in the Republic of Macedonia." *Balkan Journal of Interdisciplinary Research* 4 (1): 64–72.

Tomovska, I. 2008. "Macedonia 2001 and Beyond: New or Old War?" *HUMSEC Journal* 2:85–96.

Traughber, C. M. 2007. "Terror-Crime Nexus?: Terrorism and Arms, Drug, and Human Trafficking in Georgia." *Connections* 6 (1): 47–64.

Trifković, S. 1998. *The Kosovo Dossier*. London: Lord Byron Foundation.

Trotter, A. 2012. "Witness Intimidation in International Trials: Balancing the Need for Protection against the Rights of the Accused." *George Washington International Law Review* 44 (3): 521–38.

Trumbull, I. V., and R. George. 2012. "A Tale of Two Secessions in the Sahara." *Middle East Report* 42 (264): 30–33.

Trzciński, K. 2004. "The Significance of Geographic Location for the Success of Territorial Secession: African Example." *Miscellanea Geographica* 11 (1): 207–16.

Tudoroiu, T. 2012. "The European Union, Russia, and the Future of the Transnistrian Frozen Conflict." *East European Politics and Societies* 26 (1):135–61.

Unal, M.C. 2012. *Counterterrorism in Turkey: Policy Choices and Policy Effects toward the Kurdistan Workers' rty (PKK)*. New York: Routledge.

United Nations Office on Drugs and Crime (UNODC). 1999–2019. *World Drug Report*. Vienna: UNODC.

———. 2003. *Addressing Organized Crime and Drug Trafficking in Iraq Addressing Organized Crime and Drug Trafficking in Iraq*. Report, August. Vienna: UNODC.

———. 2005. *Crime and Development in Africa*. Report, June. Vienna: UNODC.

———. 2010. *The Globalization of Crime: A Transnational Organized Crime Threat Assessment*. Vienna: UNODC.

———. 2013. *Transnational Organized Crime in West Africa: A Threat Assessment*. Vienna: UNODC.

———. 2015. *Afghan Opiate Trafficking through the Southern Route*. Report, June. Vienna: UNODC.

———. 2017. *World Drug Report*. Vienna: UNODC.

Uzodike, U. O., and B. Maiangwa. 2012. "Boko Haram Terrorism in Nigeria: Causal Factors and Central Problematic." *African Renaissance* 9 (1): 91–118.

van Bruinessen, M. 1996. "Turkey's Death Squads." *Middle East Report* 26 (2): 20–23

———. 2000. *Transnational Aspects of the Kurdish Question*. European University Institute working paper 2000/22. Florence: Robert Schuman Centre.

van de Bunt, H. G., D. Siegel, and D. Zaitch. 2014. "The Social Embeddedness of Organized Crime." In *Oxford Handbook of Organized Crime*, edited by L. Paoi, 321–35. New York: Oxford University Press.

van der Veen, H. T. 2003. "The War on Drugs in the Creation of the New World (Dis)order." In *Shadow Globalization, Ethnic Conflicts, and New Wars*, edited by D. Jung, 105–28. London: Routledge.

van Dijk, J. 2007. "Mafia Markers: Assessing Organized Crime and Its Impact upon Societies." *Trends in Organized Crime* 10 (4): 39–56.

Vangelovski, T. 2017. "*Macedonia: Ethno-Religious Conflict (1991–2016)*." PhD diss., Australian National University.

Varese, F. 2011. *Mafias on the Move: How Organized Crime Conquers New Territories*. Princeton, NJ: Princeton University Press.

Vasić, M. 2005. *Atentat na Zorana Djindjića*. Belgrade: Vreme.

Vickers, M. 1998. *Between Serb and Albanian: A History of Kosovo*. London: Hurst and Co.

Vigh, H. 2017. "From Warlord to Drug Lord: The Life of João Bernardo 'Nino' Vieira." In *Warlord Democrats in Africa: Ex-Military Leaders and Electoral Politics*, edited by A. Themnér, 156–76. London: Zed Books.

Volkov, V. 2002. "Who Is Strong When the State Is Weak?: Violent Entrepreneurship in Russia's Emerging Markets." In *Beyond State Crisis?: Postcolonial Africa and Post-Soviet Eurasia in Comparative Perspective*, edited by M. R. Beissinger and C. Young, 81–104. Washington, DC: Woodrow Wilson Center Press.

von Steinsdorff, S., and A. Fruhstorfer. 2012. "Post-Soviet De Facto States in Search of Internal and External Legitimacy: Introduction." *Communist and Post-Communist Studies* 45 (1–2): 117–21.

Vukosavljević, D. 2012. "Nađeni posmrtni ostaci Milana Jurišića u Španiji." *Politika*, March 22.

Wahab, B. A. 2006. "How Iraqi Oil Smuggling Greases Violence." *Middle East Quarterly* 13 (4): 53–59.

Wahlbeck, Ö. 2002."The Concept of Diaspora as an Analytical Tool in the Study of Refugee Communities." *Journal of Ethnic and Migration Studies* 28 (2): 221–38.

Wallerstein, I. 1961. *Africa: The Politics of Independence and Unity*. Lincoln: University of Nebraska Press.

Walter, C., A. von Ungern-Sternberg, and K. Abushov, eds. 2014. *Self-Determination and Secession in International Law*. Oxford: Oxford University Press.

Wang, P. 2010. "The Crime-Terror Nexus: Transformation, Alliance, Convergence." *Asian Social Science* 6 (6): 11–20.

Warner, J. 2010. "Narco-TrAfrica: Why West Africa Is the World's Newest Alleyway for Illicit Substances and Why the Global Community Should Care. *Africa Policy Journal* 7:15–28.

Waters, C. 2014. "South Ossetia. In *Self-Determination and Secession in International Law*, edited by C. Walter, A. von Ungern-Sternberg, and K. Abushov, 175–91. Oxford: Oxford University Press.

Watts, M. 2007. "Petro-Insurgency or Criminal Syndicate?: Conflict and Violence in the Niger Delta." *Review of African Political Economy* 34 (114): 637–60.

Weeraratne, S. 2017. "Theorizing the Expansion of the Boko Haram Insurgency in Nigeria." *Terrorism and Political Violence* 29 (4): 610–34.

Weinreich, M. 2008. *History of the Yiddish Language*. New Haven, CT: Yale University Press.

Weiss, M., and H. Hassan. 2015. *ISIS: Inside the Army of Terror*. New York: Simon and Schuster.

Weitzer, R. 2012. *Legalizing Prostitution: From Illicit Vice to Lawful Business*. New York: NYU Press.

Wellman, C. 2005. *A Theory of Secession: The Case for Political Self-Determination*. Cambridge: Cambridge University Press.

Welt, C., and I. Bremmer. 1997. "Armenia's New Autocrats." *Journal of Democracy* 8 (3): 77–91.

West, J. 2002. "The Political Economy of Organized Crime and State Failure: The Nexus of Greed, Need, and Grievance." *Development and Change* 33:935–55.

White, P. 2015. *The PKK: Coming Down from the Mountains*. London: Zed Books.

Williams, P. 2002. "Cooperation among Criminal Organizations." In *Transnational Organized Crime and International Security: Business as Usual?*, edited by M. R. Berdal and M. Serrano, 67–80. Boulder, CO: Lynne Rienner Publishers.

———. 2009. *Criminals, Militias, and Insurgents: Organized Crime in Iraq*. Carlisle, PA: US Army War College, Strategic Studies Institute.

———. 2011. "Organized Crime and Corruption in Iraq." In *Peace Operations and Organized Crime*, edited by J. Cockayne and A. Lupel, 153–73. London: Routledge.

———. 2012. "How Globalization Affects Transnational Crime." Council on Foreign Relations interview, May 31. Accessed April 25, 2020. www.youtube.com/watch?v=Ipmpv0R1D0s.

Williams, P., and J. Picarelli. 2001. "Organized Crime in Ukraine: Challenge and Response." *Trends in Organized Crime* 6 (3–4): 100–142.

Wilson, J. M. 2006. "Law and Order in an Emerging Democracy: Lessons from the Reconstruction of Kosovo's Police and Justice Systems." *Annals of the American Academy of Political and Social Science* 605 (1): 152–77.

Wimmer, A. 2013. *Ethnic Boundary Making: Institutions, Power, Networks*. Oxford: Oxford University Press.

———. 2018. *Nation Building: Why Some Countries Come Together while Others Fall Apart*. Princeton, NJ: Princeton University Press.

Wintrobe, R. 2006. *Rational Extremism: The Political Economy of Radicalism*. Cambridge: Cambridge University Press.

Woords, E. 2016. "Weapons: Online Arms Trafficking in Russia and Ukraine." *Wired*, July 5. Accessed April 25, 2020, https://medium.com/@SmallArmsSurvey/wired-weapons-online -arms-trafficking-in-russia-and-ukraine-162291dd1a00.

Vogt, M. 2019. *Mobilization and Conflict in Multiethnic States*. New York: Oxford University Press.

Wolff, K. H., ed. 1950. *The Sociology of Georg Simmel*. New York: Free Press.

Wolff, S. n.d. "Georgia: Abkhazia and South Ossetia." In *Encyclopedia Princetonienisis*. Accessed December 10, 2014, http://pesd.princeton.edu.

Yekelchyk, S. 2015. *The Conflict in Ukraine: What Everyone Needs to Know*. Oxford: Oxford University Press.

Yiftachel, O. 2006. *Ethnocracy: Land and Identity Politics in Israel/Palestine*. Philadelphia: University of Pennsylvania Press.

Zaitseva, L., and K. Hand. 2003. "Nuclear Smuggling Chains Suppliers, Intermediaries, and End Users." *American Behavioral Scientist* 46 (6): 822–44.

Zenn, J., and Z. P. Pieri. 2017. "The Boko Haram Paradox: Ethnicity, Religion, and Historical Memory in Pursuit of a Caliphate." In *Understanding Boko Haram: Terrorism and Insurgency in Africa*, edited by J. H. James and H. Solomon, 41–64. New York: Taylor and Francis.

Zohar, E. 2015. "The Arming of Non-State Actors in the Gaza Strip and Sinai Peninsula." *Australian Journal of International Affairs* 69 (4): 438–61.

Zolberg, A. R., A. Suhrke, and S. Aguayo. 1992. *Escape from Violence: Conflict and the Refugee Crisis in the Developing World*. Oxford: Oxford University Press.

———. 1986. "International Factors in the Formation of Refugee Movements." *International Migration Review* 20 (2): 151–69.

Zoubir, Y. H. 2012. "Qaddafi's Spawn." Foreign Affairs, July 24. Accessed April 20, 2020, https:// www.foreignaffairs.com/articles/algeria/2012-07-24/qaddafis-spawn.

Zürcher, C., P. Baev, and J. Koehler. 2005. "Civil Wars in the Caucasus." In *Understanding Civil War: Africa (Vol. 2)*, edited by P. Collier and N. Sambanis, 259–98. Washington, DC: World Bank Publications.

A NOTE ON THE TYPE

This book has been composed in Adobe Text and Gotham.
Adobe Text, designed by Robert Slimbach for Adobe,
bridges the gap between fifteenth- and sixteenth-century
calligraphic and eighteenth-century Modern styles.
Gotham, inspired by New York street signs, was designed
by Tobias Frere-Jones for Hoefler & Co.

CPSIA information can be obtained
at www.ICGtesting.com
Printed in the USA
LVHW111915071020
668135LV00002B/2